AN AMERICAN REALITY: "WHITE PEOPLE" ... LOL

DR. RONALD BARNES

AMERICAN REALITY: "WHITE PEOPLE" . . . LOL

Bennett books may be ordered through booksellers or by contacting:

Bennett Media and Marketing
1603 Capitol Ave., Suite 310 A233
Cheyenne, WY 82001
www.thebennettmediaandmarketing.com
Phone: 1-307-202-9292

ISBN: 978-1-957114-50-7 (Paperback)
ISBN: 978-1-957114-51-4 (eBook)

Printed in the United States of America

TABLE OF CONTENTS

APPENDIX

Preface

An American Reality emerges in the context of "The Incident" of racism and discrimination that Dr. Ronald Barnes, the author of this book, experienced at the University of Chicago. "The Incident" is a case study backdrop to explore the reality of racism and racists in American society. "The Incident", described in Chapter IV thru Chapter VII, is microcosmic of experiences encountered by millions of minorities historically and today, on a daily basis. Anyone who gives the concept of racism any significant thought has to conclude it is a mindset that only the most simple-minded, the most ignorant, the most devious, the most unethical, or the most immoral people on earth subscribe to. The stupid mentally retarded racists are a virus in white culture and American society. For this reason, the reality of White racism is relevant to present as a topic of this book. Racism has become so prevalent and identifiable with American Society that it is normal behavior for White people to be racists or to act with "*racist residue*". It is empirically established that people have a "bias blind spot," meaning that

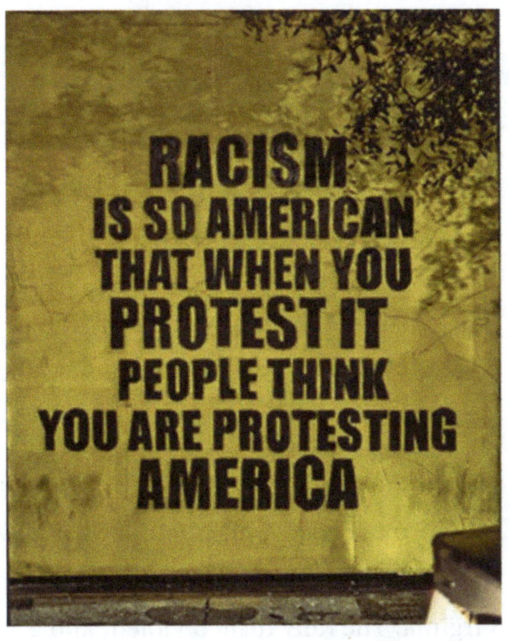

they are less likely to detect bias in themselves than others are. [1] "The Incident" Dr. Barnes experienced, caused him to research and study the psychology and sociology of racism and racist. "The Incident" encountered by Dr. Barnes did not appear to be have alignment between his perception of the individuals involved and their behavior. Because all individuals involved were associated with the University of Chicago, and normally one would think the education environment is more liberal than much of the general society. Not necessarily true. Educated White people have more subtle ways of expressing their racism. There is a "*racist residue*" in the crevices of the White personality that emerges, often without their understanding of, why. White people embrace their racism and White privilege without concern for the privilege of others and even at the expense of others who are non-White, including African Americans, Asians and Asian Americans, Hispanics and Hispanic Americans, Jewish people, people of non-western religious orientation and people who are non-traditionally gender defined. Racism is so American that when you protest it, people think you are protesting America.

When Heather Heyer (a White woman supporting equal rights) was killed in 2017 by a racist White man, she along with other members of Black Lives Matter (BLM) were counter protesting a "Unite the Right" rally in Charlottesville, Virginia. The rally turned violent and a White racist killed Ms. Heyer. Ms. Heyer represents the portion of the White culture that represents what America is supposed to stand for. Donald Trump stated, "There are good people on both sides." **This author is taking the position that racists, White Nationalist, and White supremacist are deplorable human beings, detrimental to civilized society, criminals and deserve the same treatment as ISIS, Timothy McVeigh (Oklahoma City bomber), Charles Manson, Al Qaeda, Bin Laden, and others who have harmful terrorist intentions toward American Democracy and toward the citizens of the United States of America. Racists are terrorist and destructive to America. Racists are overtly harmful and potentially harmful**

to decent White people. This book is unapologetically critical of the negative and destructive elements in our United States of America. The racists in White culture, White nationalist, White supremacist, and neo-Nazis are the negative and destructive elements referred to. **The author recognizes and believes there are many decent and good White people in America, who, themselves, deplore the negative elements in their culture.** "Attorney General Merrick B. Garland and Homeland Security Secretary Alejandro N. Mayorkas told senators ... that the greatest domestic threat facing the United States comes from what they both called "racially or ethnically motivated violent extremists. Specifically, those who advocate for the superiority of the white race," Mr. Garland told the Senate Appropriations Committee. [2] The reason the United States has not effectively dealt with racism historically, is that the terrorist attacks targeted non-White people or White people who support equality. Even the United States Armed forces are taking action to eliminate White supremacist from their ranks. [3] The government pursued and apprehended Al Qaeda, ISIS, the Oklahoma bomber (Timothy McVeigh), The Unabomber (Ted Kaczynski), with relentless effort, because their attacks were against White people. The government even arrested suspected terrorist, without any more proof than suspicion. America waged a 20-year global war against terrorism because the threat was against White America. The Ku Klux Klan (KKK), Proud Boys, the Aryan Nation, Neo-Nazis, and other White hate groups (Appendix IV list hate groups) operate with relative un-harassed freedom because their targets are non-White people. This is only one indication of the duality of justice in America. Even decent White people remain silent or ignore illegal actions by Whites, when atrocities against Black and minority people occur. This only reinforces racism and motivates racist to become more violent. Failure to address racists and racism in America only leads to White people feeling justified and empowered to behave deplorably and participate in acts of racist behavior, occurring at all levels of society. White Police throughout America kill unarmed or innocent

Black people and are virtually unpunished or receive a minimal sentence, with rare exceptions. [4]

Racism is so American that when you PROTEST IT,
People think you are protesting America

What type of People,
Mother, Father,
Country or Society
would ALLOW
THIS
To turn into
THAT????????

The diminishment of a child's preciousness is sick, and abusive.
The positive enhancement of a child's development contributes to societal well-being.

And many of these
Are
These in disguise.

Racism is embedded in America to a significant degree. It is implanted deep into White culture, and American institutions. The reason American Institutions are racist is because they are run and influenced by White people. While some White people attempt to hide their racism, many still harbor racist residue and sentiments. Too many Americans have racist beliefs embedded deep in their nature. Racist Socialization is a normal phenomenon in White culture.

The real tragedy is to witness innocent pure young children become socialized into deplorable adults who internalize hatred against other groups of people for no logical reason instead of becoming decent Americans internalizing American values. Racism is not an American value.

White racism is a cause of many American catastrophes. White racism is a primary reason America has so many problems, not only between its citizens but also between its leadership. Racism causes a "tidal wave" of problems between people in America. American racism inhibits People from getting along with each other. They do not know how to resolve differences, nor do they know how to accept non- threatening differences in different cultures, religions, appearances, or races.

Americans' inability to get along with each other causes a "constant storm of conflict ", "a constant state of disruption" in American Society. This disruptive state of chaotic mentality among Americans, not only causes problems in their relationships with fellow Americans but it also disrupts the balance in worldwide relationships. Racism is a reason for the inequalities in America. Americans cannot get along with fellow Americans, how can we expect them to get along with people who are not Americans? The non-compromising ideology and psychology creates divisions. Dysfunction is a characteristic that permeates throughout all interactive phenomena in the lived experiences of racist individuals.

Dedication I

This author reached out to those who were parties and accomplices in discriminating against the author. The author contacted Sarah Nolan, Assistant Chief Joanne Nee, Attorney Jackie Hennard, and Assistant Provost Ingrid Gould to interview and get their feedback and response to the incident referenced herein. Each of them refused interview input for this book. The author contacted Assistant Police Chief, Joanne Nee, by phone on two occasions and left voice messages for her input. She did not returned either of the phone calls but did send an email indicating her unwillingness to participate. This author also contacted Sara Nolan by phone to give her the opportunity to give input. Sarah Nolan did not return the call but did respond by email, refusing to participate. Attorney Jackie Hennard avoided all conversation on this issue. All University investigative personnel and respondents to the complaint lodged by Dr. Barnes refused to respond or give their side of the incident. (Appendix 1, Exhibit 1). Ingrid Gould refused to interview but was strategically responsible for resolving the matter with a shortsighted result. I will add that it is the opinion of this author that Ms. Gould was in a difficult position. She realized the unfairness of the action, taken against Dr. Barnes, resulting in her reversing the action on behalf of Dr. Barnes (Appendix 10). In addition, she was an administrative member of the University of Chicago and responsible for upholding the reputation of the university. People usually do not testify or respond to a complaint, especially when they are guilty, at fault, or realize there is validity to the complaint against them. In the case of Ms. Gould, the hypothesis is she was acting political correct on behalf of the university, while at the same time focused on correcting the injustice against Dr. Barnes. Dr. Barnes does appreciate the corrective action taken by Ms. Gould and applauds her for doing the right thing. Although she did fall short of evaluating the situation realistically. Ms. Gould watered down and minimized an act of discrimination as a misunderstanding. The author dedicates this book to them: Sarah Nolan, Attorney Jackie Hennard, Assistant Police Chief Joanne Nee, and Assistant Provost Ingrid Gould. Since the writing of this book, Attorney Jackie Hennard has resigned from the employ of the University of Chicago, as she should have done. This book is also dedicated to the University of Chicago and all other institutions of learning dedicated to the elimination of the divisions in society. It is important to teach equalities in attitudes and behaviors among all human beings. That is the America Way, in theory and dogma. The challenge for America is to align theory and dogma with practice and behavior.

Again, this author wants to reiterate he believes most White people are good and decent human beings. This author believes that the majority of White people believe in the dogma of the United States of America including the Constitution of the United States of America and doctrines that speak to the equality and decency of all human beings (The Declaration of Independence, The Bill of Rights for all, The Emancipation Proclamation and the Holy Bible). The author also wants to state that he believes the individuals at the University of Chicago referenced in this book are decent individuals even though the case study incident that is the backdrop of this book indicates the contrary. This circumstance indicates that even decent White people harbor the *"racist residue"* resulting from their White cultural racist history. The author hopes those to whom this book is dedicated will give a second thought if they are ever confronted with a similar situation in the future and respond with more mindful emotional intelligence. White people process information involving African American individuals differently than they do information involving White individuals.

It is astonishing how people, in this case study Chapters VII through VII, can take something so well meaning and turn it into toilet residue. Sometimes people encounter situations that reveal repressed aspects of their personality. Racist behaviors are a part of the socialization and development process to a significant degree in White culture. Racist traits are socialized in White culture as learned behavior that begins with the childhood developmental process. Early in life, when White people only interact with to other White people reinforces racist tendency. When they attend all White elementary schools and all White secondary schools, white privilege is reinforced. The perspective on the world White kids learn is influence by White culture, White parents and the limitations of an all-White environment, being the only substantial contact they have with the world they live in. White people, White youth encounters, are isolated from interaction with diverse individuals. Attending all White schools and having limited or no interaction with people of diverse backgrounds, gives White kids limited knowledge of the world they live in. This limitation leads them into a discriminating judgmental mindset. Segregated environments reinforce racist's attitudes. Media and other bias White viewpoints shape and mold the White youth's impression of Black people when their direct interactions are limited or null. How to break the cycle of prejudice behavior is a learning process. Learning institutions (from elementary schools, high schools, colleges and universities) can make a significant contribution to the student body, the alumni, American society, and be an example for the world, if they address the issue of racism and discrimination effectively. Sometimes individuals change their racist inclinations because of introduction new experiences. Sometimes individuals who are socialized into a diverse psychology become racist because of introduction to new experiences. Effectively addressing the issues of racism and discrimination will only enhance the already esteemed reputation of institutions like the University of Chicago, Harvard University and other leaning institutions throughout America that prepare young minds to influence society. Unaddressed, without resolution; the dysfunction of racism, discrimination and prejudice will continue to have negative impact and stain on White culture and White people, at the expense of non-White people, Black people, and American society. Even educated White people will act with a low emotional IQ and embrace thinking and behavior that will negatively influence their lives, if they do not learn and behave in ways that display a positive respect for diversity.

Dedication II

(Rest in Peace)

More importantly, this book is dedicated to the almost 200 unarmed Black and Brown human beings killed by police. The list only includes unarmed Black and Brown people killed by police from the 1970's up to 2020. This dedication also applies to those Black and Brown people killed after 2020 as well. The list does not include the historic, growing and ongoing violent atrocities committed against Asians, Jews, Muslims and LGBHT individuals by White people. The list of these innocent victims are as follows: [5]

Ahmaud Aubrey – 25 years old
Shot and killed by 3 White men because he was a Black man.
Shot on February 23, 2020 in Brunswick, Georgia

Charles "Chop" Roundtree Jr., September 5, 2000 - October 17, 2018
San Antonio, Texas
Shot: October 17, 2018, San Antonio Police Officer

Chinedu Okobi, February 13, 1982 - October 3, 2018
Millbrae, California
Tasered/Electrocuted: October 3, 2018, San Mateo County Sheriff Sergeant and Sheriff Deputies

Anton Milbert LaRue Black, October 18, 1998 - September 15, 2018
Greensboro, Maryland
Tasered/Sudden Cardiac Arrest: September 15, 2018, Greensboro Police Officers

Botham Shem Jean, September 29, 1991 - September 6, 2018
Dallas, Texas
Shot: September 6, 2018, Dallas Police Officer

Antwon Rose Jr., July 12, 2000 - June 19, 2018
East Pittsburgh, Pennsylvania
Shot: June 19, 2018, East Pittsburgh Police Officer

Saheed Vassell, December 22, 1983 - April 4, 2018
Brooklyn, New York City, New York
Shot: April 4, 2018, Four Unnamed New York City Police Officers

Stephon Alonzo Clark, August 10, 1995 - March 18, 2018
Sacramento, California
Shot: March 18, 2018, Sacramento Police Officers

Dennis Plowden Jr., 1992 - December 28, 2017
East Germantown, Philadelphia, Pennsylvania
Shot: December 27, 2017, Philadelphia Police Officer

Bijan Ghaisar, September 4, 1992 - November 27, 2017
George Washington Memorial Parkway, Alexandria, Virginia
Shot: November 17, 2017, U.S. Park Police Officers

Aaron Bailey, 1972 - June 29, 2017
Indianapolis, Indiana
Shot: June 29, 2017, Indianapolis Metropolitan Police Officers

Charleena Chavon Lyles, April 24, 1987 - June 18, 2017
Seattle, Washington
Shot: June 18, 2017, Seattle Police Officers

Fetus of Charleena Chavon Lyles (14-15 weeks), June 18, 2017
Seattle, Washington
Shot: June 18, 2017, Seattle Police Officers

Jordan Edwards, October 25, 2001 - April 29, 2017
Balch Springs, Texas
Shot: April 29, 2017, Balch Springs Officer

Chad Robertson, 1992 - February 15, 2017
Chicago, Illinois
Shot: February 8, 2017, Chicago Police Officer

Deborah Danner, September 25, 1950 - October 18, 2016
The Bronx, New York City, New York
Shot: October 18, 2016, New York City Police Officers

Michael Brent Charles Ramos, January 1, 1978 - April 24, 2020
Austin, Texas
Shot: April 24, 2020, Austin Police Detectives

Daniel T. Prude, September 20, 1978 - March 30, 2020
Rochester, New York
Asphyxiation: March 23, 2020, Rochester Police Officers

Breonna Taylor, June 5, 1993 - March 13, 2020
Louisville, Kentucky
Shot: March 13, 2020, Louisville Metro Police Officers

Manuel "Mannie" Elijah Ellis, August 28, 1986 - March 3, 2020
Tacoma, Washington
Physical restraint/Hypoxia: March 3, 2020, Tacoma Police Officers
4, 2019
Winston-Salem, North Carolina
Asphyxiated (hog-tied in prone position)/Heart Attack/Brain Injury: December 2, 2019, Forsyth County Sheriff Officers
Atatiana Koquice Jefferson, November 28, 1990 - October 12, 2019
Fort Worth, Texas
Shot: October 12, 2019, Fort Worth Police Officer
William Howard Green, March 16, 1976 - January 27, 2020
Temple Hills, Maryland
Shot: January 27, 2020, Prince George's County Police Officer
John Elliot Neville, 1962 - December 4, 2019
Winston-Salem, North Carolina
Asphyxiated (hog-tied in prone position)/Heart Attack/Brain Injury: December 2, 2019, Forsyth County Sheriff Officers
Atatiana Koquice Jefferson, November 28, 1990 - October 12, 2019
Fort Worth, Texas
Shot: October 12, 2019, Fort Worth Police Officer
Elijah McClain, February 25, 1996 - August 30, 2019
Aurora, Colorado
Chokehold/Ketamine/Heart Attack: August 24, 2019, Aurora Police Officers and Paramedic
Ronald Greene, September 28, 1969 - May 10, 2019
Monroe, Louisiana
Stun gun/Force: May 10, 2019, Louisiana State Police
Javier Ambler, October 7, 1978 - March 28, 2019
Austin, Texas
Tasered/Electrocuted: March 28, 2019, Williamson County Sheriff Deputy
Sterling Lapree Higgins, October 27, 1981 - March 25, 2019
Union City, Tennessee
Choke hold/Asphyxiation: March 24-25, 2019, Union City Police Officer and Obion County Sheriff Deputies
Gregory Lloyd Edwards, September 23, 1980 - December 10, 2018
Brevard County Jail, Cocoa, Florida
Kneed, Punched, Pepper Sprayed, Tasered, and Strapped into a restraint chair with a spit hood over his head/Failure to Provide Medical Care: December 9, 2019, Brevard County Sheriffs
Emantic "EJ" Fitzgerald Bradford Jr., June 18, 1997 - November 22, 2018
Hoover, Alabama
Shot: November 22, 2018, Unidentified Hoover Police Officers
Daunte Demetrius Wright, October 27, 2000 - April 11, 2021
Brooklyn Center, Minnesota
Shot: Brooklyn Center Police Officer, April 11, 2021
Marvin David Scott III, 1995 - March 14, 2021
McKinney, Texas
Peppered sprayed/Restrained with spit hood/Asphyxiated: 7 Collin County Jail Detention Officers, March 14, 2021
Patrick Lynn Warren Sr., October 7, 1968 - January 10, 2021
Killeen, Texas
Shot: Killeen Police Officer, January 10, 2021
Vincent "Vinny" M. Belmonte, September 14, 2001 - January 5, 2021
Cleveland, Ohio
Shot: Cleveland Police Officer, January 5, 20201
Angelo Quinto, March 10, 1990 - December 26, 2020
Antioch, California
Knee on neck/Asphyxiated: December 23, 2020

Andre Maurice Hill, May 23, 1973 - December 22, 2020
Columbus, Ohio
Shot: December 22, 2020, Columbus Police Officer
Casey Christopher Goodson Jr., January 30, 1997 - December 4, 2020
Columbus, Ohio
Shot: December 4, 2020, Franklin County Sheriff Deputy
Angelo "AJ" Crooms, May 15, 2004 - November 13, 2020
Cocoa, Florida
Shot: November 13, 2020, Brevard County Sheriff Deputies
Marcellis Stinnette, June 17, 2001 - October 20, 2020
Waukegan, Illinois
Shot: October 20, 2020, Waukegan Police Officer
Jonathan Dwayne Price, November 3, 1988 - October 3, 2020
Wolfe City, Texas
Tasered/Shot: October 3, 2020, Wolfe City Police Officer
Dijon Durand Kizzee, February 5, 1991 - August 31, 2020
Los Angeles, California
Shot: August 21, 2020, Los Angeles County Police
Rayshard Brooks, January 31, 1993 - June 12, 2020
Atlanta, Georgia
Shot: June 12, 2020, Atlanta Police Officer
Carlos Carson, May 16, 1984 - June 6, 2020
Tulsa, Oklahoma
Pepper Sprayed/Shot in Head: June 6, 2020, Knights Inn Tulsa Armed Security Guard, former sergeant and detention officer with the Tulsa County Sheriff's Office
David McAtee, August 3, 1966 - June 1, 2020
Louisville, Kentucky
Shot: June 1, 2020, Louisville Metropolitan Police Officer
Tony "Tony the TIger" McDade, 1982 - May 27, 2020
Tallahassee, Florida
Shot: May 27, 2020, Tallahassee Police Officers
George Perry Floyd, October 14, 1973 - May 25, 2020
Powderhorn, Minneapolis, Minnesota
Knee on neck/Asphyxiated: May 25, 2020, Minneapolis Police Officer
Dreasjon "Sean" Reed, 1999 - May 6, 2020
Indianapolis, Indiana
Shot: May 6, 2020, Unidentified Indianapolis Metropolitan Police Officer
Michael Brent Charles Ramos, January 1, 1978 - April 24, 2020
Austin, Texas
Shot: April 24, 2020, Austin Police Detectives
Daniel T. Prude, September 20, 1978 - March 30, 2020
Rochester, New York
Asphyxiation: March 23, 2020, Rochester Police Officers
Breonna Taylor, June 5, 1993 - March 13, 2020
Louisville, Kentucky
Shot: March 13, 2020, Louisville Metro Police Officers
Manuel "Mannie" Elijah Ellis, August 28, 1986 - March 3, 2020
Tacoma, Washington
Physical restraint/Hypoxia: March 3, 2020, Tacoma Police Officers
William Howard Green, March 16, 1976 - January 27, 2020
Temple Hills, Maryland
Shot: January 27, 2020, Prince George's County Police Officer
John Elliot Neville, 1962 - December 4, 2019
Winston-Salem, North Carolina
Asphyxiated (hog-tied in prone position)/Heart Attack/Brain Injury: December 2, 2019, Forsyth County Sheriff Officers

Atatiana Koquice Jefferson, November 28, 1990 - October 12, 2019
Fort Worth, Texas
Shot: October 12, 2019, Fort Worth Police Officer
Elijah McClain, February 25, 1996 - August 30, 2019
Aurora, Colorado
Chokehold/Ketamine/Heart Attack: August 24, 2019, Aurora Police Officers and Paramedic
Ronald Greene, September 28, 1969 - May 10, 2019
Monroe, Louisiana
Stun gun/Force: May 10, 2019, Louisiana State Police
Javier Ambler, October 7, 1978 - March 28, 2019
Austin, Texas
Tasered/Electrocuted: March 28, 2019, Williamson County Sheriff Deputy
Sterling Lapree Higgins, October 27, 1981 - March 25, 2019
Union City, Tennessee
Choke hold/Asphyxiation: March 24-25, 2019, Union City Police Officer and Obion County Sheriff Deputies
Gregory Lloyd Edwards, September 23, 1980 - December 10, 2018
Brevard County Jail, Cocoa, Florida
Kneed, Punched, Pepper Sprayed, Tasered, and Strapped into a restraint chair with a spit hood over his head/Failure to Provide Medical Care: December 9, 2019, Brevard County Sheriffs
Emantic "EJ" Fitzgerald Bradford Jr., June 18, 1997 - November 22, 2018
Hoover, Alabama
Shot: November 22, 2018, Unidentified Hoover Police Officers
Charles "Chop" Roundtree Jr., September 5, 2000 - October 17, 2018
San Antonio, Texas
Shot: October 17, 2018, San Antonio Police Officer
Chinedu Okobi, February 13, 1982 - October 3, 2018
Millbrae, California
Tasered/Electrocuted: October 3, 2018, San Mateo County Sheriff Sergeant and Sheriff Deputies
Anton Milbert LaRue Black, October 18, 1998 - September 15, 2018
Greensboro, Maryland
Tasered/Sudden Cardiac Arrest: September 15, 2018, Greensboro Police Officers
Botham Shem Jean, September 29, 1991 - September 6, 2018
Dallas, Texas
Shot: September 6, 2018, Dallas Police Officer
Antwon Rose Jr., July 12, 2000 - June 19, 2018
East Pittsburgh, Pennsylvania
Shot: June 19, 2018, East Pittsburgh Police Officer
Saheed Vassell, December 22, 1983 - April 4, 2018
Brooklyn, New York City, New York
Shot: April 4, 2018, Four Unnamed New York City Police Officers
Stephon Alonzo Clark, August 10, 1995 - March 18, 2018
Sacramento, California
Shot: March 18, 2018, Sacramento Police Officers
Dennis Plowden Jr., 1992 - December 28, 2017
East Germantown, Philadelphia, Pennsylvania
Shot: December 27, 2017, Philadelphia Police Officer

Bijan Ghaisar, September 4, 1992 - November 27, 2017
George Washington Memorial Parkway, Alexandria, Virginia
Shot: November 17, 2017, U.S. Park Police Officers
Aaron Bailey, 1972 - June 29, 2017
Indianapolis, Indiana

Shot: June 29, 2017, Indianapolis Metropolitan Police Officers

Charleena Chavon Lyles, April 24, 1987 - June 18, 2017
Seattle, Washington
Shot: June 18, 2017, Seattle Police Officers

Fetus of Charleena Chavon Lyles (14-15 weeks), June 18, 2017
Seattle, Washington
Shot: June 18, 2017, Seattle Police Officers

Jordan Edwards, October 25, 2001 - April 29, 2017
Balch Springs, Texas
Shot: April 29, 2017, Balch Springs Officer

Chad Robertson, 1992 - February 15, 2017
Chicago, Illinois
Shot: February 8, 2017, Chicago Police Officer

Deborah Danner, September 25, 1950 - October 18, 2016
The Bronx, New York City, New York
Shot: October 18, 2016, New York City Police Officers

Alfred Olango, July 29, 1978 - September 27, 2016
El Cajon, California
Shot: September 27, 2016, El Cajon Police Officers

Terence Crutcher, August 16, 1976 - September 16, 2016
Tulsa, Oklahoma
Shot: September 16, 2016, Tulsa Police Officer

Terrence LeDell Sterling, July 31, 1985 - September 11, 2016
Washington, DC
Shot: September 11, 2016, Washington Metropolitan Police Officer

Korryn Gaines, August 24, 1993 - August 1, 2016
Randallstown, Maryland
Shot: August 1, 2016, Baltimore County Police

Joseph Curtis Mann, 1966 - July 11, 2016
Sacramento, California
Shot: July 11, 2016, Sacramento Police Officers

Philando Castile, July 16, 1983 - July 6, 2016
Falcon Heights, Minnesota
Shot: July 6, 2016, St. Anthony Police Officer

Alton Sterling, June 14, 1979 - July 5, 2016
Baton Rouge, Louisiana
Shot: July 5, 2016, Baton Rouge Police Officers

Bettie "Betty Boo" Jones, 1960 - December 26, 2015
Chicago, Illinois
Shot: December 26, 2015, Chicago Police Officer

Quintonio LeGrier, April 29, 1996 - December 26, 2015
Chicago, Illinois
Shot: December 26, 2015, Chicago Police Officer

Corey Lamar Jones, February 3, 1984 - October 18, 2015
Palm Beach Gardens, Florida
Shot: October 18, 2015, Palm Beach Gardens Police Officer

Jamar O'Neal Clark, May 3, 1991 - November 16, 2015
Minneapolis, Minnesota
Shot: November 15, 2015, Minneapolis Police Officers

Jeremy "Bam Bam" McDole, 1987 - September 23, 2015
Wilmington, Delaware
Shot: September 23, 2015, Wilmington Police Officers

India Kager, June 9, 1988 - September 5, 2015
Virginia Beach, Virginia
Shot: September 5, 2015, Virginia Beach Police Officers

Samuel Vincent DuBose, March 12, 1972 - July 19, 2015
Cincinnati, Ohio
Shot: July 19, 2015, University of Cincinnati Police Officer

Sandra Bland, February 7, 1987 - July 13, 2015
Waller County, Texas
Excessive Force/Wrongful Death/Suicide (?): July 10, 2015, Texas State Trooper

Brendon K. Glenn, 1986 - May 5, 2015
Venice, California
Shot: May 5, 2015, Los Angeles Police Officer
Freddie Carlos Gray Jr., August 16, 1989 - April 19, 2015
Baltimore, Maryland
Brute Force/Spinal Injuries: April 12, 2015, Baltimore City Police Officers
Walter Lamar Scott, February 9, 1965 - April 4, 2015
North Charleston, South Carolina
Shot: April 4, 2015, North Charleston Police Officer
Eric Courtney Harris, October 10, 1971 - April 2, 2015
Tulsa, Oklahoma
Shot: April 2, 2015, Tulsa County Reserve Deputy
Phillip Gregory White, 1982 - March 31, 2015
Vineland, New Jersey
K-9 Mauling/Respiratory distress: March 31, 2015, Vineland Police Officers
Mya Shawatza Hall, December 5, 1987 - March 30, 2015
Fort Meade, Maryland
Shot: March 30, 2015, National Security Agency Police Officers
Meagan Hockaday, August 27, 1988 - March 28, 2015
Oxnard, California
Shot: March 28, 2015, Oxnard Police Officer
Tony Terrell Robinson, Jr., October 18, 1995 - March 6, 2015
Madison, Wisconsin
Shot: March 6, 2015, Madison Police Officer
Janisha Fonville, March 3, 1994 - February 18 2015
Charlotte, North Carolina
Shot: February 18, 2015, Charlotte-Mecklenburg Police Officer
Natasha McKenna, January 9, 1978 - February 8, 2015
Fairfax County, Virginia
Tasered/Cardiac Arrest: February 3, 2015, Fairfax County Sheriff Deputies
Jerame C. Reid, June 8, 1978 - December 30, 2014
Bridgeton, New Jersey
Shot: December 30, 2014, Bridgeton Police Officer
Rumain Brisbon, November 24, 1980 - December 2, 2014
Phoenix, Arizona
Shot: December 2, 2014, Phoenix Police Officer
Tamir Rice, June 15, 2002 - November 22, 2014
Cleveland, Ohio
Shot: November 22, 2014, Cleveland Police Officer
Akai Kareem Gurley, November 12, 1986 - November 20, 2014
Brooklyn, New York City, New York
Shot: November 20, 2014, New York City Police Officer
Tanisha N. Anderson, January 22, 1977 - November 13, 2014
Cleveland, Ohio
Physically Restrained/Brute Force: November 13, 2014, Cleveland Police Officers
Dante Parker, August 14, 1977 - August 12, 2014
Victorville, California
Tasered/Excessive Force: August 12, 2014, San Bernardino County Sheriff Deputies
Ezell Ford, October 14, 1988 - August 11, 2014
Florence, Los Angeles, California
Shot: August 11, 2014, Los Angeles Police Officers
Michael Brown Jr., May 20, 1996 - August 9, 2014
Ferguson, Missouri
Shot: August 9, 2014, Ferguson Police Officer
John Crawford III, July 29, 1992 - August 5, 2014
Beavercreek, Ohio
Shot: August 5, 2014, Beavercreek Police Officer

Tyree Woodson, July 8, 1976 - August 2, 2014
Baltimore, Maryland
Shot: August 2, 2014, Baltimore City Police Officer
Eric Garner, September 15, 1970 - July 17, 2014
Staten Island, New York
Choke hold/Suffocated: July 17, 2014, New York City Police Officer
Dontre Hamilton, January 20, 1983 - April 30, 2014
Milwaukee, Wisconsin
Shot: April 30, 2014, Milwaukee Police Officer
Victor White III, September 11, 1991 - March 3, 2014
New Iberia, Louisiana
Shot: March 2, 2014, Iberia Parish Sheriff Deputy
Gabriella Monique Nevarez, November 25, 1991 - March 2, 2014
Citrus Heights, California
Shot: March 2, 2014, Citrus Heights Police Officers
Yvette Smith, December 18, 1966 - February 16, 2014
Bastrop County, Texas
Shot: February 16, 2014, Bastrop County Sheriff Deputy
McKenzie J. Cochran, August 25, 1988 - January 29, 2014
Southfield, Michigan
Pepper Sprayed/Compression Asphyxiation: January 28, 2014, Northland Mall Security Guards
Jordan Baker, 1988 - January 16, 2014
Houston, Texas
Shot: January 16, 2014, Off-duty Houston Police Officer
Andy Lopez, June 2, 2000 - October 22, 2013
Santa Rosa, California
Shot: October 22, 2013, Sonoma County Sheriff Deputy
Miriam Iris Carey, August 12, 1979 - October 3, 2013
Washington, DC
Shot 26 times: October 3, 2013, U. S. Secret Service Officer
Barrington "BJ" Williams, 1988 - September 17, 2013
New York City, New York
Neglect/Disdain/Asthma Attack: September 17, 2013, New York City Police Officers
Jonathan Ferrell, October 11, 1989 - September 14, 2013
Charlotte, North Carolina
Shot: September 14, 2013, Charlotte-Mecklenburg Police Officer
Carlos Alcis, 1970 - August 15, 2013
Brooklyn, New York City
Heart Attack/Neglect: August 15, 2013, New York City Police Officers
Larry Eugene Jackson Jr., November 29, 1980 - July 26, 2013
Austin, Texas
Shot: July 26, 2013, Austin Police Detective
Kyam Livingston, July 29, 1975 - July 21, 2013
New York City, New York
Neglect/Ignored pleas for help: July 20-21, 2013, New York City Police Officers
Clinton R. Allen, September 26, 1987 - March 10, 2013
Dallas, Texas
Tasered and Shot: March 10, 2013, Dallas Police Officer
Kimani "KiKi" Gray, October 19, 1996 - March 9, 2013
Brooklyn, New York City, New York
Shot: March 9, 2013, New York Police Officers
Kayla Moore, April 17, 1971 - February 13, 2013
Berkeley, California
Restrained face-down prone: February 12, 2013, Berkeley Police Officers
Jamaal Moore Sr., 1989 - December 15, 2012

Chicago, Illinois
Shot: December 15, 2012, Chicago Police Officer
Johnnie Kamahi Warren, February 26, 1968 - February 13, 2012
Dothan, Alabama
Tasered/Electrocuted: December 10, 2012, Houston County (AL) Sheriff Deputy
Shelly Marie Frey, April 21, 1985 - December 6, 2012
Houston, Texas
Shot: December 6, 2012, Off-duty Harris County Sheriff's Deputy
Darnisha Diana Harris, December 11, 1996 - December 2, 2012
Breaux Bridge, Louisiana
Shot: December 2, 2012, Breaux Bridge Police Office
Timothy Russell, December 9. 1968 - November 29, 2012
Cleveland, Ohio
137 Rounds/Shot 23 times: November 29, 2012, Cleveland Police Officers
Malissa Williams, June 20, 1982 - November 29, 2012
Cleveland, Ohio
137 Rounds/Shot 24 times: November 29, 2012, Cleveland Police Officers
Noel Palanco, November 28, 1989 - October 4, 2012
Queens, New York City, New York
Shot: October 4, 2012, New York City Police Officers
Reynaldo Cuevas, January 6, 1992 - September 7, 2012
Bronx, New York City, New York
Shot: September 7, 2012, New York City Police Officer
Chavis Carter, 1991 - July 28, 2012
Jonesboro, Arkansas
Shot: July 28, 2012, Jonesboro Police Officer
Alesia Thomas, June 1, 1977 - July 22, 2012
Los Angeles, California
Brutal Force/Beaten: July 22, 2012, Los Angeles Police Officers
Shantel Davis, May 26, 1989 - June 14, 2012
New York City, New York
Shot: June 14, 2012, New York City Police Officer
Sharmel T. Edwards, October 10, 1962 - April 21, 2012
Las Vegas, Nevada
Shot: April 21, 2012, Las Vegas Police Officers
Tamon Robinson, December 21, 1985 - April 18, 2012
Brooklyn, New York City, New York
Run over by police car: April 12, 2012, New York City Police Officers
Ervin Lee Jefferson, III, 1994 - March 24, 2012
Atlanta, Georgia
Shot: March 24, 2012, Shepperson Security & Escort Services Security Guards
Kendrec McDade, May 5, 1992 - March 24, 2012
Pasadena, California
Shot: March 24, 2012, Pasadena Police Officers
Rekia Boyd, November 5, 1989 - March 21, 2012
Chicago, Illinois
Shot: March 21, 2012, Off-duty Chicago Police Detective
Shereese Francis, 1982 - March 15, 2012
Queens, New York City, New York
Suffocated to death: March 15, 2012, New York City Police Officers
Jersey K. Green, June 17, 1974 - March 12, 2012
Aurora, Illinois
Tasered/Electrocuted: March 12, 2012, Aurora Police Officers
Wendell James Allen, December 19, 1991 - March 7, 2012
New Orleans, Louisiana
Shot: March 7, 2012, New Orleans Police Officer
Nehemiah Lazar Dillard, July 29, 1982 - March 5, 2012

Gainesville, Florida
Tasered/Electrocuted: March 5, 2012, Alachua County Sheriff Deputies

Dante' Lamar Price, July 18, 1986 - March 1, 2012
Dayton, Ohio
Shot: March 1, 2012, Ranger Security Guards

Raymond Luther Allen Jr., 1978 - February 29, 2012
Galveston, Texas
Tasered/Electrocuted: February 27, 2012, Galveston Police Officers

Manual Levi Loggins Jr., February 22, 1980 - February 7, 2012
San Clemente, Orange County, California
Shot: February 7, 2012, Orange County Sheriff Deputy

Ramarley Graham, April 12, 1993 - February 2, 2012
The Bronx, New York City, New York
Shot: February 2, 2012, New York City Police Officer

Kenneth Chamberlain Sr., April 12, 1943 - November 19, 2011
White Plains, New York
Tasered/Electrocuted/Shot: November 19, 2011, White Plains Police Officers

Alonzo Ashley, June 10, 1982 - July 18, 2011
Denver, Colorado
Tasered/Electrocuted: July 18, 2011, Denver Police Officers

Derek Williams, January 23, 1989 - July 6, 2011
Milwaukee, Wisconsin
Blunt Force/Respiratory distress: July 6, 2011, Milwaukee Police Officers

Raheim Brown, Jr., March 4, 1990 - January 22, 2011
Oakland, California
Shot: January 22, 2011, Oakland Unified School District Police

Reginald Doucet, June 3, 1985 - January 14, 2011
Los Angeles, California
Shot: January 14, 2011, Los Angeles Police Officer

Derrick Jones, September 30, 1973 - November 8, 2010
Oakland, California
Shot: November 8, 2010, Oakland Police Officers

Danroy "DJ" Henry Jr., October 29, 1990 - October 17, 2010
Pleasantville, New York
Shot: October 17, 2020, Pleasantville Police Officer

Aiyana Mo'Nay Stanley-Jones, July 20, 2002 - May 16, 2010
Detroit, Michigan
Shot: May 16, 2010, Detroit Police Officer

Steven Eugene Washington, September 20, 1982 - March 20, 2010
Los Angeles, California
Shot: March 20, 2010, Los Angeles County Police

Aaron Campbell, September 7, 1984 - January 29, 2010
Portland, Oregon
Shot: January 29, 2010, Portland Police Officer

Kiwane Carrington, July 14, 1994 - October 9, 2009
Champaign, Illinois
Shot: October 9, 2019, Champaign Police Officer

Victor Steen, November 11, 1991 - October 3, 2009
Pensacola, Florida
Tasered/Run over: October 3, 2009, Pensacola Police Officer

Shem Walker, March 18, 1960 - July 11, 2009
Brooklyn, New York
Shot: July 11, 2009, New York City Undercover C-94 Police Officer

Oscar Grant III, February 27, 1986 - January 1, 2009

Oakland, California
Shot: January 1, 2009, BART Police Officer
Tarika Wilson, October 30, 1981 - January 4, 2008
Lima, Ohio
Shot January 4, 2008, Lima Police Officer
DeAunta Terrel Farrow, September 7, 1994 - June 22, 2007
West Memphis, Arkansas
Shot: June 22, 2007, West Memphis (AR) Police Officer
Sean Bell, May 23, 1983 - November 25, 2006
Queens, New York City, New York
Shot: November 25, 2006, New York City Police Officers
Kathryn Johnston, June 26, 1914 - November 21, 2006
Atlanta, Georgia
Shot: November 21, 2006, Undercover Atlanta Police Officers
Ronald Curtis Madison, March 1, 1965 - September 4, 2005
Danziger Bridge, New Orleans, Louisiana
Shot: September 4, 2005, New Orleans Police Officers
James B. Brissette Jr., November 6, 1987 - September 4, 2005
Danziger Bridge, New Orleans, Louisiana
Shot: September 4, 2005, New Orleans Police Officers
Henry "Ace" Glover, October 2, 1973 - September 2, 2005
New Orleans, Louisiana
Shot: September 2, 2005, New Orleans Police Officers
Timothy Stansbury, Jr., November 16, 1984 - January 24, 2004
Brooklyn, New York City, New York
Shot: January 24, 2004, New York City Police Officer
Ousmane Zongo, 1960 - May 22, 2003
New York City, New York
Shot: May 22, 2003, New York City Police Officer
Alberta Spruill, 1946 - May 16, 2003
New York City, New York
Stun grenade thrown into her apartment led to a heart attack: May 16, 2003, New York City Police Officer
Kendra Sarie James, December 24, 1981 - May 5, 2003
Portland, Oregon
Shot: May 5, 2003, Portland Police Officer
Orlando Barlow, December 29, 1974 - February 28, 2003
Las Vegas, Nevada
Shot: February 28, 2003, Las Vegas Police Officer
Nelson Martinez Mendez, 1977 - August 8, 2001
Bellevue, Washington
Shot: August 8, 2001, Bellevue Police Officer
Timothy DeWayne Thomas Jr., July 25, 1981 - April 7, 2001
Cincinnati, Ohio
Shot: April 7, 2001, Cincinnati Police Patrolman
Ronald Beasley, 1964 - June 12, 2000
Dellwood, Missouri
Shot: June 12, 2000, Dellwood Police Officers
Earl Murray, 1964 - June 12, 2000
Dellwood, Missouri
Shot: June 12, 2000, Dellwood Police Officers
Patrick Moses Dorismond, February 28, 1974 - March 16, 2000
New York City, New York
Shot: March 16, 2000, New York City Police Officer
Prince Carmen Jones Jr., March 30, 1975 - September 1, 2000
Fairfax County, Virginia
Shot: September 1, 2000, Prince George's County Police Officer
Malcolm Ferguson, October 31, 1976 - March 1, 2000
The Bronx, New York City, New York

Shot: March 1, 2000, New York City Police Officer
LaTanya Haggerty, 1973 - June 4, 1999
Chicago, Illinois
Shot: June 4, 1999, Chicago Police Officer
Margaret LaVerne Mitchell, 1945 - May 21, 1999
Los Angeles, California
Shot: May 21, 1999, Los Angeles Police Officer
Amadou Diallo, September 2, 1975 - February 4, 1999
The Bronx, New York City, New York
Shot: February 4, 1999, New York City Police Officers
Tyisha Shenee Miller, March 9, 1979 - December 28, 1998
Riverside, California
Shot: December 28, 1998, Riverside Police Officers
Dannette "Strawberry" Daniels, January 25, 1966 - June 7, 1997
Newark, New Jersey
Shot: June 7, 1997, Newark Police Officer
Frankie Ann Perkins, 1960 - March 22, 1997
Chicago, Illinois
Brutal Force/Strangled: March 22, 1997, Chicago Police Officers
Nicholas Heyward Jr., August 26, 1981 - September 27, 1994
Brooklyn, New York City, New York
Shot: September 27, 1994, New York City Police Officer
Mary Mitchell, 1950 - November 3, 1991
The Bronx, New York City, New York
Shot: November 3, 1991, New York City Police Officer
Yvonne Smallwood, July 26, 1959 - December 9, 1987
New York City, New York
Severely beaten/Massive blood clot: December 3, New York City Police Officers
Eleanor Bumpers, August 22, 1918 - October 29, 1984
The Bronx, New York City, New York
Shot: October 29, 1984, New York City Police Officer
Arthur Miller Jr., 1943 - June 14, 1978
Brooklyn, New York City, New York
Chokehold/Strangled: June 14, 1978, New York City Police Officers
Michael Jerome Stewart, May 9, 1958 - September 28, 1983
New York City, New York
Brutal Force: September 15, 1983, New York City Transit Police
Eula Mae Love, August 8, 1939 - January 3, 1979
Los Angeles, California
Shot: January 3, 1979, Los Angeles County Police Officers
Randolph Evans, April 5, 1961 - November 25, 1976
Brooklyn, New York City, New York
Shot in head: November 25, 1976, New York City Police Officer
Barry Gene Evans, August 29, 1958 - February 10, 1976
Los Angeles, California
Shot: February 10, 1976, Los Angeles Police Officers
Rita Lloyd, November 2, 1956 - January 27, 1973
New York City, New York
Shot: January 27, 1973, New York City Police Officer
Phillip Lafayette Gibbs, September 1, 1948 - May 15, 1970
Jackson, Mississippi
Shot: May 15, 2970, Jackson State University Police Officers
James Earl Green, 1953 - May 15, 1970
Jackson, Mississippi
Shot: May 15, 2970, Jackson State University Police Officers

Henry Dumas, July 20, 1934 - May 23, 1968
Harlem, New York City, New York
Shot: May 23, 1968, New York City Transit Police Officer

Fatal police shootings of unarmed Black people in US are more than three times as high as with Whites. Racism alone does not explain this phenomenon say researchers. Research findings indicate, "The influence of an insidious anti-Black and anti-Indigenous logic in police violence warrants further exploration into the role of these factors in fatal police encounters." [6] Investigation of police brutality and civil rights violation needs to be standard in every cases of killing unarmed Black and Brown people. "Police brutality refers to the excessive use of force by a police officer against a victim or victims that is deemed to go beyond the level required to sustain life, avoid injury, or control a situation." [7] Each of the cases mentioned in the dedication involved unarmed Black and Brown people killed by police. One hypothesis a White police shoots and kills an unarmed Black man, other than being a racist hater, is because the White police officer feels physically inferior to the Black individual, the police officer is scared.

While most interactions with police by Black and Brown people do not involve violence, one has to consider, what is the mental state, the psychology of police that steers them into situations of violence and acts of brutality, especially, when they use deadly force on an unarmed individual? Often police have backgrounds in the military, and many have experienced war and violent conflict encounters prior to becoming a police officer or entering the field of law enforcement. The mental health of law enforcement personnel may play a role in their response to Black and Brown individuals. A 2019 study found that officers reported to engage in abusive police practices tended to have higher levels of post-traumatic stress disorder (PTSD) symptoms. [8] Police officers with PTSD tend to be more suspicious toward others, especially people of color, if the police are White. PTSD can involve problems of aggression, which can cause a police officer to overreact and use unwarranted deadly force unnecessarily. [9] "Some researchers theorize that traits of "psychopathy", also called *Anti-social Personality Disorder* (APD), may be more prevalent in police officers than the general population. Traits such as "fearless dominance" or "cold-heartedness" can be adaptive in dangerous or emotionally charged situations, but they can also make an individual more likely to engage in excessive use of force or to feel that they do not need to follow the rules. [10] In addition, some White police are outright racist themselves, which diminishes their level of empathy for non-White and black people. White police exercise higher levels of suspicious behavior when they encounter non-White, Black and Brown people. They bring a predetermined sense of suspicion and guilt into any encounter involving Black and Brown individuals. The unprofessional and untrained use of White police racial profiling gives them a predetermined perception that Black and Brown people are guilty. The objective thought that a Black or Brown person is innocent is disregarded. [11] Fatal police shootings of unarmed Black people in US are more than 3 times as high as with Whites, even though whites commit more crimes.[12]

There is a significant movement throughout America to defund the police. This movement gained momentum after the unnecessary murder of George Floyd in Minneapolis by White police officer, Derek Chauvin. Floyd was unarmed and presented no resistance to his arrest. Trust in the police by the Black and Brown American communities is low, distrustful, and mixed with resentment and anger. Defunding of the police sprang from the belief that police are the enemy to Black and Brown people instead of protectors. According to Karissa Lewis, "The root cause of crime is poverty, but instead of making investments in our communities, people in positions of power are pushing for more money for police". [13] This statement by Ms. Lewis should come as no surprise. That America does not invest in Black and Brown communities but wants to increase police patrols to arrest or kill Black and Brown people is consistent with America's racism. It also speaks to the racism in the political infrastructure of America. Nevertheless, defunding the police is an extreme idea. Communities need police. The bad police need to be identified and eliminated. There are many good police. The budgets for police need to be increased but for the purpose of educating police, to train police in the behaviors of interacting in a diverse environment with Black and Brown people in ways that give them a positive image instead as being seen as enemies. Police need training in the mental attitude and psychology when interacting with minorities, especially White police. Racist police need to be eliminated from the police force and the police know who the racist police are. It is common knowledge that police protect racist police, which only jeopardizes the safety and quality of work of the good police. Police do dangerous work. The danger involved in police work requires a psychology different from that of the average citizen and worker in society. Defunding the police is not a good idea. Increasing the police budget for psychological and diversity training is a better solution, along with eliminating the racist police from their ranks. Police departments in America should also hire individuals who have a psychology that compliments diversity and is compatible with law enforcement in minority communities. This does not mean police should be soft on crime. Criminals are criminals regardless of their color. Police just need better training.

The case study backdrop described in Chapter IV thru Chapter VII of this book is not nearly as drastic as life threatening encounters. However, the author, Dr. Barnes did have an encounter with the police that involved presumption of guilt. The police encounter with officer Nee involving Dr. Barnes was a microcosm of those incidents mentioned above and an example of police mentality when dealing with Black people. The police interaction with Dr. Barnes assumed his guilt without getting his side of the story. The police interaction with Dr. Barnes took the word of a White person rather than approach the situation objectively. The fact that the complaint against Dr. Barnes was reversed; is an indication that White people often act with inadequate responsibility (irresponsibility), especially, and too often, when it comes to White police dealings with Black and Brown people. The encounter Dr. Barnes had with the White persons and White police described in the Case study referenced in this book, is an example of how White people act irresponsible when they encounter Black people. ***Black people harbor the awareness that every encounter they have with White police has the potential to end up in their death. This is a constant awareness in the minds and lived experience of Black and Brown people, a constant awareness White people do not have to deal with.***

It is with regret and sympathy that I dedicate this book to those Black and Brown individuals who have lost their lives unfortunately because they had an encounter with a police officer who probably should not have been a police officer in the first place. Loss of life is permanent, a situation in which there is no resolution. Many of the police involved should not have been a police officer in the first place.

Claims / Disclaimers

The author claims that every word of the Case Study (Chapter IV thru Chapter VII) in this Book describing the incident of racism encountered by Dr. Barnes is accurate according to what he experienced and observed. His communication with University of Chicago employees, his lived experience, the researched literature references from qualified professionals, and the description of events referenced by Dr. Barnes' experiences is accurate. The events referenced and documented by literature and that occurred in American society are empirically true. The author's experiences of the events and the assessments of events occurred as recounted. The respondents herein mentioned, were given many opportunities to provide input into this book, but refused. Dr. Barnes' intention is not to defame, disrespect, or bring a lawsuit against the individuals involved or the university. Dr. Barnes has great admiration, respect, and appreciation for the privilege of being an Alumnus of the University of Chicago (high school and graduate school). Dr. Barnes does not seek any negative recourse against those he feels discriminated against him. It is his believe they are decent people with "*racist residue*." His hope is for them to receive diversity training, along with the entire University of Chicago community, grow as individuals, and contribute to the university and society with mindful emotional and intellectual intelligence.

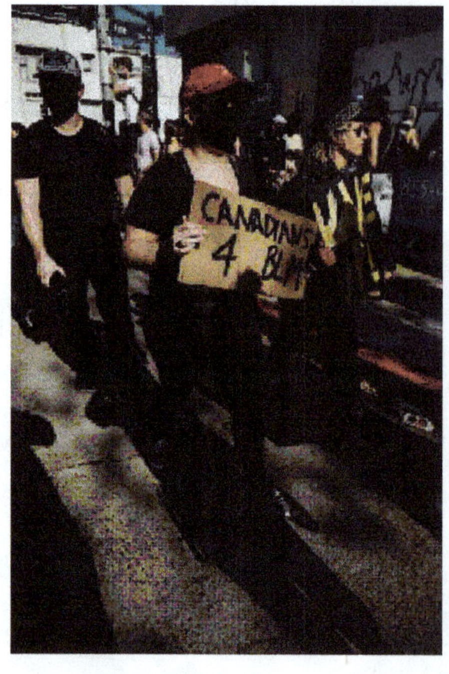

It is also important to note, again, that **not all White people are racists**. The tone of this book is strongly in disfavor of racism, racists, discrimination, prejudice, White supremacy / White supremacist, White Nationalism / White Nationalist, and Nazis. Distinction needs to be made between the deplorable White people and the decent White people. Decent White people know their culture is infiltrated with the virus of sick White others, who shame and stain White culture. **There are many good White people**; at least the 85,000,000 people who voted for Joe Biden. That, however, needs to be put into perspective with the 75,000,000 mostly White people who voted for Donald Trump. Hypothetically and figuratively, alluding to Biden voters labeled as non-racist and Donald Trump voters labeled as racist. Realistically, some Biden supporters could be racists and some Trump voters could be good people. The point is that there are a significant number of racist in America and the residue of America's racists history still permeates itself to this modern day 21st. Century.

Throughout this book, generalized, seriously meant, derogatory, empirically researched and sarcastic references are made about "*White people.*" These references apply to that significant segment of the White race and culture who harbor racist and White supremacist beliefs. These are not contextual reference about all White people in America. **Excluded from the derogatory references are those White people who support democracy, equality, those who are anti-racist, those who are not racist, and those who believe in the equality and equal rights for all human beings. Those White people who have transcended and escaped the "*Matrix*" of White privilege, White superiority, White nationalism, and racism are assets to American society**. The others are destructive liabilities. The generalized, derogatory, and negative references to "*White people*" in this book refers to those who exists in the "*matrix*" of systemic racism that internalizes and supports discrimination, prejudice, White privilege, White Nationalism, White superiority, and White supremacy. These are the, "*White people ... LOL*". LOL is a contemporary acronym for "Laughing Out Loud." Aside, from their deplorable racist mentality, racist have a "clown like" presence that makes them pathetically funny. However, realistically, they are dangerous and a threat to American democracy. If it were not for the atrocities and inhumane acts that have occurred over the centuries because of racism, discrimination, and prejudice then for any human being to think they are better than another human being because of skin color would be a funny joke. The reality of racist behavior is not funny, nor is it a joke. Nor is it true that skin color is basis for determining human value. People who think that, lack intelligence. People who believe it are stupid.

I realize that many references to White people mentioned in this book are offensive. The author's intent is to be honest, straightforward, and to tell the truth. The truth about White culture is offensive. It is offensive to Black people. It is offensive to decent White people and it is offensive to the human race. It is also offensive to the United States of America. While White culture has made many positive contributions to the world, they have also contributed to some of the most negative, devastating, and destructive acts humanity has ever witnessed or experienced. The truth often is painful. Black people have lived in pain for centuries. If references to racist White people in this book are offensive, or if White people find distaste in how White culture is portrayed, then they should change and become better human beings. The references to White racists are distasteful, because they are distasteful human beings.

Abstract

Appropriately titled, "*An American Reality: White People ... LOL*" includes a case study, on an incident of discrimination experienced by this author, as the backdrop to a more extensive psychological and sociological exploration into White racism, White racist, White supremacy, White privilege, White nationalism, prejudice, and discrimination in America. The backdrop incident, described in Chapter IV thru Chapter VII, is a repercussion of a broader catalyst, the racist environment and influence in America. With surrounding context of reinforcing information, the author evaluates and analyzes the socialization, sociology, mentality, and psychology, which is influences White racist behavior. The reinforcing information speaks to the oldest sickness phenomena in America, racism, discrimination, prejudice, White privilege, and White superiority. If America believes there is any future in racism, irrespective of the past, then the divisions in America will only continue to create circumstances that make America weak, susceptible to outside influence and threaten our democracy. This Book includes a case study based on the lived experience of Dr. Ronald Barnes subsequent, to receiving his Master of Arts degree in Religious Studies from the University of Chicago Divinity School and prior to receiving his PhD in psychology. The book recounts his lived experience, as a Black man and an alumnus of the University of Chicago (UChicago), with discrimination levied by personnel in the University of Chicago (UChicago) Alumni Association and supported by other University of Chicago (UChicago) personnel.

Even many good and decent White people have the "*residue of racism*" of discrimination, and prejudice because it is natural to their cultural socialization process. It is not easy for White people to escape the long history of their racist socialization process or transcend the racist dysfunction they have witnessed, experienced, learned, or been taught during the developmental stages of their life. There is significant disassociation and dissonance between the dogma of American doctrines and the behavior of White Americans. This is a problem for White people. There is significant misalignment between the way White America describes itself to be and the way many White Americans really are.

This book will give insight into the psychology that motivates racial incidents, explore how the environmental situation at the higher education level is microcosmic of the general society, and explore how the education environment feeds racist behavior. The author will also give rationale to why the learning environment allows racial behavior to manifest. The author will recommend effective solutions to address the dysfunctional behaviors that will complement policies already in place at the University of Chicago and other institutions in America. The strategic position of learning institutions in society qualifies them to mitigate the issues of racism, prejudice, and discrimination, effectively.

Definition of Terms

For the sake of having a common understanding of the terms used in this book and the context in which the terms are used, it is important to give definition to them.

Alternative Right (Alt-Right) - Some may think this term is all encompassing, but "alt-right" is an umbrella created by the P.T. Barnum of racism, Richard Spencer. It describes a range of racist philosophies that fall under the big tent of racists. It is a branding strategy.

Cognitive ability — "broadly defined as a set of mental skills that allow an individual to learn from experience, adapt to new situations and solve problems, understand and manipulate abstract concepts, and use knowledge to act on the environment—is widely held to have a profoundly liberalizing influence on racial attitudes". [14]

Ideological Refinement Theory - "contends that cognitively sophisticated members of a dominant racial group are no more committed to racial equality than their peers with lower ability. They are, however, better equipped to understand, analyze, and act on their group interests; to develop effective legitimizing ideologies for extant inequalities; and to articulate an astute defense of their social position". [15]

Implicit Bias - Implicit bias is an unconsciously triggered belief in the inferiority of, or negative attitude toward, an individual or group(s). According to cognitive psychology research implicit biases influences attitudes, behaviors, and actions, such as, unconscious negative beliefs and feelings about racial groups and individuals of different ethnicities. These attitudes, behaviors, and actions are often displayed in everyday, interpersonal interactions at work, at school or on the street with daily encounters.[16]

In-group - In-groups are groups to which a person belongs. Normally, an exclusive, typically small, group of people with a shared interest or identity. There many groups to which a person can belongs, depending on how he or she categorizes the social world and their social location in the social world.

Institutional Racism – The expansion of racism from individual beliefs and behaviors to racism being manifested in the structure, policies and practices of non-human entities such as the social processes, policies, norms, and practices of institutions (the court system, the legal system, the law enforcement system, the education system, the employment system, the economic system or the political system).[17] "Institutional racism refers to particular and general instances of racial discrimination, inequality, exploitation, and domination in organizational or institutional contexts, such as the labor market or the nation-state."[18] Institutional racism can be overt (formalized policies that promote exclusion of people because of race, religion, sexual orientation, or gender). Often implicit bias is displayed in terms of disparate impact, where organizations or the government distributes more resources to one group over another without exercising overt racist intent. Disparate impact racism is considered institutionalized or systematized because the rules, processes, policies, and opportunity structures are constructed in favor of one group over another.[19]

Outgroups - Outgroups are groups to which a person does not belong and does not identify with (and which could therefore become a target for in-group bias). There many groups to which a person can belongs, depending on how he or she categorizes the social world and their social location in the social world.

Prejudice – "Prejudice is an unjustified or incorrect attitude (usually negative) towards an individual based solely on the individual's membership of a social group."[20]

Much of the research on prejudice is focused on how people's negative attitude constructs stereotypes that contribute to the intolerance of others (based on race, religion, gender etc.). However, new research suggest that emotions may also be a predictor of the formulation of racial prejudice toward certain groups. Emotions such as pity, envy, jealousy, disgust, insecurity, lack of self-esteem, and pride may play a bigger role in the development of prejudicial attitudes. People's emotions may better predict intolerant behavior toward certain groups than can stereotypes, according to a social psychologist's research. People are entitled to their thoughts and feelings, what is more significant is their behavior. [21]

Psychology – Psychology, simply put, is **the science of the mental (mind) alignment with the behavioral functions of an individual, individuals, a group, or a society. Psychology i**ncludes the study of conscious and unconscious phenomena, as well as feelings and thought. For the purpose of this book, the term psychology explores how an individual's thinking aligns with how they act and behave. The purpose is to understand how the role of mental functions and behaviors in individuals, groups, and society influences their social behavior and their social behavior toward others.[22]

Race – While race is thought to be determined by skin color, and physical characteristics, the consensus among social scientist is that "race" is generally thought of as a social construct and a biologically meaningless term when applied to humans. Race is distinguished from ethnicity. "Physical differences such as skin color have no natural association with group differences in ability or behavior." The primary significance of race categorizations is in structuring a social location, even if it is a false social reality. [23] Races are distinguished by perceived common physical characteristics, which are thought to be fixed. Ethnicities are defined by perceived common ancestry, history, and cultural practices, which are seen as more fluid and self-asserted, rather than assigned by others.[24] It can be misleading to categorize race in terms of skin color because ethnicities vary in skin colors from light to dark. Black, Asians, and Hispanic people are examples of ethnic skin color variations.

Racial Discrimination - racial discrimination refers to unequal treatment of persons or groups based on their race or ethnicity. Racial discrimination is manifested in behaviors. Up to 50 years ago, discrimination was consistently overt, widespread, and unashamedly practiced by White people against Black people. Today acts of discrimination are often not as overt and direct as in the past. Discrimination is more subtle, subconscious and covert, however, still today, overt, and direct acts of racism occur with too much frequency. It is not as easy to assess the degree to which an individual's everyday experiences and opportunities involve ongoing forms of discrimination. Nevertheless, it exists and is often evident in the difference between the ways White people treat White people compared to the ways White people treat Black people.[25] Racial discrimination in behavior is motivated by racial attitude and racial ideology.[26]

Racism – Race is a socially constructed term to categorize people. Racism is an ideology or an attitude that influences and supports the marginalization and/or oppression of people of color based on a socially constructed hierarchy that privileges white people.[27]

"Racism is a system of structuring opportunity and assigning value based on physical properties such as skin color." [28]

"Racism is often defined as disliking or mistreating others because of their race, but that definition has come under criticism. Racism is now seen as a system of advantage based on race, fueled by everyone, whether they mean to or not, and whether they identify as racist or not.[29]

Racism is rooted in an ideology of racial domination. [30] There is a presumption that biological or cultural superiority of one or more racial groups justifies or warrants the inferior treatment or subservient social position(s) of other racial groups. Racialization, perceived patterns of physical difference, such as language, skin color or eye shape, are used to differentiate groups of people, thereby constituting them as "races. Racialization becomes racism when it involves the hierarchical and socially consequential valuation of racial groups, establishing justification for discrimination. [31]

Racist – A Racist is someone who believes that their race makes them better, more intelligent, more moral, etc. than people of other races and who does or says unfair or harmful things as a result. A Racist believes people who belong to other races are not as good, intelligent, moral, etc. as people who belong to their own race. A practitioner of racism, a believer in White supremacy, a believer in White superiority, and a supporter of racial discrimination. A stupid, ignorant, and deplorable human being.

Racist / Racial Residue – Racial residue refers to the lingering socialized perceptions White people have of Black, Brown, and minority individuals. For example, many White people exposed to the term "nigger" and other derogatory references to Black people, internalize a negative perception of minorities. Consistent reinforcement of negative perceptions of minorities causes White people to embrace racist attitudes and exhibit racist behaviors. White people, who have life experiences contrary to the defamation of minorities, realize the negative influence of racism in their lives and grow to eliminate racism from their thinking and behavior. However, racist socialization has deep roots in White culture. Eliminating racism is a process that causes decent White people to have periodic racist response to phenomena involving minorities. Periodic racist response to racial interactions by decent White people is "racist residue".[32]

It is empirically established that people have a "***bias blind spot***," meaning that they are less likely to detect bias in themselves than others are. In addition, People exhibit a "***bias blind spot***": they are less likely to detect bias in themselves than they are to detect bias and racism in others. [33] Even good White people may have hidden bias. [34] The "***bias blind spot***" is often associated with the "***racist residue***" that indicates the depth and degree to which racism is implanted into White culture. White people who consider themselves non-racist can recognize racism in others easier than they can recognized their own subtle acts of racism.

Relational Balance - Relational Balance refers to an environment in which people interact with each other, and each person or persons understand their respective cultural locations relative to other individuals. Individuals embrace and respectfully appreciate the individual differences in others.

White Privilege – White Privilege is "The concrete benefits of access to resources and social rewards and the power to shape the norms, values, and rewards of society which Whites receive, unconsciously and consciously, by virtue of their skin color in a racist society." [35]

White Supremacy / White Supremacist – "White supremacy groups espouse white supremacist or white separatist ideologies, often focusing on the alleged inferiority of non-whites, including, Jews, Blacks, Muslims, Asians, Hispanics. They believe all others are physically, mentally, and morally weaker than the Caucasian race. The concept of white supremacy is one of the oldest racist philosophies, which originated from their effort to explain their need to rape, pillage and conquer the world.

A variety of groups are known to practice White Supremacy and are considered White Supremacist, sometimes called White Nationalist —Ku Klux Klan, neo-Confederate, neo-Nazi, racist skinhead, Proud Boys, Christian Identity and many more — are commonly known white nationalist. White Supremacist are also referred to as White Nationalist who are supporters of White Supremacy. They believe that white identity should be the organizing principle of the countries that make up Western civilization. White nationalists support policies to reverse changing demographics and the loss of an absolute, white majority.

Ending non-white immigration, both legal and illegal, is an urgent priority for white nationalists. They seek to preserve white, racial dominance.[36]

White Nationalist / White Nationalism- White nationalism is different from white supremacy in that white nationalists seek to maintain a white identity for America. Of all the different kinds of racists, white nationalists have the most selective of memories. They completely forget the fact that the only reason America became an economic superpower is that it benefited from 250 years of free labor. A comprehensive list of hate groups can be found in **Appendix 15.**

White Superiority – A superiority complex is a behavioral construct that insinuates a person believes they are superior to others. People with this complex often have exaggerated opinions of themselves. They may believe their abilities and achievements surpass those of others. However, a superiority complex most likely hides low self-esteem or a sense of inferiority. Psychologist Alfred Adler first described the superiority complex in his early 20th century work. He outlined that the complex is really a defense mechanism for feelings of inadequacy. Psychologists suggest that a superiority complex may be the result of multiple failures. "A person tries to complete a specific goal or achieve a desired outcome in life, but they don't succeed. They learn to handle the anxiety and stress of the failure by pretending to be above it. A White superiority complex can be a defense against the reality that Whites, consciously or subconsciously feel inferior to Blacks and other minority groups. [37]

Chapter I
Introduction
Background on American Reality

There are those of you who will read this book and find it insulting. It may arouse disturbing emotions. You may even have a problem with the way the author presents arguments. You may not like what is written. Reading this book might arouse feelings of anger. Good, to all of the emotions that erupt, if you find this book disturbing. That only means there is a section of decency in your soul or it could mean that you are unapologetic about your stupidity and deplorable personality. Nothing is more disturbing that a racists society. Complete reading the book to the end and understand White psychology and White culture better. Better, understand the reasons for the inadequacy in White culture. Maybe informed insight might give White culture reason to change and become an American entity worthy of the heritage.

Conservatives (Republicans) are disagreeable obstructionist. Liberals (Democrats) are angry and frustrated. Stop being disagreeable obstructionist and start being bipartisan collaborators. Stop being angry and frustrated and start being smart. Trying to change people is difficult but everyone cares about something. In America, bipartisan cooperation is a concept in the phantom zone. America is a melting pot of Americans. Americans who want to see America thrive and inclusive of all Americans are true Americans. Americans who want to control with exclusive intent, who create divisiveness and conflict are anarchist, traitors to democracy and criminals. In today's society, the difference is so distinct it is clearly recognizable.

Then there are those of you who will read this book and resonate with its contents and perspective. You will agree with the author's perceptions and arguments presented. However, none of you that can say the contents of this book is not based on empirical information or applicable. The focus of this book is primarily about racists, and racist's behavior, White people who are racist, and White people who harbor *racist residue*. The author has no intention in being "soft" in his references to racists. His intention is to be harsh, to identify racist as the deplorable human beings, destructive to society that they are. God did not create humanity to include racists. Racists are mutations to God's creation. The God given privilege of "freewill" shows us the depth to which human depravity can sink. Racists are an aberration of God's magnificent creations. The problem with racist is that they create racist and stain the dignity of being a human being. This first Chapter sets the stage for the rest of the book. The author explores the psychological foundations and developmental process that motivate the sickness and depraved behavior of White racists. American society has been far too lenient on allowing White racists to have voice in America. That is the same thing Germany allowed Hitler to do in 1933, have voice. **The author hopes to reach the abundant majority of good and decent White people who are contributing assets to society.** The only fault of good and decent White people is they are a "silent majority" when it comes to speaking and acting out against racism, and eliminating the threats posed by racists. Racists are not only a negative influence on minorities, they are also a negative and embarrassing influence on White culture. Racist overpopulate White culture. **Not all White people are racist** but too many are. This book speaks to the American problem of the sick deplorable racist that live in America. This book speaks to the decent White people and encourages them to purge America and White culture of racists and remove the legacy of the racists stain on their past and present. The decency in White culture was benign during slavery, during the post slavery period of the Black laws, during the many lynching's and killings of Black people, during the Jim Crow era and during the over 400 years of the racism, discrimination and prejudice. In the past and in our modern era, there have been symptoms of White revolt against racism (John Brown's revolt against slavery and White participation in Black Lives Matter). However, the White effort to make America the country it thinks it is falls far short. Black and minority people have suffered throughout and endured since they were kidnapped, and brought to the shores of Jamestown Virginia as slaves, in 1619. What should White people have done? What should White people do? White culture should never have allowed their lived experiences to create such depraved and deplorable creatures, but that is hindsight. The issue that matters at this point is what should White culture do. Much talk has been circulating about reparations. The mentality of White culture believes money is a solution to all problems, even a way to mitigate the loss (death) of a loved one. That is how White people think. In America, money is the only thing White people have to offer. Money acts as a substitute for decency. Equality is a natural right of human beings. It does not have to be bargained for. Equality is not experienced unless suppressed people believe they are equal.

Black people should not pay taxes for as long as the entire period they have been repressed, from 1619 to the present. Why? Because Black people essentially experience taxation without representation in these contemporary times. In a review of history, "*taxation without representation*" was the battle cry of the American colonist (revolutionist) in 1775 that motivated them to engage the Revolutionary War. The opportunity cost of being subjected to White racism is incalculable. Tax exemptions without any denial of government services is only a token reparation because lives lost and the sufferance of inhuman situations, and the opportunity cost of racism has an infinite cost value. The human lives of loved ones cannot be compensated for. This is not an avocation of any illegal act. It is a proposed reconciliatory suggestion in common with reconciliation.

What is sufficient compensation for the murders of hundreds of thousands people? What is the compensation for centuries of suffering and enduring acts of indecency? How much will be sufficient to erase the history of racism suffered by Blacks, inflicted by Whites? The problem is that White people do not want to pay for their crimes. When Black and minority people pay taxes, it is a form of robbery with informed consent, and taxation without representation. Tax dollars do not flow into Black communities in the form of community development or jobs. White people want to commit crimes and get away "Scott free" The repercussion effect of centuries of suppression, repression, depression and the denial of equal rights to Black and minority individuals is incalculable in terms of dollars, cents and sense.

What is the GNP of Black people? According to statistics, Black people are major consumers in the American economy and spend more than $1 trillion a year on goods and services but lack wealth. [38] Black workers make up 12.9 percent of the US labor force today but earn only 9.6 percent of total US wages.[39] In 2020, African American economic spending energized the U.S. consumer market as never before. The buying power of African Americans rose to $1.6 trillion, or 9% of the nation's total buying power. [40] These statistics give African Americans a basis to formulate a strategy to become a more effective force in America. Being objective and honest, it has to be recognized that Black and African Americans are discriminated against, and endure prejudice and racism because they allow it. Yes, there is a deviant and deplorable characteristic in White culture that infects the United States of America. However, just like any other disease or virus, people should learn how to take precautions to cure and avoid infection. Knowledge of how to cure disease is basic to a healthy life. There is a theory that the oppressed often emulate the behavior of their oppressor. This was the case in the way the colonist treated the Native American Indians and Black slaves. Colonist who came to America to escape oppression acted toward the Native American Indians and Black slaves in the same ways their oppressors acted toward them, but worse. Black people should study and learn the concept of the "*Pedagogy of the Oppressed*". Paulo Freire wrote the book entitled the "*Pedagogy of the Oppressed*" (Appendix 6). It gives guidelines on how oppressed people can recover their dignity. Freire advances the belief that teaching should challenge learners to examine power structures and patterns of inequality within the status quo. People should learn to challenge the structures of power that oppress them. He demystifies democratic authority or power, and encourages a transformative discourse focused on social equality. Some people will argue that his views are socialist but the people that argue that are those who are oppressors. Democracy is an equal opportunity system. If Democracy does not exercise equality, it is not Democracy. America is a hybrid case of oppression. Some African American individuals are reaping the economic benefits of the "*American Dream*". However, the general and overall relationship America (White America) has with the vast majority of Black Americans is oppression, discrimination and prejudice. Even educated African Americans, ethical and moral African Americans, African Americans who spend their lived experiences primarily in White society, and who embrace the benefits of White society, will encounter White racism, interacting with White people. It is inevitable because White culture is a racist culture. Nevertheless, African American and minority people should define their own cultural perspective. There are symptom in Black culture of frustration aggression. Black people are too violent against each other. Their frustration causes them to exercise aggressive behavior toward each other. There are too many incidents throughout America involving Black people acting dysfunctional and violently toward other Black people. This is an example of frustration aggression. It is also an example of Black individuals taking on the behavior of their oppressor and directing their anger toward each other. Because African Americans do not control their livelihoods (jobs and money) and because money is needed to survive, Black people too often pursue alternative methods of survival, which further complicates their victimization. Controlling ones destiny requires commitment, dedication, education and love for oneself. The confidence of knowing the quality of one's character is a valuable asset toward problem resolution. Historically, African American and Black people have always had quality character. Proof of this is the longstanding religious devotion of Black people to God and to the church. Wrong knows wrong. The initial decision to make is, does wrong want to be right. Black people are considered the most religious individuals in America. [41] The civil rights movement to address the wrongs White America have inflicted on Black people sprung out of the Black church. The civil rights movement was based in ethical and moral cause to address the unethical and immoral injustice of White culture and White attacks on black people. Any and every intelligent individual in America knows this. The ignorant, deplorable racists, and those who want to perpetuate the sickness of racism will try to spin or argue with the fact that the civil rights movement was based on an immoral cause to fight against morality. Racists, in their ignorance and stupidity believe they are right. White culture is a destructive culture.

A racist White mob destroyed 30 blocks of a thriving Black economy, known as Black Wall Street, in Tulsa Oklahoma. The massacre began during the Memorial Day weekend, May 31 – June 1, 1921, after 19-year-old Dick Rowland, a Black shoe shiner, was falsely accused of assaulting Sarah Page, the 17-year-old white elevator operator in the Tulsa Drexel Building. As this lie spread throughout the White community in Tulsa, a White mob formed. Incensed by the false accusation the white mob rioted and set fires that destroyed a prominent Black area in Tulsa, Oklahoma. At least One thousand Black people were injured or killed. The exact number is unknown. The Tulsa race riot or the Black Wall Street massacre is considered one of "the single worst incident[s] of racial violence in American history", and is believed to be one of the deadliest terrorist attacks in the history of the United States.

The attackers burned and destroyed more than 35 square blocks of the neighborhood – at the time one of the wealthiest Black communities in the United States, known as "Black Wall Street". [42] Black Wall Street was a symbol of economic hope and success, due to the entrepreneurial spirit demonstrated by Greenwood residents who thrived together at a time when it was not common, in the face of racism and segregation in the early 1900s. Approximately 10,000 Black people were left homeless, and property damage valued at more than $1.5 million in real estate and $750,000 in personal property (equivalent to $34.18 million in 2021). Many survivors left Tulsa, while residents who chose to stay in the city, regardless of race, largely kept silent about the terror, violence, and resulting losses for decades. The massacre was largely omitted from local, state, and national histories. Naturally, White people do not want to talk about this incident or have it publicized. German Nazis do not want to talk about the holocaust either. Many fake propaganda racists spread rumors the holocaust is a hoax. [43] What is the opportunity to Black people because of White mobs destroying the opportunities and lives of Black and minority people historically since 1619? The pathetic irony in American jurisprudence is that White people who are caught red-handed committing crimes against Black people, heinous crime, go to court and plead "not guilty", and are exonerated. Even today, White people argue that the historical truths about racism should not be taught in schools. History talks about the Revolutionary War, where colonist and the English killed each other. History teaches about the civil war, where Americans kill Americans. History talks about the War of 1812, The Mexican-American War, the Spanish American War, World War I, World War II, the Korean War, the Vietnam War and American involvement in the Middle East; yet White people do not want to talk about the war White American racist have engaged with Black Americans for over 400 years. They know it is shameful and revealing insight into the degenerate and deplorable nature of White human beings. The real problem is they do not face the truths about their culture and continue to socialize racism into their culture. White people still, to this day, behave in the same deplorable degenerate ways. Much of the contemporary racism is subtle, but it is still rampant in America. White people do not display desire to become better people. Realistically, racism is unchecked in White culture and it is rampant. **Again, this author reiterates, not all White people are deplorable racist but too many are.**

Similarly, a young 14-year-old Black boy was falsely accused of offending a White woman in Money, Mississippi in 1955. His name was Emmett Till. Emmett was abducted, tortured, lynched, and then dumped in the Tallahatchie River. Emmett was from Chicago, Illinois. He was spending the summer with relatives in Mississippi. He spoke to 21-year-old White woman named Carolyn Bryant, who was married and the proprietor of a small grocery store in Mississippi. Emmett was accused of flirting with or whistling at Bryant. Till's interaction with Bryant, violated the unwritten racist code of behavior for a black male interacting with a white female in the Jim Crow-era South. Several nights after the incident in the store, Bryant's husband, Roy, and his half-brother J.W. Milam, who were armed, went to Emmett's great uncle's house and abducted Emmett. They took him away, beat and mutilated him, before shooting him in the head and sinking his body in the Tallahatchie River. Three days later, Emmett's mutilated and bloated body was discovered and retrieved from the river. [44]

In September 1955, an all-white jury found Bryant and Milam not guilty of Till's murder. Protected against double jeopardy, the two men publicly admitted in a 1956 interview with *Look* magazine that they had tortured and murdered the boy, selling the story of how they did it for $4000. [45] Till›s murder was seen as a catalyst for the next phase of the civil rights movement. In December 1955, the Montgomery bus boycott began in Alabama and lasted more than a year, resulting eventually in a U.S. Supreme Court ruling that segregated buses were unconstitutional. According to historians, events surrounding Emmett Till's life and death continue to resonate. The Emmett Till Anti-lynching Act makes lynching a federal hate crime, and was signed into law on March 29, 2022 by President Joe Biden. [46] In 2017, Carolyn Bryant admitted that she lied about Emmett flirting and acting inappropriately with her. [47] This is one of the worst atrocities of violent terrorist acts against a Black person in the history of the United States of America and the culprits got away "Scott free". That was in 1955, yet the racist institutionalization of America have not significantly addressed the issue of racism. The hypocrisy in the way White American culture behaves under the veil of the Constitution of the United States of America and Civil Rights Laws indicates the worthless character of the White American cultural concept of humanity.

An American Reality is the appropriate title for this book because it recounts a reality that has existed since the first Europeans landed on Plymouth Rock in the 15th century, in the early 1600's (1607-1625), the reality of White racism. [48] The reason it is important to write this book is because White culture has initiated acts of hostility, brutality, racism, prejudice, and discrimination against non-White indigenous and all other people who came to America that were non-White for centuries. White brutality against non-White people has been ongoing since the day White people came to America. The oldest and most consistent phenomenon in White American behavior is their history of racism, discrimination, prejudice, and White supremacy. Disrespect and disregard for the culture and rights of non-White people is a character trait in White culture that has not changed since they arrived in the Americas in the early 1600's. It is *An*

American Reality, that White culture's disrespect for non-White human beings manifest as the most stable and consistent trait in White culture, their racism, prejudice, and discrimination. Racial discrimination is the "unequal treatment of persons or groups on the basis of their race or ethnicity." There are two aspects to discrimination, ***Differential treatment***, and ***disparate impact***. "*Differential treatment* is when individuals are treated unequally because of their race, ethnicity, religion, or difference. *Disparate impact* occurs when individuals are treated equally according to a given set of rules and procedures but when the latter are constructed in ways that favor members of one group over another". [49] An important factor of discrimination is that it is manifested in behavior. Discrimination is distinct from, but motivated by, racial prejudice (attitudes), racial stereotypes (beliefs), and racism (ideologies) and may be associated with racial disadvantage. [50] These attitudes, beliefs and ideologies have been, consistently, the most profound influence in America than any other phenomena. American history is severely incomplete without learning the history of slavery, racism, discrimination, and prejudice. Current American history taught in schools misrepresents, or excludes facts about, the true *American Reality.* The reason this book is important is that White racism, White discrimination, White prejudice, White supremacy, White privilege, and White inequality are despicable, anti-American behaviors that are destructive to America and our society, even destructive to White society. White people need to know the truth about their history, their psychology and their behavior. They are delusional about how they perceive society, themselves, and non-White people. As stated, racist are destructive to society, other decent White people, and especially non-White people.

The misrepresentation of American history in history books and movies portray White culture as conquerors and heroes. The truth is that White culture has conducted the most heinous acts against other human beings of any people on the face of the earth (Pizarro and the Inca's, Hitler against the Jews and Europe, Stalin against his own people, American colonist and the Indians, American Soldiers and the Indians, White Americans, and Slavery). White people attempted to commit genocide against the Indians, stole their land, and disregarded their culture without respect.

Black / White Intelligence

Early studies on race and intelligence found that White people were more intelligent than Black people were. This argument was advanced based on the hypothesis that the superior intelligence of Whites is based on their genetic makeup. Recent studies found that those early studies were not scientifically based. They served as a means to reinforce White racism and White privilege against non-White people. Subsequent research studies published in the National Library of Medicine, found evidence that race is a social construction with no scientific validity, socially constructed to rationalize advantage of one group over another. More recent valid and empirical research studies found that there is no scientifically link between race and intelligence. There is no gene that has been conclusively linked to intelligence. Research evidence further finds that heritability, a behavior-genetic concept, is an invalid and false argument, a null hypothesis, concerning any argument that intelligent and race are genetically connected. The hypothesis that White people, as a group, are intellectually superior to non-White people, as a group, is racist propaganda. [51]

The myth of White superiority has been promoted in many venues of White Culture, especially in the media, and movies that appeal to the racist conditioning of America. What is wrong with the White American Male Cowboy / Calvery hero image? It is a lie. It is true that the White man conquered the Native American Indians, but to steal their lands. Portraying White men as hero's when they were actually criminals and thieves is what should be considered the "*Great American Spin*". John Wayne, the actor, the White American hero, is a White American illusion. John Wayne was a racist himself. One of the great American White heroes was a bigot and racist, a concoction of the *Great White American Lie.* Wayne made the statement that he "believes in White supremacy." He can believe whatever he wants. Belief in White supremacy only shows how stupid he is / was.[52] Ironically, John Wayne applied to the U.S. Naval Academy, but was not accepted because his grades were poor, below acceptable standards, typical, considering his racism and ignorance. [53] Ironic, that John Wayne, below average in academic performance, thinks he is better than anyone is. He had learning disabilities and was learning impaired. It is stupid to believe a lie. That he was, and is embraced by American culture as a hero, is telling. Racists want to be superior but, in reality, they are not. John Wayne as a White American hero is a fantasy illusion, and only indicates the character of White America and the lengths of deception they will concoct to lie and spin the truth. People, who believe in a lie and base their behavior on a lie, are stupid.

What is the relationship between intelligence and racism? The influence of cognitive ability on racial attitudes is ambiguous and multifaceted. "***Enlightenment theory***" advances that "*higher cognitive ability is linked to mental processes that are less vulnerable to the faulty, uninformed, and inflexible generalizations that underlie prejudicial attitudes. It also contends that cognitive ability promotes a genuine commitment to liberalism, defined in terms of a greater willingness to make personal sacrifices to improve the welfare of unrelated others.*" [54] An open mind learns. Nothing enters a closed mind.

The ideological refinement perspective, conversely, advances that dominant group members with higher cognitive ability are no more committed to the welfare of others than those with lower ability. It argues, "*high-ability whites are simply better equipped to recognize and act in accordance with their group interests and to mount a more sophisticated ideational defense of their group's social position that avoids the appearance of intergroup negativism.*" [55]

Findings indicate that whites with higher verbal ability are significantly less likely than comparable whites with lower ability to overtly display racist behavior and less likely to report anti-black prejudice. In addition, high-ability whites, compared with low-ability whites, are significantly more likely to support racial integration in principle and to acknowledge discrimination against blacks. However, despite their more favorable views about blacks, greater support for racial equality in principle, and greater awareness of discrimination, whites with higher verbal ability are generally no more likely than their counterparts with lower ability to support specific policies designed to realize racial equality in behaviors. Whites with higher cognitive ability are vulnerable to the racist White "*Matrix*". Even if they escape the "*racist matrix*" higher cognitive decent White people are subject to the stain of "*racist residue*"

Whites with higher cognitive ability are significantly less likely than whites with lower cognitive ability to support school busing programs and workplace racial preferences. The relationship between verbal ability and policy support is not strictly monotonic. [56] In other words, Whites with more intelligence have more skill to shadow their racial beliefs than Whites with less intelligence. Whites with higher intelligence know racism is wrong. They know it is socially unacceptable and they know it is wrong. That is why they attempt to hide their overt racism, at least as a visible characteristic. However, this does not mean White individuals of higher intelligence are not racist. White racism at the higher intelligence levels is more subtle. They might believe that it is to their advantage to eliminate competition, competition in the workplace, for jobs. Higher intelligent Whites might also have racist residue. Then again, higher intelligent Whites might actually believe White people have higher cognition than minorities. White educated people can have a low emotionally IQ and they can be stupid. Protecting their social image is more important than verbalizing their real feelings. Avoiding the issue is a normal course of action. Not to support equality and not to appear racist are the dilemmas of the White person with higher intelligence or who is educated. Educated and intelligence are not necessarily the same (refer to the Central Park Karen discussed later in this Chapter, p. 56). They may not mind Black acquaintances on a casual basis (at work or impersonal acquaintances, etc.) but Black friends on a personal basis (visiting each other's homes, socializing together, friendships), is more scrutinized. The racial complexities of White people with a higher cognitive ability is complicated and variable. Some are genuinely liberal. Some are subtle and strategic racists. Many have "*racist residue*" and some are blatant racist.

The arguments and research on racial intelligence is phenomena with deep complexities. There is evidence that studies measuring intelligence have been prejudicially constructed. Scientists have measured intelligence in a variety of ways, and the main conclusion remains stable. A study of white children found that some were less able to see that a short wide glass holds the same amount of water as a taller skinnier glass. This mental ability is known as "conservation" in the field of intelligence measurement. Conservation in psychology, advanced by Jean Piaget, is a psychological logical assessment thinking ability that determines an individual's ability to determine that a certain quantity will remain the same despite adjustment of the container, shape, or apparent size. His theory posits that this ability is not present in children during the preoperational stage of their development at ages 2–7 but develops in the concrete operational stage from ages 7–11. [57] Psychological conservation is considered an important mental ability. Research indicates that children who demonstrate greater fluency in conservation have a higher cognitive ability than children who demonstrate lower conservation ability. [58] Research further indicates that the kids who lacked conservation ability held more negative views of black children. Other researchers conducted an ambitious meta-analysis, a statistical aggregation of findings from many studies, and documented a link between cognitive style and ability, on the one hand, and authoritarian attitudes on the other. Low intelligence and "low effort thinking" are strongly linked to right-wing attitudes, including authoritarianism and conservative politics. There seems to be a noticeable causal link between children who grow and develop poor mental skills and develop to be strongly right-wing adult. [59] This is not a criticism of republican politicians, it is an empirical finding of research.

Additionally, according to Dhont and Hodson, there is a causal linkage between conservative ideology and prejudice. Research evidence indicates that conservative ideology predicts a number of prejudices, prejudice against ethnic and racial minorities, the disadvantaged, LGBT, non-Christian religions, Hispanics and Jews, any outgroup. Right wing individuals are much more likely to see outgroups as a threat to traditional values and social order, resulting in heightened prejudice. Dhont and Hodson tested and confirmed this mediation model: "Lower childhood intelligence clearly predicts right-wing ideology and attitude, which in turn predicts prejudice in adulthood." [60]

Intelligence and thinking determine how people assess threats in the world. Those with lower ability, lower level reasoning skills, less capable cognitive processing speed, and slower comprehension prefer simple and predictable answers, because that is what they are capable of processing. Uncertain situations are threatening. "They respond to such threats by trying to preserve what is familiar and safe, the status quo. These conservative reactions are basic and normal. Minimal cognitive effort reduces anxiety. Over time, the minimal effort to cognitively process phenomena develops into more stable and pervasive worldviews, which include stereotypical thinking, avoidance, prejudicial attitudes and overt discrimination. [61]

The *Ideological Refinement Perspective* of racist behavior has variable patterns of racial conflict. This perspective, rejection of overt prejudice and superficial support for racial equality in principle. Research indicates that reinforcement of verbal ability on a comprehensive set of racial attitudes, including anti-black prejudice, views about black-white equality in principle, and racial policy support; strengthens the Ideological Refinement Perspective to support equal opportunity. It also investigates cohort differences in the effects of verbal ability on these attitudes. Results suggest that high-ability whites are less likely than low-ability whites to report prejudicial attitudes, and are more likely to support racial equality in principle. Despite their liberal appearance, high-ability Whites are no more likely to support a variety of remedial policies for racial inequality than lower intelligent Whites are, unless they have lived experiences that reinforce equality. Research evidence indicate that liberal attitudes and perspectives on anti-black prejudice and views about racial equality develop systematically over time in Whites who subscribe to the "*ideological refinement theory*". [62]

A hypothesis is that higher cognitive abilities promote racial tolerance and a greater commitment to racial equality, but an alternative theoretical framework advances that higher cognitive abilities merely enable members of a dominant racial group to articulate a more refined legitimizing ideology for racial inequality.

Based on this perspective, *ideological refinement* occurs in response to shifting patterns of racial conflict, characterized by exposure to overt prejudice, superficial support for racial equality in principle, and an ambiguous position on policies that challenge the dominant group's status. Experiencing the spectrum of racial experiences confronts the individual with the reality of their commitment to civil rights or their commitment to racism. In other words, exposure to racist incidents and racism confronts higher cognitive individuals with taking a position on the issue or confronts them with developing a strategy on how to respond to racism. Results suggest that, realistically, high-ability whites are less likely than low-ability whites to report prejudicial attitudes and more likely to support racial equality in principle. However, "*Ideological refinement*" theoretically does have a liberalizing effect on high-cognitive ability whites. In reality, the ostensibly liberalizing effects of verbal ability on anti-black prejudice (speaking out against racism) and views about racial equality in principle can emerge slowly over time, based on "*ideological refinement theory*". [63] However, higher cognitive ability Whites are still challenged to rid themselves of "racist residue". Higher cognitive ability Whites are more articulate about hiding the degree of their racism and are skilled at presenting an ambiguous reality depending on their situation. Realistically, higher cognitive ability Whites placate subordinate group members by avoiding inflammatory attitudes and situations. They display a superficial support for racial equality in principle.

Racism, Discrimination and Prejudice Behavior Manifestations

Indians are the original Americans. White culture stole their land. White culture showed and continues to show disregard for non-White human beings. That is a problem for humanity. Keeping to the subject of this book, we will not discuss slavery, an inhumane system of Black servitude to Whites, constructed because Whites were not capable of doing their own work. They were too lazy and ethically, and morally deficient.

The backdrop of this Book is based on the lived experience of Dr. Ronald Barnes subsequent, to receiving his Master of Arts degree in Religious Studies from the University of Chicago Divinity School. This book recounts his encounter, as a Black man and as an alumnus of the University of Chicago, with discrimination levied by personnel at the University of Chicago Alumni Association, then reinforced by the Campus Police, prejudicially investigated by the university investigative attorney, washed over by the provost office, and the University general counsel regurgitated the falsehoods. Everyone believed the lie presented to him or her. White people are in the habit of believing other White people and disputing minorities, often at the expense of the truth, as in this case. Integrating this experience into the cultural phenomena of racism and conversation on discrimination that exist in our American society will give a focused perspective to the psychology of White culture, racist White people, and Black and White relationships. The discrimination experienced by Dr. Barnes does not rival the extreme acts of racism, discrimination, and prejudice frequently experienced by African Americans, historically and in the present day. Focusing on the experience of Dr. Barnes, however, will help the reader understand how racism is institutionalized and systematic in American society and how it filters down to daily encounters that impact Black and White interaction. The racial climate in America gives White people a false sense of security to behave in racist ways. In acting out their racist false sense of security, most often their ignorance is displayed. The case study of Dr. Barnes' experience identifies the reality of White people and Black people interaction. It gives insight into how White people mentally and authoritatively exercise, frivolously and freely, their "assumed authority" over Black people, without intelligent thought, but with mindless impulse. The book also gives insight into their lack of sincere interest to resolve their racist issues and their ignorance about how to deal with racial problems. White people cover up for each other even when they are wrong. Many good and decent White people have residue of racism, discrimination, and prejudice because it is deeply rooted into their culture. Figuratively and humorously speaking, it may take an exorcism for White culture to extricate racism from their culture. This book describes an example of "*racist residue*" in decent White people, who probably do not consider themselves racist or prejudice at all. They probably become insulted if someone referred to them as a racist. Some may even claim to have Black friends. Such action is common among many White people who consider themselves good people or non-racists. However, a racist's action, remark, a display of insensitivity, and White / Black interactions reflecting low emotional intelligence are examples of "racist's residue." That decent White people have "*racist's residue*" represents the degree to which racism is rooted in White culture. The process of eliminating racist residue is a challenge. It begins with accepting the fact they have a deplorable racist cultural history. Understanding the developmental process of how White culture socializes racism, and then correlate their interactions with how White people interact with other White people, if there is a difference in how White people respond to White people compared to how White people respond to minorities, that is racist. Until White culture can evaluate people based on character and not on skin color, they will always be inadequate as human beings. Understanding that White culture is a racist culture then becoming motivated and educated to change, is a first step toward mending the gap between races. The problem is that White people have a dichotomy in the way they relate to other White people, how they relate to Black people and how they expect Black people to relate to them. The dilemmas need resolution. Black people are giving more pushback to discrimination they encounter. Instead of finding equilibrium to the racist problems, American society seems stalwart to hold on to its outdated deplorable values and morals of inequality. Colonist fought the revolutionary war because of "taxation without representation." White people want what they themselves do not give. The colonist, who fought and won the revolutionary war, then took on the same character traits as their suppressors, regarding the Native American Indians. This is an ironic psychological phenomenon. One psychological explanation is because being in a subservient role and understanding the distaste of subservience, the only role and behavior colonist were familiar with was to emulate their suppressors. Colonist that came to America did not experience fairness in their lived experiences. Their lived experiences lacked decency. Their lived experiences lacked the nourishment of decency; otherwise, they would not have come to America for freedoms and opportunity. White people coming to America for freedom and opportunity, denied freedoms and opportunity to those who were already here and to slaves they brought here. To this day, American society has not made any sincere effort to construct a fair and equal society for all Americans.

Racism permeates and is institutionally ingrained, through in, and throughout White Culture and America. White Americas are perpetrators of racism, prejudice, and discrimination. Racism permeates in the lives of African American culture and non-White people, as victims of racism, prejudice, and discrimination. While this book will only address racism, discrimination, and prejudice by White culture toward Black individuals, However, White racism affects the lives of Asians, Hispanics, Jews, Muslims, people who are gender re-defined from traditional roles, and even White people that support equality. All are subject to and victimized by White racists, discrimination, and prejudice. The common denominator in the experiences of racism minority's encounter is that the perpetrators are usually White.

Sociologically, race is a social construct, without scientific foundation. During the 18th century, racial groups were defined with assertions of moral, intellectual, spiritual, and various other forms of "superiorities" (Whites) and "inferiorities" (non-Whites). The definitions and constructs given to various others was the basis for Europeans to rationalize the domination over racialized and indigenous others.

> *"Racist ideology served as justification for land appropriation and colonial violence towards Indigenous peoples as well as the enslavement of Africans starting in the sixteenth century. It was later used to justify state-sanctioned social, economic, and symbolic violence directed at blacks and other minorities under Jim Crow laws."* [64]

In the opinion of this author one reason racism, prejudice and discrimination exists in American society is because Americans are socialized to categorizations and relate to people based on color, race, sexual orientation, religion, and extrinsic factors instead of intrinsic factors that identify character, ethics, morality, and humanity as the primary catalyst for human interactions. Focus on extrinsic human factors rather than intrinsic human factors is catalyst for

White people to discriminate and behave despicably against minorities. How people identify define and categorize individuals is a determinate factor in how they relate, respond to and act towards each other. Much of the human dynamics of interpersonal relationships are how people define each other and how they prioritize their human definitions and categorizations. The dynamics resulting from how people attach definitions to each other is a factor in societal structure, values, norms, equality, inequality, behavior, racism, prejudice, education, economic equality, standard of living, health, friendships, marital paring, and the engagement of interpersonal relationships. In other words, the *relational perspectives* individuals have of each other in a society has a far-reaching impact in almost all areas of their lived experiences. The foundational dogma that governs the United States of America (The Constitution of the United States of America) states that in American society, all people are equal. The foundational religious dogma (The Bible, The Torah, and the Quran) of most Americans, who claim to be religious states that all individuals matter and are equal in the eyes of God. Yet there are a significant number of deplorable racists in America that only want privilege for White people. To give a proper perspective to this book it is important to establish the fact that racism, discrimination, and prejudice is a White cultural construct. The cost of hating another person without substantial cause is to love yourself less. There is hypothesizes that racists do not like themselves, are insecure or have unresolved issues. Dana Harron, a Washington, D.C., clinical psychologist advances that "the things people hate about others are the things that they fear within themselves." [65] Likewise, the things people do not like in others are the things they do not like in themselves. An objective of this book is to enable White people to begin their journey for resolution and growth as human beings and as a culture. The Golden rule, "Do unto others as you will have them do unto you." or "Do not do to others, that which you do not want them to do to you," practically is more rhetoric than meaningful behavior orientation, as a general practice in America. It is ironic that many of the negative attributes Whites label onto minorities are the same attributes they demonstrate and act out in their behavior toward minorities.

There is a correlation between racism and psychological health. "Racism is a symptom of psychological ill-health. It is a sign of a lack of the psychological integration of qualities that nurture a positive self-image, a lack of self-esteem and a lack of inner security. Psychologically healthy people with a stable sense of self and strong inner security are not racist, because they have no need to strengthen their sense of self through group identity. They have no need to define themselves in distinction to — and in conflict with — others." [66]

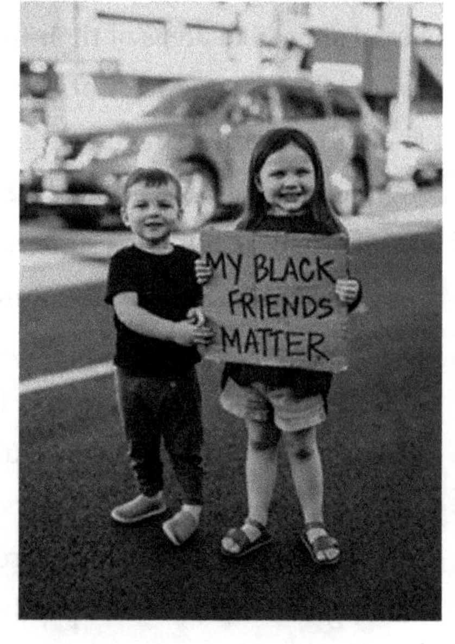

Racism, prejudice, and discrimination is learned behavior. Children are born without these deplorable personality traits. Adults socialize and teach kids to internalize deplorable traits. In the case of racism, prejudice, and discrimination, it is the White culture process of socialization. "Social scientists believe that implicit biases are learned as young as age 3 and may be fueled by stereotypes perpetuated in the media, or beliefs passed along by parents, peers, and other community members." [67] The Kirwin Institute defines *Implicit Bias* as attitudes or stereotypes that are activated unconsciously and involuntarily. *Implicit Bias* is different from *overt bias* or bias that people attempt to hide or repress because of unpopular or incorrect social behavior or protocol. *Implicit bias* is often reactionary and based on subconscious response caused by socialized learning.

White racism and prejudice are stupid, ignorant and laughable, traits (LOL). Words do not adequately describe the pathetic character of White racist. Dr. James Whitfield, a Black man, who was the principal of Colleyville Middle

School from 2019-2020 and the assistant principal for the high school from 2018-2019, was criticized in a school board meeting for posting photos on Facebook of him and his "White" wife embracing. They shadowed his showing love for his wife with other criticisms: for supporting anti-racist organizations and for speaking out about the death of George Floyd. [68] White people cannot help themselves. White people are silent when Neo-Nazis, White Nationalist, Ku Klux Klan, and other racist organizations commit violent acts of terrorism. Dr. Whitfield was showing love for his wife. The white pushback was not because Dr. Whitfield was showing love to his wife. It was because Dr. Whitfield was showing love to his "White" wife. White people … LOL.

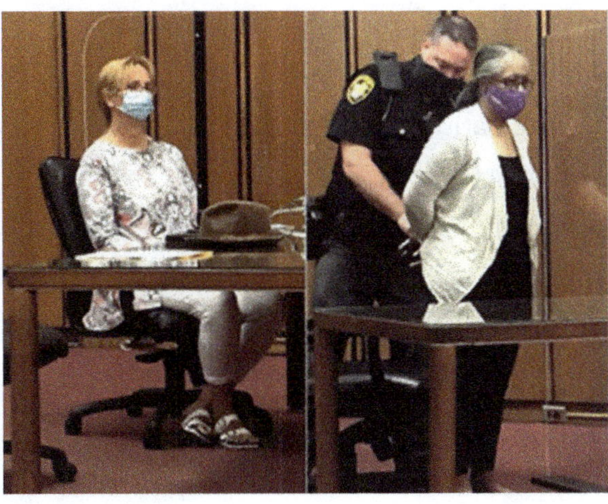

Another example of White American racism that is significantly damaging to our country is evidenced in two separate court case occurring in the same country, same state (Ohio), same city (Cleveland) and the same courthouse (Cuyahoga County Common Pleas Court). The court convicted a White woman who stole $250K, but she received probation, while a Black woman who stole $40K went to jail. A white woman, Debbie Bosworth, stole nearly $250,000 from the village of Chagrin Falls in 2019. Judge Hollie

Gallagher sentenced her to two years of probation. A Black woman, Karla Hopkins, stole $40,000 from Maple Heights City Schools in 2020. When she went before Judge Rick Bell, he sentenced her to 18 months in prison. [69] Ms. Bosworth ruling (2019) occurred before the ruling of Ms. Hopkins (2020), so the court had precedent when the judge made the ruling on Ms. Hopkins.

The 14th Amendment of the Constitution of the United States of America guarantees all American citizens Equal Protection under the Law. Equal Protection refers to the idea that a governmental body may not deny people equal protection of its governing laws. ***The governing body, state or country, must treat one individual in the same manner as others in similar conditions and circumstances.*** [70] This is a clear violation of the constitutional rights of an African American person and a clear example of discrimination and racism. In America, this is a frequent occurrence. Dr. James Whitfield was victimized for speaking out against this type of behavior. White People … LOL. In all honesty, it is not funny. It is ridiculously despicable. White Criticism about Dr. Whitfield's "doing the right thing," only indicates that some White people in America are racists and not only those who are poor and destitute, but also those who are educated and in positions of authority. The case in Ohio is a prime example of systematic and institutionalized racism that exist in America. When the legal system acts racist, it is no wonder that White police and White people are exonerated for murdering Black people in cold blood. It is no wonder that Sarah Nolan felt justified to discriminate against Dr. Barnes. That Joanne Nee, as a police officer, felt justified acting unjustly against Dr. Barnes, enacting punishment without knowing Dr. Barnes' side of the story. It also explains why Ingrid Gould and Attorney Stamatakos easily believed the lie. The investigation conducted by the White Attorney, Jackie Hennard, misrepresented the truth and conducted an investigation prejudicially, in an effort to defend Sarah Nolan. If she did not conduct a prejudicial investigation then she conducted an investigation partial to White perspective influenced by her "*racist residue*". White people with racist residue think it is normal to relate to Black people different than they relate to White people. Decent White people, even those with "*racist residue*", suffer from dissonance to behave prejudicially toward a Black person. However, their "*racist residue*" instinctively causes them to express their racist socialization. All of the persons involved in the discrimination case against Dr. Barnes, all of them White, responded protectively to the White person because Dr. Barnes was a Black man. It was normal behavior for White people. In essence, this makes all of them accomplices to racist behavior. Their actions were consistent with *American Reality*. The decency of White culture is at stake. Minorities will not tolerate the deplorable behaviors demonstrated by Whites, nor should America. Nor should decent White people. It is up to the decent White people to establish and reinforce ethical and moral diversity values in their culture and save the White race from itself. White culture has a destructive and negative backlash on society. Not all White people are deplorable. Good White people, especially good White people with *racist residue* need to work on eliminating that deficiency in their culture. Too many White people in America behave with racist tendency, some consistently, some periodically. While Dr. Barnes' experience was quite insignificant compared to others mentioned in this book, it is microcosmic of the American society in which we live. The values and norms internalized by White culture supports racist's behaviors and inevitably acts of discrimination such as experienced by Dr. Barnes will continue to occur, consistently.

White Culture has some of the most despicable human beings on earth. Their racism is so obvious that it is an insult to the human race to have such individuals called human beings.

Paul and Tenisha Austin, the Black couple pictured on the right. Spent years investing in their Marin City, Northern California home. When they decided to sell the home, they got an appraisal for $995,000 from a White appraiser, Janette Miller, a principle in the firm of Miller and Perotti. Mr. and Mrs. Tate suspecting

their home was under appraised for less than its value, arranged for their White friend to pretend to be the owner of the home. They then got another appraisal. The Tate's "whitewashed" their home by hiding family photos and artwork reflecting ethic interest. When confronted with a White owner, the home appraised at $1,482,500.00, a difference of almost $500,000. The condition of the home was the same with the Black owners and with the White person impersonating the homeowner. The couple are suing the appraisal firm for discriminatory practices. The Tate's contend that Janette Miller, the White woman appraiser, devalued their home because they were a Black family. in a Black neighborhood. The Brookings Institute found that owner-occupied homes in majority-Black neighborhoods throughout the U.S. are undervalued by an average of about $48,000 per home. Racism in America is rampant in every sector of the society. [71] This is clear indication that the socialization process in White culture is racist. White individuals in every aspect of American society are infected with discriminatory prejudiced racist ideology. Not all White people are, but too many White people across all sectors of American society are ignorant racist bigots.

One of the most despicable examples of the reality of our American society is evidenced by the actions of an Iowa woman, Nicole Poole Franklin, who, on December 9, 2019, purposefully ran her car into two children because of their race. One child was a 12-year-old Black boy. The other child was a 14-year-old Mexican girl. Both children were walking on the sidewalk when Franklin plowed her car into them with intent to kill two children simply because they were non-White human beings. This is one of the sickest examples of *American Reality.* It indicates the state to which American society has evolved or should I say, declined. Franklin was sentenced to 25 years in prison for attempted murder. The social and political climate in America is catalyst to this and numerous other acts of deplorable violence, enacted on minorities by Whites, historically and in this present day. These occurrences happen too often in America. This and other acts of racial violence committed against minorities by Whites are a result of the benign efforts on the part of American law enforcement, American leadership, politicians to address the problems, and unfortunately good White people who ignore the problem because it's not happening to them. This indicates that American politicians, lawmakers, and law enforcers, not only do not care, but they covertly support conflict that divides America. Some of the most dedicated racist in America are in the United States House of Representatives and the United States Senate. America has also had presidents who were racist. President 45 was widely considered racist, in the words he muttered and in his behavior. They will deny it but their actions are more vocal than their words. When White mentality has become as reprehensible and disgraceful as to act with intent to kill children because of their race, then that is an indication of the extent to which racist influence has on American society.[72] Consider the many, too many, number of unarmed Black people killed by police and the fact that the police were exonerated for murder. The fact is that unless lawmakers act with strong conviction to establish an America in the true sense of the Constitution of the United States, incidents like this, lesser racist incidents, and violent racist incidents will become more frequent. How the United States of America morphed into a country of immoral and unethical intolerance evidenced in the relationship between White culture and Native Americans, White culture and Black Americans, White culture and Jewish Americans, White culture and Hispanic Americans, White culture and Asian Americans, White culture, Muslim Americans and White culture and anyone else who is non-White. Without change, racism is the cornerstone legacy of White culture, unless decent White people take responsibility to change the "deplorable others" in their culture.

Another case of White racist psychology and definitive evidence of how racism is in-grained in White culture and White people is in an incident that occurred at a mall in New Jersey on February 2022. A Black teenager (White hoodie) and White teenager (Dark hoodie) were fighting. Fortunately, the video was captured the proof of White police racism. The police, the White police, arrived to break up the fight. The police separated the teenagers and instinctively, sat the white teenager on a bench, leaving him unattended, then, proceeded to tackle, restrain, and handcuff the Black teenager. When they separated the teenagers, the White teenager was on top of the Black teenager beating him. The police automatically assumed the Black teenager was at fault, the guilty culprit, even though the White teenager was in the dominant aggressive position. The evidence clearly shows both boys were equally engaged in aggressive physical violence against each other. From the evidence shown in the video both teenagers had an equal role in instigating the conflict, but the White police instinctively assumed the Black teenager was at fault. That is the ***American Reality.*** [73] That incident depicts the truth about the psychology of White culture regarding Black people. Racism is socialized into the fabric of White culture, and they cannot help themselves when it comes to the reality of White racism.

These police probably have cordial relationships with their Black colleagues, their fellow police who are Black. However, when it comes to their *racist residue,* their honest core feelings, they are racist and cannot help themselves. Too many White police in America are racist or harbor *racist residue.* Too often incidents between White police and Black men / Black boys result in the unjust death of the Black man or the Black boy. The incidents mentioned above give an accurate cross-section of how racism permeated and manifested through in and throughout America's legal justice system, America's law enforcement system, in the general behaviors of White American culture, and in the professional areas of America, including the education system. The unaddressed area of American racism in the above-mentioned incidents of judicial, legal, social, criminal, economic, and financial injustice are perpetually common in America. It is be a challenge to rid America of racism and racist, comparable to exterminating rats and roaches from an infested building structure. For America to be the country it professes to be, White people need to address this element that stains their culture.

It is common and customary practice in America for racist to frame and spin their acts of racism as benign incidents without any racial overtone. In other words, consistent with their deplorable character, they lie. Failure to confront and identify racists and racist acts for what they are only perpetuates racism, discrimination and prejudice in American society. It weakens American society because the conflict is constant. In a society that is based on equal opportunity and equal rights, the racist in America are anti-American. The many decent White Americans need to understand America and American democracy is at risk and threatened by the deplorable racist elements in their culture.

The civil rights in America has been, at the least, stagnant since before 2016. There is significant consensus that civil rights has been in the decline since the death of Dr. Martin Luther King, Jr. General consensus also advances that civil rights for Black and minorities has been in a backslide since Dr. King's assassination. Critical Race Theory (CRT) argues this exact issue (Chapter VIII). Since the 2016 election of Donald Trump, hate crimes against African Americans, Asians, Muslims, Jews, LQGBT, and minorities have all increased.

"In New York City hate crimes were reported to have increased by 76%, as of April, 2022 compared to the same period last year, according to data from the NYPD's Hate Crimes Task Force. To date, there have been 35 hate crimes committed against Black people in the city, 51 against Asians, 149 against Jewish people and only one recorded against a White person, according to the NYPD Hate Crimes Dashboard". [74]

Donald Trump's support in the 2016 campaign was clearly driven by racism, sexism, homophobia, and xenophobia. FBI data show that since Trump's election there has been almost a 25% increase in hate crimes concentrated in counties where Trump won by larger margins. It was the second-largest uptick in hate crimes in the 25 years for which data are available, second only to the spike after September 11, 2001. [75] Studies indicate that the Trump administration instigated and influenced the increase in hate crimes. Anti-Asian hate crimes increased approximately 150% in 2020, driven by the rhetoric of Donald Trump, labeling Covid-19 the "*Asian flu*".[76] Even after Trump lost the election to Joe Biden in 2020, the momentum of Trump's toxic administration and policies caused lingering effects of hate crimes as residue of his administration. White racists now feel they have liberty to surface and actively spread their depravity. [77] It is an accurate hypothesis that Donald Trump was inadequate in the job of fulfilling the primary duty of a president, which is to protect the safety of all Americans, which makes him unfit to hold the job. He contributed to the harm of Americans. In addition to Donald Trump, at least three other members of his Administration are considered ardent racist. Steve Bannon, associated with Breitbart News, "a white ethno-nationalist propaganda organization", served as

Trump's Chief Strategist. Stephen Miller who has an extensive history of racist statements served as Trump's White House Senior Advisor. Miller also orchestrated the separation of kids at the southern border from their asylum-seeking parents. Trump nominated Jeff Sessions as Attorney General. Sessions has a long-standing history of hostility to civil rights and is known for his animosity to minorities. [78] Sessions background clearly indicates he was unfit for the job of Attorney General of the United States. The Republican controlled Senate voted him in anyway. The approval of Sessions as Attorney General is a testament to the political ideology of the Republican Party and is insight into the direction of America when there is a Republican controlled government, Senate or House of Representatives. Sessions approval as Attorney General speaks to the platform ideology of the Republican Party in general. Many of Trump's cabinet, judicial, legislative, and government appointments were substandard. His basis for selection was not qualification but loyalty to him and his own incompetence. This author is not the only opinion concerning Trump's incompetence. The New York Post editorial board is on record regarding a 2024 Trump campaign, "calling him 'unworthy' to serve in the White House for another term" [79] Consider the number of Trump's close associates and campaign workers who have been criminally charged: [80]

Steve Bannon: "Trump's political Svengali was charged with fraud in August 2020 for a fundraising swindle tied to raising dollars to build Trump's much bally-hooed border wall".

Tom Barrack: "Barrack was charged on seven counts on Tuesday. The allegations, according to the indictment, center on the idea that Barrack used his closeness to Trump to "advance the interests of and provide intelligence to the UAE while simultaneously failing to notify the Attorney General that their actions were taken at the direction of senior UAE officials." Following Trump's 2016 victory, Barrack, acting under the direction of the UAE, asked UAE officials to provide him with a "wish list" they hoped for from the administration over the first 100 days of Trump's presidency".

Elliott Broidy: "Broidy, a top fundraiser for Trump's 2016 presidential campaign, pleaded guilty in October 2020 to conducted a secret lobbying campaign in exchange for millions of dollars. "Broidy was charged earlier this month with conspiracy for failing to register and disclose his role in a lobbying effort aimed at stopping a criminal investigation into massive fraud at a Malaysian investment fund and advocating for the removal of a Chinese billionaire living in the US.""

Michael Cohen: "The one-time fixer for Trump, Cohen was sentenced to three years in prison for a series of crimes, most notably secret hush-money payments made during the final months of the 2016 presidential campaign to two women alleging affairs with Trump. Cohen turned informant on Trump and, in sworn testimony in front of Congress in 2019, Cohen called Trump "a racist," "a conman" and "a cheat" – and insisted that the president was fully aware of the hush-money payments".

Michael Flynn: "Flynn spent a brief stint as Trump's national security adviser before being forced to resign after he failed to disclose the depth and breadth of his contacts with Russian officials during the transition. Later that year, Flynn admitted that he had lied to the FBI about his contact with Russia and had also done work for Turkey as an unauthorized lobbyist".

Rick Gates: "Gates, deputy to the campaign chairperson of Trump's 2016 campaign, pleaded guilty to aiding and abetting Paul Manafort in concealing $75 million in foreign bank accounts. Gates turned informant for the government as part of the broader probe into Russian meddling in the 2016 election, and was sentenced to 45 days in jail".

Paul Manafort: "Trump's campaign manager for part of the 2016 presidential campaign, Manafort pleaded guilty in 2018 to on count of conspiracy against the US and one count of conspiracy to obstruct justice due to attempts to tamper with witnesses – and agreed to cooperate with the ongoing Russia probe. Manafort was sentenced to 47 months in prison in 2019. Trump pardoned Manafort, who wound up serving just under two years in prison, in the final weeks of his presidency."

George Nader: "An informal foreign policy adviser to Trump's 2016 campaign, Nader cooperated heavily with special counsel Robert Mueller's probe into Russian interference in the 2016 election. In early 2020, he pleaded guilty to two counts of sex crimes involving minors".

George Papadopoulos: "Papadopoulos, a relatively junior adviser to Trump's campaign, was sentenced to 12 days in prison for lying to investigators about his contacts with individuals tied to Russia. Papadopoulos was defiant about his innocence; "The truth will all be out," he tweeted the night before reporting to prison. "Not even a prison sentence can stop that momentum." Trump pardoned Papadopoulos in December 2020.

Roger Stone: "Stone spent years advising Trump although he was only formally affiliated with the 2016 campaign very briefly. He was convicted in November 2019 for lying to Congress and threatening a witness regarding his efforts for Trump's campaign. According to the judge, Stone's actions "led to an inaccurate, incorrect and incomplete report" from the House on Russia, WikiLeaks and the Trump campaign. Stone was pardoned by Trump in December 2020."

Allen Weisselberg: "The longtime chief financial officer for the Trump Organization was charged with tax crimes tied to benefits he was given in lieu of salary. "All told, the indictment alleged, Weisselberg evaded taxes on $1.76 million in income over a period beginning in 2005. He avoided paying city income taxes."

The commonalities in each of these individuals is 1) they are all White. 2) Their crimes revolve around financial crimes, greed, espionage (conspiring and developing relationships with foreign countries without informing the United States), and dishonest conspiracy in election fraud. One has to consider and acknowledge the people Trump surrounds himself with, the "birds of a feather" syndrome. Does any intelligent life on earth believe Donald Trump was ignorant of the activities of his closes associates? Was he complicit? Studies indicate there is often an alignment between White criminality and racism.

There is a term called "*distraction*", strategic actions, dialogue or propaganda that prevents someone from giving full attention to something else. Rooted in the country's white supremacy is the lie that black men are a physical threat to white people. The narrative that black men are inherently violent and prone to rape white women has been prevalent for centuries. This idea has served as the primary justification for the need to oppress black people and to protect white people. The idea that black people are wantonly attacking white people in some sort of race war is an untruthful and damaging narrative with a very long history in America. The distraction is that deflecting the attention of society on the issue of "*race conflict*", gives White people a cover to commit crimes, to steal money, to govern without scrutiny, and to promote and support their racist ideologies.[81] The truth is that White culture is committing grave injustices and crimes against the American people, while using the pretext of "*Black people being a threat to White people*" as justification for White criminal and racist behaviors.

The racist scapegoat for instilling fear in White people has expanded to Asians ("*The Asian Virus*"). According to Donald Trump: [82]

> "Wuhan. Wuhan was catching on, coronavirus, kung flu," he said, repeating it as the crowd roared. "I could give you many, many names. Some people call it the Chinese flu, the China flu, they call it the China."

Trump blamed the Asian culture for the Coronavirus. Trump's use of racially insensitive slurs against China is considered the primary catalyst causing the increase in hate crimes against Asians.

Regarding Hispanics, quoting Donald Trump: [83]

"When Mexico sends its people, they're not sending their best ... They're sending people that have lots of problems, and they're bringing those problems with us. They're bringing drugs. They're bringing crime. They're rapists. And some, I assume, are good people".

More Donald Trump racism: [84]

"It's coming from more than Mexico. It's coming from all over South and Latin America, and it's coming probably — probably — from the Middle East ... Islamic terrorism is eating up large portions of the Middle East. They've become rich. I'm in competition with them"

"They just built a hotel in Syria. Can you believe this? They built a hotel. When I have to build a hotel, I pay interest. They don't have to pay interest; because they took the oil that, when we left Iraq, I said we should've taken.." Donald Trump made this statement in 2017. During his 2016 Presidential campaign, Trump stated the following:

"Trump told Fox News Radio on August 29: "Look, we should have never been in Iraq. I've said that from day one and I was a civilian and it was covered but it was – you know, I was a civilian so who cares, right? But I said from day one, we should not go to Iraq."

"In his 2000 book "The America We Deserve," Trump argued that a military strike on Iraq might be necessary. Trump wrote that the US still did not know the true status of Iraq's nuclear program. He then wrote, "I'm no warmonger. But the fact is, if we decide a strike against Iraq is necessary, it is madness not to carry the mission to its conclusion. When we don't, we have the worst of all worlds: Iraq remains a threat, and now has more incentive than ever to attack us." [85]

The one thing that has been consistent about Donald Trump is that he only cares about himself and he is a racist who supports discrimination against non-White individuals. His believes, principles and ethics are conditionally situational. His positions are rooted in only one thing; Donald Trump. He does not care about anything or anyone else. Trump is a user. What father would bring his kids into the cest pool environment of the lived experiences he creates and attracts? Everything behavioral phenomena about him is situational and based on his personal interest.

The concept of "*deflection*" creates the pretext used by unsavory individuals to label an entire group of people with disdain, deflect public attention, and create racist sentiments against the target group of people to justify target group oppression. While the general public is being misdirected, the deflecting group can plumage or exercise White power to dictate the lives of the target group. This is the type of "*thing*" American people elected as President of the United States of America in 2016. It is also the "*thing*" America voted out of office in the 2020 Presidential election. It is also a "*thing*" that has permeated in America for centuries. A major result of Donald Trump's occupation of the White House is an increase in hate crimes. The relevance of Donald Trump to the issue of racism, discrimination and prejudice is that his administration was catalyst to the White racist supremacy element in America becoming more visible and more vocal.

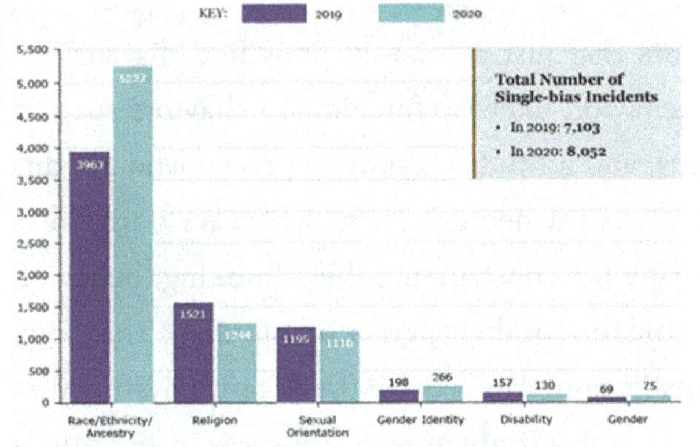

Of the 6,780 known offenders:

- 55.1% were White
- 21.2% were Black or African American
- 15.7% race unknown

Source: Department of Justice [86]

Psychology studies indicate that racially tolerant individuals display good psychological health and racially prejudiced individuals demonstrate poor psychosocial functioning and poor decision-making. Prior studies have found dysfunction in the interpersonal relationships for prejudiced individuals in childhood. "Blatant racists aggressively assert that members of minority groups are inferior. Subtle racists blame social inequities on minority group cultures and customs. A questionnaire to distinguish tolerant individuals from blatant and subtle racists was employed. Tolerant individuals were shown to be psychologically healthier than both blatant and subtle racists were. Both blatant and subtle racists show maladaptive patterns in psychosocial functioning. Both blatant and subtle racists report predicted disturbances in parental relationships, as well as insecure and hostile ties with peers."[87]

Harvard University conducted a test that revealed subconscious racial bias against African Americans. The study "showed that White Americans consistently received more help than Black Americans. The only harm done to Black Americans in those studies was the consequence of inaction — the absence of helping. This left them without advantages received by Whites, who received help. We can call this ***hidden discrimination*** . . ." Additional analysis of the data showed that "Automatic White preference is pervasive in American society." [88]

An American Reality suggests that just as racism, prejudice, discrimination is learned dysfunctional behavior, likewise functional behaviors such as developing positive relationships, and attitudes regarding people who are different physically and ideologically is learned behavior. Babies are born, metaphorically, as a blank canvas ripe for constructing their thinking, behavior, and ideology according to the guidance of their parent or guardian. This book further suggests that learning institutions can counter the negative dysfunction of implanted racist, prejudicial, and discriminating impressions in the minds of babies, youth, adolescents, and students from kindergarten through college. Unfortunately, learning institutions deal with these dysfunctional issues in a peripheral manner, if at all, comparable to "putting a band aid on a shot gun wound." The traditional function of learning institutions in America is to teach subject matter (math, English, social studies, science, etc.). Traditional learning is important to get jobs for a successful orderly life, theoretically. These subjects are important; however, human beings receive less attention in developing and maintaining interpersonal relationships. Intellectual Intelligence (IQ) is the primary focus. Learning institutions neglect Emotional Intelligence (EQ) in the learning process. Learning institutions take for granted that people know how to interact with each other. Historically, Kids learned respect, social values, norms and mores (functional behavior) in the home. Numerous, ongoing, consistent, and daily negative phenomena in American tell a different story. The many racial conflicts and violent acts that occur in America daily and constantly make us wonder if people even learn functionality. Current learning methods fall short of resolving cultural interactive people problems. Dysfunction between cultures are frequently occurring experiences in American society. White culture is not willing to resolve the root cause of racism, prejudice, and discrimination. The root cause is White culture and their socialization process, how they relate to people who are different from themselves and in many cases how they relate to other White people. White culture does not take responsibility for the seriousness and destructive problem they have caused and continue to perpetuate for minorities, people with gender differences, and religious difference. White people cause problems for themselves and for the United States of America by perpetuating racism, discrimination, and prejudice. Some White people give little value to the seriousness of the race problem in America. Many feel race issues get too much attention. Ironically, many Whites blame Black and minority people for their shortcomings, unemployment, disadvantage they encounter. Many White people profess the discrimination is not a barrier to Black and minority success. [89]

An American Reality identifies the subtle, the cultural manifestations of racism and the depth to which racist behavior permeates White culture. "*An American Reality*" case studies describes an incident of racism, discrimination and prejudice embedded in one of the most prestigious

learning institutions in the world, The University of Chicago (UChicago). This book will recount a specific incident and the environmental constructs that support racism, discrimination, and prejudice at an outstanding academic institution, The University of Chicago. The University of Chicago (UChicago) is one of the best higher education learning institutions in the world (depending on the source, it ranked in the top 10 in the world, among all studies in the top 20).[90] This author, Dr. Ronald Barnes, is a product of the University of Chicago, having attended the University of Chicago Laboratory High School and the University of Chicago Graduate School. Dr. Barnes earned a master's degree in religious studies from the University of Chicago Divinity School. This author has nothing but high praise to bestow upon UChicago as a learning environment and an institution dedicated to give its students one the best academic learning experiences with some of the most capable instructors in the world. UChicago is not necessarily a racist institution and has policies dedicated to address the problems of racism, prejudice, and discrimination. [91] However, like the broader White culture UChicago is part of, it harbors and employs people with culturally socialized, conditioned, and ingrained *racist residue.* Likewise, as an institution whose purpose is to educate all students, the construct of the University of Chicago is White focused and oriented, in practice, realistically benign to diversity. Individuals reflect aspects of their true nature in all situations they encounter. It is not easy for people to escape their socialization process. White people cannot repress their racism, be it subconscious, conscious, subtle, or overt. It is part of their socialization, and an integral part of their nature. This does not necessarily apply to all White people. There are exceptions. Numerous White people in America who understand and internalize the concept of equality and value equal rights and have a common humanity for all law-abiding individuals. This is an accomplishment for those who escaped from the "*Matrix*" of White privilege and recognize "**privilege**" should be an equal opportunity phenomenon. While the "American Dream" has historically been a mirage for most Black people, it is becoming a fleeting memory even for White people. As the renowned theologian and scholar, James Cone, would say, Good White people are White people who have "transcended their Whiteness." [92] While UChicago is not a racist institution, they, like many other institutions, do not adequately deal with the problem of racism, racist attitudes, and racist behavior, existing in the mist of their institution. While their intentions convey a concerted effort to address diversity issues, their results are very different from being effective in addressing the root of the problem. Metaphorically, analogous to weeds in the ground that are not pulled out from the roots. The weeds simply grow back. Education institutions have outreach programs that cultivate learning experiences for youth and create "safe zones" for diverse groups, but they do not sufficiently develop the infrastructure of the institution. Diversity training and awareness for management, instructors, professors, and administrators in many education environments is neglected. When diversity training is offered, it is either inadequate or not comprehensive or continuous. Diverse students exist in a predominately-White learning environment that socially and mentally is conditioned for diversity. As a result, diverse students face social and learning challenges White students do not encounter. *An American Reality* addresses positive recommendations to resolve this problem. This author realizes that UChicago is not alone in its share of racist occurrences. When people are present in a diverse environment, positive interpersonal interaction between individuals or groups is more the exception than the rule. Most likely, individuals associate predominately with members of their own cultural and social groups. It is common for people to associate in environments and groups where they are most comfortable. It is a negative personality flaw, and unfortunately occurs too often, when people disrespect others in different groups, especially without valid criteria for judgement. This author is writing about UChicago because he experienced racism, first-hand, in that environment and because UChicago is, in many respects, microcosmic of the overall American society.

Some will argue that a college or university's primary and only purpose is to teach minds to learn traditional subject matter. If this were the case, it would resolve many challenging issues. However, this viewpoint is absurd because colleges and universities are social environments as well as learning environments. People are social creatures more than they are mental creatures. A hypothesis is that when the social climate is improved the mental acumen results in higher achievement.

It is not at all the intention of this author to defame the greatness of UChicago. This author is a proud product of the UChicago learning environment. It is the intention of this author to provide insight that will make UChicago a greater institution than it is now. However, perfection is a fleeting goal we strive to attain. Achieving perfection is a nebulous concept. The devotion and desire to achieve and improve has been a constant motivation for human beings since the beginning of time. It is in this spirit that drives the intentions of this author to write *An American Reality*. UChicago, like many institutions in America needs to devote more financial resource and education resource to teaching people how to get along with each other, to improve human interactions. Learning positive diverse human interactions should be central to the education process, instead of peripheral to the education process. People with diversity awareness value others and are better prepared to learn, to teach and to live in society. It seems elementary to state that people need to learn how to interact with other people but evidenced by the state of our society, behaviors in interpersonal relationships are "trial and error." Leaning institutions neglect teaching basic human needs. How to balance a checkbook, how to select a mate, how young people should manage their sexuality, how to have successful relationships (friendships, marriage or professional), how to deal with individual difference, how to resolve conflict, or how to be a parent are among the most basic of human needs that are ignored in the learning process. They are often unaddressed in the home. How people should interact with each other, is essential among basic human needs and critical to learning. All of these circumstances are threats to the benefit of people who are skilled in the traditional learned skills. Analogously, learning institutions are building a fantastic house on a weak foundation. Therefore, it should not be a surprise when the perfect designed house collapses.

Consider the plight of Amy Cooper, known as the Central Park "Karen." She attended the University of Chicago, Booth Business School, graduated and took a job in New York City. In a videotaped encounter with a black man, Christian Cooper, in Central Park. It is ironic that both the culprit and the victim have the same last name. Mr. Cooper asked Amy to abide by park rules and put her dog on a leash. He recorded the incident on his smartphone, she charged him in a threatening manner, coming within inches of him. She initially refused to put her dog on a leash, instead threatening the 57-year-old man, Christian Cooper, a Harvard graduate who works in communications. She screamed that she would call the police, to file a report. "*A Black man*" was putting her life in jeopardy, stating, "I'm going to tell them there's an African American man threatening my life." Amy Cooper, who worked as a vice president and head of investment solutions at Franklin Templeton Investments in New York City. Cooper earned her MBA at the University Of Chicago Booth School Of Business, was let go by Franklin Templeton after an internal review of the videotaped encounter with the black man, Christian Cooper, in Central Park. Mr. Cooper, simply, asked Amy to abide by park rules and put her dog on a leash. Clearly, the park posted signs that dogs "MUST be leashed" at all times. The incident is another example of white people calling the police on African Americans making false accusations and for incidents, they initiate and lie about. It is an example of racism, running rampant in America. [93] It also indicates the failure of the education system to address issues of emotional intelligence (EI). This is an example of how a low EI can sabotage the professional career of a person with a high IQ.

The Reluctant Activist is also a graduate of The University of Chicago Booth School of Business. She is also a self-identified White woman who has chronicled her antiracist awakening and journey toward intersectional feminism on Instagram. Her insights on the University of Chicago environment gives some explanation regarding how White culture influences or supports the racist mindset of educated people, stating:

> "*The only reason I could believe this lie was because I am White. So many of our American systems and institutions are built in a way that benefits White people while oppressing others. These systems are designed to be invisible to White eyes. We are told we are smart and hardworking, and we earned what we have achieved. As a result, I failed to recognize the truth back then: By not actively fighting racism, I was reinforcing it. So, although I do not hold the University of Chicago directly responsible for my beliefs or the actions of Amy Cooper, I have to name what I saw. And that was an* ***institution that through its inaction reinforced White supremacy****. They conferred degrees on me and my classmates letting us believe that we had wholly earned them. They aided and abetted my racist views by doing nothing substantial to disabuse me of them.*"[94]
>
> The Reluctant Activist further stated, "*The leaders of the future need to be antiracist. Until intentional effort is put into cultivating antiracism, our leading educational institutions will continue to provide the same racist education that I, Amy Cooper, likely you and countless others received. And people like George Floyd, Ahmaud Arbery, Breonna Taylor, Nina Pop and Tony McDade will continue to be harmed by a system that goes unchallenged by those it benefits.*"[95]

The reason these insights are valuable is because, the Reluctant Activist echoes the values and norms of inaction at the University of Chicago that reflects Dr. Barnes' experience. She echoes the values of most White educational institutions in America. She gives substantial reason why diversity and anti-racist education is critical as a foundation for professional growth. Her insights also substantiate the importance of making diversity education central to the education process. Amy Cooper is a perfect example of a great mind that failed because she lived in a narrow-minded, foundationally weak, "White world" instead of the real world. One person commented: *"What has this country become?* Then answered his own question: *"The same as before, but with video phones to document it."*

Historically and in these contemporary times there, have been and are so many incidents of racism and White atrocities against Black and minority people that it will fill a library to document the details of the injustice against minorities by Whites. However, the pinnacle of awareness on how White people demonstrate their disregard for other cultures is evident in an investigative report issued by the U. S. Department of Interior on Federal Indian Boarding Schools. Between 1819 and 1969, Native American (Indian) children were forcibly kidnapped from their families, to physically and psychologically separate them from their tribes and their native culture to attend Federal Indian Boarding Schools. The United States directly targeted American Indian, Alaska Native, and Native Hawaiian children in the implementation of a policy to cultural assimilation these groups. This action coincided with Indian territorial dispossession. Whites established Four-hundred eight (408) Federal Indian boarding schools across 37 states to destroy the native culture of the target groups and assimilate them into the White culture. Investigation of this abhorrent practice discovered at least 53 burial sites for children across this system.[96]

The intent of the U. S. government was to educate the Indian kids to the "ways of White culture". White culture's purpose was to assimilate the indigenous culture of children and "civilize" the Indian children. This meant alienating the kids from their family and native culture, housing them in federally funded boarding schools run by missionaries. In this case, we have the institution of education, and the government collaborating with the institution of religion to change the way of life of Indian children, to reconstruct their internalized cultural heritage. The result of this collaboration was a failure; destructive to the Indian tribes, the children, the Indian parents and especially the perpetrators. The boarding schools often mixed children from different tribes, required the kids to speak English, cut the children's hair, made them wear uniforms, and subjected them to military-style regimentation, specifically meant to sever their link to their former lives. Most often the conditions were poor, resulting in health problems ranging from gall bladder disease to cancer rates much higher among Native American adults who had attended boarding schools than those who had not. It was an effort that gave White culture the freedom to exercise their racist ethnocentricities in a failed effort at forced assimilation. White culture does not respect other cultures. Their intent was to change the indigenous culture to adopt to White culture. The ironic hypocrisy is that parents on the Right worry about "woke" indoctrination of their children. White parents fear the Left will implant progressive ideologies into the minds of their children. White parents fear their children will learn the truth about their culture. This attempt on the part of the "White right" to denigrate and minimize the Indian culture and the minority groups' contributions to society is the exact behavior Whites fear from "the left woke". White culture fears their children will learn the truth about their culture, the way they are and behave. Immoral and unethical acts such as those imposed on the Indian children reveals the truth about White culture. Indian children were taught to believe that the ideal is a straight, white male. This action was reinforced by the power of the U.S. Government and the Christian Religion. [97] This incident gives insight into the nature of White culture. Who in their right mind should want to be White? White people, themselves, should be ashamed to be White, and many are. We need to ask, what does White culture fear? Do they fear the superiority of other cultures or the inferiority of White culture?

Tim Scott, the only Black republican in the United States Senate, profoundly stated "Hear me clearly: America is not a racist country." [98] That statement by Tim Scott causes one to think. The doctrine and dogma that governs America is not racist, despite the existence of too many racists in America, the persistence of racial disparities and wide racial gaps in the US healthcare system, its criminal injustice system, its discriminatory educational system, and its unequal economic system. In fact, these gaps have grown over time. Additionally, despite the significant number of deplorable racist individuals and the atrociously violent acts against African Americans and minorities that have occurred historically and since they arrived in the slave port of Jamestown Colony, Virginia in 1619, up until this present day, America is not a racist country, in its dogma. America just has too many racists inhabiting this great land. It is a conundrum but while America is not a racist country according to the Constitution of the United States, America is infected with significant hordes of racist individuals, many of whom supported and voted for Donald Trump (74,000,000 out of a population of 300,000,000. Approximately, 25% of the American population). In response to Scott, journalist Soledad O'Brien commented, "It sounds like a racist country to me," [99] At the least, America is based on hypocrisy. Like, the Native American Indians say, "White man speaks with forked tongue. In other words, White men lie, with a consistency that caused Native American Indians to brand the White man as speaking with a forked tongue.

President Joe Biden and Vice President Kamala Harris also weighed in on racism in America, with both acknowledging there is much work to do, President Joe Biden stated, "We have a real chance to root out systemic racism that plagues America." The reluctance to brand America as a racist country is not a commonly held opinion by everyone. However, there is little doubt that America is over populated with racists. The issue certainly evokes cognitive dissonance among many of our elected leaders and people who believe in American dogma. The "*Great Replacement Theory*" is that there are too many deplorable White people, whose actions overshadow and replace the actions and behavior of the many good and decent White people. The fact that America condemns other countries for civil rights abuse, then displays the same behaviors against minorities gives the international community the impression of America being hypocritically racist, which increases the cognitive dissonance in Americans. Pulitzer Prize winner Isabel Wilkerson appeared on the Don Lemon Show and compared racism in America to a caste system, yet America condemns other countries for subjugating the human rights of their citizens.[100] It makes many Americans defensive when hearing America criticized for being a racist country and when others claiming that racism breeds racism in the social institutions of America. One theory is that people are aware they are benefitting from the discriminating policies of America, their assets are unearned, and the advantage of being American is not shared with minorities.[101] Most often, this defensive position is associated with Whiteness and the strategy to deflect focus away from unearned benefits. Scott, Harris, and Biden understand this and frame their positions politically. They balance the reality of America, overburdened with racist, with their concern for voters nationally. In a state like South Carolina, Tim Scott has to be expert at balancing his act because he is an elected Black senator in the South. As Scott mentioned, America is not a racist country. American dogma is not racist, but too many Americas are racists.

There has not been one President in the history of the United States, not one session of the United States Congress, nor one session of the United States Senate that has done anything to mitigate racism, racists, or inequality on a significant scale. Abraham Lincoln accomplished the most significant act to advance the cause of freedom for American and for Black people. Lincoln issued the "Emancipation Proclamation" in 1863 to eliminate slavery at a great cost to our nation, the civil war, as well as a great cost to Lincoln, his life.. Unfortunately, a southern sympathizer assassinated Lincoln. His successor Andrew Johnson was a pro-southern racist who supported the White southerners in halting the post-slavery progress made by Blacks. When Lincoln freed slaves from slavery, the institution of slavery was not totally dismantled. Freeing human beings from an inhuman, immoral and deplorable systematic condition was revolutionary. However, the residue of that deplorable institution still exists today. The problems and problem is that hordes of deplorable racist terrorist still exists in America.

Dr. Martin Luther king, Jr. dedicated his life, literally dedicated his life, to the cause of civil rights. He was killed because the racist's component in American society feared he was making progress, and he was, in terms of making America a better country. President Barack Obama was the first Black man elected president in the history of the United States. His major contribution to racial equality was being the first Black president of the United States of America. I have great respect for President Obama. He was the president of all Americans. He is a moral and ethical man. A decent human being. The opposite from his successor. It is just that his tenure as president did little to progress the cause of Black America. President Obama was confronted with a Republican congress and a Senate leader (Mitch McConnell) who obstructed as many of his proposed policies as they could. Much of President Obama's opposition was based on the fact he is Black. There is a racist pathetic faction in the highest bastions of our government, that herald the behavior that not even a Black man who is elected President of the United States of America, by the American people is immune to racism. His tenure maintained the status quo. However, during the Obama administration the White domestic terrorism against Black, minority, Hispanic, Asian, Jewish, Muslim and LGBT groups was not nearly as aggressive as it was during the Trump administration and is today.

What is the problem with America that our legislators, government officials and White culture are more concerned with nonrestrictive gun laws and the bribes they receive from the gun companies than they are about America's children? Police arrested a 12-year-old White boy after the kid pulled out a weapon and robbed a gas station in Michigan. The 12-year-old White kid robbed the gas station in broad daylight in the presence of other customers in the gas station. He pointed the gun at the clerk, demanded money and fired a shot into the ceiling to assert himself.[102] This incident does not involve racism because the kid robbed a gas station owned by a White proprietor and the clerk was White. It is merely an example of the dysfunction in our society that victimizes our children. In the White kid, this dysfunctional behavior is an entry into other area of dysfunction developing in his life, including racism, which has direct linkage to White criminality when experienced early in life. This situation is not unique to White kids. Black kids also encounter misguided phenomena and experience dysfunction in their early development stages. This lack of guidance leads kids to become American casualties. A child is a terrible thing to lose. Consider the following examples of Dylann Roof, Salvator Ramos, and Payton Gendron. Three young boys (21 years old, 18 years old and 18 years old respectively). These boys are American casualties to the hatred and racism in America. The hatred in the minds of these boys did not immediately develop at the time they committed their racist acts. They became racist as a process of their development.

On June 17, 2015, Dylann Roof (pictured left), a 21 year old, American white supremacist, neo-Nazi, mass murderer, and domestic terrorist, killed nine African Americans during a Bible study. This hate crime at Emanuel African Methodist Episcopal Church, included the murder of the church pastor and state senator, Clementa C. Pinckney. Roof entered the church, sat in the bible study session for a few moments then opened fire on the group of African American Christians attending the bible study. Roof confessed that he committed the shooting in hopes of starting a race war. Roof's actions in Charleston are acts of domestic terrorism. [103]

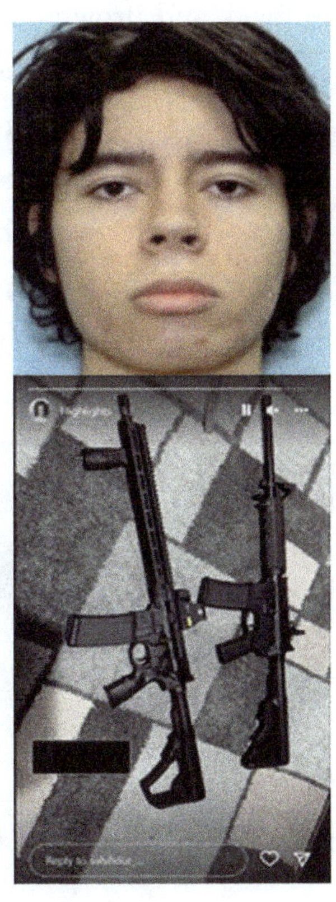

Salvator Ramos, an 18-year-old individual, entered Robb Elementary school in Uvalde, Texas and murdered 19 people 21 people, 2 adults and 19 children in grades 2 to 4. It was the nation's most deadly school shooting, since the 2012 massacre at Sandy Hook Elementary in Connecticut, but one of the many acts of terrorism in America. Before he set off on his murderous rampage, he shot his grandmother. Ramos was a worker at Wendy's fast food restaurant and high school dropout. The gunman used an AR-15 assault weapon, (pictured left). This weapon has high capacity bullet magazines and is made for use in military warfare. The gunman used this weapon to kill 21 unarmed people including 19 children, ages 7-10. [104] The thought of this happening to children beings tears to one's eyes. It makes decent Americans angry. It does not develop love for America among American citizens. The United States of America has serious problems. The legislators in America, especially the Republican faction of politicians, are seriously inadequate in their ability to solve America's violence and terrorism problems. American politicians shoulder the blame for many of the violent acts in America. American politicians are accomplices in the murders of all schoolchildren after the first incident of school violence. A number of the people who commit these acts of violence are kids themselves, under 21 years old. The violence problems in America, the racism, and the many incidents of dysfunction in America are all related to the psychology that governs America. The political ideologies and mentality of America's political leadership does not serve American citizens. America's politicians serve personal and special interest and money. Why does America elect these people to office? That these acts of violence occur mostly in Black and Brown communities, the White politicians are not motivated to act. However, when these acts of violence happen in White communities, the politicians are still not motivated to serve the interest of the American people over the bribes they take from gun companies. America has the most pathetic group of politicians in the World. America is considered a world leader. Leader in What? Almost all other civilized countries have a better record of protecting its citizens than America. Why? A country that does not protect its children is not great, it is pathetic. Its understatement to say the leadership is pathetic.

Payton Gendron (pictured left), an 18 year old, white supremacist teenager who shot 13 people at a Buffalo, New York market on May 14, 2022. Eleven of the 13 people shot were African American. Gendron who lives in Conklin, New York traveled approximately 200 miles to Buffalo, where he massacred 11 people and attempted to kill all 13. Before the shooting Gendron specifically researched neighborhood's demographics to target a predominantly black community, Investigations revealed Gendron repeatedly visited sites espousing white supremacist ideologies and race-based conspiracy theories. He specifically researched the 2019 mosque shootings in Christchurch, New Zealand, and the man who killed dozens of people at a summer camp in Norway in 2011, authorities indicated. "The US Department of Justice is investigating the shooting "as a hate crime and an act of racially motivated violent extremism," according to a statement from US Attorney General Merrick Garland". [105]

One motivating factor in Gendron's action was his belief in "*The Great Replacement Theory*". "*The Great Replacement Theory*" is a philosophy held by White Nationalist, White Supremacist, and far right conspiracy theorist. French author Renaud Camus started this absurd conspiracy theory. One hypothesis regarding this unfounded conspiracy theory is that Camus started the theory because he had personal feelings of uselessness and inadequacy in the first place. Hypothesizing he had feelings of replacement because he had low self-esteem issues and feelings of inferiority is a reasonable perspective considering his theory is unfounded. Why else would he advance an unfounded theory he was replaceable and Whites are being replaced, especially since it was not and is not true? Possibly he had subconscious belief, he was replaceable? Who are White Americans being replaced with, immigrants, other Americans? If Whites are concerned about being replaced, they should develop skills that are in demand. This is a concern among uneducated, unskilled, ignorant White people who have nothing to contribute but dysfunction in the first place. Replacement theory advances that, assisted by society elitist, the White French and European populations are being demographically and culturally replaced with non-European peoples specifically Arab, Berber, Turkish and sub-Saharan Muslim populations because of mass migration, demographic growth and a drop in the birth rate of White Europeans. [106] Specifically, Camus was a fear monger against Muslim presence in Europe. In America right wing racist, White Nationalist, White supremacist and neo-Nazis have adopted the "*Great Replacement Theory*" out of the fear that Blacks, Hispanics and other minorities will become the majority population and the White population is projection to be the minority population by the year 2045. The thought Whites are being replaced would not surface if Whites were secure and confident in their social location. According to census projections, Whites will comprise 36% of the population by 2060. [107] Republican congressional representative Steve King endorsed this conspiracy theory. Florida State senator Dennis Baxley referenced this theory in the context of the abortion debate. "Nick Isgro, Vice Chair of the Maine Republican Party endorsed the conspiracy theory after claiming financial subsidies were promoted for abortions in the U.S. to kill our own people», and those asylum seekers were human pawns who are being played in a game by global elites and their partners here in Augusta.» Greg Kesich, a writer for the Portland Press Herald, reported that the current Mayor of Waterville's speech displayed the sentiment of the Great Replacement.[108] United States President Donald Trump has made reference to the theory to appeal to the right wing and alt-right voters, characterizing Hispanic migrants as invaders taking American jobs and arguing to 'send them back.'" [109] In April 2021, Tucker Carlson prominently mentioned the replacement conspiracy theory on his show, as one of the many stupid propaganda themes Carlson's spouts. [110] Former speaker of the House of Representatives, Newt Gingrich and Republican congressional representative Scott Perry have echoed the theory in a supportive way.[111] Proponents of the "*Great Replacement Theory*", believe that national-born Americans, native-born Americans are being replaced and this will permanently transform the landscape of America. Some believe that the election of Donald Trump as President was due in part to his campaign reference to the "*Great Replacement theory*". What White culture did to the Native American Indians is irrelevant from the viewpoint of the "*Great Replacement Theory*", unless White America reflects on their own White past. The landscape of America was transformed when Whites came to America and stole the land from the Indians. It is deplorable how people inflict behaviors on others; they themselves do not want inflicted on them. The people, who believe in the Replacement theory, need to be replaced. It is an un-American racist belief.

The alarming issue regarding this conspiracy theory is that some individuals who govern America, lawmakers, support it. It is a White nationalist, White

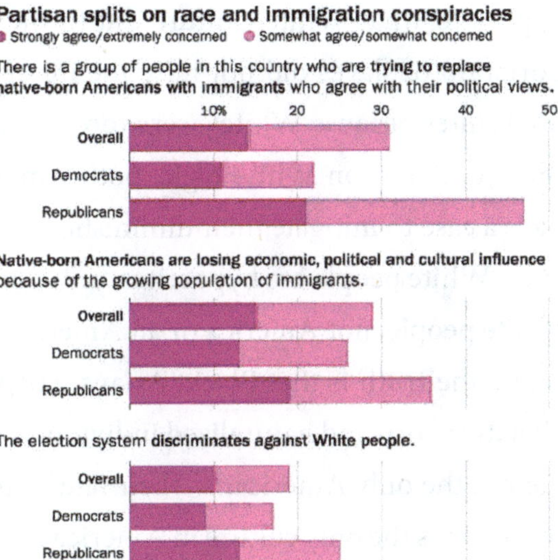

supremacist theory and support for the theory is based on White nationalist and White supremacist belief. What difference does it make who is the minority or majority population, if America is a fair, ethical, moral and equality-based country? According to the Washington Post, nearly half of Republicans agree with '*Great Replacement Theory*' and 30% of Americans agreed with the idea that native-born Americans were losing influence, and intentional replacement of Whites was taking place. Approximately 20% of Americans think the election system discriminates against Whites. [112] The irony in this belief is that the American political system is based on Republicans and Democrats aggressively campaigning to select candidates, at all levels of government (local, County, State, and National) who agree with their political views. The concept and foundation of American politics rejects the policy of the best candidate for America and the American people. The best candidate is a relative concept. The concept of the best candidate for America and the American people is mute. The foundation of American politics is the best candidate for the party, their donors, their constituents, and themselves. The American voter is often influenced by factors that have no relevance to their best interest. The fact that politicians complain about immigrants diminishing the influence of Native-born Americans is a joke. All White people in America are immigrants or offspring of immigrants. Their ancestors took the economic, political and cultural influence away from the Native American Indians and imported slaves to build America into the country it is. If anything, the "Great Replacement Theory" applies to what White Culture did to the Native American Indians. The importation of slaves did not raise the ire of immigrant Whites as replacements for Whites because Whites were too lazy and weak to do the work slaved performed. Based on White logic, both American Indians and American Blacks have a case to mitigate their diminished economic, political, and cultural influence. White people are hypocrites, only concerned with issues in the interest of White people, not America or all Americans. However, grounded in common sense; the truth is that Black, Asians, Hispanics, Whites, Muslims, LGBT and all native born and naturalized individuals are American citizens. White people are not the only Americans. Their failure to recognize other cultures and their behavior as the only culture in America is catalyst to their racism, prejudice and discrimination. White people consider themselves the only culture in America worthy of America's benefits. White Immigrants to America did not mutually collaboration with the Indians. White culture is only concerned about White culture and attempt to dictate who can participate in the fruits of America. Non-Whites who comply with the rules of White culture have limited participation. Senator Tim Scott of South Carolina is an example of a non-White person allowed to participate on a limited basis. Immigration to America is or was the source of the American way of life and opportunity for most, including the ancestors of all White people in America.

Intelligent, clear minded, emotionally intelligent and decent individuals need to understand the ignorance and stupidity in the "*Great Replacement Theory*". Fox news, Tucker Carlson, the media, politicians, and the right-wing racist that promote this theory are a danger and a threat to America, The American way of life, and all American citizens.

Pollsters also asked respondents what cable news channel they preferred found those who preferred Fox News were more likely than Americans overall or than those who preferred CNN or MSNBC to agree with the replacement

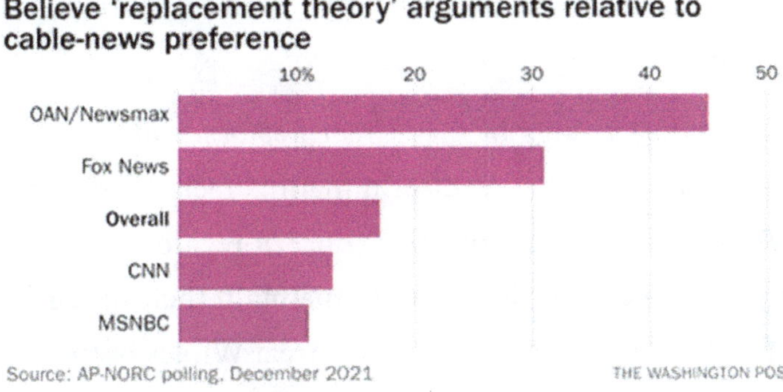

theory idea. Three in 10 of those who prefer Fox News held the agree/concerned positions on the first two questions above. Among those who watched cable news closer to the right-wing fringe, "One America News and Newsmax, the figure was 45 percent". [113] This is because Fox news and One America are more propaganda news channels that deliver a one-sided right-wing perspective on the news. CNN and MSNBC are left of Fox and One America but deliver a more balanced perspective on the news.

The belief that immigrants come to America to influence the outcome of elections or to change the American way of life is ridiculously stupid. Some human beings are incredibly ignorant in their beliefs and ideology. Immigrants come to America for a better way of life. They come to participate in the American way of life, (same as the ancestors of the Whites who are here now), the American Dream (assuming it still exist). Immigrants do not want to change the American way of life. They want to participate in it. White people are socialized only to get along with other White people and often, White people have difficulty getting along with White people.

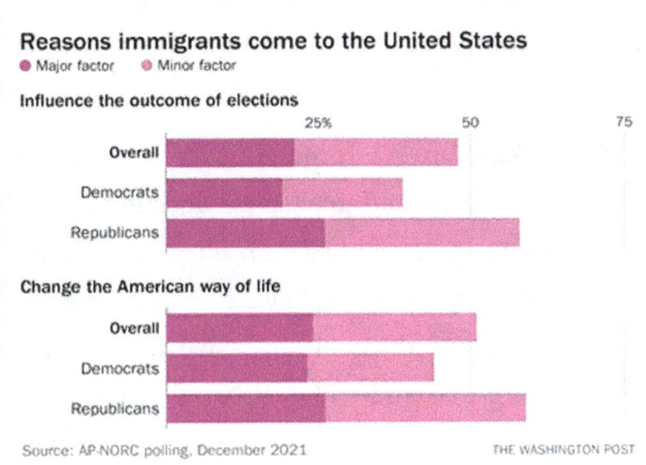

It is especially a challenge for White people to get along with others who are not White.

The psychology of the "*Great Replacement*" concept indicates that White America is an insecure, discriminating, racist faction of America. The fact that Whites have such a protective concern regarding "*The Great Replacement Theory*" indicates their intention to maintain their unfair policies. It could also be a fear that the "new majority" will treat Whites in the same way, Whites treated minorities, as Whites are the majority. Is this White guilt complex? This is an important issue and requires further analysis to understand the depth of ignorance in the thinking associated with the "*Great Replacement Theory*". Whites fear they will become a minority. How do humans populate? They populate when they copulate. White people are becoming a minority because they do not copulate, not because of other cultures gaining in numbers. Sexual inadequacy or sexual adequacy in White culture, and the impotence in White men, need to be studied. A study on the physical and psychological impotence in White culture will possibly uncover reasons why White culture is on track to become a minority. Yet they blame their sexual inadequacy, and diminishing population rates on minorities. When will White culture take responsibility for their own shortcomings and inferiorities? If White people become a minority, it is because they have sexual diminished activity compared to other cultures. That is simple logic.

Traditional hereditarianism thinking on White superiority claimed that Western civilization was doomed to "cultural and intellectual decline because of "*dysgenic overbreeding by the less intelligent and under breeding by the more intelligent.*" Despite the evidence of steadily rising intelligence among the non-White population, the hereditarians, advanced the ideology that unavoidable and obvious racial differences in intelligence and morality would lead to new understanding and acceptance of average differential outcomes of Whites over non-Whites in wealth, education, criminal conviction, and social position among Whites and non-Whites. Hereditarianism hypothesizes that the inevitable acceptance of White privilege and the accompanying racism, which is said to be caused by Black frustration and White resentment (e.g., over affirmative action), would be greatly reduced, with the inevitable evolution of White privilege. [114] Some traditional society racists, from a psychological viewpoint, advance hereditarianism, as genetic inheritance that is a major influence on behavior. There is considerable debate on this position. An alternative viewpoint is the belief that environment and learning account for the major differences between people, not genetic heredity.

The "*Great Replacement Theory*" circulating among White racists as a motivation for their dysfunctional behavior has a sexual overtone. A research study should be conducted on the sexual dissonance in White culture. While most cultures accept the natural sexual interaction between males and females, White culture appears to have gross confusion in the way they engage sexuality in their lived experiences. White sexual protocol previously assumed that it was intellectually and culturally superior to minimize and scrutinize the number of offspring produced. The White race now supports anti-abortion policies that will increase childbirths. The variety of strategies deployed by White culture to maintain their dominant and racist ideology is absurdly pathetic. They deploy every strategy other than a strategy that is collaborative and that recognizes the multi-cultural nature of American society.

There are reasons the White population is at risk of becoming the minority in America.

1) Whites are less sexual than other cultures.

2) Whites are less potent or less fertile.

3) Whites use birth control more often today than in the past. This indicates, Whites do not want to have babies. For centuries, White men have not only suppressed the lives of minorities but they have also suppressed the lives of White women and restricted the opportunities for White women. Now that women have opportunity to become educated and pursue professional careers, they are prolonging marriage and having children.
4) White women have more abortions than women do in other cultures (Appendix 3).

Statistics indicate that White women and Black women of color have the most abortions. Non-Hispanic White women and non-Hispanic women have the most abortions (Appendix 3). Black women and White women accounted for the largest percentages of all abortions (33.4% and 38.4%, respectively).[115] The number of births for White women and Black women is decreasing. However, the number of births for Hispanic woman and other is increasing (Appendix 14). If the population of the White race is decreasing, it is their own fault. White people are not having babies at the same rate as Hispanic and other women. Yet, characteristic of the nature of White culture, they blame others for their problems, fears, and shortcomings. Led by the right-wing Republican Party, the extreme changes in laws against abortion could be strategically a way to maintain the White population majority. When will White people learn, that other cultures behave with more humanity than they do. As a standard political norm, White Republicans commonly institute policies that infringe on the rights of others or policies that diminish the rights of others. White fear and White racism motivates their behavior, ethics, morality, and the violence and hostility White culture enacts toward other cultures, and those who are non-White.

White culture seems to be suffering from a mass hysteria of "Frustration-Aggression. **The frustration-aggression theory advances that human aggression is a result of frustration.** Frustration is any event or stimulus that prevents an individual from attaining a goal and its coinciding reinforcement quality. When people experience frustrated, they manifest a need to be aggressive towards the object of their frustration. Often, however, it is impossible or inappropriate to confront the source of their frustration, so their aggression focuses on something or someone else. [116] Considering the source of White frustration is the insecurity and inadequacy in their own culture, rather than confront their own short-comings they violently and with vengeance act out against others, Blacks, Asians, Muslims, Jews, LGBT, minorities, or anyone else other than fix themselves.

White culture should exercise its humanity and eliminate the sick deplorable racists and racism in their culture. Maybe it is a good thing that the birth rate of White people is decreasing. Possibly, over the years there will be fewer domestic terrorist and racist in America. The "*Great Replacement Theory*" is a conspiracy theory that reflects the ignorance and diminished capacity of racists White people. The decent White people in America who believe in democracy and a fair and just America as reflected in American dogma, need to take responsibility for eliminating the stain of Domestic terrorism and hate mongers from their culture. America seems to have a serious dilemma regarding how to deal with domestic terrorism and hate crimes. The American legal system and the American system of law and order seem to struggle about how to stop domestic terrorism and hate crimes. One suggestion is to round up members of the domestic terrorist groups and members of hate groups and take them to Guantanamo for interrogation and to determine their plight. Use the same tactics deployed with ISIS and AL Qaeda. The threat of Domestic terror and hate crimes is greater to America than is international terrorism. White supremacist, White nationalist, neo-Nazis, and racists are traitors, dangerous to American democracy and American citizens: Black, Hispanic, Jewish, Asian and White. Another important step to mitigate domestic terrorism is to change the gun laws and curtail the strangle hold the gun industry has on American politicians.

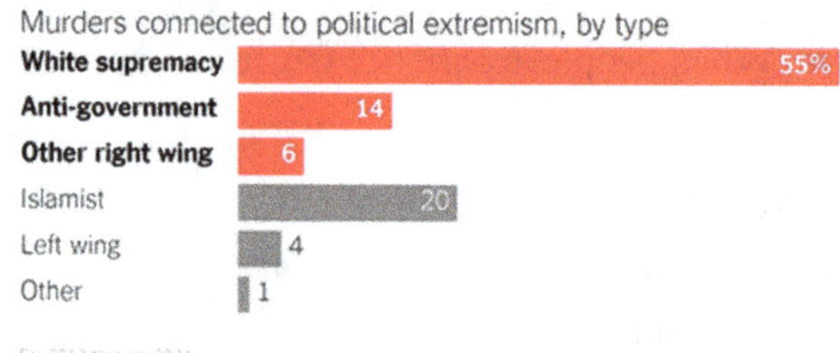

That our country's legislators support "*The Great Replacement Theory*" is especially concerning because it indicates these people are not qualified to protect democracy or defend the Constitution of the United States of America. They are traitors operating in the midst of our United States government and society. When America sees these traitors for the destructive force that they are, then America will have clarity regarding how to deal with them.

Over the past decade, there have been approximately 450 US murders committed by political extremists. Right wing extremist are responsible for about 75% of the terrorist violence. Over one-half of the murders connect to White supremacists. The American political right has violence problems. The primary right-wing politicians belong to the Republican Party. A number of Republican Party members have denounced the violence on the part of their followers but many Republican Party members condone and support the violence. That is evident from the stance and lack of cooperative support the Republicans have taken regarding the January 6 insurrection investigation. The Republican Party, especially Donald Trump's faction and a substantial number of legislators (in congress and in the senate) who fail to denounce the right-wing acts of violence, including the Republican House Speaker, Kevin McCarthy and the Republican leader in the Senate, Mitch McConnell. Representative Liz Cheney and Senator Mitt Romney are two of the few Republican who have honorably denounced right-wing terrorist violence. Cheney stated, "History has taught us that what begins with words ends in far worse." America needs politicians (Republican and Democrat) who are not ambiguous about rejecting violence but who unambiguously expel antidemocratic terrorist and terrorist sympathizers from their party, even maintain surveillance on them as suspects that support terrorist activity. [117] This generation of American politicians is populated with a pathetic lot of inadequate substandard individuals who have no place in government or in any capacity that deals with the welfare of the United States of America and its citizens.

Both Roof and Gendron reinforced their racist's beliefs by subscribing to White supremacist and White nationalist sites on the internet, where they communicated with others who are likeminded racists. When freedom of speech promotes violent behavior, it is illegal. White racists agendas to "start a race war", to conduct acts of violence against law abiding American citizens, or to ethnic and minority Americans as targets to commit acts of violence is a crime against America. Authorities need to eliminate these groups, designate their internet activity as aggressive acts of terror against America and punish members of these domestic terrorist groups the same as ISIS and Al Qaeda. Statistics indicate that domestic terrorism is a much bigger threat to our democracy than International terrorism. [118] Another terrifying aspect of these incidents is that the perpetrators were young White men, 21 and 18 years old. The philosophy of racial hatred, internalized by young White youth, is a startling condemnation on White culture and the White socialization process. It waste young minds, indicating the ignorance and immoral character that permeates in White culture, a waste of human resource. The lives of these young men are gone, wasted. The only thing they have to look forward to is to become "pet boys" for the White racist in prison culture. Maybe they will become "party favors" for other prison inmates.

Recently, in May 2022, White high school students at Colerain High School in Cincinnati Ohio, taped "Whites only," and a "Blacks only" signs above a pair of water drinking fountains in the hallway. This is reflective of life under the Jim Crow laws. This incident mirrors a number of racist acts by young White youth. In 2022, student-athletes in several states, including Georgia , Washington, Vermont, Minnesota and California, have reported hearing competitors or spectators yelling racial slurs at them during or after games. Racists are developing at a younger age. That White culture, in these contemporary times, are enacting racist behavior signals the disgraceful, deplorable life direction White youth consider as alternatives to decency. [119]

The Internet and social media plays a significant role in Domestic and racist terrorism. International and domestic violent extremists have developed an extensive presence on the internet through messaging platforms, blogs, online images, videos, and publications. These mediums facilitate the groups' ability to radicalize and recruit individuals who are weak-minded and receptive to extremist messaging. Social media has also allowed both international and domestic terrorists to gain unprecedented, virtual access to people living in the United States and throughout the world, in an effort to enable homeland attacks. International and domestic terrorist communications and mediums has resonated with supporters in the United States and abroad. Domestic terrorist groups like the Ku Klux Klan, the Proud Boys, Aryan Nations, neo-Nazis and others of the like, have adopted methods of recruitment to spread their terrorist and racist philosophies. [120] Social media and internet operators, along with government authorities need to act on multiple fronts to eliminate the threat of domestic terrorism and hate crimes, starting with the means of recruitment deployed by domestic terrorist. Also the social media operators must monitor the activity over they networks much better. The "free speech" "hands off" policy of social network providers is no longer feasible. This outdated policy only opens the door for terrorist activity. One has to wonder how many lawmakers in the congress, in the senate and in the State legislatures are supporters of domestic terrorism and racism. The January 6 attack against our capital and the politicians who defended the attack against the capital should give the American people insight into those who lean toward having sympathy for domestic terrorist. How strong their sympathies are, is worthy of investigation. To have sympathy for domestic terrorism at all, hints of treasonous inclinations. There is strong reason to believe that there is a linkage between social networks, domestic terrorism and hate crimes. *"Research sponsored by the National Institute of Justice has found that study samples of individuals in the United States who have engaged in violent and non-violent hate crime and other forms of extremist crime were influenced by social media."* [121] Interrupting the developing cycle of hate crimes and domestic terrorism is a process that requires action on multiple fronts. The government needs to criminalize and prosecute anti-American, domestic terrorism, hate crimes and racial violence aggressively. At the same time Americans, need to learn and become socialized to adopt behavior that mitigates dysfunction in our society. The learning process needs to take place in our learning institutions; primary, elementary, secondary and higher learning institutions.

At present, the prestigious learning institutions in our great country are reflective of the overarching society. The institutions themselves may not be racist, but racism inhabit all environments in America. Administrators that govern our learning institutions are sensitive to the issues of racism, prejudice, and discrimination. As a result, diversity policies and programs are established. Frankly, White school administrators lack the insight, knowledge, and ability to institute programs and policies that change the behaviors and culture of racism on their campuses. Students still stratify with few exceptions, along racial, gender, cultural and religious lines. Asians primarily interact with Asians. African Americans primarily interact with African Americans, LGTBQ students primarily interact with other LGTBQ students, Islamic students primarily associate with other Islamic students and White students primarily associate with other White students. People have the right to make these choices. Individuals are more comfortable with those whom they share common interest. People have the right to choose their associations. The disadvantage is that understanding other cultures and other people is limited to perception, rather than fact, based on personal interaction. Multiculturalism and interpersonal relationships with others should be part of the learning process, especially during the years in the college and the university learning environment. The college and university learning environment is the perfect stage to facilitated multicultural exposure, diversity interaction and learning in a positive framework. Unfortunately, our society and the world has not evolved to the point where people are comfortable with exploring individual differences with purpose that is not restricted. Likewise, the learning institutions have not established an environment that eliminates the resistance to diverse interaction among students. While the major focus of learning institutions is traditional learning, even the most prestigious of learning institutions are deficient in teaching life learning and diversity learning. The fact that there is significant disassociation and dissonance between the dogma of America and the behavior of Americans is a problem. There is significant misalignment between the way America describes itself to be and the way Americans really are. The gap between America in theory and *American reality* has to close. Learning institutions can make a significant contribution to closing the gap. Individuals would probably they have more in common with diverse individuals than differences, if they ventured to find out.

An American Reality recounts an incident of racism in the UChicago environment, experienced by this author. This book gives insight into the psychology that motivates racial incidents. It explores how the environmental situation at the higher education level is microcosmic of the general society, and explores how the higher education environment feeds racist behavior. The author will also give rationale to why the learning environment allows racial behavior to manifest. More important, this book presents recommendations on effective solutions to address the dysfunctional behaviors that will complement those solutions already in place at UChicago and other learning institutions in America.

Qualitative methodology is used to collect Information for this study. Case study design will focus on one institution and the discrimination phenomenon that occurred at UChicago. Using descriptive techniques allows the author / researcher to describe the observed phenomena he experienced. Descriptions of Phenomena allows the author to describe the phenomena and lived experiences he encountered. The method and case study designs mentioned above integrates into this book as a non-fiction real life accounting of the irony in the "*Existence of racism in a perceived "non-racist*" environment. What history and current phenomena shows is that "*American Reality*", is accepting of White Racist. "*White people ... LOL.*" Verification that America is accepting of racism is the fact that racists are actively involved in the operational fabric of America culture. Racists, domestic terrorist and domestic terrorist sympathizers are in Education, American law enforcement, legislators in the halls of government, and even including racists and domestic terrorist sympathizers who have occupied the office of President of the United States of America.

The purpose of this Chapter I was to set the stage for the rest of the book. The intent of Chapter 1 is to give background and perspective for the reader to understand the manifestations of White cultural psychology, and the behavior resulting therefrom. The White cultural development process will also be explored further in the subsequent chapters.

The truth is not racist. The truth is merely the truth. The information in this Chapter 1 is foundation for the remainder of this book and reveals foundational truths about White culture and their racist cognitive and behavioral nature.

Notwithstanding the statement above, the fact remains, **not all White people are racist**. The majority of White people in America are decent law abiding citizens, assets to American society, who believe all people are created equal. Yet the fact still remains that America is infested with too many racist, at all levels of American society.

CHAPTER II
THE NATURE OF PREJUDICE

The landmark research of Gordon Allport propelled the phenomenon of ethnic stereotyping into the mainstream of behavioral science. He focuses his research on the process of cognitive functioning. How people think about phenomena they encounter determines how their mental functioning manifest in their behavior. The thinking of the mind manifest in human behavior. How people think is not evident until they express themselves in speech or behavior. However, behavior reveals the influence of an individual's cognitive functioning. Allport studied prejudice in terms of intergroup relations. He defined ethnic prejudice as ". . . *an antipathy based upon a faulty and inflexible generalization. It may be felt, or expressed. It may be directed toward a group, as a whole, or toward an individual because he is a member of that group.*" A significant aspect of his research was to bring the topic of ethnic stereotyping into the mainstream of behavioral science, focusing on prejudice as a manifestation of "ordinary cognitive functioning." [122] Another finding was there is a non-reversible quality of ethnic stereotypes, which gives a grim prognosis that prejudice will change. Racial stereotypes are ingrained into White America so deeply it is analogous with the psychology of White America. However, the conflicting norms in American society cause a dissonance that America is still struggling to resolve. The *American reality* of social stratification and racial inequality conflict with the America that theoretically perceives and defines itself as a "land of freedoms, equality, and equal opportunity. Reconciliation of the *American Reality* and the perception of America can be significant in the process of restructuring the psychological and cognitive thought process and behavior of White America, as well as improving the relationship between races.

Allport saw a link between prejudice and other negative social attitudes. Even though, racial prejudices are based on unfounded information and stereotype, research concludes that racial prejudices held firm even when contradictory information was evident. [123]

Learning Racism and Prejudice

Babies are born with a "pure soul," all babies. They are a blank canvas, primed for shaping their minds and behaviors in almost any form and shape their caretakers (parents) desire. It's a tragedy for a baby, a child, a miracle from God, to be influenced by parents or caretakers that condition their minds and behaviors to internalize racist, prejudice and a dysfunctional value system based on ignorance, bias against other human beings, only based on a different color, race, religion, or gender.

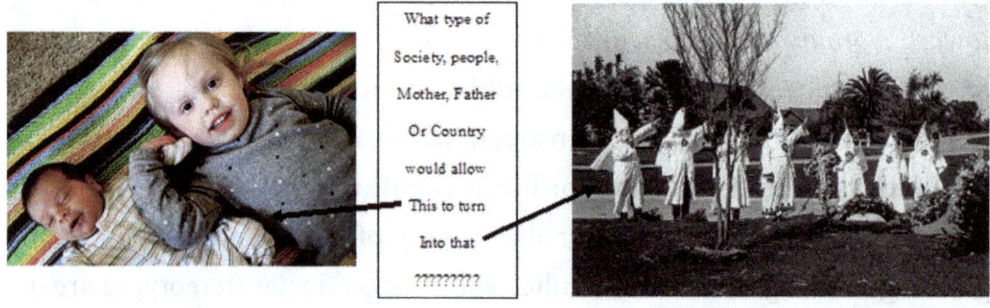

What type of
Society, people,
Mother, Father
Or Country
would allow
This to turn
Into that
?????????

Learning is a process that takes years to internalize and stabilize the mindset to motivate behavior. Experiences reinforce the fermentation process of cognition and behavior into human nature. Cognition that manifest in behavior, with consistent reinforcing stimulus / conditioning and aligned behavioral responses defines the individual. Sometimes people learn a behavior pattern then change because of exposure to other values, norms, experiences, and beliefs. Considerable challenge often accompanies mindset and behavior change. Individuals experience conflict, anxiety, and dissonance when new ways of thinking challenge prior ways of thinking. It is a normal and consistent foundation of White culture to encounter racist influence. Even good White people who do not embrace racist attitudes, beliefs or behavior encounter other White people who do. It is almost virtually impossible for White people to escape racists, prejudice and discriminating influence. White culture nurtures the depth and broad implantation of racism in White lived experiences. Attending all White schools, living in all White neighborhoods, encountering other White people who have racist and prejudicial beliefs, and worse of all racist reinforcement in the home, are all methods of conditioning White youth to adopt and internalize racist attitudes and behaviors. Often many of these encounters are subtle and unintended to cause a racist impact. However, without other influence that deals with diversity and the equality of all human beings, the subtle nature of racism and prejudice is, over time, implanted in the nature of White youth. White culture does not reinforce diversity. In many cases, Whites avoid introducing their kids to diverse experiences.[125] Research in social psychology, cognitive psychology, and anthropology indicates that learning occurs in environments that have established cultural and social norms and expectations and that these settings influence learning and facilitate the transfer of information in significant ways. This research is significant when applied to how people learn, internalize and manifest racism, prejudice and discriminating behaviors. [126] The formal and environmental learning process in White culture establishes racism as a norm. This conceptual realization alludes to racism as a significantly established, reinforced, supported and maintained value, integral to being White. While White culture is a racist oriented, however, individually, there are White people who avoid the negative racist entrapments of their culture. They are fortunate to escape any of the "*racist residue*" that is usually a byproduct of being White.

The Committee on Developments in the Science of Learning advances that learning is a multi-dimensional process that includes:

The brain (a person's cognitive ability and conditioning);

The Mind (the reasoning ability of the mind and how information is processed);

The life experiences (an individual encounters throughout their life and how these experiences are reinforced by subsequent experiences or how individuals encounter experiences that contest or conflict with other lived experiences), and

Schooling or education (influences an individual encounters that expose them to different concepts, data and information, as well as the individual differences in people). [127] The formal learning experience of youth is structured. In the White communities the structure rarely included issues and learning about diversity. Therefore, White kids understand diversity conditioning without structure or educational guidance. Their understanding of diversity is often a result of news media, peer group influence, or family influence, most of which often lacks direct substantial experience with other diverse individuals. In integrated learning environments, interaction with diverse individuals is a significant and fortunate learning experience that allows youth to experience diversity on a first-hand basis. Intergroup contact is a factor that eliminates prejudice.[128] One of the conclusions of the research by The Committee on Developments in the Science of Learning is that emphasis be placed on learning with understanding. The problem is that understanding in theory is different from understanding developed from experience. Students are often limited in their opportunities to understand diversity because of their lack of exposure to diverse environments and diverse ideology. Learning curricula that only emphasizes learning from textbooks or lecture is limiting the understanding of the concepts and truthful presentation of topics and issues introduced to the students.

At the least, most White youth are uninformed about diversity issues, and most are influenced by the attitudes and values of their parents, family, and peers. Some kids are fortunate to have parents that expose them to diversity influence in a positive manner. Many White families prefer to avoid issues on diversity altogether when interacting with their kids. Some parents and families are deplorable racist themselves and transfer that belief and behavior to their children. Without any type of diversity exposure during the life, learning process kids are highly likely to adopt the views of their racist parents. This logical presentation of the learning process does not ignore the fact that kids can have parents that socialize them with positive diversity values, yet they encounter life experiences that cause them to adopt racist and prejudicial behaviors. The point is that learned behaviors is a multi-dimensional process that depends on many factors. How these factors are presented, the environments in which they are presented, and the strength of their reinforcement are critical in the process of behavior manifestation and how an innocent baby develops into a decent human being or a deplorable racist. The White kids who are exposed to diversity in schools, in their neighborhoods, and whose parents socialize their kids to understand the value of appreciating diversity among individuals are fortunate. Kids who live in primarily segregated environments are exposed to diverse individuals because they are drawn the diverse music. They watch TV and see people who are different or inadvertently notice diverse individuals when they are out in public. In any event, without personal contact and meaningful significant experiences with diverse individuals, people (both Black and White) develop distorted views of different cultures.

The Committee on Developments in the Science of Learning presented the following basic concepts as necessary to the learning, internalization, and behavioral process. [129]

1. Students come to the classroom with preconceptions about how the world works. If their initial understandings are not engaged, they may fail to grasp the new concepts and information that are taught, or they may learn them for purposes of a test but revert to their preconceptions outside the classroom.

1. To develop competence in an area of inquiry, students must: (a) have a deep foundation of factual knowledge, (b) understand facts and ideas in the context of a conceptual framework, and (c) organize knowledge in ways that facilitate retrieval and application.

1. A "metacognitive" (**awareness or analysis of one's own learning or thinking processes**) approach to instruction can help students learn to take control of their own learning by defining learning goals and monitoring their progress in achieving them.

These findings and concepts make it important to teach and expose kids to the fact they live in a diverse world. If White youth do not learn this, then they will lack the skillset to live in the real world. Learning institutions need to sort out their education priorities. What values should schools teach? Should schools teach kids to get along with others in the world, along with reading, writing, and arithmetic? This author suggest that learning should be inclusive of teaching kids how to interact with others who have a different color, race, religion, education, gender, and background than themselves. This applies to all kids. Otherwise, our education system is insufficient in preparing kids for their future. The state of our modern contemporary society gives more sufficient evidence that human beings have serious problems with individual differences. If the cycle of dysfunction is not broken, then the future looks bleak. Obviously, society cannot completely depend on family values to address the range of diversity issues. The issue of racism, prejudice and discrimination is a White cultural created problem that minorities are impact by and suffer from. That is a historical fact. The learning process is not as effective for White kids who are taught racist concepts in the home then encounter minorities who are smarter, stronger, more athletic, and financially better off. The point is that when kids are taught prejudice then encounter conflicting experiences, dissonance is created that diminishes their ability to process information. Their intellectual process becomes retarded. Dissonance is expressed in a variety of ways from insecurity to confusion to anger, resulting in violence.

Reskin (2005) researched the processes that link the ascribed characteristics of groups and how ascribed characteristics contribute to racism and prejudice. Some ascriptive characteristics are primarily hereditary, such as Race, sex, age, class at birth, religion, ethnicity, species, and residence. Ascription is determined by **"social class or stratum placement and is primarily hereditary."** Society stratifies people by methods often beyond the individual's control. [130] Mechanisms that support ascription and contribute to inequality, racism and prejudice are as follows: [131]

Intrapsychic Ideas, conflicts, pertaining to impulses or other phenomena that is psychological and arises or occurs within the mind or psyche.

Interpersonal relates to relationships or communication between people. Interpersonal skills include the following: **Active listening. Collaboration. Problem-solving. Conflict resolution. Empathy. Diplomacy. Adaptability**

Societal Relates to society or social relationships.

Organizational Relates to an organization or the way it is set up or relating to the action of organizing something or relates to the structure of an organization or entity.

Alternatively, these mechanisms can support ascriptions that contribute to equality and the development of positive social interaction.

These mechanisms when used to support racism, prejudice and discrimination are personal and institutional. The point is that the mechanisms of racism are ingrained in society to the extent that reinforces White racist behavior. The White cultural developmental process shaping the intrapsychic and interpersonal and their White oriented lived experiences reinforces their racism, discrimination, and prejudice. Institutions, including the workplace, schools, law enforcement, courts, and work environment all support the personal mindset of White culture, thereby further reinforcing the personal, systematic, and institutional function of racism, discrimination, and prejudice. Because minorities have no or very limited voice or little influence in the construction of the American institutional and societal constructs, their interest are ignored, and their welfare is not adequately addressed. If the needs of all people in a society are not addressed, whether it be consciously, subconsciously, covertly, overtly, subtly or by oversight, conflict and discord is the natural result. The result is that people suffer. The group that constructs the mindset of kids, the group that establishes the policies of institutions and the group that is predominant in society, establishes rules and policies in their own interest. In the case of *American reality*, society, government, economic and social constructs are determined with priority White interest, and minimal regard to non-White people. Minorities construct the mindset of their kids to deal with the adversities and challenges in society. White culture constructs the mindset of their kids to embrace White privilege. As a result, Americans: White, Black, Hispanic, Asian, Jewish, Muslim are all socialized with different perspectives of *American Reality*. To understand the result of the various human differences and the juxtaposition in the socialization of White and minorities we can look to the mindset of Muhammed Ali. His position and response when being drafted and refusing to go into the Army and fight for the United States of America (stating, "Viet Cong never called me "Nigger"). Why should minorities support a society that discriminates against them? This is not a question of policy, responsibility, duty or feeling. It is a simple psychological viewpoint and conditioning, a practical and a normal result of living in a society that has no responsibility to minorities. This causes minorities to have the same reflective responsibility to America, as they perceive America has toward them. Another truth is that the construct of American society does not even nurture responsibility to the country on the part of White or minority people. Although people will chant; "God Bless America" or "We love America," that even is a misconception because the America that people live in is an American of dysfunction, greed, racism, hatred, and discrimination. Contemporary America is not an environment constructed by people who have high regard for their country. It is an environment maintained on principles of hatred, selfishness, greed, racism, discrimination, and prejudice. These are not foundational values of God, the Constitution, or any type of positive construct. Perceptions of America are based on positive values as expressed in the Constitution of the United States, The Bible, the Bill of Rights, and principles set forth by the founding fathers and religious doctrine. The *American Reality* is that it operates on values of racism, prejudice, discrimination, greed, that reflect and reinforce basic core values and norms of White culture. White norms and values that dominates American society naturally and innately causes conflict.

Now, let us take a straightforward look at the problem and nature of prejudice, and how it is socialized into American culture, how and why is it sustained in American culture, and why it is allowed to exist in American society.

Scholars, psychologist, anthropologist, historians, and politicians all theorize about racism, discrimination, and prejudice in American society. The problem is that their research, opinions, findings, and conclusions have been important, but practically impotent. While they are theorizing, many other people are suffering. How long did the colonist "theorize" before they acted in the Revolutionary war? I am not advocating any form of revolution; I am merely saying that White culture embraces their racist, discriminating, and prejudicial value system and cultural norms, without sincere intention to change. Those who investigate the problem identify and state the problem, but do nothing to solve the problem. The question to ask is are these ways of decent people or a decent culture. The colonist went to war over "taxation without representation." Not only do minorities suffer "taxation without representation" they are jailed; murdered, and discriminated against for having different skin colors, a different ethnic heritage, different religions, or a different creed. What is the worth of people who discriminate against "others" when those "others" have differences, but have commendable character qualities? Think Nazis. Think Ku Klux Klan. Think terrorist, ISIS, Al Qaeda. Racist fit into the same category as these deplorable groups. So why does America continue to support inequality, racism, discrimination, and prejudice? That is the question to ask and the issue to expose. America supports it because …? America allows the problem to exist. It is "*An American Reality*". Scholars raise the issues because they exist. The reasons racism exist is just as ignorant and deplorable as the fact that it exist. Racism, discrimination, prejudice, and people who harbor such characteristics, are deplorable and detrimental to America, detrimental to White Americans, minority Americans, detrimental to democracy and to the world

Why Do People Hate

Arguably, racism, prejudice, and discrimination are manifestations of hatred. Hate is a destructive and self-destructive emotion. A person who experiences emotions and feelings of hate may have emotional challenges and problems with their own self-esteem and self-worth. Hate is an extreme emotion. The Oxford dictionary and the Merriam Webster Dictionary respectively define hate as "to feel strong aversion or intense dislike for," hate implies an emotional aversion often coupled with enmity or malice. Hate is to turn dislike into an active desire to hurt someone else — and not necessarily physically. To truly hate, you must reach that dark place inside yourself that you do not want to admit exists. An individual admits they have it in them to hate, to think vile thoughts, to fantasize about hurting someone. Hate can be a motivation causing people to commit crimes against others. Hatred is a feeling of hostility directed toward another person or group. Hate crimes were limited to crimes in which the perpetrators acted based on a bias against the victim's race, color, religion, or national origin. [132] Arguably, hate is "one of the most destructive affective phenomenon in the history of the human nature. [133] Hate develops as the hater internalizes an ongoing negative perception of a target group. Hate intensifies with reinforcement of that negative perception. Hate is associated with the emotional state of an individual. The hater often has intentions coupled with maliciousness, repugnance, and willingness to harm and even annihilate the object of his hatred. Hatred also motivates individuals to exclude others from their social environment. *"Hate is based on perceptions of a stable, negative disposition of persons or groups. Racial hate for persons and groups is more because of who they are, than because of what they do. Hate has the goal to eliminate its target ..."* Hate can be reassuring and self-protective, because its message is simple and framed to sustain the cultural worldview of the hater. [134] Often White people hate Black people without ever having contact or knowing a Black person. This mentality is destructive to America, Black Americans, All Americans and more so, decent White Americans. It is also stupid, ignorant and, without cause, a mental condition that needs intervention.

Hate is a complex phenomenon. It has varying levels of degrees that determine how a person responds to their feelings of hatred. Intrinsic bias is a lesser form of hatred that normally does not result in violence but does manifest in subtle acts of discrimination. Hate manifest when individuals mistreat or humiliate someone, or when an individual's deliberate and purposeful actions are intended to obstruct the goals of the target individual. Other negative emotions accompany hate, such as, anger, contempt, or moral disgust. "*When individuals experience hate, they typically perceive their hate target as having malicious intentions and being immoral, which is accompanied by feelings of lack of control or powerlessness.*" [135]

Research suggests there are three ways that hatred spreads and perpetuates.

(1) First, hate seems to develop and perpetuate among in-group members who have shared values that are reinforced within the members of the group and among peers.

(2) Another way hate is developed and perpetuated is based on generalization socialization. The accumulated manifestation of immoral and violent behavior of a "hater" affects the future of the group in terms of maintaining their homogenous malicious perceptions of target groups or individuals. Even though the "hater" group did not suffer from the target of their hatred, they still internalize emotions of hatred because it is socialized into their nature.

(3) The third way hatred is manifested, and spreads is because of the absence of any personal interaction or contact between the hater and the target individual or group. Lack of knowledge and ignorance are predominant characteristics of racist

In this 21st century, why is there still so much hatred in American and in the world? One would think that based on the history of widespread conflicts and violence; humans would have figured out how to get along by now. After all, they did figure out how to get off the horse and get in the automobile. They figured out how to go from firewood light and heat to electricity. They figured out how to air travel around the world. They figured out how to cure a number of diseases. So why cannot humans figure out how to get along with each other and "stop the hate?" Why is something seemingly so simple, compared to other human accomplishments, practically, so hard to accomplish?

Laws, policies and legislation addresses discriminatory, prejudicial behavior and violence-based hate crimes (the Emancipation Proclamation, The Civil Rights Laws, Equal rights voting laws) but there is still hatred that dilutes the impact of these laws. Why? Unfortunately, laws cannot dictate the human psyche or human behavior. Even-though these the laws are on the books, people still hate. According to Andrea Mathews, LPN, NCC, hate of a whole race of people (Blacks, Hispanics, Asians) or an entire set of people (LGBHT, Jews, Muslims) indicates a psychological concept called "projection. In other words, a person hates groups of people without just cause because they are insecure in themselves. They are insecure in their own cultural identification or insecure in their own sexual orientation. They project hate onto others to keep from hating themselves. When people hate people because they are different, it gives insight into the "hater" and says nothing about the hated. [136] These type haters are completely irrational and self-consciously insecure.

"Hate is a feeling of intense hostility and aversion usually deriving from fear, anger, or a sense of injury. It is extreme dislike or disgust. Hatred is an emotion. Extreme hatred can inspire violence." [137] Doctors Rohini Radhakrishnan and Shaziya Allarakha state that hate breeds negative emotions that effect personal and professional relationships. Emotions of hatred alters the chemistry in the brain, stimulating the part of the brain that dictates planning and execution of motion, triggering aggression. This causes the individual hater to defend or attack or ignites a "fight or flight" response. Medically and physiologically, hormone levels of cortisol and adrenaline increase, potentially causing weight gain insomnia, anxiety, depression or chronic illness. Hatred also stimulates the mind to perform delusional possibility thinking, causing the hater delusional predictions of how the hated person might respond to being hated. This triggers additional feelings of anxiety, restlessness, obsessive thinking and paranoia in the hater. Obsessive hate is a mental disorder that can lead to health problems. [138] Some people hate because they are mentally or physically ill. Their state of mind and being lacks the health to experience normal balance.

People hate because they are scared, they fear those who are different from themselves. This type of hatred is ignorance and indicates a lack of interaction or negative interactions with people who are different. According to Allison Abrams, LCSW-R, "Hatred is driven by two key emotions: love and aggression: One's love for the in-group—the group that is favored; and one's aggression for the out-group—the group that has been deemed as being different, dangerous, and a threat to the in-group." [139] Ms. Abrams references Dr. Dana Harrow and further reintegrates the projection theory, "the things people hate about others are the things that they fear within themselves" [140] or the things they hate in themselves. Sigmund Freud first introduced the concept of projection. While analyzing people, Freud discovered that patients expressed resentment of behaviors in others, they themselves demonstrated. Other theories on hate are: [141]

> "When hate involves participation in a group, it may help foster a sense of connection and camaraderie that fills a void in one's identity. He describes hatred of individuals or groups as a way of distracting oneself from the more challenging and anxiety-provoking task of creating one's own identity"

> "Acts of hate are attempts to distract oneself from feelings such as helplessness, powerlessness, injustice, inadequacy and shame. Hate is grounded in

some sense of perceived threat. It is an attitude that can give rise to hostility and aggression toward individuals or groups."

Why people hate is conceptually and theoretically variable. The complexity of hatred that leads to racism, prejudice and discrimination is rooted in many factors and sources. The psychology makeup of a person, their family history, their cultural history, their political history, and the lived experiences they encounter, all contribute to an individual's hate quotient and their capacity for racism. The one that is common about hate that leads to chronic and obsessive racism is that it is a negative emotion. It has destructive tendency for both the hater and the hated. Racism based in hate, causes the hater to behave aggressively toward the hated. The dilemma is that racist often have no substantial basis for hate other than ignorance.

There are behaviors that have symptoms of discrimination and prejudice, that may appear racist but, do not have a direct foundation in racism. The American capitalist system fundamentally promotes concepts of individualism and greed. Individual and greed are catalyst that can give the impression of racist behavior. These characteristics harbor discriminating and individualistic behaviors that give the presence of inherent racist because they are characterize by behaviors that emulate prejudice and discriminating behaviors. Whites predominantly control the American economic and political systems. Minorities, for the most part, are excluded from the mainstream of American economics, politics, and Wall Street, International trade, business financing and venture capital, and business deals that require collaboration. The elimination of minorities from these venues are not just based on racism, even though for the most part they are race based. White people, in practicing their greed and reinforcing their individualistic behaviors, inscribed as integral to the capitalistic system, interact predominantly with other Whites when transacting business. Familiarity breeds security. The Lack of interaction and an "open door" between races in financial transactions breeds an insecurity, common to unfamiliarity. While the economic environment in America is not necessarily "hate" based, it is discriminatory because minorities are essentially "left out" and, for the most part, "Kept out." American segregation in housing, education, and economics restricts the familiarity that opens doors to opportunity. American individualism and greed keep the doors closed that promote familiarity and trust. It is racist behavior that keeps the doors closed and that restricts opportunity for minorities. It is racist not to allow minorities participation in the American systems with national, international, and widespread impact. The driving discriminating factors in economics, business, and finance is not only racism. It is also individualism, greed and green (money). The racism is relevant to the exclusion of Black and Brown minorities, but greed is also a significant factor.

Rohini Radhakrishnan and Shaziya Allarakha, MD offer insight on how to get rid of hatred, indicating that people often repress their emotion of hate and blame others for their shortcomings. When emotions accumulate, and are not mitigated, they intensify. The mind, the body, and behavior can be affected by allowing feelings of hatred to manifest. Rohini Radhakrishnan and Shaziya Allarakha, MD suggest the following "hate remedies." [142]

- Acknowledge that you feel hateful. Acknowledging this can begin to deal with this emotion and find a solution to the problem.
- Understand the root cause of hate. Hate usually stems from fear, insecurity, or mistrust.
- Do not compare yourself with others. Strive to be the best version of yourself instead.
- When you feel hate or anger, it is best to take a step back and avoid reacting in heat of the moment. It is difficult to make the right decisions when you are feeling hateful and angry.

- While feeling hate or anger, you may consider taking a break from the situation, going for a walk, mediation, playing with pets, or doing an activity you find enjoyable.
- Face the problem instead of ignoring the issue. Try to find a solution to the problem. You may consider talking to someone, you trust, such as a close friend, family, or partner. You can also consider seeking the help of a therapist or counselor. They can assess you to understand your emotions and the origin of hate. Treatment generally involves counseling to help manage negative emotions and develop coping mechanisms. Medication may be prescribed if needed.

The problem with these "hate remedy" recommendations is that they are considerations for people with a higher cognitive ability. Many or most racist are of low cognitive mentality. Often they are so fermented in their racism; intelligent resolutions are not an option. In addition, these remedies are for individuals who want to mitigate their racist thinking, feelings and behavior. Most racists do not want to change. Racism is a deep-seated emotion that often develops in the socialization process of White individuals. Their environment and associations constantly reinforce white racist. Racism remedies are more comparable to exorcism than intelligent solutions. However, no amount of White hate for non-White individuals will work unless White culture ostracizes the negative elements in their culture and address this White problem. Decent White people need to stigmatize racist psychology, mentality, behavior and the individuals, themselves.

The Psychology of Racial Hate between Individuals and Groups (Appendix 4 – Hate Groups)

People do not hate. Hate is not a naturally ingrained instinct. Hate is socialized, learned, and reinforced. Hateful intergroup conflict may be motivated by the following: "in-group love,» a desire to positively contribute to the group to which one belongs, or «out-group hate,» a desire to injure a foreign group.[143] For the most part, "in-group love is a stronger influence on negative feelings, hate and violent acts against minorities than "out-group hate". However, both motivations can be significant factors in causing dysfunction toward others. There is potential for intergroup conflict to diminish if group members devoted more energy to positive in-group improvements than to out-group competition. [144] When groups or individuals do not establish themselves in competition or as adversaries, their relationship becomes salient and has opportunity to establish without negative overtures. Collaborative interaction indicates that groups formed around a set of moral codes are more likely than non-morality-based groups to exhibit "out-group hate" as a response to their especially strong sense of "in-group love." [145] Intergroup and interpersonal conflict can be caused when one group's interest threatens another group's interest, goals or well-being.[146] The reason one can consider the hypothesis that White culture has a viral sickness, an intergroup psychosis is because many of the attacks and conflicts initiated by Whites are unprovoked, baseless and without rational reason. Individual and Intergroup "*threat theories*" provide a framework for intergroup biases and aggression.[147]

> "***Realistic Group Conflict Theory***", *addresses competition between groups by positing that when two groups are competing for limited resources, one group's potential success conflicts with the other's interests, which leads to negative out-group attitudes.* [148]

When groups have common goals, their interactions are more likely to be positive. Opposing goals will cause intergroup conflict. Intergroup conflict may increase in-group unity, leading to a larger disparity and more conflict between groups.

> "***Symbolic Threat*** *Theory" advances that intergroup bias and conflict result from conflicting ideologies, not from perceived competition or oppos-*

ing goals.[149] *Symbolic threat bias tend to be stronger predictors of practical behavior towards out-groups than biases based on realistic threat.*[150]

The phrase, "agree to disagree" is characteristic of "Symbolic threat Theory." Another example of Symbolic Threat Theory is the relationship between Democrats and Republicans. The contemporary political environment of no-compromise, no-collaboration, partisan politics characterize American politics. Realistic group conflict theory and symbolic threat theory are, in some cases, compatible.

"***Integrated-Threat Theory***" *recognizes that conflict can arise from a combination of intergroup dynamics and classifies threats into four types: realistic threat, symbolic threat, intergroup anxiety, and negative stereotypes.*[151] *Intergroup threat theories provide a framework for intergroup biases and aggression.*[152] *Intergroup anxiety refers to a felt uneasiness around members of other groups, which is predictive of biased attitudes and behaviors.* [153]

Negative stereotypes correlate with these behaviors, causing threat potential based on negative expectations about an out-group. [154]

According to the 7-stage hate model, a hate group, if uninterrupted, experiences seven stages.[155] In the first four stages of the hate model, hate groups vocalize their beliefs (1) the Haters Gather; (2) the Hate Group defines itself; (3) the Hate Group Disparages the Target; (4) the Hate Group Taunts the Target). In the last three stages, they act on their beliefs; (5) the Hate Group attacks the target without weapons; (6) the Hate Group Attacks the target with weapons; and (7) the Hate Group Destroys the Target. Factors that contribute to a group's likelihood to act include the vulnerability of its members and the group's reliance on symbols and mythologies. There is a transition period, according to the hate model, that exist between verbal hate speech advocating violence and violent action. What happens indicates which haters are hardcore, and which haters are rhetorical. Hate speech is considered a prerequisite to hate crimes, and indicates a potential of hate crime occurrence. Historically, one can refer to the rise of Hitler and the Third Reich to understand the development and consequences of hate. Hate group intervention to mitigate any violence is possible if a group has not yet gone from the speech phase to the action phase. Mitigation interventions on immature hate groups are more effective than interventions on groups that are firmly established. [156] Intervention and rehabilitation is most effective when an individual or individuals who can identify with the hater individuals, or the hate group, lead the process. Deconstructing personal insecurities of group members, contributes to weaken the intensity of hate in the group. One of the most critical strategies to rehabilitating the hate-centered motives in a hate group is to prevent the recruitment of new members. Supporting those who are most susceptible, especially children and youth, in developing a positive self-esteem and a humanized understanding of out-groups is important to constructing cultural worldviews based on positive life experiences.[157] Giving more attention to addressing the lacking security needs, the insecurities and self-esteem issues of young people can be mitigating factors in eliminating hate and aggression in young people. This is one reason, the learning institutions are better forums for addressing these issues than leaving it up to the internet or social media, which is a catalyst of dysfunction in children when kids are longing for attention or become involved with the wrong influences.

The Psychology of American Racism

Steven O. Roberts is an assistant professor in the psychology department at Stanford University.

Michael T. Rizzo is a postdoctoral research fellow in the psychology department at New York University and with the Beyond Conflict Innovation Lab. These professionals studied and researched racism. The interesting and empirical content of these researchers and the research of the majority of references in this book is that the researchers are White individuals. Not only do the research studies support their claims and conclusions, but also the researchers are White and have firsthand knowledge based on lived experiences into White culture and the White lived experience and psychology. Almost every White person in America has had contact with racism, either directly or indirectly. They have experienced the nature of racist psychology. Their social location as White individuals highly increases the odds they have encountered racist phenomena. How White people who encounter racism handle it becomes a matter of other lived experiences and the influence or multiple life experiences they encounter, that either reinforces racism or counters racist influences. That White researchers and psychologist present data and insight into the nature and psychology of White racism has significant meaning.

Contemporary Americans have inherited a racist system and as a result, to maintain the system of racism White Americans are socialized with a value system that supports and sustains American racism. Roberts and Rizzo argue that racism is as American as apple pie. Psychologist Steven O. Roberts and Michael T. Rizzo advance seven factors they indicate as contributing to and maintaining racism. [158] [159]

Categories. "People see races, not individuals. Early on, children start categorizing according to race; racial biases emerge in children as young as 3 years old."

Factions. "People treat their own race like a team. Children feel that their own group requires their loyalty, trust, and cooperation."

Segregation. "People separate themselves on the basis of race. Most Americans have more contact with White people than with people of color, which contributes to people often seeing persons of color as homogenous stereotypes."

Hierarchy. "White Americans are granted a status above all others. As one example, even God is often portrayed as White, which leads people to perceive White people as God-like."

Power. "White Americans have the power to set norms and structure society. This extends to politicians, educators, and even parents. White parents rarely talk with their children about race and racism, which gives White children the illusion of post-racialism."

"Post-racialism means society has reached a stage or time at which racial prejudice no longer exists or is no longer a major social problem." However, realistically this is a fantasy White parents want their children to believe. This psychology also feeds the objection White parents have to teaching Critical Race Theory in elementary schools. The problem is that a significant case of dissonance is caused when White children are confronted with the truth. White kids develop a confused psychology about how to relate to Black people in relationship to their White value system. Then things become more confusing when White kids discover they were lied to.

Media. "White Americans are portrayed as superior to Americans of color. Over the past 20 years, the proportion of low-status Black TV characters has tripled."

Passivism. "People ignore and deny that they do any of this, thus allowing the system to persist."

Anti-Racism has two modes: Proactive Anti-Racism and Reactive Anti-Racism. ***Proactive antiracism*** addresses and attacks racism with the knowledge it exist and to challenge its existence when it appears or in anticipation of its appearance. Examples of Proactive antiracism include establishing and maintaining environments that prevent individuals from acting in racist ways; such as having an understood policy in the workplace that racist behavior is cause for dismissal. Another example is passing legislation that deters racist policies. The Federal Government department that prosecutes hate crimes is established as a Proactive antiracist measure. Proactive antiracism is future-oriented and a preventative measure. [160]

Reactive antiracism attacks and challenges racism whenever it appears. Examples include protesting police brutality, calling out existing racist systems and beliefs, by voting to remove racist policies and policymakers, and enacting legislation that corrects systemic inequalities and injustice. All of these actions occur after the fact. Protesting the murder of George Floyd, an unarmed Black man killed by White Minnesota police officer, Derek Chauvin. This incident prompted national antiracist demonstrations. Demonstrations and protest against the changes in voting laws by various states that are seen as limiting the voting rights of minorities are an another example of reactive antiracism.[161] That the voting laws were legislated to be more restrictive against minority voters, based on a lie, spawned by Donald Trump and supported by the majority of the Republican Party, that the 2020 election was stolen, indicates the rampant and widespread existence of racism in the American government among American leglislators.

New York Post editorial board throws commented on the 2024 Trump campaign, calling him 'unworthy' to serve in the White House for another term. The New York Post endorsed Donald Trump the Democratic presidential nominee, Joe Biden in the 2020 presidential election. (In 2016, the paper withheld a general election endorsement, but backed Trump in the New York GOP presidential primary that year.). [162] Americans have had a front row seat to witness the character of Donald Trump. He is an alleged racist, an alleged rapist, a misogynist, a serial cheater, and considered an incompetent unfit leader whose purpose is to grift from the American people. Therefore, why would anyone vote for this person to be president of the United States of America, considering his character? The only logical reason Trump will garner supporters is because he is a racist and a considerable faction of Americans are more racists than they are American. The Trump saga of American history is reminiscent of the rise of Adolph Hitler.

Roberts and Rizzo cite an interesting analogy by child psychologist Beverly Tatum. Ms. Tatum addressing racism using the following analogy. She compares "racism to a moving walkway in an airport. To be actively racist is to know where the walkway is headed, and to choose to move along with it. To be passively racist is to stand idly by as the walkway moves in the same direction as those who are actively racist. An inaction that maintains and reinforces racial hierarchy. To be antiracist, she argued, is to turn around and to actively move in the opposite direction." [163]

Understanding the psychology of Racism and gaining an insight into the White racist and how their discriminating and prejudicial behavior is formed and perpetuated is valid and credible insight when it comes from the lived experiences of White people themselves. White people who understand the destructive and deplorable system of racism and who have intention to rid our United States of America from this virus disease are better positioned to do so. Up to this present day, the disease of racism and racism virus is still a pandemic. America is a sick country to allow the disease to manifest in the country. Eliminating racist and racism will cure America. America is a hypocrite to criticize other countries for acting in the same manner as America. The question one has to ask is; what kind of human being are you? What kind of human being do you want to be?

Chapter III
The Purpose of "An American Reality"

Why is a book like *American Reality* even necessary? The Answer is simple. 1) Because racism is rampant in America and permeated into the fabric of American society; including America's legal system (law enforcement, legal, judicial and penal), social system, economic system, health system, education system and the interpersonal relationships between White people and minorities. As long as racism exists in America, books like *An American Reality* will continue and be necessary to write. It would be much better to write about the greatness of America instead of the shortcomings of America. However, America's shortcomings exceed America's greatness, unfortunately at least in terms of the experience of Black Americans, minorities, Jewish Americans, Muslim Americans, LGBT Americans and Americans who are non-white.

The reason the author wrote *An American Reality* is personal and educational. It is personal because the case study (Chapters IV thru Chapter VII) describes an incident of overt discrimination experienced by this author because of his color. The author of this book directly encountered an overt racist incident at the University of Chicago. The reason the incident is racist is because ***if Dr. Barnes, the author, were a White person, this incident of discrimination never would have occurred***, or the misunderstanding would have been handled in a different more cordial manner, or the motivation for the act of discrimination would not exist. The racist incident that Dr. Barnes experienced does not even come close to the violent and abusive acts of racism that occur daily between White and Black people. The racist incident experienced by Dr. Barnes is the backdrop that caused Dr. Barnes to further explore and evaluate the historical and contemporary racial climate in America. *American Reality* is a psychological and sociological hermeneutical approach that describes the case study incident. The hermeneutic approach advances that the most basic fact of social life is in the meaning, manifested in the accurate description of actions. Social life is constituted by social actions, and actions are meaningful to the actors and to the other social participants. Actions are an indication of thinking. The incident Dr. Barnes experienced, while relatively insignificant, to be honest, is significant in the fact that the racial climate in America is a catalyst that allows all racist incidents to occur. White people act with a sense of privilege based on lies, such as, "Donald Trump won the 2020 election" mentality or that White people have a right to privilege. Astonishingly, a White woman was stopped for a traffic violation in Anchorage Alaska on her way to a rally featuring former President Donald Trump. She showed the police a "white privilege card" instead of her driver's license and was not ticketed. [164]

Misperceptions often begin with the belief and internalization of false information and lies.

Dr. Barnes has been in integrated environments since High School. He attended the University of Chicago Laboratory High School, and Coe College in the republican state of Iowa. Throughout his post-graduate education, Dr. Barnes attended McCormick Theological Seminary and graduated from The University of Chicago Divinity School with a Master degree in Religious Studies. During his working career Dr. Barnes served the First Presbyterian Church in Cedar Rapids, Iowa; the Chicago Board of Education; the Illinois Bell Telephone Company; Western Electric; AT&T Bell Laboratories; Motorola Corporation and IBM. In all environments, his interactions and relationships with White people have been very good and cordial. Some of his best friends are White, to state a cliché often used by Whites ('some of my best friends are Black'). He was an athlete, inducted into his Coe College athletic hall of fame. He is an inducted member of Psi Chi, the International Honor Society for Psychology. He is not, at all, naïve to the racism, discrimination and prejudice that exist in America, nor protocols of disrespectful and respectful interpersonal interaction. Incidents of racism or discrimination just did not come directly or blatantly into his sphere until the incident that occurred in 2019 at the University of Chicago Alumni building. Having encountered an incident of discrimination at this point in his life was a startling experience for Dr. Barnes. After completing his master's degree in religious studies from the University of Chicago and finishing his PhD in psychology, it was a startling revelation for Dr. Barnes, that not even an accomplished, law-abiding Black man, who is an American citizen, is immune to racism and discrimination by White people in America. The irony is that usually racists are usually less accomplished and less intellignet White people. The humorous irony of racism is that racists are referred to as the *"Less Entities"*; less qualified, less intelligent, less educated, less law-abiding, less successful, less secure, and less attractive White people are those who usually act out racially towards African Americans and others who are non-White. This incident caused Dr. Barnes to revisit White mentality, sociology, and psychology. Being honest, one should feel sorry for White people who harbor discriminating sentiments. One can argue that in many cases, it is an indicator of an unhappy insecure aspect of White culture, an indicator that White people need help and education to change the negative heritage of their culture and character, a sign of suppressed inferiority. They are unable to escape their defiled past. Again, **I want to reiterate this does not apply to all White people. Some white people are not racists** but too many are racists. Some White people have escaped the "*matrix*" of racism. These individuals understand the nature of innate and emotional intelligence to judge people by the content of their character, and not by the color of their skin. **The majority of White people are decent human beings** but it is the deplorable, too many, White racist that stain White culture and the White race. Many decent White people have "*racist residue*." White people, caught in the "*matrix*" of racism, are detrimental and destructive to American society, to other White people, to the White culture, to themselves and especially to minorities. A problem for many White people is that they exist in a racist environment, surrounded by racist people expounding and reinforcing racist ideologies. Instinctively, however, many know and feel discomfort and have cognitive dissonance with the truth, which is contrary to racist ideologies that influence racist thinking and racist behavior.

Which brings us to the next reasons Dr. Barnes is writing *An American Reality*, which are:

1. To educate American society and White people on the underlying deplorable realities of their culture with intention to help them become better human beings.
2. To give White people an insight into their psychology, and how their psychology is manifested in their behavior, with intent to motivate them to change their thinking and behavior.
3. To give White people insight into their negative dysfunctional socialization and developmental process and how it does not prepare them for functional behavior in the diverse world, with intention to motivate them to change for their own benefit.
4. To resonate with decent White people to inform them of the subtleties of racism and aspects of racism hidden to their awareness and to resonate awareness of the danger to America that *racist residue* permeates

in their culture, historically and contemporarily, with intention to motivate them to influence others in their culture to change.

5. To sincerely message the authors belief and intent that not all White people are racist and that many White people are decent human beings and to let them know they are valued human beings in American society.

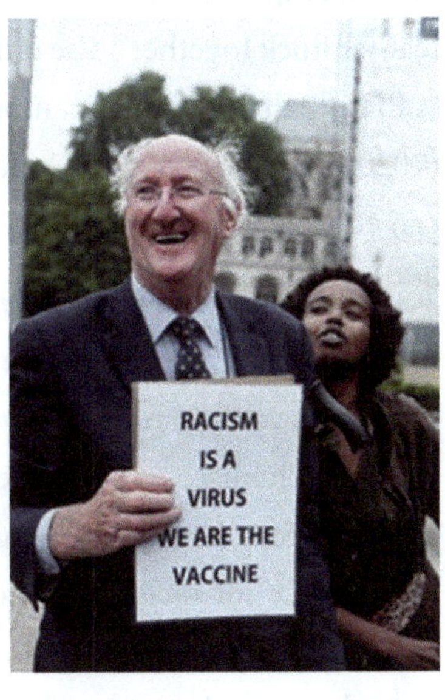

White racist, White people and the White culture need to take their blinders off and see themselves for whom they really are. Ironically, some White people are so ignorant; they are unaware of the deplorable nature of their behavior. They believe it is normal behavior to act racist. This book is an effort to help White people be better human beings, and as a motivator for White people to educate themselves and change their cultural heritage from one of racism, discrimination, and prejudice against non-White people to one of good decent human beings who are assets to the world instead of liabilities. Racism is a virus infecting White culture, a sickness, a sick virus that only they, themselves, can cure. **Again, it is also important to note that not all White people are racists.** There are many good White people at least the 85,000,000 who voted for Joe Biden. That is in perspective with the 75,000,000 White people who voted for Donald Trump. Hypothetically and figuratively, alluding to Biden voters labeled as non-racist and Donald Trump voters labeled as racist. Realistically, some Biden supporters could be racists and some Trump voters could be good people. The point is that there are significant numbers of racist in America. The residue of America's racists' history permeates itself and is abundant in American society to this day. There is significant evidence and widespread opinion, among Black and White people, that Trump is a racist. "Birds of a feather flock together". Racism, discrimination, and prejudice is a virus in White culture that infects a significant number of America's White population. One has to explore the reasons our American culture would elect a liar, a cheater, a misogynist, an accused rapist and an alleged racist like Donald Trump as the 45th president of the United States (2016-2020). That Trump resonated with so many Americans is a tragic foretelling. "Birds of a feather flock together". The only redeeming quality of the Trump administration is that finally the American people came to their senses and elected Joe Biden (2020) after one term of Donald Trump. Only other enlightened White people can educate and improve the lot of their cultural counterparts.

As obvious as the "*racist residue*" in White people may be to black people, ironically, many White people are ignorant to their racist behaviors. I hope that awareness of their *racist residue* will enable White people to work on eliminating it, in themselves and others of their kind. This author recognizes that his objective may be mute among many Whites. Those who are hopelessly lost to the "*matrix*" of racism threaten American democracy and American citizens, all American citizens, including White Americans. Some Whites are a hopeless cause because they accept and internalize racist ideology without desire to be otherwise. Most White people know their culture is infected with deplorable racist, yet they allow them to exist and have significant voice in American Society. Society must confront the reality that White people who know and accept they are racist, are a potential threat to our democracy and to American society in general. Some are so stupid they believe the lie that, "*they are better than other people*" because they are White. Some White people infected with racism are plain deplorable human beings and contrary to their belief, they are the worst of the lot America has to offer. Again, **I want to reiterate, not all White people are a negative influence on our society. Many are fine people. It is just that too many are deplorable racist.**

CHAPTER IV
BACKGROUND OF THE UNIVERSITY OF CHICAGO ALUMNI PROBLEM
CASE STUDY: PART 1

The listing and description below is of the individuals who are the participants and catalyst to the racist incident that happened to Dr. Barnes. They are also participants in the Case Study describing the actions of the events that took place in detail, with corresponding documentation in the Appendix. It is important to mention that these people are not bad people. They are educated. They possibly have good intellect (IQ). This incident, however, does raises a question about their emotional intellect (EQ). They very well may have "*racist residue*" and at the same time there are probably African Americans with whom they have a positive relationship. That is an irony. White people can accept minorities on an individual basis but accepting African Americans as a group, they often display subtle racist inclinations.

The Primary Participants (main characters)

The Author of this book – Also referred to as

Dr. Barnes or Dr. Ronald Barnes

Dr. Ronald Barnes is a graduate of the University OF Chicago Laboratory High School. He has a Master of Arts in Religious Studies from the University OF Chicago Divinity School, therefore is an Alumnus of the University of Chicago. Dr. Barnes will complete his PhD degree in psychology in 2022. Dr. Barnes is also 25% finished with a Masters' degree in Political Psychology from Arizona State University. Dr. Barnes is an inducted member of Psi Chi, the international honor society for psychology. Dr. Barnes doctorate GPA is 3.62 out of 4.0. Dr. Barnes is a published author with considerable article publications, with two books published, and 3 books in publication, prior to this title. Dr. Barnes is a member of Kappa Alpha Psi Fraternity, a fraternal organization of upstanding men. The fraternity prides itself for its service work in established programs like the Kappa League and Guide Right, mentoring young men and providing them with leadership and education direction.

Paul Casperson

Paul Casperson works in the University of Chicago Alumni Office and assisted Dr. Ronald Barnes in reaching the proper party regarding publishing an article in the Alumni magazine. Mr. Casperson is not an object of this books reference to discrimination. He was very helpful in facilitating Dr. Barnes' effort to collaborate with the UChicago Alumni Association.

Laura Demanski

Laura Demanski is the editor of the University of Chicago Alumni Magazine. Paul Casperson introduced Dr. Ronald Barnes to Ms. Demanski. Ms. Demanski is not an object of this books reference to discrimination. She was very helpful in facilitating Dr. Barnes' effort to collaborate with the UChicago Alumni Association.

Ms. Sarah Nolan – the respondent

Sarah Nolan is editor of the University of Chicago Alumni Magazine. Sarah Nolan informed Dr. Barnes that she is responsible for the publication of articles such as his, instead of Laura Demanski. She is the person who requested Dr. Barnes be banned from the Alumni building. Ms. Nolan lodged the complained with the University of Chicago Campus Police to ban Dr. Barnes from the Alumni building.

Assistant Chief of Police

Joanne Nee

Joanne M. Nee is the Director of Professional Accountability for the Department of Safety & Security. Ms. Nee provides oversight of Compliance, UCPD Internal Affairs and the complaint process, as well as the campus safety accreditation programs. Officer Nee holds a Bachelor of Science in Criminal Justice from Chicago State University. At the time of the incident, Chief Nee served as Deputy Chief for the University of Chicago Police Department. Officer Nee is the person contacted by Sarah Nolan and the representative of the UChicago Police Department who issued the ban order restricting Dr. Barnes from entering the Alumni building.

Attorney Jacqueline (Jackie) Hennard

The University of Chicago attorney responsible for investigating the racial discrimination and diversity complaints initiated by Dr. Barnes. Attorney Jackie Hennard is the Associate Director, Office for Access and Equity. She reports to the Director of the Office for Access and Equity. In this role, Attorney Hennard was the Lead Investigator for the Office for Access and Equity regarding this current case study. As of the publication of this book, Attorney Hennard is no longer employed with the University of Chicago. Attorney Hennard erroneous found no racism, conducted a racist investigation, and demonstrating her own racist residue.

Ms. Ingrid Gould

Associate Provost Ingrid Gould is responsible for various human resource-related concerns of the faculty such as leaves and retirement.

She leads the University's institutional accreditation and licensure and helped bring onsite childcare to campus. She works closely with deans, department chairs, directors, and campus administrators to address a broad range of sensitive academic and interpersonal matters with faculty and other academic appointees. These collaborations guide policy development and refinement and require the sound and equitable application of policies and principles.

Her UChicago career has spanned Campus and Student Life, the Booth School of Business, and the Office of the President. She served twice as the interim affirmative action officer, a role that then encompassed all protected-class and Title IX issues.

Ms. Gould earned her BA in romance languages and literatures at the University of Chicago and completed her MA at the Harris School of Public Policy. In her free time, she enjoys books, birding, and cooking.

Ms. Gould, as assistant Provost was responsible for reviewing the complaint initiated by Dr. Barnes and after reviewing the entire situation, Ms. Gould rescinded the ban issued against Dr. Barnes, yet she supported the no-racism report by Jackie Hennard. Mrs. Gould was in a tough situation to do the right thing and at the same time defend the university's racist residual environment.

Attorney Theodore C. Stamatakos

Attorney Stamatakos is the Senior Associate General Counsel for the University of Chicago. Dr. Barnes' attorney Amanda Gray contacted Mr. Stamatakos requesting a copy of the investigation report. Attorney Stamatakos indicated that as a private institution the University was not required to release a copy of the report. Attorney Stamatakos, like Office Nee and Ingrid Gould believed the false information they were told and supported the findings of Attorney Hennard, instead of learning or knowing the truth. At least his response to Attorney Gray indicated he supported and believed the incorrect information on no more than the word of people who did not present the facts correctly.

Mr. Angelo Chavers,

Angelo R. Chavers, LLC. Consulting Firm

Mr. Chavers is the consultant contracted by Dr. Barnes to provide input on how Dr. Barnes should handle this situation. Mr. Chavers has a master's degree from the University of Chicago Graham School of Continuing Liberal and Professional Studies. He has been a counselor in the Chicago Public School System for over 30 years and has years of experience in problem resolution. He was extremely helpful in consulting with Dr. Barnes to construct a positive strategy to address this situation in an intelligent, constructive, and resolute manner.

The broader problem of discrimination in America is revealed in the microcosm of this incident. Chief Jennifer Nee issued a "No trespass" letter banning Dr. Barnes from the UChicago Alumni building, at the request of Sarah Nolan. (Appendix 1, Exhibit 5). The miscellaneous entities, listed below, were unnecessarily copied on the ban letter. Why? Dr. Barnes has never met nor had contact with any of these individuals,

Eric Heath, Carlton Hughes, Brett Leibsker, Sarah Nolan, Suzanne Baker, Philip Gold, and Gary Wenzel

The fact that the above persons who Dr. Barnes has never met, nor have they met Dr. Barnes, leads one to wonder if Dr. Barnes' picture circulated, among those mentioned, depicting Dr. Barnes as an unsavory character. When it comes to a Black man, White people, especially White police use overkill to damage the reputation of a Black man. Do White police deal with a White respondent with more discretion? Probably. In any event, Assistant Police Chief Joanne Nee acted with complete incompetence in issuing the ban letter and distributing it to others without getting Dr. Barnes' side of the story, an example of incompetent police work or discrimination or **NO** police work at all, just the mindless exercise of power. The actions and methods deployed by Sarah Nolan and Jennifer Nee are indicative of how White people go to extravagant measures to magnify the accusations of Black people. The problem is that the wrongful discriminating actions by White people, especially White police, are easy to implement, yet a huge problem to correct the stain on the character of Black individuals. It is an irresponsible action on the part of officer Nee.

Background of the Problem based on the Lived Experience of Dr. Barnes

The alleged racist incident started when the complainant, Dr. Ronald Barnes, went to the University of Chicago Alumni office to request the publication of an article in the Alumni magazine (Appendix 2, Exhibit 1). Dr. Barnes' intent was to let the public and the University of Chicago community know how much the University of Chicago contributed to his self-actualization and positive life experiences. When Dr. Barnes inquired with the security guard in the lobby as to who is responsible for publication of articles in the alumni magazine, the security guard did not know. The guard called the upstairs offices and fared no better. Directory information at the guard's disposal did not indicate the person(s) responsible for alumni article publications. The security guard advised Dr. Barnes to go upstairs to the fourth floor and make a personal inquiry regarding the alumni magazine editor in question. Dr. Barnes presented his University of Chicago ID and signed the building log. When Dr. Barnes went to the fourth floor, he encountered Paul Casperson. Dr. Barnes conveyed to Mr. Casperson his reason to meet with the editor of the Alumni Magazine (for the purpose of having an article complimentary to the University published (Appendix 1, Exhibit 2). The article commented on how Dr. Barnes valued the education he received at the University of Chicago and the difference it made in his life and the realization that, if he can achieve, then anyone can. Mr. Casperson did not know who the editor was and promised to find out and connect Dr. Barnes with the appropriate person. Mr. Casperson followed up with Dr. Barnes and introduced him to Laura Demanski, Alumni Magazine editor (Appendix 1, Exhibit 3). Dr. Barnes and Ms. Demanski corresponded and scheduled a meeting (Appendix 1, Exhibit 4). The correspondence and meeting between Ms. Demanski and Dr. Barnes were fruitful, hopeful, and cordial. Dr. Barnes left the meeting with Ms. Demanski on a positive note (Appendix1, Exhibit 4).

There is no concrete reason that explain how events went awry, however, the only thing Dr. Barnes can point to as the seed creating the turning point for the change in Alumni responsiveness is a comment made by Dr. Barnes to Paul Casperson and Laura Demanski. Dr. Barnes made the comment that the Alumni magazine mostly published articles about Black people as artist, dancers, singers, or sports (stereotypical black images) but when it comes to the professional, intellectual, and academic accomplishments of Black people the Alumni Magazine, and media in general, does not write much about those people or their accomplishments. The statement was well meaning and one of the reasons Dr. Barnes approached the Alumni Association to have his article published in the magazine. Dr. Barnes has noticed that the Alumni Association has published diverse articles since their encounter however, their effort and subject matter is still inadequate. There are an abundance of accomplished University of Chicago Black Alumni. Many are accomplished doctors, lawyers, businesspeople, educators, and professions whose legacies are neglected by the University of Chicago Alumni magazine. The real dilemma in this situation is; what would have been the most beneficial result to all parties, including the Alumni Association, the University of Chicago and to Dr. Barnes; to publish the accolade of praise letter Dr. Barnes wrote about the University (Appendix 1, Exhibit 2) or to ban Dr. Barnes from the Alumni building? White people … LOL.

The next correspondence I received from the Alumni Office was from Sarah Nolan. She indicated that this matter fell under her responsibility more so that Laura Demanski, which was no problem. Dr. Barnes' objective was to have the article published. Ms. Nolan listed dates and times she would be available to meet. Ms. Nolan also indicated that there are rules for interacting with the Alumni Association and entering the building, which was agreeable to Dr. Barnes (Appendix 1, Exhibit 5). The fact is that no rules of entry were published for notice, and in reality, Dr. Barnes did not violate any of the rules of entry into the building. The guards at the front desk were not aware of any rules, and each, and every, time Dr. Barnes entered the building, he was directed to go up onto the offices by the security guards or did have an appointment, contrary to Ms. Nolan's perception. The guidelines given to Dr. Barnes by Ms. Nolan for entering the building are:

> "Separately, I want to make sure we are in agreement about the appropriate ways to interact with this office. Access to Harper Court offices is restricted to staff and tenants of the building. According to the security rules of Harper Court, non-staff visitors must contact us ahead of time and make an appointment before visiting our offices. Alumni badges may not be used to access the building. I understand that you have come to our offices in Harper Court several times without an appointment, which is contrary to our security rules and is not possible for our staff to accommodate" (Appendix 1, Exhibit 4).

Clearly, Ms. Nolan did not have reliable information, nor did Dr. Barnes understand the reason for Ms. Nolan saying this because each time Dr. Barnes entered the building, he was authorized by the security guard or had an appointment with an employee in the building.

Dr. Barnes entered the Alumni building on the 4 occasions listed below:

1. Dr. Barnes' encounter with Paul Casperson to learn the identity of the editor of the University of Chicago Alumni Magazine. Unscheduled Appointment but authorized by the security guard to go to the 4th floor to get the information requested. Paul Casperson did not know the person to direct Dr. Barnes but agreed to find out. Paul Casperson connected Dr. Barnes with Laura Demanski.

2. Dr. Barnes scheduled a meeting with Laura Demanski, because of the effort by Paul Casperson, sde to discuss the article for publication in the University of Chicago Magazine. Scheduled Appointment

3. Dr. Barnes's went to the Alumni building to present a woman he met at Alumni weekend with a copy of his Book. They met at the Alumni building in 2019. She worked at the Alumni building. Scheduled Appointed. Dr. Barnes does not remember her name.

4. Dr. Barnes entered the Alumni building to attend a job fair that was open to the public. Dr. Barnes signed in to attend the job fair at the Alumni Building lobby. Valid Appointment.

It was after visit number 4 to the Alumni Building that the problem with Dr. Barnes occurred.

Chapter V The Problem

Case Study: Part 2

The basic problem that frames the perception of the racial ideology between Black and White people is based on White stereotyping, media projection and White racism. Black people, as a group, are stereotypically judged without any commonsensible knowledge, except for what is printed and projected in the media, historical stereotype, internalized prejudiced in White socialization, *racist residue*, and by White racism. Integration is when Black people integrate into White neighborhoods, White schools, and White environments. Blacks encounter Whites in the workplace. The point is that when there is Black and White interaction it most often takes place by Black people integrating into White environments. As a result, Black people get a first-hand experience into White people operating in the comfort of their own environment. White people, on the other hand, seldom experience Black people in a Black environment. As a result, it can be argued that Black people have more insight and first-hand experience into White culture than White people have into Black culture. White people base their knowledge of Black people, as mentioned, on second-hand stereotype information. Therefore, it can be argued that White people have an opinion and perception of Black people based on ignorance.

Most of the conversation and society understanding relating to crime involves black people, who are too often projected in a criminal context. Blacks are called thugs and gangsters, but the "Most Violent People" are Whites. Daily, throughout America, people die at the hands of White people. White people are killing their own kind. According to the US Department of Justice statistics, 84 percent of white people killed every year are killed by other whites. In 2011, there were more cases of whites killing whites than there were of blacks killing blacks. From 1980 to 2008, white people committed a majority (53.3 percent) of gang-related murders, with most of the homicide victims being white as well. [165] This stereotype of Black people, especially Black males, filters into the perspective of White working people, White family people, White businesspeople, the normal White person, as a result they respond to Black people with a skewed perspective. The irony is that White culture is unaware of their own proclivity for criminal behavior which is more profound and numerous than that of Blacks, or any other race of people for that matter. This background influences White culture in their response to Black and minority people, a subtle contributing cause to the nature of Black / White interactions and relationships.

The Cause of the Problem

The problem was caused because Sarah Nolan, Alumni Association Magazine Editor, discovered Dr. Barnes was in the alumni building, attending a job fair, which he was authorized to attend and was open to the public. Ms. Nolan considered this a violation of her edict directing him as to the proper procedure for entering the alumni building. The fact of the matter is that Dr. Barnes attended a job fair that was open to the public, and registered for the event in the lobby of the alumni building. If Ms. Nolan had taken the time to gather the facts, she would not have acted impulsively or displayed behavior that can be considered *implicit bias.* To this day Dr. Barnes has never seen nor met Sarah Nolan. He could not pick her out of a crowd of five people, nor could he confidently pick her out of a gathering of two people. This could be an indication of some unresolved issues Ms. Nolan has regarding Dr. Barnes or Black people in general, since she has never met him personally. Maybe Ms. Nolan has control issues. Maybe Ms. Nolan had other problems brewing that day and took it out on Dr. Barnes. Maybe Ms. Nolan had a bad experience with a Black person and that experience was projected onto Dr. Barnes (an implicit bias response). Only Sarah Nolan knows her state of mind and reason for acting impulsively mindless on that day. Contrary to the charge made by Deputy Chief Nee, Dr. Barnes was never in the building without authorization. The first time Dr. Barnes entered the building he was instructed by security to go to the offices to find the person he was looking for. The second time Dr. Barnes entered the alumni building was for a scheduled meeting with Laura Demanski, editor of the University of Chicago Alumni magazine. The third time Dr. Barnes entered the building was to deliver a copy of his book, "*Practice what you preach, preach what you practice*" to an individual he met at Alumni week, who worked in the alumni building, a scheduled appointment. The fourth and final time Dr. Barnes entered the building was to attend a job fair, for which he registered and was open to the public. Maybe Sarah Nolan was offset by the comment Dr. Barnes made about the neglect of the Alumni magazine to publish articles on the academic, intellectual, and professional success of Black individuals. Maybe she felt the comment was reflective of her incompetence as the editor of the Alumni magazine. Maybe she was having a bad day and personal problems. Maybe she subconsciously had a negative impression of Dr. Barnes without ever having met him. Whatever the reason, **this incident would never have occurred under the conditions described, if Dr. Barnes was a White man**. Had Sarah Nolan took the time to get better information then she could have avoided making an uninformed and bad decision.

Anytime there is negative interaction between a Black and White people, the first impression is that it is race based. That is not always the case. Sometimes people have personality and ideological differences but usually their differences can be mutually resolved by interaction and communication. When there is no reason or just cause for negative action initiated by White people, one must

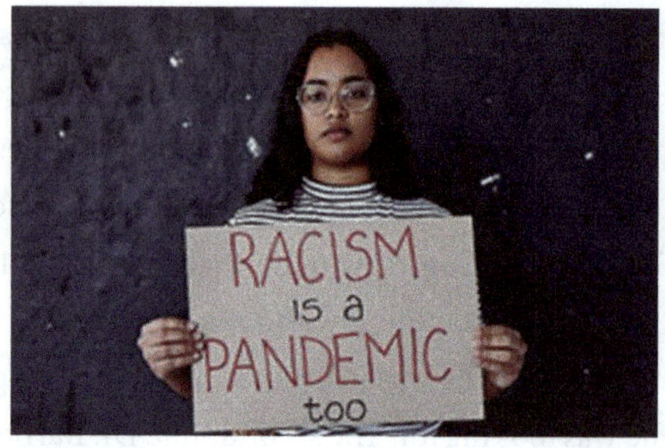

wonder, what is their motivation? **Again, if Dr. Barnes were White, this incident would never have occurred.** This is what makes this incident one of racism and discrimination. I am not saying Sarah Nolan or Assistant Chief Nee are racists or prejudice, per se. This act however was one of racism and discrimination. White people are challenged to eliminate the "*racist residue*" of their racist history from their personality. "*Racist residue*" is ingrained in White culture, by socialization. Until they realize this, they will always have character deficiency and suffer from the virus of racism and prejudice, a virus that often spreads to future generations. Racism is the longest lasting pandemic in America, it's contagious if not contained or treated.

Problem 1

The first problem is that Dr. Barnes was unjustly and without cause banned from the Alumni building and given a "No Trespass Notice" under the threat of being arrested Appendix 1, Exhibit 5). Dr. Barnes asserts that ***if he were White this situation would never have occurred.*** This is the reason the incident is racist and discriminatory. Dr. Barnes made a visit to the Alumni building a fourth time to attend a job fair that was open to the public. The job fair was held on the top floor of the Alumni building and was the only location visited by Dr. Barnes. Dr. Barnes registered for the job fair in the lobby of the Alumni building and was instructed to go to the top floor. Dr. Barnes attended the job fair for a period of no longer than one hour. It was after Dr. Barnes attended the job fair that aggressive, hostile, and discriminating action was taken against him. Within the next seven days, Dr. Barnes received "A No Trespass Notification" correspondence from Deputy Chief Joanne Nee of the University Campus Police Department informing him he was banned from entering the Alumni building under threat of arrest (Appendix 1, Exhibit 6). At the same time, Dr. Barnes received an email from Deputy Chief Nee reinforcing the ban from the alumni building (Appendix 1, Exhibit 7). For the record, the University Campus Police, in general, are dutiful and from my experience perform their job with responsible dedication. Dr. Barnes has the honor of knowing and interacting with several of the Campus police officers including the Chief of Police, Rainey. They are fine people who are dedicated to protect the students, faculty, and staff of this great University. In his opinion however, Deputy Chief Nee had a lapse of duty in this situation. The first mistake she made was to act without hearing Dr. Barnes' side of the story. Had she done this, it is probable the incident would have been reconciled and this book would not have been written. With good judgement, Deputy Chief Nee could have diffused the situation, which she did not. Dr. Barnes was guilty until being proved innocent. Which is a typical perspective of White people when it comes to Black people. It can be assumed but it cannot be certain that Deputy Chief Nee would have acted different if Dr. Barnes were White, but it can be said she did not perform dutiful police work in this situation. She took the word of Sarah Nolan, who requested the Ban without sufficient cause. Another unfortunate action Deputy Chief Nee made was to send copies of the "No Trespass Notice" to several people in the University community. Frankly, this was embarrassing to Dr. Barnes, especially since he was blindsided by the notice and believed there was no good cause for this action. It was also unnecessary. Circulating the notice to several members of the University community was also damaging to the reputation of Dr. Barnes. **One must consider the question; would the same procedure have occurred if Dr. Barnes were White?** White culture is full of serial killers, Bank robbers, rapist, even kids who kill each other in schools, yet White people escalate the alleged misdemeanors of Black people, and unjustly attack and kill Black people. Why?

Maybe because of fear. Maybe because of racism. Maybe because of a lack of their own self-worth. It is a documented fact and studies have proven that Black people receive longer jail sentences for the same crimes White people receive lesser sentences. Specific examples are cited in the Introduction of this book. White people are even exonerated for cold-blooded murder of Black people. Thank goodness, this situation was not criminal nor required any reprimand beyond a ban from a building.

Immediately upon receipt of the email from Deputy Chief Nee, Dr. Barnes called Chief Nee and requested a meeting. She was accommodating and made an appointment to meet with Dr. Barnes within an hour of the call. Deputy Chief Nee was accompanied by an overweight White man when she met with Dr. Barnes. During the meeting, the man accompanying Chief Nee made the statement to Dr. Barnes, "You should not be concerned because it was only one building on campus that you were banned from." With all respect, that was the dumbest thing Dr. Barnes has heard in the last 20 years and he cannot remember another comment made to his person that was as dumb as that one. Who wants to have any stain on their record, especially for no valid reason? Maybe White people consider it inconsequential for a black person to have a stain or two on their record. Considering, Dr. Barnes is an alumnus of the University of Chicago, and that he was banned from his Alumni building, is ridiculous. Then the Alumni association turns around and periodically during the year request Dr. Barnes to send them money, ironic. The meeting with Chief Nee was cordial. She informed Dr. Barnes of the appeal procedure to contesting the ban and indicated she was only doing her job. While Chief Nee's actions were explained, it would have been better police work to get both sides of the story before acting, and even better to act in a manner that would have diffused taking unwarranted disciplinary action. In this case, there is subtle indication that some White people have a low intellectual (IQ) and emotional (EQ) intellect when it comes to Black people and minorities in general. It indicates the necessity for White people to be trained on how to interact with diverse people. **If Dr. Barnes were White, this incident would never have happened, or it would have been handled much different.** Emotional intelligence (emotional quotient or EQ) is the ability to understand, use, and manage your own emotions in positive ways to relieve stress, communicate effectively, empathize with others, overcome challenges, and **defuse conflict.** [166]

Problem 2

In addition, Chief Nee circulated the "No Trespass Notice" to numerous persons in the University of Chicago community, people who Dr. Barnes has never seen or met. Did she circulate Dr. Barnes' picture as well? The point is, Assistant Chief Joanne Nee, while not to blame, could have handled the situation much better. She put herself in the position as a servant to a middle management individual. She acted without question or just cause. The methodology with which Sarah Nolan and Joanne Nee handled this situation made a mountain out of a molehill. This is characteristic of how, too often, the dynamics of White and Black people interactions play out, in far too many circumstances in America. The only conclusion

Problem 3

Although the basic problem was resolved, and the ban on Dr. Barnes to enter the Alumni building was lifted. The ban would not have been lifted, if there were a valid reason for the ban to in the first place. However, the residue of the ban still lingers. The fact that the investigator, Jackie Hennard, contacted Dr. Barnes' high School and graduate school under negative investigative circumstances, cast Dr. Barnes in a negative light. This is a problem. How does a person eliminate a smear to their reputation? Accusations have a lingering impact. The White investigators and White accusers do not care about the reputation of an innocent Black man. That indicates insensitivity, random impropriety, incompetence, and a low EQ. If Dr. Barnes were white, and if Dr. Barnes acted improperly, at least they would have been discreet. Their investigation was conducted in racism. This is an example, characteristically, of how White people displays a disregard for Black people. White people have a presumption of guilt when a Black person is accused, and they behave based on that presumption of guilt.

Another objective of this book is to explore the range of shortcomings in the way White people relate to Black people. In the extreme sense and unfortunately in too many circumstances in our society White people will murder a Black person, or the White police will shoot or incarcerate a Black man, a Black man who is completely innocent, then the White person or White police will declare their innocence and argue the murder or incarceration was justified. Ridiculous. American White society supports this inequality. On a much smaller scale, this is an analogy of what Dr. Barnes encountered at the University of Chicago. The White people referenced herein the case study, believed their actions were justified, even though they were not. Their belief only exemplifies the lack of knowledge, the lack of emotional intelligence, and the ignorance of White people when it comes to interacting with Black people and diverse individuals. White People … LOL.

Problem 4

The most irresponsible display of racism and prejudice on the part of the University investigation was that Attorney Hennard investigated Dr. Barnes, who appealed the ban. Attorney Hennard contacted Dr. Barnes' high school (The University of Chicago Laboratory School) and the graduate school Dr. Barnes attended (The University of Chicago Divinity School) and inquired with them as to Dr. Barnes interaction with them. First, how Dr. Barnes interacts with his Alma Maters is irrelevant in this case. Attorney Hennard reported that Dr. Barnes has a habit of "dropping in" on previous schools he attended. Is it abnormal for alumni to return to previous schools they attend to say hello or revisit staff, professors, or administrators? It happens all the time. Alumni drop in on their alma maters all the time. In addition, not one of the individuals at the University of Chicago Laboratory School or The University of Chicago Divinity School ever complained. In fact, each time they expressed they were happy to see Dr. Barnes. This is smoke screen and an example of how Jackie Hennard conducted a racist investigation. The investigation was conducted to find fault in the behavior of Dr. Barnes. The investigation was misleading and inaccurate, a false representation of the truth and an effort to find reason to exonerate the real culprit, Sarah Nolan. It is also, an example of a racist incompetent investigation and an incompetent investigator. It is also an example of the extent to which White people will go to defend their weak position and protect other White people. In reality, it demonstrates their lack of intelligence. Educated people are not necessarily intelligent or smart. I am not saying Jackie Hennard is overtly prejudice. I am saying her actions were influenced by "*racist residue*".

Dr. Barnes visited the University of Chicago Laboratory School to get information on his high school counselor, Ms. Carolyn Smith. Dr. Barnes credits Ms. Smith with being a significant guiding force in Dr. Barnes life and he wanted to get in touch with her, to thank her and give her his gratitude.

Ms. Smith called Dr. Barnes and his parents into her office when he was graduating from high school. She informed his parents that, in her opinion, Dr. Barnes would do better at a small college. As a result, Ms. Smith arranged for Dr. Barnes to attend Coe College in Cedar Rapids, Iowa. This turned out to be a critical crossroads in Dr. Barnes life. Attending Coe College Dr. Barnes was inducted into the Coe Hall of Fame and more important, he graduated from college. That is a foundational catalyst of his achievement today. He is a PhD in psychology, and a member of Psi Chi (the international honor society for psychology). Dr. Barnes has a doctoral grade point average (GPA) of 3.62 out of 4.0). He has written six books, including this current one. It is Dr. Barnes' belief these things never would have happened without the insight and guidance of his high school counselor, Ms. Carolyn Smith. This fact was of no concern to the investigation. They only wanted to gather misleading information to give credibility to their racist investigation. Ridiculous. Dr. Barnes established meaningful relationships while attending the University of Chicago Divinity School. He did occasionally visit the school to say hello to special people. They never complained and were always happy to see him. He would make appointments with, then Dean Richard Rosengarten for advice and insight. Furthermore, the investigator, Jackie Hennard, never consulted Dr. Barnes about his reasons for visiting his alma maters.

The problem is that the investigation cast Dr. Barnes in a controversial light when they contacted his past schools. They were not concerned about finding out the truth. They were concerned about protecting their racist, prejudice and discriminating behavior, white people protecting and covering up for White people. The truth did not matter. As a result, Dr. Barnes is self-conscious about visiting the schools he attended because of his name cast in this type of controversy. The irresponsibility of the investigation indicated that Attorney Hennard was not qualified for the job, nor was she interested in the truth. Maybe one of the reasons the university hired her is because they believed she would cover up the truths in racists and discrimination inquiries.

Just as discriminating is that the provost office, Ms. Ingrid Gould "bought" her story, as did the University general counsel when confronted with Dr. Barnes request to get a copy of the investigation report (Appendix 1, Exhibit 12). This case study reveals an example of the discrimination, prejudice and institutionalized of racism in a prestigious learning environment and the logistics that support and maintain discrimination. Entire institutional infrastructures supported false representations, misinformation, and lies that unjustly frame the behavior of Black people. The Campus police, the investigator, the provost office, and the University attorney, Theodore C. Stamatakos all believed false and misleading information. This is the kind of incompetence that permeates itself throughout American institutions. White people believe White people, even when they lie or misrepresent the facts. Donald Trump falsely claiming to have won the 2016 election that he lost, is an example of how gullible White people are. Normally, when Alumni return to their Alma Mater they are welcomed with open arms. The University of Chicago employs people who only welcome the return of White people. Often the institutionalization of discriminating behaviors is a process of collaborating behaviors by numerous individuals in key positions in an organization. It usually involves the mindless ignorance to believe, repeat and spread a lie, spread untruth, or spread misinformation. It is a cognitive mindless ignorant process White people in an organization use to cover up their racism, while maintaining their racists behaviors. The manifestation of racism in institutions is a strategic phenomenon. In this case the misinformation and untruth were originated by Sarah Nolan, then believed and acted upon by Assistant police chief Joanne Nee. Then covered up and framed untruthfully by Attorney Jackie Hennard. The false information and racist investigation was believed and accepted by Associate provost Ingrid Gould, and then when Dr. Barnes requested a copy of the report, the matter was referred to the UChicago attorney Theodore C. Stamatakos, who repeated the false information (Appendix 1, Exhibit 12). The entire chain that establishes an institutional position on this case involved a mindless ignorance to discover the truth. This is a textbook example of how a lie can become believable. The real absurdity is that it could have been avoided with simple academic institutional communication and intelligence. Smart people sometimes act stupid.

Problem 5

One of the most damaging impacts of experiencing racism and discrimination is that it creates distrust. When an individual experiences discrimination on the part of police or White people, they develop an intensified awareness of the interactive roles between others they encounter, especially police and other White people. Victims of racism are cautious to interact with police and harbor a suspicious viewpoint of White people and the police. Subconsciously, a discriminatory experience causes a Black person to harbor a resentment for White people and police. They become aware of the callous and malicious nature in White culture. Imbalance is created in the way Black people, White people, and the police interact. Superficial interaction instead of substantial exchange becomes the norm. However, the most impactful result of discrimination is distrust and resentment.

Chapter VI Aftermath of the Problem: The Appeal and Investigation

Case Study: Part 3

After the appeal process for contesting the ban was explained by Assistant Chief Nee, Dr. Barnes proceeded to initiate the appeal to reverse the ban. Dr, Barnes wrote a letter to the provost office explaining his side of the story (Appendix 1, Exhibit 9), requesting the ban be lifted. As a result, an investigation into the matter was initiated. Attorney Jackie Hennard was assigned to investigate the complaint on appeal by Dr. Barnes. However, prior to contacting the University of Chicago provost office, Dr. Barnes sent an email to Sarah Nolan and Assistant Chief Nee proposing to resolve the matter between themselves (Appendix 1, Exhibit 8). Dr. Barnes was sensitive to the embarrassment of the situation that befell him. Sarah Nolan nor Officer Nee responded. It was at that point Dr. Barnes initiated contact with the University provost office to appeal the ban. In addition, at this time in the process, before acting on the ban appeal, only three people were involved (Sarah Nolan, Officer Nee and Dr. Barnes), aside from the miscellaneous others that Chief Nee copied on the "No Trespass Notice." Since no resolution or positive collaboration could be gained from Ms. Nolan or Officer Nee, Dr. Barnes filed an appeal to the Ban with the provost office. What is insightful in this case is that neither Office Nee nor Ms. Nolan were willing to resolve the issue amicable between themselves and Dr. Barnes. Obviously, they felt they were right. The irony is that they were wrong. One of the characteristics of White privilege is that White people always think they are right, in encounters with Black people, even when they are wrong. In many cases, they get away with it. The extent of White naivety and ignorance is that they believe in their negative social location. C Wright Mills defines social location as the corners or place in life that people occupy because of where they are located in a society. Factors such as gender, class, race, and religion are four of the main factors in determining one's social location. [167]

Attorney Jackie Hennard was put in charge of the investigation. Dr. Barnes met with Attorney Hennard. Initially she seemed to have an open mind and an objective interest in the investigation. She indicated she was and independent investigator and did not report to the University. That was a lie. She has a university email, a university phone number, and business cards with the University logo. She is in university offices, and her boss who she reports to is University personnel and she receives a university paycheck. Attorney Hennard was not honest from the beginning. Even during her investigation, she was "tight lipped" about the investigation, about the information she discovered, and about the method in which she conducted the investigation. Attorney Hennard did not disclose any detailed or significant information to Dr. Barnes about how she was conducting the investigation. She kept her conversations short and shallow. The Appendix list the details of communication between Dr. Barnes and Attorney Hennard (Appendix 1 Exhibit 10). When Dr. Barnes requested a report update on the investigation, Attorney Hennard only replied, she could not disclose any details.

Attorney Hennard told Dr. Barnes the investigation would take 30 days to conclude. The investigation wound up taking more than three months (over 90 days). One would suspect when the investigation took considerably longer than normal something is not right. There are extenuating circumstances that cause a considerable time delay, as the investigation took three times longer than planned. One can conclude it took that long to compile information on Dr. Barnes and investigate him instead of focusing on the incident in question.

When Attorney Hennard completed the investigation, she did not give Dr. Barnes any report. She directed Dr. Barnes to contact Assistant Provost Ingrid Gould. When Dr. Barnes requested copies of the investigative report, she told him that it is not the university policy to provide complainants with a copy of the report. Attorney Hennard stated to Dr. Barnes that the matter would be resolved by Associate Provost Ingrid Gould. Ms. Gould had a copy of the investigative report, and it was Ms. Gould's responsibility to judicate the matter.

The issue of the competence and ability of the investigators to handle racism and discrimination complaints became a question. The way the investigation was conducted, and the findings demonstrates the investigators have no substantial understanding of racists' issues or discrimination behaviors. White culture is socialized to consider it normal behavior to be skeptical about the behavior of Black people even when Black behavior is the same as White behavior. 1) Either the investigators are compliant with racist and discrimination behavior. 2) The investigators do not understand the subtle behavior of racism. 3) Either the investigators do not have the ability or skillset to address the issue of racism and discrimination, 4) the investigators are just plain unaware and do not know how to deal with racism and discrimination, or 5) because the investigators are themselves racists, 6) or the investigators have "*racist residue*"

To present such a weak case that focuses on the behavior of the complainant rather than the behavior of the person the complaint was made against is ridiculous and mindlessly ignorant. To present a rationale for action taken against the complainant such as: "he has a habit of dropping in" is ridiculous. In other words, to stop by and say hello to people that are former associates and valuable to Dr. Barnes' learning process, is objectionable behavior. Being that was the only rational reason the investigators could come up with for finding, "no discrimination" for the ban placed against Dr. Barnes is so ridiculous that one must pity the people who defend discrimination in this case. Attorney Hennard appeared to have an empathy for discrimination or an empathy for White people who demonstrate discriminating behavior. The way White racists conduct themselves completely contradicts the fact they are intelligent or smart, even if they are educated. Their conduct in this case indicates they are not smart about how to resolve problems within their own culture nor smart, in general. This case study is a perfect example of people who may have a high IQ (intelligence quotient), but a low EQ (emotional quotient). This is a reason White people need to be educated, learn, and influenced on how to positively relate to diversity. Dr. Barnes understands the behaviors of the institutional participants. He understands their ignorance, because he is an educated, PhD psychologist. He has been in White environments for a substantial part of his life, which gives him an insightful depth into White psychology. He understands the actions of White people and the foundational impact their racism has on their behavior. More so, however, when an individual believes the are better than another person, merely because of skin color does, and that the difference in skin color is a justified basis for privilege, the person who believes this, is ignorant.

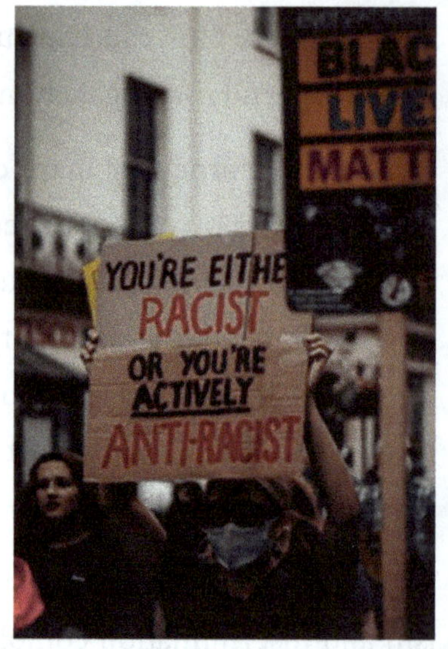

CHAPTER VII
RESOLUTION OF THE PROBLEM
CASE STUDY: PART 4

The entire discriminatory situation described in the case study that Dr. Barnes experienced could have been avoided if Sarah Nolan, Chief Nee and Dr. Barnes met to resolve the issues. The entire matter could have been resolved as a misunderstanding and we all could have forgotten the matter. White people, however, have an inability, an inhibiting restrictive characteristic called "White Privilege" that does not allow them to admit wrongdoing, especially in the case of wrong perpetuated against Black people. When White wrongdoing against African Americans goes unchecked, that is a reinforcement of their White privilege and their "*racist residue.*" If White people keep resisting the reality that they have "*racist residue*", they will always be racists and wrong. They cover-up their wrongdoing. They are too insecure to admit their mistakes. Consider the caricature that Donald Trump never apologizes. Throughout his life and presidency, and all the deplorably bad decisions he made (with bankruptcies, misogynistic relationships with women including rape accusations, adulteries, coronavirus management, separating kids from their parents, and fracturing the people in America against each other). He never apologizes. He never thought he did anything wrong. Many others thought he mishandled the pandemic and was responsible for hundreds of thousands of deaths. Fortunately, Dr. Barnes' situation is not that serious, but it is characteristic of how White people who make mistakes and are unapologetic for their inadequacy. As a result, White people do not become better people. They become human beings that are more deplorable. Many incidents have been recorded of Whites (female Karens and White Male idiots) berating Asians, Blacks, Hispanics, Muslims, and Jews in public without cause. These are examples of the degree to which racism is internalized in White culture. Their racist culture is reinforced without significant counteraction.

Dr. Barnes contacted Associate Provost Ingrid Gould to find out the results of the investigation. A person he contracted as a consultant, Mr. Angelo Chavers, accompanied Dr. Barnes to the meeting with Associate Provost Gould. Mr. Chavers of Angelo R. Chavers, LLC. Consulting firm was instrumental in giving Dr. Barnes a constructive perspective on this matter from its inception and provided positive input on how to proceed as a victim of discrimination, a situation Dr. Barnes had never encountered in his life, until now. The meeting with Ms. Gould was cordial. She explained the University position and diligently listened to Dr. Barnes' position. Frankly, she completely misunderstood the situation because she was given misleading information by the investigator, Attorney Jackie Hennard, and she believed it. The investigator outright tried to cover up the racist allegations and focused the investigation on Dr. Barnes, the complainant, rather than they did the respondent, Sara Nolan. The entire investigation was racist. To her credit, Associate Provost Ingrid Gould lifted the Ban and for that, Dr. Barnes is grateful. The truth is that if there was legitimate cause for the ban it would not have been lifted. Ms. Gould did show deference to the truth and did the right thing, in this case. However, the process of the investigation and the conclusions they drew were completely negligent and indicated the inadequacy of the investigator and the investigation process. It also was an example of how White people cover up for White people and have an inability to admit they are wrong, even when they are.

The correspondence with Ms. Gould lifting the ban contained errors, false statements and lies. In the correspondence letter lifting the ban, it was obvious that Attorney Hennard was unqualified to conduct this type of investigation and that the objective of the University was to protect their White employee. The statement below is an excerpt from the lifting of the ban letter that indicates this point (Appendix 1, Exhibit 10).

Jackie Hennard, Associate Director/Lead Investigator in the Office for Access and Equity, assessed the alleged discriminatory basis, finding no discrimination. Her rationale is, in part, that there is no evidence that those responsible for implementing the directive were aware of your race at the time. She also found evidence of a plausible non-discriminatory reason for the directive. I suggested that you speak with Melissa Gilliam about your Alumni Association & Development (ARD) concerns.

The statement that Attorney Hennard rationalized there was "*no evidence that those responsible for implementing the directive were aware of my race at the time*" indicates that either Attorney Hennard did not do a competent job of investigation. Either she intentionally was trying to cover up the incident, or she lacked the skills and knowledge for the job, or she outright lied, or all of the above. I gave Laura Demanski a copy of the article for publishing, which included my picture (Appendix 1, Exhibit 2). Laura Demanski gave the article to Sarah Nolan. She saw my picture, read the article then contacted me to inform me publishing the article fell under her responsibility. She also gave me guidelines for entering the building. Therefore, this part of the investigation report was inaccurate. Either Sarah Nolan lied, or Attorney Hennard misrepresented the facts or lied or was a co-conspirator in the lie. If Sarah Nolan did not know what Dr. Barnes looked like or what his race was then how would she be able to know when he entered the building or whether it was Dr. Barnes? How would she know he attended the job fair?

This statement in the lifting of the ban letter also indicated in the excerpt above that she also found "*evidence of a plausible non-discriminatory reason for the directive*" (the ban). What she is referring to is the fact that Dr, Barnes was accused of entering the building without legitimate reason. This is false.

Attorney Hennard in collaboration with Sarah Nolan framed the investigation scenario to cover up the facts and the truth. Attorney Hennard was incompetent in her investigation and Ingrid Gould bought her story. Typically, White people cover up for other White people because they have a compatibility in their mindset toward non-White people (racist residue). They will taint and re-arrange the facts to cover up the "real truth." This is a common practice by White people when Black people accuse them of racism and discrimination. In this case, it shows the extent to which White people will go to protect their White privilege, their wrong and irrational behavior.

However, the most ridiculously flawed part of the investigation was when Dr. Barnes discovered Attorney Hennard spent considerable time investigating Dr. Barnes. The excerpt below from the letter lifting the ban indicates Attorney Hennard spend more time investigating Dr. Barnes than she did investigating the person who was the subject of Dr. Barnes' complaint (Appendix 1, Exhibit 10). Attorney Hennard contacted the University of Chicago Laboratory High School to inquire as to Dr. Barnes' interaction with the school. She also contacted the Divinity School to inquire about Dr. Barnes' interactions, as is evidenced below in the excerpt from the ban lift letter.

Further, as I reviewed your petition, I learned that you sometimes drop in on others on campus. While some people enjoy an occasional impromptu visit as much as you do, many UChicago employees find it disrupts their work to receive surprise visitors. You would extend a courtesy by scheduling time to meet with Laboratory Schools, Divinity School, and other staff. You bridled at this suggestion and stated that Americia Huckabee, the Divinity School assistant to the dean of students and someone you described as a friend, welcomes your unscheduled visits. While you may be right, consider that her supervisor expects her to work during work hours. You would avoid problems by calling ahead.

Interactions with previous schools was irrelevant to the appeal initiated by Dr. Barnes and was an effort by Attorney Hennard to find reasons to disqualify and discredit Dr. Barnes' appeal complaint. The investigation was racist in the way it was conducted. Attorney Hennard's objective was to find ways to clear Sarah Nolan rather than to objectively find the truth. Attorney Hennard was unqualified for this job, or she was qualified for the job of covering up any complaints against the University. White people will lie when Black people are involved. The excerpt above shows that Attorney Hennard alleged that Dr. Barnes "*sometimes drop in on others on campus.*" She framed this as a problem caused by Dr. Barnes. This is total misrepresentation, and another example of the extent to which White people will go in order to cover their bad judgments, shortcomings and wrongdoing. Dr. Barnes did, on more than one occasion visit the University of Chicago Laboratory High School he attended. The first time was to inform them of the book he wrote and to gain notice in the Lab notes magazine. Which the school did accommodate. As mentioned previously, and to reiterate, two other times Dr. Barnes visited the Lab School Alumni office was to find the contact for his High School counselor at the time of his attendance. Reflecting on his journey, Dr. Barnes credits his high school counselor, Ms. Carolyn Smith for providing valuable guidance at a critical time in his life. Ms. Smith recommended Dr. Barnes attend a small college because his attention span needed focus that a small college would better accommodate. Ms. Smith set a meeting with Dr. Barnes and his parents and gave them insight and direction. All agreed. As a result, Dr. Barnes went to Coe College in Cedar Rapids, Iowa. He graduated with a B.A. degree in Economics. Dr, Barnes saw this as a pivotal moment in his life and made visits to the High School Alumni office to find out how to contact Ms. Smith to tell he how much he appreciated her guidance. In addition, the High School alumni office never complained. They welcomed Dr. Barnes each time he met with them without complaint. Attorney Hennard was not interested in the reason Dr. Barnes "dropped in" on his high school. For Attorney Hennard to frame this situation in any other manner is misrepresentation and shows an overt effort to cover up the real issue, the truth, the fact Dr. Barnes was discriminated against, or to defend her White counterpart. Again, this is an example of "*racist residue.*" It shows that attorney Hennard was unqualified for the job, as well as an accomplice to this incident of racism. It would not be surprising if the university wanted someone in that job who would defend the university, cover up incidents of racism and manipulate the facts so as not to confront the university with the truth that might damage the university's reputation. This only perpetuates the problems. Instead, the university should use these incidents as an opportunity to address the issues in a resolving manner, as an education endeavor. Instead, the university perpetuates the problem, like an ostrich putting their head in the ground so as not to encounter reality. This is not the purpose of a learning institution. Most learning institutions are remiss to teach people how to interact with other people. What is more important, teaching students about business, religion, psychology, economics, humanities, sociology, and the traditional disciplines, or teaching students how to get along with others in this world or at the least on the campus. While Traditional disciplines are valuable to life, they do not touch the perimeter value of human relationship and interactions. The dysfunction of people relationships is so prevalent in America that even these traditional subjects are mute unless people learn how to relate to people. It almost seems like a trivial pursuit to raise the necessity that people need to learn how to relate to each other. However, consider the situation involving Central Park "Karen," in addition to the vast number of dysfunctional interactions occurring in American society on a consistent and daily basis.

A white woman, Amy Cooper, in Central Park, NYC, falsely accused a Black man of attacking her. The Black man was merely birdwatching and requested that the White woman put her dog on a leash, in compliance with posted park rules. She became so offended that she called the police and falsely reported that the Black man attacked her. Completely and totally a lie. Amy Cooper was a University of Chicago MBA graduate of the Booth School. She was probably a brilliant person academically, but a lying stupid idiot when it came to exhibiting the emotional intelligence when it comes to interacting with others, especially minority others.[168] This is one example of why it is important for Academic institutions to teach the educated minds they produce how to interact with other people. It is analogous to giving an individual a Rolls Royce Car but not teaching them how to drive. In response to this incident, the New York City District Attorney's office responded as such:

"As alleged in the complaint, Amy Cooper engaged in racist criminal conduct when she falsely accused a Black man of trying to assault her in a previously unreported second call with a 911 dispatcher. Fortunately, no one was injured or killed in the police response to Ms. Cooper's hoax," DA Cy Vance said in a statement. "Our office will pursue a resolution of this case which holds Ms. Cooper accountable while healing our community, restoring justice, and deterring others from perpetuating this racist practice." [169]

I reviewed the no-trespass warning itself, the reasons for its imposition, and the rationale for it to remain. I concluded that the no-trespass directive should be lifted. You are again welcome to enter the Harper Court office tower as long as you, like all other visitors, respect that building's rules, which are more restrictive than on other parts of campus.

Above all, Associate Provost Ingrid Gould lifted the ban (Appendix 1, Exhibit 9).

One can rationalize that the decision to lift the ban was made because it was the right thing to do. By falsely finding no discrimination the universities objective was probably attempting to find a win-win situation. Ms. Gould did the right thing. It is the opinion of this author that Ms. Gould was in a tough position. Politically and based on job security, she protected the university. However, in the sense of fairness and doing the right thing she lifted the ban. Ms. Gould most likely realized, the entire situation was unfortunate and overreaction. However, there is no, win-win in an untruth, a cover up, deception or conducting a racist investigation. The University of Chicago is not alone in the phenomena of diversity challenges. One can understand the dissonance in a White person accusing another White person of being racist. "*Racist residue*" infects good White people. It gives them a sensitivity to racism that makes it difficult for a White person to accuse another White person of exhibiting racist behavior.

CHAPTER VIII CRITICAL RACE THEORY

The University of Chicago case study incident emphasizes the importance of integrating Critical Race Theory (CRT) into the learning environment. Repressing incidents of White racism (past and present), condones and potentially perpetuates the dysfunction of White culture and its sickness into future generations. Understanding the concept of Critical Race Theory (CRT) will give perspective to the subtle and destructive characteristics of racism, as it integrates with the legal system and society. Incompetent and corrupt police, lawyers, and judges, who mishandle civil rights cases or racist investigations, fail all individuals involved. They fail the individual, the institution, the society, and the country. They become catalyst to racism. Just as important, they fail themselves and their profession. CRT advances that the legal system and laws in America affect the social, cultural and legal issues as they relate to race and racism. CRT examines the institutionalization of racism and how the legal systems, in America is governed by Whites who execute the laws to the advantage of White culture and to the detriment of Black culture. [170] Several White people reject CRT and object to including it into the learning curriculum or even debating it as an issue. Rejection of CRT can be viewed as rejection of equal rights, equal opportunity, a rejection of the Constitution of the United States of America, as well as the inability of White culture to deal with the truth. White people want to perpetuate and maintain White privilege, racism, and discriminatory behaviors in their favor.

In response to the objection of teaching CRT in the education system, it is important to give young minds a positive perspective as they proceed through the process of life and learning. Presenting and implanting the atrocities of White culture (past and present) into young minds may do more harm than good and taint the development and learning perspective with cynicism and negative foundation. Young people should be taught in elementary schools and in high school (grades kindergarten thru 12) that all people are equal. They should be taught respect for all people. They should be taught the truth about human evolution originating in Africa. They should be taught respect for humans of all races, cultures, religious orientations, and gender preferences. In the formative years of leaning, students should be taught positive foundational values and principles of relating to others in a non-discriminating manner. The blame for racism most people erroneously attaches to CRT is ridiculously stupid. The blame for racism lies with White people. This author agrees that CRT should not infiltrate the elementary education system (before grades K-6). However, in the junior high school levels students should be introduced to discriminating and prejudicial behaviors manifested in White culture. A CRT curriculum should be expanded in secondary education environments. CRT should be further taught in college and universities when students are matured in their learning process and able to process CRT with cognitive responsibility. The purpose of CRT should not be taught to make Whites feel guilty or to make Blacks feel resentment. Teaching CRT should present the reality of historical phenomena and current phenomena of racism, racist, discrimination and prejudice that exist in America. The intention of teaching CRT introduced into the learning environment at junior high school, high school and colleges is because that is a time when students have a matured mind for learning and processing the history and phenomena they learn. The purpose of CRT should be to tell the truth, for developing constructive positive interpersonal relationship, to facilitate learning and reconstruct negative learning that has taken place in the past-lived experiences of students. Avoidance or lying will not resolve society issues of racism, discrimination, and prejudice. The teacher in the classroom needs to control the interactions and reactions between students. It is critical for the teacher to maintain a learning environment not a critical environment of anger and defensive insecurity. Contemporary White kids are not responsible for the acts of their ancestors unless they internalize racist values. Contemporary Black kids are no longer slaves. A purpose of CRT should be to deter White kids from internalizing racist values and keep Black kids from feeling victimized. Teaching CRT should give kids a security in dealing with the truth and proceeding into life with an ability to deal with reality securely.

CRT originated in the United States at Harvard law school during the mid-1970. It advances that racism is the product of individual bias, but and is embedded in legal systems and policies. [171] Researchers and legal professionals wanted to know why the advances gained by the Civil Rights movement resulted in so little improvement in the condition and lives of minorities. They hypothesized that the gains were neutralized and undermined by White resistance and the courts. The institutionalized and systematic racist practices by White Americans obstructed equal opportunity policies. The counterstrategy to gains made by the Civil Rights movement is reminiscent of the White backlash after the Civil War. Whites proceeded to undo the gains made by Blacks economically and politically. While the end of the Civil War marked the end of antebellum slavery, it was not the end of White racism, discrimination, and black disenfranchisement. The Southern Black Codes of 1865-1866, were instituted by Southern Whites to neutralize the impact of freed slaves and to institute a system that restricted the freedom of people of color. [172] It was during the post-Civil War period that Whites formed the Ku Klux Klan (KKK) to further intimidate and disenfranchise Blacks and their advancement, mostly using criminal violence. Today, Whites have become strategic about Black disenfranchisement. They use the legal system to disenfranchise Blacks. Whites are especially vocal against the inclusion of teaching about the brutality and evils of slavery in the schools, as part of the learning process. Advocates of CRT argue it "lays bare the hidden machinery of systemic racism." It tells the truth and recounts the reality of American history. Critics argue it is racist, because it positions white against black and teaches negative ideologies about White privilege and White supremacy, as well as makes a virtue of victimhood. [173] Some people advance that to promote CRT is a threat to Western Civilization. Considering slavery as the reality, that it is, is a denial of the truth. This is a flaw in White culture, the inability to deal with the truth. The inability to deal with the truth caused the ongoing manifestation of lies that falsely project reality. We witness this happening in multiple occurrences in today's contemporary phenomena (Global warming is fake news, Trump won the 2020 presidential election, President Obama was not born in America, just to name a few). The brutality of slavery is a reality. The truth is that sometimes "the truth hurts", especially when the truth is based on negative actions. White people should be ashamed of their participation in the system of slavery. Does the truth set you free? As for the future, this is a lesson in the adage advanced by C. L. Barnes, "*if you can't stand up to it, don't do it*." So, if White people are ashamed of the truth, then why do they consistently persist in being racists, discriminating and acting prejudicially? Is the teaching of CRT more a threat to Western Civilization than racism, discrimination, and prejudice? Do the White critics want to cover up the truth about the history of slavery and at the same time perpetuate the practices embedded in systematic and institutionalized racism? That is a joke and no one who tells it is funny. Critics argue that to teach CRT portrays Whites as villains and Blacks as victims. Both cases are true. Denying the truth will not resolve the issues and it is weak and shortsighted. People who take these positions will only perpetuate the problems.

White parents in many of United States school districts do not want CRT taught in the elementary and high schools. The first false argument and misunderstanding they present against CRT being taught is that CRT focuses on racism. CRT is a broad-based concept and certainly, racism is integral to CRT, but the primary ideology of CRT is that institutions, especially the legal system, are so infested with systemic racism that discrimination and racism has become as American as "apple pie and baseball."

One can argue that White people do not want any interference with their being racist. White people want to be racist. They want to discriminate, and they want to "Make America White Again." White people want the America they stole from the Indians, the America that was built on the backs of Slavery and Black people. White people do not want to make America great again. It can be argued that America has never been great. White people want America to be White America. The dilemma is that America is not White. America has never been White. America is a melting pot of many ethnicities, races, religions, and cultures. A basic problem with White America is they want to construct an irrational, fake and unrealistic image of America. White people are so out of touch with reality they want to construct an America that has never existed. They want to live in a White fantasyland America. What do they call adults who believe in fairy tales … immature, retarded, slow learners, ignorant or plain stupid? An even bigger problem is that the kids of these White people inherit the same retarded psychology and thinking as their parents. This creates the potential to perpetuate future generations of immature, retarded, slow learners, ignorant or plain stupid White people. Progress will be to break this cycle of ignorance. Some believe teaching CRT will accomplish this. What will accomplish this is "the truth". Being sensitive to the development of young minds who are born innocent and have no direct involvement in creating the system of racism, nor do they have any involvement in perpetuating racism until they are taught racism behaviors by other White people, internalize racist values, and behave as racist. Otherwise, it is important to construct and preserve the character quality in the minds, of all young people. Young minds are impressionable. The process of constructing young minds is a layered process. Subjects taught in kindergarten, through grades 12 are building blocks to the curriculum in the subsequent grades. Subjects taught in the first grade lay the groundwork for what students learn in the second grade. This process is ongoing throughout the formal elementary and high school students learning process. CRT involves the legal apparatus of racism in large part. It is true that young White people played no role in the development of racism. It is not fair for them to internalize guilt for something they are not responsible. However, White kids benefit from White racism, discrimination and prejudice. If White culture does not break the cycle of racism, prejudice and discrimination then those very same White kids who did not create racism will become racists.

Another hypothesis on why White people are against CRT theory and it being taught in schools is that many white people, especially white people with lower levels of education and income, understand that whiteness comes with a premium and an advantage that exceeds economics but includes the cultural and social capital of privilege. President Lyndon Johnson commented, "If you can convince the lowest white man he's better than the best colored man, he won't notice you're picking his pocket. Hell, give him somebody to look down on, and he'll empty his pockets for you." [174] This is a direct quote from Lyndon Johnson, 36th President of the United States, referring to the mentality of White people, with condescending reference. Realistically, it makes sense that White people would rather repress the truth about their American history. Low class and poor White people even want to realize some form of dignity, even a perpetuated false dignity. There are aspects of White history that are inhumane and that are catalyst to contemporary White culture and behaviors toward minorities. If the truth sets you free, then White people need to know the truth. White people are incarcerated in the "*matrix*" of their lies and insecure sense of worth. Maybe it will also give minorities freedom along with White people. In every realm of common sense; where, when, and how is uneducated and poor better than educated and economically comfortable? White people will embrace an unrealistic fantasy to perceive a semblance of self-worth. Many White people are ignorant to the fact that they, themselves, are being "fleeced" and manipulated by White people. The average White person has more in common with Black people than they realize. All lives matter. It is just that White people are misdirected to the extent they do not realize Americans have no conflict with Americans, regardless of skin color, religion, or gender. We all want the same things in life. Like Lydon Johnson reveals, perpetuate a lie that causes chaos and conflict between people then the distraction allows others to benefit. Black people understand White America are manipulating them. White people exist in a "*matrix*" of lies, untruths and ignorance. The same White America that represses minorities manipulates white people. Upward mobility and financial success do not eliminate the racist encounters that Black people are prone to experience. If that were the case, Dr. Barnes would have no reason to write this book. The American journey for Black people is rampant with hurdles obstacles and challenges while for many Whites, the path to success does not have the same degree of obstructions.

It is understandable that White people want to protect their children from the historical stigma of White culture. Racist stigma is so deeply embedded in White Culture that they have the need to repress every thought of their past deeds; or rationalize their past atrocities as justified. However, current actions of many Whites still resonate the residue of racism. White people simply misunderstand the concept of Critical Race Theory.

> U.S. Rep. Jim Banks of Indiana sent a letter *to fellow Republicans on June 24, 2021, stating: "As Republicans, we reject the racial essentialism that critical race theory teaches ... that our institutions are racist and need to be destroyed from the ground up."* [175]

White people have a false understanding of CRT. Obviously, "racism" is a sensitive subject to many Whites as it is to many Blacks. However, misunderstanding between races has always been the rule rather than the exception. A more accurate way to frame CRT is as follows:

> Kimberlé Crenshaw, a law professor and a primary influence in the development of critical race theory, indicated that critical race theory just says, *"let's pay attention to what has happened in this country, and how what has happened in this country is continuing to create differential outcomes. … Critical Race Theory … is more patriotic than those who are opposed to it because … we believe in the promises of equality. And we know we can't get there if we can't confront and talk honestly about inequality."* [176]

Ms. Crenshaw explains CRT with more intelligence than Mr. Banks' objection to CRT. Mr. Banks is obviously a White person who is so entrenched to the "*matrix of racism*" that he intellectually is ignorant to understand the tenants of CRT. Mr. Banks represents the numbers of White individuals who are obstructionist to the truth and obviously, insecure to confront truth. Why is a person like this even in government? Perpetuating a lie is not leadership. Obviously, as Mr. Banks clearly states, he is more Republican than he is American.

Critical race theory **does not** assert the following: [177]

(1) One race or sex is inherently superior to another race or sex.

(2) An individual, by virtue of the individual's race or sex, is inherently privileged, racist, sexist, or oppressive, whether consciously or subconsciously.

(3) An individual should be discriminated against or receive adverse treatment because of the individual's race or sex.

(4) An individual's moral character is determined by the individual's race or sex.

(5) An individual, by virtue of the individual's race or sex, bears responsibility for actions committed in the past by other members of the same race or sex.

(6) An individual should feel discomfort, guilt, anguish, or another form of psychological distress solely because of the individual's race or sex.

A proper understanding can be reason for people to see the value of being educated in CRT.

Intrinsically, consciously, or subconsciously resistance to CRT being part of the education curriculum can be seen as a perpetuation of racism, a reason that aligns with the objectives of White culture, past and present. White culture looks at America and see "Blue Skies, opportunity, and a system that works for them." Black people look at America and see "A brick wall obstructing opportunity, a racist discriminating system, and a system detrimental to the welfare of Black people." These polarized viewpoints need to be reconciled or America will always be dysfunctional, racist, and hypocritical to its professed core values.

The following is a completely accurate scenario described by Ray Rashawn of the Brookings Institute that could not be stated any better: [178]

"Black people who succeed often walk on pins and needles because they realize that their success, and more so maintaining it, is precarious. As a result, some Black people aim to make white people feel comfortable.

Many of us are mostly socialized to do so. It is often a survival strategy for our lives during police encounters or economic survival in boardrooms. Some of us who succeed may experience "survivor's remorse" because we are some of the few to "make it." We actually embody the American Dream and become the in-person example to people who do not want to admit that systemic racism exists. We may even convince ourselves that racism is more prominent on the individual level than the institutional level. We simultaneously represent racial progress but are also most likely to be subjugated to racial discrimi-

nation because of the predominately-white spaces we are embedded within. We experience a chronic form of double-consciousness and admitting as such can often lead us to being conscious of the slow death we often experience through the cumulative racist cuts and hurdles we encounter. The American Dream being achievable for a few does not absolve the system and an imperfect union, even when some of those successful people try to rationalize systemic racism away.

In most instances: When Black parents worry about their straight-A student's traffic encounters with the police more than they do a potential accident, this is because of experiences with racism. When a Black couple is about to have a baby and has to think consciously about what hospital to deliver in so they can obtain equitable care, this is racism. When a Black parent worries about their child attending a prestigious university outside of an urban area, this is often because of the racism they worry about them encountering driving to the school and even once physically on the campus of the school. And even more urban universities are not absolved from racism.

Systemic racism is not simply a thing of the past. It is up close and personal in the present."

Another scenario is regarding *Black delusion* and has no bearing to the success of Black individuals. It is characterized by the "*Black Caterer*". Colloquially, the "*Black Caterer*" is referred to as an "*Uncle Tom*" but it goes much deeper than that. These individuals have an identity crisis and problem with their own self-esteem. There are some Black individuals who respond to White people with a polite catering subservient respect, while relating to people of their own race with disrespect. The White people they cater to can be less educated, less successful and poorer than the "*Black Caterer*". The Black individuals they disrespect can be more educated, more successful and smarter than the "*Black Caterer*". The "*Black Caterer*" views himself as inferior to Whites, and has diminished self-respect, wishes he / she were White and bears shame of his own culture. This can apply to people in general. There are some White people who wish they were Black and who value the "Black persona" above their White social location. Likewise with Asians and other minorities. The "*Black Caterer*", too, is caught up in the "*Matrix of racism*". It is a challenge for African Americans and minorities in general to have "*relational balance*" in contemporary American society because racism is historically and contemporarily ever present and dominates diverse relationships in American society. It is also a challenge for White people to have relational balance because they either have "*racist residue*" or are entrapped in the "*Matrix of racism*". Racism blurs the lines in human relationships in American society. Everyone in the world has being a human being in common, yet they relate to each other in uncommon terms.

Chapter IX
Overview of a University Diversity Initiative

The University of Chicago, like other higher education institutions in America, is not blind to the issue and challenges of diversity. Many higher learning institutions have programs and policies in place to deal with the issues of diversity however; they can address the issues of diversity more effectively. A most significant component of the university diversity strategy is that they need to have an ongoing program that teaches and trains students and university personnel. Without this, the origin and root of racism will not be addressed. Serious, capable, and dedicated people who are dedicated to creating a positive university-learning environment run the existing diversity programs at UChicago. They consider a successful diverse learning environment a "core institutional value." Their efforts warrant high praise and respect. The recommendations mentioned in Chapter V of this book is intended to supplement what they are already doing.

University of Chicago Diversity & Inclusion Statement

"Diversity is critical to the process of discovery. Here, different backgrounds, viewpoints, and perspectives are not only sought after and encouraged, they are the building blocks that make rigorous inquiry possible. While there is still much work to be done, we are committed to enabling all people to participate in the life of the University." [179]

The University of Chicago Diversity Commitment Statement

"Diversity is not only an ideal to which we strive, but a core institutional value."

We are dedicated to creating an environment where people of different backgrounds feel valued and where their ideas and contributions can flourish. While the University has made significant strides in creating a more inclusive campus, there is still much work to be done.

We promise to remain vigilant and dedicated—ceaselessly working to identify and remove barriers to full participation. For our efforts to be successful, this work needs to happen at a grassroots level and an institutional one. " [180]

It is one thing to have a diverse environment, a commitment to diversity, and a core value as an ideal to which one strives; however, it is a completely different thing to construct an environment supportive of diversity goals and ideals. Without a reinforcing environment, goals and ideals will operate in an ambiguous state or fail. Most institutions have noble goals for diversity but operate in an environment that is not supportive. A supportive environment needs to be developed, constructed by training, and conditioning the institutions infrastructure.

I sincerely believe the diversity staff is dedicated to their mission however, they are limited as to what they can accomplish by budget restraints and a lack of diversity educational programs that extends to students, the university staff, personnel, instructors (to construct a supportive environment), the alumni association employees. Investigators and investigations, such as conducted by Attorney Jackie Hennard, subjugate Diversity & Inclusion efforts. Denial of racist incidents is counter-productive to diversity efforts. These incidents should be used as learning tools instead of being covered up. They are aware that discrimination is a problem in the university environment otherwise; they would not have a diversity initiative. Budget allocation is an indicator of how dedicated the university is to diversity. The problem should be of primary concern not only in educational institutions but also as a learning process that develops people to live constructively in the general society, starting in the elementary schools. Institutions of higher learning should be training grounds for students to participate productively in society, not just professionally but in relationship to others. White people understand racism, discrimination and prejudice is a widespread problem in America. If they took it seriously, the problem would be resolved. That the problem has existed for over 500 years is evidence that White people are overtly conscious, subtly conscious, unconscious, and / or complicit racist. Polio, the Flu, HIV, Cancer, Chickenpox, Measles, Mumps, Rubella, Diphtheria and many more diseases that have been cured because Americans made the effort and provided the resources to fix the problem. Racism, discrimination, and prejudice is also a disease in America. It a virus that spreads to White youth, innocent beautiful babies that develop into deplorable ugly adults. That racism has been infectious far longer than those diseases mentioned indicates the true nature of White America. The reason racism and discrimination are not yet been resolved is because White people are not the victims. They are the culprits. They are the disease, and they are the cure.

Diverse Interactive Constructs among the Student Body

The University of Chicago, like other institutions, addresses the issues of diversity. The following section identifies some of their efforts and initiatives to create collaboration and change. It is a challenging task to induce students to interact across the lines of their comfort zone. While the university has programs and policies in place with intent to bridge the gap between an advantaged lived experience and a disadvantaged lived experience, still students show little motivation to interact with diverse groups. The following gives an insight into the efforts the University of Chicago has implemented to address the issues of diversity and inclusion. [181]

Existing University Strategic approach to change (including diversity strategies from the University of Chicago, Duke University, Rutgers University, and Harvard University)

"We tackle issues related to diversity and inclusion in a variety of ways, from tapping into behavioral science techniques to using human-centered design to create individualized solutions. But no matter the challenge we're addressing, all our work is grounded in solution-oriented strategies in one of four distinct areas."

A) INFRASTRUCTURE

"Create the conditions and resources needed for sustained efforts across campus."

Programs: D+I Studio, D&I Planning Toolkit, Faculty Diversity Liaisons, Equal Opportunity Programs

B) CLIMATE

"Build a culture of full participation and high engagement for all members of our campus community."

Programs: Inclusive Pedagogy, UChicago Inclusion Workshops, Center for the Study of Race, Politics, and Culture, Center for the Study of Gender and Sexuality, Center for Identity + Inclusion, UChicagoGRAD, Inclusive Climate Grants, Diversity Leadership Awards

C) PEOPLE

"Increase the diversity of our faculty, other academic appointees, postdoctoral researchers, student body, professional staff, and senior leadership. "

Programs: Faculty and Staff Search Training, Provost's Postdoctoral Fellows Program, Pathways Program, Leadership Alliance, Mellon Mays Undergraduate Fellowship, Ivy Plus Reimagining Pathways to the Academy Consortium

D) COMMUNITY

Create skills and opportunities for meaningful scholarly, professional, and personal engagement with our community in a context of partnership and collaboration.

Programs: Community Engagement Grant Program, Office of Civic Engagement, Student Civic Engagement Center

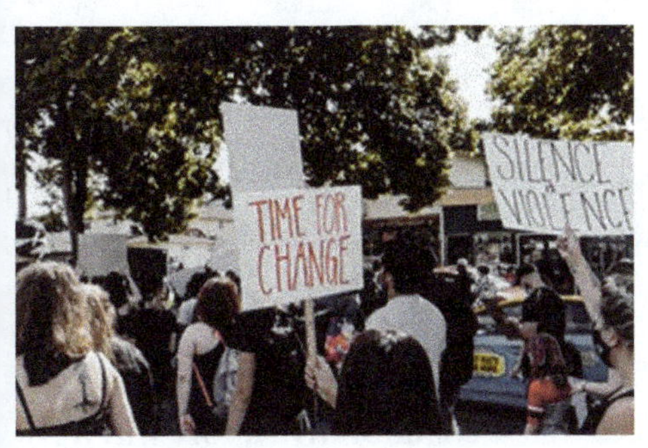

It is encouraging that young White Americans are becoming supportively aware and active against the injustice that has been ongoing for America. Young White youth have more respect and concern for American society than Whites do in prior generations. What is the problem with people who live in hate? They must be sick and unhappy human beings. Being sheltered within the constraints of their secluded mindless ignorant environmental circumstances, they have most likely not experienced unprovoked hostility against them by Black Americans. The good thing is that many young White people reject the negative ignorance of their prior generations and their dysfunctional racist peers. When a young White person was asked what it would take to end racism, discrimination, and prejudice; his answer was: "*The older generation needs to die off.*"

Dr. Barnes' intention is to complement the initiatives at UChicago and in other higher education environments regarding Diversity and Inclusion on the basis they exist. Being honest, and observation of the accomplished results, it is common that institutions and individuals present their "Strategic approach to change" in an idealistic framework more so than with a real commitment to the accomplishment of objectives. Often the individuals responsible for enacting diversity initiatives do not have the required knowledge. They do not make the monetary budget commitment, or they lack the social location to understand the problems and solutions to resolve the problems. This section recommends complements to the already established diversity and inclusion efforts the learning institutions have in place that will make them more effective. There are organizations that are involved in the same effort of developing the minds of young people, same as the University. Kappa Alpha Psi (KAY) men's fraternity is active in working with young people to engage their minds to learn. The fraternity prides itself for its service work in established programs like the Kappa League and the Guide Right Program to assist young men and provide leadership. The same interest is prevalent with women's sororities. Alpha Kappa Alpha (AKA) women's fraternity located at 57th and Stoney Island Avenue is a potential resource. The DuSable Museum is proximate to the University Campus on 57th and Cottage Grove. These are resources that a collaborative effort will have mutual advantage to all involved. In addition, the exposure and experiences with these organizations should not be limited to African American students, but all individuals in the student body should be exposed to these resources. Collaborating with resources in the community will benefit the University and the community. It is challenging for students to integrate their experiences, interacting with others outside of their comfort zone and common cultural interest. The university can construct activities, events and programs that induce and motivate students to interact across their cultural lines. They type of activities that motive students to interact across cultural barriers needs to be brainstormed. It will be a mutually beneficial learning experience to all involved.

The University of Chicago is not alone in its dilemma regarding how to address diversity. Duke University has established a Center for Truth, Racial Healing & Transformation. Duke University was selected by the Association of American Colleges and Universities (AAC&U) as one of 10 inaugural Truth, Racial Healing & Transformation (TRHT) Campus Centers. In theory, The Duke Center for Truth, Racial Healing & Transformation (Duke TRHT Center) is working towards becoming "a formidable and influential vehicle for facilitating transformation at Duke, in Durham, and beyond." The Objectives of The Duke University Program are: [182]

Vision

A world without racism: where empathy, equity, and unity prosper; human variation is valued and seen as an asset essential to the progress and flourishing of the human family; and the life outcomes of all are radically improved.

Mission

To dismantle deeply rooted beliefs in racial hierarchies and disrupt persistent structures and impacts of racism at Duke, in Durham, and beyond.

Goals

1. Uncover, produce, and share accurate and complete narratives about race and racism.
2. Cultivate relationships that celebrate our common humanity, embrace our diversity, and expand the circles of individuals willing to work towards transformation.
3. Foster systemic change wherein every life has equal value and the consequences of a false belief in a racial hierarchy no longer shape our individual and collective experiences or outcomes.

Rutgers University also has incorporates a "*The Truth, Racial Healing, and Transformation (TRHT) Center*" on its campus. Newark (RU-N) is one of 28 national, comprehensive, and community-based initiatives developed by the Association of American Colleges and Universities (AACU) with initial funding from the W. K. Kellogg Foundation. Their Vision, Mission and Goals are; [183]

VISION

The TRHT Campus Center at Rutgers University – Newark (RU-N) will foster and strengthen the collective knowledge and wisdom of the diverse communities in and of the City of Newark, throughout the state of New Jersey and the Northeast Corridor. Drawing on the methodologies and strategies of the humanities and the arts within a social justice framework, RU-N and our community partners will engage in an arc of interactive programming designed to change the narrative about race and race relations in Newark and beyond. The Center will also leverage and support new and existing RU-N and city-wide initiatives to effectively respond to economic and social disparities in our communities and promote equitable growth

MISSION

The Truth, Racial Healing, and Transformation Campus Center at Rutgers University-Newark pursues community engagement and democratic collaboration focused on changing the dominant narrative/perception all marginalized communities in and of the city of Newark and beyond by:

- Connecting our citywide partner network through initiatives that leverage existing and emerging resources to promote equity, access, and transformative positive narratives about the City of Newark and its peoples.
- Exhibiting positive change reflected in measurable outcomes.

GOALS OF THE TRHT CENTER @ RU-N

- Increase Understanding about the Importance of Positive Narratives about Newark.
- Increase positive engagement and perceptions of Newark amongst RU-N administration, faculty, staff, students, and alumni.
- Increase the number of specialized on and off-campus activities utilizing dialogue and dialogic techniques around issues of truth, racial healing, and relationship building.
- Decrease segregation and increase access and equity for Newark Residents by leveraging RU-N resources to reduce poverty and unemployment and strengthen the city's economy by the beginning of the next decade.
- To embed TRHT framework into the ethos, culture, and environment of anchor institutions and other community-based organizations.
- Among all of the Colleges and Universities that recognize the necessity to address diversity, Harvard University seems to take the more aggressive stand and positive initiative in addressing diversity.

"*Harvard University* has released a report *detailing the school's involvement in the U.S. slave trade, including faculty and staff owning slaves and professors teaching racial eugenics. In 2019, Harvard President Lawrence Bacow formed a committee that included representatives from all the schools on campus, and asked them to uncover Harvard's ties to slavery. The committee found that Harvard faculty and staff enslaved 70 people from the school's founding in 1636 to the banning of slavery in Massachusetts in 1783. Some of those who were enslaved lived on campus and were responsible for providing care for Harvard's presidents, professors and students.*"

"Harvard outlined several next steps it said it would take in an attempt to atone for its involvement in the slave trade, including monetary reparations for Black and Indigenous students who are descendants of enslaved persons in the U.S.

"The profound harm caused by the university's entanglements with slavery and its legacies cannot be valued in monetary terms alone," the study said. "Nevertheless, financial expenditures are a necessary predicate to and foundation for redress."

The Legacy of Slavery Fund will be kept in an endowment "strategically invested to support implementation of these recommendations," the report said.

The Ivy League school also plans to further partner with Historically Black Colleges and Universities (HBCUs) through initiatives, such as appointing visiting HBCU professors to Harvard for one year and subsidizing summer, semester or yearlong studies at Harvard for HBCU students.

The school said it is working to identify Black and Indigenous students who are direct descendants of people enslaved in the U.S.

"We further recommend that, in recognition of this lineage, the university engage with these descendants through dialogue, programming, information sharing, relationship building, and educational support," it said."

Harvard University is setting aside $100 million for an endowment fund and other measures to close the educational, social and economic gaps that are legacies of slavery and racism. This policy by Harvard sets an example for other organizations, colleges and universities. Harvard's actions are a commentary on a wider conversation about the impacts of centuries of slavery, discrimination and racism. While Harvard had notable figures among abolitionists and in the civil rights movement, "The nation's oldest institution of higher education ... helped to perpetuate the era's racial oppression and exploitation." Harvard recommended offering descendants of people enslaved at Harvard educational and other support so they "can recover their histories, tell their stories, and pursue empowering knowledge." Harvard should be commended for taking responsibility for the injustice done to Black people by Whites, even well-meaning White people. While the contemporary offspring of Harvard's White culture is not to blame for the sins of their ancestors, by making this gesture, Harvard is taking initiative to correct past wrongs and setting a base standard for what should be an example for other organizations, institutions, colleges and universities. This action by Harvard exemplifies what it will take to put America on the road to greatness. [184] The difference between Harvard's perspectives on addressing diversity is that most other programs are theoretical. Harvard's program is actionable. It is a well-known fact that meaningful behavior and commitment on the part of White culture is based on how the money is spent.

Diversity programs in America's learning institutions, colleges, and universities indicate good intentions to integrate America and resolve some of the dysfunction and racial problems in the country. However, while intentions are good, the logistics of addressing the problem fall short in most cases. The main shortcoming is the individuals most institutions have directing diversity programs. White people direct the diversity programs in many universities and organizations. White people whose social location alone puts them out of touch with the issues and needs confronting minorities. Their knowledge, instincts and skills to address and implement effective solutions in addressing diversity problems are lacking. Consider the incident mentioned in the Introduction of this book, Chapter I, describing the intent of the U. S. government to assimilate the indigenous culture of Indian children into American culture, to "civilize" the Indian children. Most White people have no awareness of how to interact with cultures who are not White. This same situation exist with White people directing diversity programs in universities aimed at minority and diversity initiatives. I am not saying that no White people have the ability to make a difference. However, my experience at the University of Chicago is that the Diversity initiative, while noble in its intentions, does not have leadership that is effective in addressing the problems. One of the primary issues is trust between Whites and minorities. White people in positions of leadership require much more from minorities to gain their support while with other White people they will support on a handshake. It is an example of "*racist residue*" that exist in the most liberal of White people. Most Whites do not understand the basic and core issues of the problem confronting diverse communities and their efforts will not resolve the problem. It is comparable to a garden of flowers where only the flowers are picked, and the weeds remain. I cannot apologize for stating the facts, based on my opinion and observation. A 25-year-old person is 4'11 inches tall. They are short. To say they are short can be taken as an insult, but it is the truth. The fact that they are short does not mean they do not internalize greatness. Furthermore, to focus on their height, in itself is a bias. Minorities want the same equal rights as Americans to participation in America. White people deny minorities the instruments of domestic tranquility and prosperity that they value for themselves. My intention is not to be insulting. It is to construct what works. White individuals with a middle class social location often have "racist residue", often subtle in its manifestation, but significant enough to obstruct the trust in White people who don't know what to do, but lack trust in qualified minorities to do what works. These people are not qualified to effectively direct a diversity program, especially a community oriented diversity program that involves minorities, whether it is university or government sponsored.

Chapter X
Recommendations for Diversity Program Implementation In a Higher Education Environment

This section of the book outlines recommendations for educational institutions with a diverse student body to consider implementing. An objective of this book is to motivate education institutions to create more comprehensive diversity programs that incorporate its instructors, personnel, employees, staff, students, and a program curriculum that significantly addresses diversity issues. Effective diversity programs involve multiple dimensions of learning and synergy development but, definitely, include programs that teach people how to relate to each other, with respect. Unless racism and discrimination are addressed with resolve to eliminate alienating behavior on college campuses throughout America, racism, discrimination, and prejudice will continue to exist, perpetuate, and increase in society. If the purpose of education is to teach and learn, then what is more important than teaching and learning how to live in a society that works for all, a society where people get along with each other? What is more important than for people to get along with each other? American institutions have failed in that area. Diversity learning must be distributed throughout the university community. It is important for both Minority and White individuals to undergo diversity training. Is it wishful thinking to have a diverse environment, bring people together with different backgrounds, and expect synergy? Synergy must be facilitated. Learning about other cultures is a crucial component of the learning process, a critical part of developing mutual respect, and basic to being a self-actualized human being. In most learning environments diversity issues are addresses in a token manner. Frankly, they are ineffective in resolving diversity problems in the long-term. That they create awareness in the short term is a good thing, but they will not induce a long-term change in behavior, nor will they have any long-term benefit to society. The traditional subjects that students learn have long-term benefits for career and professional achievement. Once learned, people never forget, 1 + 1 = 2, or the States in America, or the fact the chemical formula for water is H_20. However, the exposure students get regarding diversity is not as substantially internalized. People leave the learning environment and interact in a society exposing them to a multitude of ideologies. Many that are racist and discriminatory against others. Are the current format of diversity programs designed to withstand the racist influence people will encounter once they enter "the real world?" Unlike learned traditional subjects that are applied in the "real world" and developed to produce long lasting effective results to sustain careers, diversity learning does not influence the "real world" in the same substantial way. If it did then America would be a different society than it is. Ideologies can be and often are challenged. Diversity issues are addressed in learning institutions as a temporal condition, rather than as a central condition, an issue that is meant to have a lasting impact on society. Diversity should have reference to ideologies that give a stable and positive reflection to individual differences, open discussions in learning group sessions instead of negative reference to or focus on individual's skin color, religion, or gender orientation. People will relate to each other as human beings and discussions about individual differences will be comfortable and easy to deal with. Admittedly, this is optimistic in terms of our present society perspective but realistic in terms of what America can achieve.

There is another reason it is important to resolve the issue of racism and discrimination, **NOW**. One theory that White people are such ardent racist and resistant to equality for minorities because they fear that if minorities were equal, minorities would treat Whites the same way Whites treat minorities. This indicates a guilt complex based on fear and insecurity.[185] The current tone and standard for interpersonal relationships involving the races in American is conflictive and discriminatory. If this does not change now, it will not change in the future. Remember, the colonist came to America and treated the Indians in the only way they were accustom, aggressively dominating and destroying their way of life. That is the way Whites were treated by the nobility in Europe. In turn, they treated the Native Americans the same way.

According to Forbes: [186]

- 80% of the population identified as white in 1980; by 2000 that had dropped to 69.1% and by 2019 it is estimated to stand at 60.1%.
- Estimates released by the U.S. Census Bureau ahead of the 2020 results show that in 2019 more than 50% of those under 16 identified as a minority.
- The 2010 to 2020 decade will be the first in the nation's history in which the white population declined in numbers.

By the year 2060, White people are projected by the U.S. Census Bureau to comprise 36% of the United States population. Hispanics (32%) and Blacks (16%) will make up 48% of the U.S. population, others (13%) and Asians (8%). The point is that Whites are going to be a minority in the foreseeable future, within the next 40 years, within this generation.[187] This could explain the reason Donald Trump and the Republican Party wants to stop immigration of Hispanics into the United States. However, the population shift is inevitable, and Whites are scared and insecure that they will become minorities and suffer the same fate they, themselves, inflicted on minorities. Frankly, everyone in America should be treated fairly, as American citizens, including Blacks, Hispanics, Asians, Others and Whites. However, the current tone of American interpersonal interracial relationships is discriminatory. It is important to change this tone to assure Americans are socialized today, to treat people fairly, in the future. Then, some think that White people will destroy America before they accept the reality of the population shift. Is White psychology conducive to getting along with others, different from themselves, without conflict? That is questionable and a significant reason for educational institutions to focus on diversity education. History and contemporary conditions, say **"NO"**, they cannot. In a sense, a stronger focus on Diversity education can be seen as a program to save the future of America, including White America.

This author will present recommendations that will give positive contribution to issues of diversity in the higher education learning environment (Appendix 1, Exhibit 10). One of the main reasons Dr. Barnes wanted to have his article printed in the University of Chicago Alumni magazine was to inform the public and University Alumni of the accomplishments of Black people, beginning with the accomplishment of a Black person. There are hundreds of thousand, millions of successful and accomplished Black people. However, White culture only hears of Black gangs, Black violence, Black athletes, and Black entertainers. They stereotype Black people based on the news media and half-truths that only convey the negative aspects of Black culture or the intellectually benign characteristics. The truth is that White culture has considerably more deplorable incidents of gang violence, murders, and criminally despicable behaviors. Black culture is thriving with an abundance of professional individuals. However, the White media keeps this a secret from White people to repress the reality of White feelings of inferiority, White jealousy, and White insecurity and to perpetuate White superiority.

Recommendations

Develop / Establish *Relational Balance* in the Learning Environment

Relational Balance refers to an environment with-in which people interact with each other, and each person or persons understand their respective cultural locations relative to other individuals. Individuals embrace and respectfully appreciate the individual differences in others. The following are reasonable assumptions for a diverse learning institution:

1. Some White students come into the learning environment with racist residue.
2. Some minority students come into the learning environment with an defensive and apprehension that they are entering a discriminating environment (an unfriendly environment).
3. Some minority students come into the learning environment with resentment against White culture and harbor feelings of anger.
4. Students Black and White have reluctance to interact with each other unless the institution constructs proximity (dormitory roommates, integrated dormitories, collaborative class assignments etc).

Relational Balance requires positive interaction between individuals, inclusive of their respective differences, cultural location, social location, and cognitive location. The focus should be based on common values with appreciation for differences. In other words, if a White person from Australia interacts with a Black person from Mississippi, they would relate based on common values rather that stereotypes. Establishing relational balance accomplishes this. Learning about each other's differences based on *relational balance* is considered a growth experience. The foundation of a working diversity program is first to put everyone involved in a *relational balance*. Constructing the Relational Balance in Americans is a learning process. This includes all students in the student body, professors, instructors, administration, and everyone at the institution in a position to facilitate learning among the student body. The method for achieving a relational balance is to have the people take a designed curriculum on Diversity education. The purpose is to create a universal awareness of the diverse cultures at the University. Students should have an insight into the diverse entities they will encounter during their attendance at the education institution and in society. In addition, this is a program session to establish the social position of the variety of diverse entities, allowing them to confront their predisposed opinions and attitudes and be exposed to the opinions and attitudes of others. The basic objective is for everyone is in the learning community to achieve a common goal, to learn about others, discover common interest and appreciate differences. This experience should confront individuals with their predetermined attitudes in conjunction with the realities of the diverse groups they will encounter. The positive impact of *Relational Balance* should have a lifetime impact.

Professors responsible for the education of students are human. They bring into the teaching process predetermined attitudes. The elimination of bias, by learning bracketing techniques is important for professors and instructors to learn. This allows the instructors to evaluate the objectivity with which they can educate and teach students. Successful bracketing techniques on the part of the instructor can also have motivational results for the student.

Provide extensive and periodic ongoing diversity training for university personnel on a regular basis. Especially personnel in positions that deal with minority and diversity encounters, (The Alumni department personnel, The University police, Professors, University Staff, and the students themselves). Issues facing America relative to Islamic issues, African American issues, Asian issues, Hispanic issues, LGQTB issues and Caucasian issues should be openly dialogued so everyone is on the same page of understanding with a positive perspective (relational balance). For example, Asian students, for the most part, are a close-knit group and find comfort in their own group settings. However, Asians have much to offer this, other university environments, and all students therein. Asians can contribute to all students in providing insight into what gives them the academic focus they stereotypically possess. This insight will be helpful to all learners in this institution. If there is isolation and discrimination in the university environment, without committed and qualified programs, the Universities will only achieve mediocre success in contributing to society. A dedicated effort to diversity education will bring people together to enhance learning and improve relationships and conditions on campus and in society. There is more to teaching and training the complete human being than book knowledge. The lack of social skills and acceptance of all human beings regardless of race, color, creed, or gender orientation, the lack of which makes book smart people appear stupid and ignorant. "*The Central Park Karen*" proves that. The sharing and exchange of knowledge on diverse cultures is one thing that students can learn in a university or college environment that brings people together from all over the world. It is a wasted opportunity not to learn about the positive aspects of other cultures when one has the opportunity. The university is the perfect setting to take advantage of this unique opportunity. Cultural exchange is an advantage of campus life that has not been fully nurtured. The diverse and integrated environment of college campuses in America does not take full advantage of the opportunity of cultural exchange.

Another activity associated with establishing Relational Balance is to assign incoming freshmen another freshman of a different ethnic background in an exchange program. Have them correspond and communicate with each other on a regular basis (daily or weekly for a significant period). These students should then keep a log of their interactions / conversations and submit it as a writing assignment at the end of the prescribed period.

Deploy Students as Academic Coaches and Adjustment Coaches for New Students

Students can serve as academic and adjustment coaches for other students. Incoming freshmen are confronted with new experiences adjusting to college and university life. New experiences can have an overwhelming effect for culturally diverse students coming into a new environment. Adjustment can be challenging; culturally, socially, and academically. During the four years in college or university life have sophomores coach incoming freshmen, juniors coach sophomores, and seniors coach juniors. The knowledge and experience of upper class (upper grade class) individuals should filter down to freshmen and subsequent lower class (lower grade class) individuals after the first four-year cycle, then on an ongoing basis. This program will allow lower-grade class individuals, respectively to gain from the insights and experiences of senior students who have been through experiences lower-grade class individuals have yet to face.

Publication and Distribution of Information including American Association of University Press (AAUP) strategies for Minority Academic Publications

The publication of literature is one way people practice their first amendment right. It is also a way people can express their ideas, opinions, and viewpoints to the public forum. Whites control the college and university publications apparatus at all levels. Minorities have little to no voice in what is published nor is there significant minority presence in their publications. This is considerable restriction to enacting equal opportunity in college publication and in the general society.

At the University undergraduate, graduate and alumni levels, Minority Students should have publications that address their interest. For example, a publication, theoretically called *The Minority Report*, will involve the dissemination of news, articles, and information relative to the respective groups. The dissemination of information is currently White controlled. Whites control articles that are published in campus and Alumni publications. Their primary interest is proven not to give significant or positive attention to the needs and interest of minorities. One thing for sure, the articles published on minorities in the White media are mostly published by Whites that do not deal with core issues concerning minorities in the way minorities would deal with their own issues. Learning is to get the information from the person whom it is relevant to, instead of someone with a limited perspective on the needs of minority cultural issues is important. For example, a Publications relating to the following, as a suggestion:

The Asian Minority Report
The African American Minority Report
The Hispanic Minority Report
The Islamic Minority Report
The LQGBT Minority Report

Minority students and minority Alumni should have their own university publication separate and apart from the White University Student body and the White Alumni Association. Call it the Minority Report (Undergraduate, Graduate and Alumni). An Alumni publication that addresses relevant society phenomena, the accomplishments of Black and minority individuals who are students or university Alumni will form a tighter bond between the university and alumni, resulting in increased minority alumni contributions. Making the general student body, the alumni and the public aware of minority accomplishments will enable positive perceptions. Certainly, most individuals graduating from a prestigious university have a great story to tell and most likely have a life direction worth sharing. Regarding the accomplishments of minority individuals, White media does not accomplish this adequately and in the general society, White media rarely gives adequate positive coverage and publication to minority phenomena. Awareness of the many accomplishments of minority students and alumni can reconstruct and destruct stereotypes that are unaddressed or not factual. This can have potential to facilitate more collaboration and exchange between diverse factions of the student body. Minorities should have their own publication separate from that of the White controlled University undergraduate, graduate, and alumni publications. The backdrop issue, the catalyst of this book, and the impetus for the Case Study (Chapters IV thru VII) is because of controversy to have an article printed in the University of Chicago Alumni magazine. An article written by a Black Alumni praising the University. When it comes to positive effort by Black people often Whites are blinded by their own racism or *racist residue. Racist residue* restricts White people from seeing the beauty in the forest because they have blockage by the rotten trees in their culture and heritage.

This problem is not limited to publications on the college or university campus or in the university community. This is a problem throughout the entire college and university publications industry and throughout the society. Discriminatory practice in the American Association of University Press (AAUP) is a problem. The Association of American University Presses (AAUP) is an organization of more than 150 international nonprofit scholarly publishers. Since 1937, the Association of University Presses advances the essential role of a global community of college and university publishers whose mission is to ensure academic excellence and cultivate knowledge. The Association holds intellectual freedom, integrity, stewardship, and diversity and inclusion as core values. The inclusion and diversity claim in their mission appears to be promotional "fluff" that truth. AU Presses members are active across many scholarly disciplines, including the humanities, arts, and sciences, publish significant regional and literary work, and are innovators in the world of digital publishing." They forgot to add that their service is primarily available for White authors. The AAUP is considerably neglectful of publishing literature authored by Black authors. At the University level and in the academic arena the AAUP controls the literature they publish. The decisions they make when publishing Academic or meaningful literature is significantly in favor of White authors and discriminating against minority, especially Black, authors. First, their discrimination is evident when the works they publish is examined. Another reason the AAUP is prone to be discriminatory in its' selection of works is evident when one looks at the demographics of the leadership governance of the AAUP. The fact that the leadership in the AAUP is over 80% White can contribute to the lack of the publication of minority literature. However, the bigger reason is not that the leadership is White; White leadership lacks diversity in the literature they select to publish. Literature that expresses different viewpoints is limited because the AAUP significantly limits the viewpoints of minority and African American authors. This is a form of racism. The fact that the AAUP leadership is almost 90% white and lacks diversity is a possible factor in their mindset lacking the perception to acknowledge quality literature from minority authors.

TABLE 1

Race and Ethnicity of Governance Leaders and of All Full-Time Faculty Members at Four-Year Institutions

Race/Ethnicity	Governance Leaders	Full-Time Faculty Members
American Indian or Alaska Native	0.8%	0.4%
Asian	3.2%	11.5%
Black or African American	4.7%	5.7%
Hispanic or Latino	2.2%	4.9%
Middle Eastern	0.2%	n/a
Multiracial	1.4%	1.1%
Native Hawaiian or Other Pacific Islander	0.2%	0.1%
White	87.3%	76.2%

Sources: 2021 AAUP Shared Governance Survey and IPEDS Human Resources component, 2018–19.

Note: The reported IPEDS percentages exclude the categories "race/ethnicity unknown" and "nonresident alien." The category "Middle Eastern" is not among those used in IPEDS. The other categories are taken from IPEDS. The survey percentages on senate chairs exclude respondents who did not wish to report their race/ethnicity (4.9 percent of respondents).

This author performed an unofficial research study (Appendix 2). Ten AAUP publishers were contacted, including the University of Chicago Press. The author sent a copy of his manuscript (not this manuscript but one on the environment) to each of the AAUP publishers along with his credentials. The credentials of the author made him significantly more qualified than most authors whose books the AAUP does publish. Another difference is that the experiment provided a picture of the author who is a Black man. Upon receipt of the manuscript and request to publish, each of the 10 AAUP publishers rejected the manuscript, including the University of Chicago Press. All providing the same boilerplate response, while at the same time supporting the necessity to address the subject matter. It is obvious that the AAUP does not contribute to the academic community except in a way to scrutinize published literature and selectively publish literature that does not address the issues viewpoints of minority authors. In other words, this author considers the AAUP part of the same America that has "*racist residue*" and limits the voices of Black intellectuals. The fact that each of the publishers rejected the manuscript was not as telling as the fact that the manuscript was rejected with the same boilerplate responses (Appendix 2).

The solution to this problem is for the Historic Black Colleges and Universities (HBCU's) to establish their own publication organization that gives a voice to Black and minority authors. Since African American and minority authors cannot depend on the AAUP to publish their literature, the AAUP should be eliminated from consideration by Black and minority authors.

Qualified Personnel to Investigate Racial and Discrimination Complaints

In general, White people are not qualified to investigate White racism, except in rare cases. At least this is the case with Jackie Hennard, She is / was not qualified in the opinion of this author, to be a University of Chicago discrimination investigator. It is a challenge to find a White professional person void of "*racial residue.*" That does not mean White professionals cannot do a fair and competent job of investigating discrimination complaints. It does mean that few are able to understanding the subtle, subconscious, implicit bias, and covert acts of racism, prejudice, and discrimination. **Most White people are good and decent people** who, by environment and social location, are likely to be influenced by a "*racist residue.*" Many reject the overtures of racism encountered in the early stages of their developmental process and throughout their lived experiences. Someone who has background and knowledge of racial phenomena in a diverse environment is better qualified. Someone such as a person of minority status would be better qualified, educational qualification not excluded. The depth of implicit and explicit bias in White culture is widespread, to the extent that they cannot hide it or cover it up. It is natural to the personality of many White people, too many, to empathize behavior with overt or subtle acts of racism, prejudice, and discrimination. [188]

Someone of minority status who has background and understands the overt and subtle acts of racism is better qualified to reconcile conflicts and educate the perpetrators with empathy. Theoretically, but not necessarily, Black individuals, are more qualified to detect and adjudicate incidents of racism based on their social location. White individuals who have escaped the "*matrix of racism*" and who are void of "*racist residue*" can potentially serve the role as *diversity compliance investigator*. The person investigating the discrimination complaint, regarding the situation herein, Attorney Jackie Hennard, was not qualified to understand the realm of racist behaviors. Based on her investigation process / procedure, her being white, her social location, her perspective was influenced with a "*White empathy*" (*racist residue*) that was skewed with a skeptical perspective toward Black behavior, behavior that would be totally acceptable if White people acted in the same manner. The reason Attorney Hennard is considered inadequate is because she spent more time investigating Dr. Barnes than she did investigating the situation that occurred between

Dr. Barnes and Sarah Nolan. Often White people are prone to cover up racist acts by White people rather than condemn White racism or provide education that gives more understanding to the problem. Recommending that White people receive diversity education is an admission of White "*racist residue*." Some White people feel shamed with the confrontation they harbor "*racist residue*." They would rather stay racist than fix themselves. Sometimes people who are sick refuse to get medical attention.

Benefits to the University

If Black people felt the University of Chicago or other institutions Black students attend were more responsive to their needs and more opened to Black participation, then post-graduation (alumni) Black contributions to the University would increase. Dr. Barnes has talked to several Black Alumni who have no interest in giving money to their University alma-mater. They feel the score is even. They got the great education, and the University got paid. Even score. In my opinion, this attitude on the part of both parties needs to change. It is in everyone's best interest to see their alma-mater university flourish and as great as the university is, it can get better. The more resources the university has the better it can get. This is the attitude of many Black and minority alumni through the college and university community, nationwide. However, improvement also involves improving the cultural values and the mindset of the university community and the student body of all cultures. This can only be done when racist incidents are addressed with a strong resolve and when the issue of diversity in a diverse environment is competently addressed. Dr. Barnes' case was handled to protect the culprit (Sarah Nolan and the University Alumni Association) and rationalize (in a very weak manner) justification for the ban. However, if the ban were justified it would not have been lifted by Ms. Gould, the university associate provost. This incident that happened to Dr. Barnes is an example of why Black Alumni do not have any monetary empathy for their alma-mater institution after they graduate. Dr. Barnes would like to see this changed, but first Black students have to see change in the White universities.

Revision of Investigative Policy

Dr. Barnes recommends that the University modify their investigation policy. In the case described herein, the Police acted solely on the word of a University of Chicago employee, against a University of Chicago Alumnus. The police should have gotten both sides of the story before they acted. Is it their policy to enact restrictions against people who are the objects of complaints rather than get to the bottom of the issue, find out the truth? Is it university policy to consider an individual guilty without investigating the incident? It is when the incident involves a White person accusing a Black person. When a White person is accused, is the same procedure involved? Probably not and in this case obviously not. The campus police failed to act responsibly in this case. This procedure needs to change, especially for minor controversies. The procedure by Assistant Police Chief Nee was flawed.

The investigation procedure by Attorney Jackie Hennard was also flawed. She investigated Dr. Barnes, the complainant. The way Attorney Hennard proceeded to investigate Dr. Barnes gives the impression of preconceived intent to find guilt in Dr. Barnes. Or, Attorney Hennard had preconceived intent to find no-charge against Sarah Nolan. Or Attorney Hennard was inadequate and unqualified for the job. Or Attorney Hennard, herself, was racist or compliant with racist behaviors. The fact that Attorney Hennard did not want to disclose any information in her report and findings is suspect.

Therefore Dr. Barnes recommends that investigations include the following:

1. Campus Police should, in such cases, investigate both sides of the story before acting.

2. The investigative person should disclose findings of the investigation to both parties, the complainant and respondent. Procuring information in the beginning can alleviate escalation of minor problems or misunderstandings. It will also save time.
3. If possible, the parties involves should be confronted in proximity with each other in a session mediated by the diversity investigator for the purpose of resolution of complaints and resolving misunderstandings.
4. The investigative person should be someone who understands the nature of interpersonal interactions, the subtleties of racism, the overtness of racism, prejudice, discrimination, and who understands the difference between misunderstanding and wrong, someone who understands Black and White cultural values and norms, as well of stereotypes. Finally, this person should be someone with a reconciling oriented mindset.
5. The investigation should focus on resolution, learning, understanding and reconciliation rather than guilt, punishment, or defamation. This applies to all parties involved in the complaint, unless it involves blatant racist or violators with intent. In that case they have no place in the academic learning environment. Institutional policies and programs need to reflect this position.

Problem Resolution Training

It is embarrassing for individuals to be perceived with controversy, especially when framed in a negative light. First impressions people have of Dr. Barnes, who were made aware of the incident that do not know him, is based on controversy. Dr. Barnes' reputation is at stake, his professional image is at stake. All of which could have been prevented. Both, Joanne Knee and Sarah Nolan refused to resolve the matter before it escalated to the provost level and required more

University resources to resolve than necessary. This demonstrates a lack of ability to resolve conflict with mindful intelligence, a low emotional IQ. If they had approached this incident in a more intelligent manner, it would have reflected positive on the University. Problem and conflict resolution is an area that the University of Chicago Police Department (UCPD) and obviously, persons of leadership positions in the university need to learn. The university should have ongoing training in problem and conflict resolution for its police and management and it will be a good idea to have students take seminars on this topic. This is a diverse environment, with different cultures, ideologies, religions, and views. Learning tolerance and understanding individual differences only creates and enhanced the learning environment. It is also an area the University of Chicago can take leadership thus enhancing the university's already established reputation for academic excellence. One of the privileges of attending The University of Chicago is that it gives students the opportunity to experience and learn from diversity. To offer a series of workshops for students on various aspects of diversity, problem resolution and collaboration would be valuable.

Emotional Intelligence as it Relates to Conflict and Problem Resolution in Racism, Discrimination and in Life

The reason it is important to understand the value of Emotional Intelligence in life and lived experiences people encounter is because racism, discrimination and prejudice is a characteristic of people who display a low emotional intelligence or emotional quotient (EQ). In the case of the situation experienced by Dr. Barnes described herein, it can be argued that the people who were directly involved in the complaint against Dr. Barnes, demonstrated characteristic of people with a low emotional intelligence. Their exhibition of a low EQ may not be pervasive in all situations they encounter but in this specific situation involving Dr. Barnes, one must consider it was handled by people who exhibited a low EQ. Emotional intelligence (or emotional quotient or EQ) is thought to be a quality that impacts almost area of life and an individual's lived experiences. Many experts believe that EQ is more important than IQ in determining life success. A low EQ can negatively impact not only your interpersonal relationships but also your mental and physical health. [189]

Self-emotional appraisal concerns an individual's capacity to understand his/her emotions and to be able to exhibit these emotions. The self-appraisal by people who interact with others in the performance of their work, is important, especially if there is high amount of interaction with customers in service jobs. An individual should understand their own emotions, feelings, and beliefs before they understand those of others, because emotions, feelings and beliefs have a direct influence on social interactions. EQ becomes more important when people operate in a capacity where their jobs and livelihood are dependent on the people they interact with. "Researchers have found the need of service employees to manage their emotions in order to manage emotions of the customers, and this is applicable across education industry to the hospitality industry."[190]

The EQ of individuals directly influences the culture of the work environment especially if an individual is in a position of leadership. The EQ of leadership in the work environment has an influence on the other employees. Whether that influence is positive or negative depends on the EQ demonstrated by the management or leadership of the organization. The effectiveness of an organization is often a factor of the EQ prevalent in the organizational culture based on the EQ of leadership.

- "Perception of other's emotions: Accurate social perception allows individuals to gain considerable knowledge of other group members' attitudes, goals, and interests, which should enable influence by identifying, understanding, and addressing members' unstated needs and creating goals that might be accepted." [191]

- "Understanding of others' emotions: EI members may improve the performance of their group. The ability to orchestrate one's emotions as per the need of the group helps in accomplishment of the group task, which in turn influences group performance." [192]
- "Manage emotions: The effective management of emotions enables a member to influence the group by changing other members' emotional reactions to particular courses of action; these influencers draw upon past experience and apply on them." [193]

People with higher socioeconomic status often (SES) have lower emotional intelligence, especially at high levels of inequality. *"Studies published in Social Psychological and Personality Science found that people of higher socioeconomic status (SES) score consistently lower on tests of emotional intelligence, especially when they perceive high levels of inequality in their community. The researchers suggest that high SES and high subjective inequality promotes increased self-focus and less motivation to attend to others' emotions."* [194]

People of higher SES are more concerned with themselves and less concerned about others. This characteristic has considerable psychological implications but in terms of racism, discrimination, and prejudice, definitely aligns with the behaviors of racist. This does not necessarily indicate that people of higher SES are racist or prejudice. SES individuals can be White, Black, Hispanic, Asian, Jewish, or Muslim. The benign neglect of SES individuals for others is not dependent on race, ethnicity, or culture. The dependent factors in this case are wealth, economic status, and money which determines privilege. Their lack of concern can be directed at anyone of lesser means and economic standing. However, some misdirected white people consider themselves to be better than Black, Hispanic, Jewish, Asian, and Islamic people merely because they are White. They perceive themselves as privileged (White privileged). The perception of greater superiority and privilege along with the notion that others are not equal to the White race, "*intensifies the magnitude of the differences between those who are low and high in SES, the differences in emotional intelligence among those with varying levels of SES should be more pronounced when people perceive more inequality.*" [195] According to the study, there was no significant difference in emotional intelligence for people who perceived little inequality. This indicates that racism, prejudice, and discrimination are characteristics that can result from people who perceive unequal status between themselves and others or who perceive themselves superior to others. [196]

"*Role of EI in achieving organizational effectiveness is significant. However, assessment and predictability of EI leading to success is still a very important issue to be addressed. Available literature suggests that facets of EI align well within the framework of achieving goals of the organization and ultimately leading to job satisfaction.*" [197] People who are racist, who discriminate and who demonstrate prejudice behavior towards others often have emotional problems and dysfunctional relationships with others. [198] It is important to understand the EQ of others when considering or putting them in a position of influence in an organization or education environment. The following charts give examples of the characteristics of healthy and unhealthy EQ individuals.

Characteristics of High Emotionally Intelligent people to resolve conflict

Emotional intelligence in this context is a practiced awareness of how emotions affect your communication and organizational efforts, along with thinking through how to leverage emotions (both yours and other people's) to make your points clearer and more relatable and to become more persuasive. Emotional intelligence often leads people to treat others more nicely and to develop empathy for them. But these benefits are tangential positives. They are not the core definition or goal.

1. Before you start arguing, decide how you want it to end.

2. Think how you can make it end well for the other side.
3. Control the circumstances (When are you talking? How are you talking? Who's initiating the call or traveling to the other person's location? Is this all over email or text? Are other people listening in?).
4. Control the emotions.
5. Do not skip the small talk.
6. Adjust (not react) in real time.
7. Listen — and look as if you're listening.
8. If you interrupt, do so strategically.
9. Seek to understand.

Characteristics of people with Low Emotional Intelligence to resolve conflict

What Is Low Emotional Intelligence?

"Low emotional intelligence refers to the inability to accurately perceive emotions (in both yourself and others) and to use that information to guide your thinking and actions."

1. They are argumentative
2. They don't listen
3. They Always Have to Be 'Right'
4. They're Oblivious to Other People's Feelings
5. They Behave Insensitively
6. They Blame Others for Their Problems
7. They Have Poor Coping Skills
8. They Have Emotional Outbursts
9. They Struggle with Relationships

People with partisan mindsets cannot give positive contribution to a university or learning environment. In the case of racism, discrimination, and prejudice they only reinforce the negative and dysfunction that create conflict between people. The work environment and the learning environment does not need people with partisan racist mindsets interacting with others. The university needs people who have knowledge of overt and subtle forms of racism and discrimination to address claims, diffuse conflicts and to establish an environment of collaboration and cooperation. The initial purpose of identifying racism and discriminating behavior in organizations should not be to punish the person demonstrating racism but to educate them and help them to identify the subtle racist and discriminatory characteristics in their behavior. In extreme cases, other remedies may be necessary. [199]

The Critical Importance of Diversity Education as a Central Discipline

What do good White people think about racists? If they believe racists are deplorable then why don't they become active in subjugating the racists to the low-life status in America where they deserve to be? Racist display the same behaviors as ISIS, Al- Qaeda, and other terrorist groups. Or, at least become active in addressing the virus of racism in White culture. According to one journalist, *'There Is No Neutral': 'Nice White People' Can Still Be Complicit in a Racist Society.* [200] It is ironic that good minority people suffer more discriminatory acts in America than deplorable White racist. A primary reason it is important for education institutions to centralize the process of diversity learning is because the education environment is a place to have the continuity that can institutionalize the values of fairness and equality that is currently restricted from minorities in our American society. Additionally, all individuals encounter and pass through the learning system (Elementary through College / University). The Leaning environment is institutionally stabilized in the American socialization process. The Establishment of Relational Balance in a high school environment and on a college campus is a challenging task. However, the process starts with learning. The learning institutions in American are the ideal environment for diversity learning to take place. The learning institutions also have a stable quality which can give stability to a diversity learning program. Positive human relationships can replace the dysfunctional human interactions that have become so prevalent in America. Good White people must take responsibility for allowing the ugly counterparts of their culture to have voice and a significant presence in America. Robin DiAngelo in her book "*White Fragility*" indicates the question that white people should be asking themselves is not *have* I been shaped by race, but *how* have I been shaped by race? DiAngelo is the author of *White Fragility: Why It's So Hard for White People to Talk About Racism.* DiAngelo posits that *"the status quo in the United States is racism."* She further states that *"it is comfortable for me, as a white person, to live in a racist society."* The topic of race needs to have ongoing and have consistent interactive communication. It cannot be avoided and assume progress will be made. Avoidance will only result in stagnation. The education environment is appropriate to positively construct a curriculum and effective program of discourse on diversity. It is the most logical place to effectuate change. [201] In a structured learning environment white people can be encouraged to reflect on how race has shaped their lives, likewise with minority individuals. In a structured learning environment, the process will be ongoing, and the impact can have lifelong potential. White people need to explore and evaluate, how they are complicit in racist systems and recognize their own racism. Nice, white people who passively respond to racism and find solace in being nice people can be racist, themselves. They are complicit with racism and discriminating behavior by doing nothing. "*There is no neutral place.*" This applies to learning institutions who have the capability and responsibility to make a difference and change society, but do not. They are also complicit. [202]

A structured learning environment and curriculum on diversity will help White people and Black people explore, more constructively, issues surrounding, what is means to be White in America as well as what it means to be Black and how these labels have shaped their lives. Sharing these insights will enable both Black and White individuals to develop the relational balance so they can relate with understanding empathies. It should be pointed out, that Dr. DiAngelo is White. It is refreshing to know a White person who tells the truth and has a resolve to address and correct racial inequities. The process of escaping the "*matrix of racism*" eliminating "*racist residue*" begins open acknowledgement and discussion, as Dr. DiAngelo suggests.

According to Dr. Robin DiAngelo "*racism is what happens when you back one group's racial bias with legal authority and institutional control. ... When you back one group's collective bias with that kind of power, it is transformed into a far-reaching system. It becomes the default. It's automatic. It's not dependent on your agreement or belief or approval. Its circulating 24/7, 365*" [203]

Dr. DiAngelo is honestly candid to present an insight into how White people learn values and how they learn to identify with people of color. She states that, "*Pretty much everyone has been taught by white people who were taught by white people who were taught by white people who were taught by white people using textbooks written by, for and about and centering white people but presented as objective and neutral,*" DiAngelo comments. "*Do you feel the weight of that whiteness?*" The culture of racism perpetuated in White culture is learned. That is why it is critical for learning institutions to break the cycle of learned behavior that results in dysfunction in the way Americans interact and relate to each other. Breaking the cycle of racial dysfunction in the learning environment will make America a better country. It will also give our learning institutions a higher purpose. Dr. DiAngelo has issued a challenge to the leaning institutions in America, stating, "*WHITES WILL ALWAYS BE RACIST.*" For the sake of America, we hope this is the one area of her expertise that is inaccurate. If this is to change, learning institutions need to take up the challenge.

It is refreshing to hear White people telling the truth, especially in the learning environment. A Pennsylvania State University sociology professor Sam Richards singled out an "average White guy" in a lecture and used him as an example of how his skin color benefits him over any Black student, even if they have comparable backgrounds and resumes. Richards presented the following scenario to the class:

> *"If I match him up with a Black guy in class, or a Brown guy, even ... who's just like him, has the same GPA, looks like him, walks like him, talks like him, acts in a similar way, has been involved in the same groups on campus, takes the same leadership positions, whatever it is ... and we send them into the same jobs ... the White guy has a benefit of having White skin."* [204]

It is common for Black individuals to work harder, longer, confront more obstacles, and are more challenged than White individuals to achieve the same rewards. A White person in the learning environment or the work environment receives more support than a Black person in the same environment (hidden discrimination). When Black people achieve the same degrees, grades and knowledge or do the same work accomplishment, as bestowed on a White person, it generally takes them more effort. As a result, it can be argued the Black person is potentially smarter and better qualified because they have learned the art of accomplishment despite the obstacles.

Based on this phenomenon, the issue then becomes how the society can enfranchise Blacks and minorities without disenfranchising White people. The one thing that should be a certainty is that Black people need to be integrated into the economic and educational systems in American society. White people created this dilemma and to expect minorities to suffer and pay the price for White racism is asking too much. That is what racism is about; expecting others to suffer so White people can have privilege. Being fair, ethical, moral, or doing the right thing is not part of the White agenda.

Chapter XI
Summary

"Racial categories did not emerge simply as the products of energy – and time-saving cognitive devices, but as functional entities constructed in the service of social power and cultural domination".

(Eberhardt & Randall, 1997)

(Eberhardt & Randall, 1997) [225]

"But suppose God is black, I replied. What if we go to Heaven and we, all our lives, have treated the Negro as an inferior, and God is there, and we look up and He is not white? What then is our response"?

(Kennedy, 1966)

(Kennedy, 1966) [226]

An anomaly is an abnormality, a blip on the screen of life that does not fit with the rest of the pattern. If you are a breeder of black dogs and one puppy comes out pink, that puppy is an anomaly. America gives billions of dollars to Ukraine so Ukrainians can defend themselves against Russian aggression, while neglecting the needs of the American citizens.[205] How does one explain that? Americans are suffering. American cities are deteriorating and American legislators ignore the welfare of Americans. I am not saying America should not help Ukrainians. I am saying that America's first obligation should be to its own citizens. The "*American Reality*" is hiding in clear site.

"An American Reality" is a more insightful and honest look into America's reality than many of the psychology, sociology, and history books in American's schools, learning education system or in America's libraries. White American history avoids teaching the truth about American history or only teaches a portion of truth. They either spin or lie about American phenomena involving White America and the Indians, White America and Slavery, and White America and their racist, discriminating, prejudice cultural socialization process. Even movies spin "so called American heroes" falsely (Cowboys and Indians, Colonist and Native Americans, and White people and Slavery.). White people be a pure race is a lie. *"An American Reality"* tells the truth. At the best, different viewpoints from the contents of this book is merely a different interpretation of the facts (alternative facts). Donald Trump's political advisor Kellyanne Conway coined the term "*alternative facts*". We all know how truthful Trump's administration was and how they invented facts. The only basis for evaluating this book is to comment on the facts presented. American history taught in the schools is a bunch of some truth, some half-truths, misrepresentations, eliminations of facts, and lies. Reluctance to teach the truth about American history is because White people object to the truth being known. They are afraid the truth will cast them in an unfavorable image. They fear the truth. They fear the influence the truth will have on their children. The truth about White cultural reality penetrates the weakness and insecurity in White culture. Inability to handle the truth is weakness. It can be argued that racism, prejudice and discrimination is a manifestation of hatred, hatred for the difference in others and / or because the hater hates himself or herself and reflects the feelings of themselves onto others in order to feel better about themselves. The *self-reflective* process in White people instinctively creates a self-diminishing perspective. Because White people are socialized to hate, discriminate and internalize

prejudice feelings and behaviors, those same criteria are applied to their own self-image. Inability to deal with the truth is an insecurity and a weakness.

People are so focused on being White, Black, Asian, Hispanic, Muslim, or LGBT, that they ignore the fact everyone is a human being. People relationships are constructed without regard to consider the human element in us all. That is one reason people can kill, harm, discriminate, and abuse other human beings without remorse. Seeing someone as Black instead of as human or as Asian or Hispanic or Muslim or Jewish instead of as human makes abuse or harm to others easier, Failure to see others primarily as a human being, disassociates the guilt of doing harm to someone who, in reality, is the same as oneself. Imagery reconstruction allows an individual to envision people different from themselves, which makes it easier and acceptable to treat them different. One obvious example is when a person is labeled as a "criminal". That label allows others to construct a different pattern of relationship with the "criminal". While the "criminal" label may justify different treatment, White culture applies the same analogy to minorities.

Let us take the blinders off and take a capsule view into the truth about White people, their reality, their hypocrisy, and their "*bullshit*." The following is an example of the reality of the character and reality of the true nature of White culture, many, far too many, not all, but enough to damage our United States of America. Consider the following reality of the White American role model, the White American hero. A person respected by White America.

***"Essie Mae Washington-Williams** (October 12, 1925 – February 4, 2013) was an American teacher and author. She is best known as the eldest child of Strom Thurmond, Governor of South Carolina (1947–1951) and longtime United States Senator, known for his overt racism, pro racist, anti-immigration, and anti-segregation policies. **Essie Mae Washington-Williams** is mixed race, she was born to Carrie Butler, a 16-year-old African American girl who* *worked as a household servant for Thurmond›s parents, and Thurmond, then 22 and unmarried. Washington-Williams grew up in the family of one of her mother›s sisters, not learning of her biological parents until 1938 when her mother came for a visit and informed Essie Mae, she was her mother and Strom Thurmond was her father. Essie Mae graduated from college, earned a master's degree, married, raised a family, and had a 30-year professional career in education."* [206]

This historical recount of Strom Thurmond, Governor of South Carolina (1947–1951), longtime United States Senator, ardent racist, sexual abuser, child rapist but in White culture an upstanding citizen and patriot. Frankly, he is a sick, perverted and pathetic individual when it comes to ethical morality and honest decency, but he is a White man who abused and raped a black child so White culture elect him as a senator of the United States of America. Black people have long known the true despicable nature of White culture. White people know how they are also. They know how despicable their culture is and how racist it is. If decent White people want this type despicable 'Strom Thurmond type" "Donald Trump type" human beings to define their culture, then that only indicates the unfitness of White people to be part of the human race. Remember it is the racist behaviors that go unaddressed that perpetuate and motivate the ongoing racist behaviors. While White people are not socially disenfranchised by their racism, racism has a constant negative disenfranchising impact on the lives of Black Americans. However, White people are psychological disenfranchised. White people are inadequate, uncomfortable and experience anxiety, and dissonance when confronted with interracial encounters. White people know racism is wrong. Those who believe it is justified are ignorant stupid deplorable idiots who are a malignancy to America, democracy, the human race, especially to decent White people, and definitely to minorities.

One of the most misleading and false beliefs White people have, is that the White race is a "pure" race. Nothing could be further from the truth.

"Dr. David Emil Reich, a genetics professor at Harvard, and his colleagues analyzed the genetic variants of 846 non-African people, 175 people who live in the sub-Saharan region of Africa, and a 50,000-year-old Neanderthal man. Africans are the only race that has 100 percent human DNA while the rest have Neanderthal DNA in them. While this seems controversial another separate study colludes with the Harvard study."[207]

It can be argued that the White race is a mutation, an evolution of the Black race. Migration into different areas of the World caused humans to evolve. Neanderthals, Homo Sapiens, and other human species of the contemporary human being through the process of genetic adaptation, adopted the characteristics they needed to survive in the geographical climates they migrated to out of South Africa. Northern, colder Climates, into Asia, North America, South America and throughout the world. Migrants into the colder climates did not require the skin and genetic characteristics of the southern warmer climates. Skin colors of individuals in colder regions lost pigmentation to become compatible with survival in colder climates. This is a scientific fact supported by archeologist, geneticist, and historians.

Scientists who compared the skulls and DNA of human remains from around the world say their results point to modern humans (Homo sapiens) having a single origin in Africa." [208]

"Scientists are sure that Homo sapiens first evolved in Africa, *and we know that every person alive today can trace their genetic ancestry to there."* [209]

Why is it important to present information on the origin of the human race, to point out the fact that humans originated in Africa and to establish the fact that White people are mutations that evolved from the African continent? It is important because the basis of White racism is on the false foundational belief in White superiority, and that the White race is a pure race. The entire platform of racism is a concocted falsehood that White people are superior to other races because of the color of their skin. White people have white skin because the mutation process of genetic adaptation genetically altered their characteristics to survive in colder climates, outside of Africa. A better and more understandable argument upon which to base anti-diversity beliefs is "personality differences." In this case, people need to interact to determine the differences in their personalities, values, norms, and beliefs. Argument on race as a demarcation between human beings is flawed and based on misinformation and ignorance. White culture has insecurity to deal with their truth and their reality. That is why they make up their evolutionary origins. Insecurity and a false sense of self-efficacy can be reasons racist characteristics are socialized into White culture. Racism and the socialization of racists are a means White people use to escape their reality. If a person does not accept or like himself or herself, it is difficult for them to accept or like others. The only other rationalization for White racism is that White culture has an evil gene in their DNA that responds to those who are non-White. If that is the case then White racist are unfit to live in the United States of America or in the world among other human beings and are a dangerous threat to humanity. However, let us face it; **all White people are not evil racists**. It is a dilemma how human beings can treat other human beings with violent acts of inhuman indecency. While racist, exist under a false premise of human origin, their ignorance, insecurity, diminished self-esteem, and their racist desire to construct a cultural social location supporting their racist ideology, keeps them from embracing the truth about their reality. Charles Darwin's scientific theory tells the truth.

Charles Robert Darwin is a renowned English naturalist, geologist and biologist, best known for his contributions to evolutionary biology. His theory that all species of life have descended from a common ancestor is now widely accepted and considered a fundamental concept in science.[210] The Theory of Evolution by natural selection is published in Charles Darwin's book "On the Origin of Species, published in 1859. In his book, Darwin describes how organisms evolve over generations through the inheritance of physical or behavioral traits. The theory starts with the premise that within a population, there is variation in traits. According to Darwin's theory, individuals with traits that enable them to adapt to their environments will help them survive and have more offspring, which will inherit those traits. Individuals with less adaptive traits will have survival difficulty and restrictions to passing them on. Over time, the traits that enable species to survive and reproduce will become more frequent in the population and the population will change, or evolve. Through natural selection, Darwin advances that genetically diverse species could arise from a common ancestor.

The process of *Genetic Adaptation* is a biological characteristic with a heritable basis that changes reproduction and/or survival and results from evolution by natural selection. Genetic adaptation is a mutative process that causes organisms to evolve so they survive in the environments in which they inhabit.[211] The best example of human genetic adaptation to climate is skin color, which likely evolved as an adaptation to ultraviolet radiation. Variation among populations in body size and shape also may be at least partially related to adaptation to climate.[212] Since the humanoid species originated in Africa, the truth, explained in Darwinian Theory, clearly evidences that White people are mutations, derived from the African species of humanoids through the process of Genetic adaptation and natural selection.

This is a difficult reality for some White people to embrace, even if it is the truth. White people cannot accept the truth about their reality. This is a basic and substantial weakness in their developmental and socialization process, denial that causes innate insecurity. Despite the abundance of empirical evidence from the fossil record, genetics and other fields of science, some people still question the theory of evolution's validity. Politicians and religious leaders denounce the theory, invoking a higher being as a designer to explain the complex world of living things, especially humans. Naturally the White racist elements in the world pushback against the Darwinian Theory of Genetic Adaptation and Natural Selection, coupled with the empirical evidence that the human species originated in Africa. School boards debate whether the theory of evolution should be taught alongside other ideas, such as intelligent design or creationism. Credited scientists see no controversy.

"Evolution is well supported by many examples of changes in various species leading to the diversity of life seen today. Natural selection, or in other words — variation, heredity, and differential fitness — is the core theory of modern biology".[213] Unfortunately, one can hypothesize that a root of the world and society problems may be attributed to the failure of White culture to accept the truth about themselves. If White people do not accept the fact that Donald Trump lost the 2020 presidential election, understanding the truth about their origin is far beyond their intelligent rational ability.

There are signs of hope when we look at the college campuses around America. White students and minorities from around the United States and around the World interact and attend classes together. Students discover by exposure to common levels of intellect and cognitive congruence that conflict with stereotype presumptions. College students of all cultures and races often have alignment in their thinking about world events, situations, phenomena and visions of the future. The fact that they occupy the same environment gives students awareness of their commonalities. This breaks down barriers of racism and promotes mutual respect for others of different cultures and races. This is one reason education is a valuable tool to mitigate the "race problem."

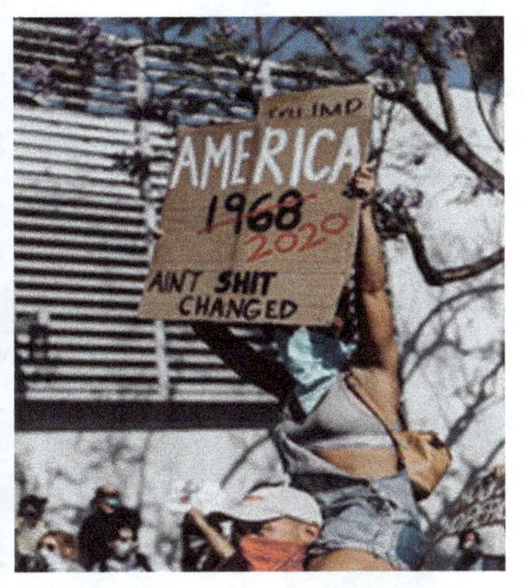

If racism did not exist, slavery would not have existed. The civil war may not have occurred. Thousands of Southern and Northern lives would have been spared. Racist Whites would not have killed black people in the Jim Crow south. Emmett Till would be alive. Dr. Martin Luther King, Jr., Malcolm X, John Kennedy and Robert Kennedy would be alive. However, the truth is that racism did and does exist, causing atrocities in America that are deplorably atrocious and based on a false premise. Racism exists but it does not have to follow us into the future. Intercollegiate integration addresses the questions / issue; Are human beings wired to get along with each other, or not? Can human beings overcome the retarded mentality of racism? Are human beings predisposed to conflictive interactive behavior? According to the examples in the learning environments (elementary, high school, college and universities), racism and conflict is relational abnormality. This state of negative perception between Black, non-White, and White people not only is destructive to America but is also a cause of dysfunctional human behaviors. These dysfunctional behaviors range from minor mental deficiency to atrociously deplorable criminal behavior.

Dr. Martin Luther King Jr. (1929-1968) along with many others gave his living life and died for civil rights and the equality of all people. The Civil War was fought in part to end slavery. Thousands of Americans lost their lives to end slavery. The United States of America fought

World War II against the racist deplorable Nazi regime. Hundred's Thousands of lives were lost in the conflict. From 1619 when slaves were brought to America to the civil war in the 1860-1865, to World War II 1940-1945 to the assassinations of Emmett Till (1955), Dr. Martin Luther King Jr. (1968), Medgar Evers (1963), Malcolm X (1965), and many thousands of other Black people have been killed and lynched by White people throughout the years. White culture is sick. White culture is infested with pathetic deplorable and worthless human beings. White people, themselves, need to address the sickness in their culture. When you consider the atrocities, White people have inflicted on the Indians and the destruction they have conducted on every indigenous people they have encountered, one must ask, what is wrong with these people? While these incidents are extreme in comparison to discrimination on a college campus. Failure to address the "White problem", manifested in White behavior throughout American society on a daily basis is a threat to democracy, America, White people, all decent people and especially minorities. It is common and accepted, by White people, for White people to be racists. Racism seems to be imprinted in White DNA. Racists White people are mutations of the human race. When will it stop?

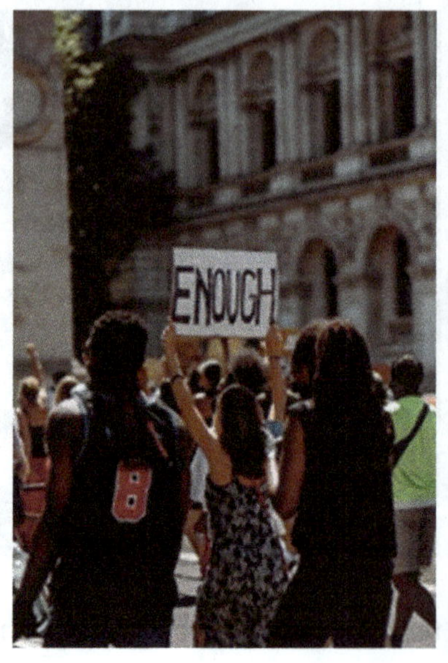

According to Stanford psychologist Sandra Feder there are seven factors that contribute to American racism. [214]

> *"Of the seven factors the researchers identified, perhaps the most insidious is passivism or passive racism, which includes an apathy toward systems of racial advantage or denial that those systems even exist."*[215]

The first three factors are based on categorizations that label people into distinct groups; *factions*, which create **in-group loyalty** and **intergroup competition**; as well as **segregation.** This construct reinforces racist ideology, preferences, and beliefs. "*Simply put, the U.S. systematically constructs racial categories, places people inside of those categories and segregates people on the basis of those categories.*"

The other four factors that contribute to American racism include:

"***Hierarchy,*** *which emboldens people to think, feel and behave in racist ways;*

Power, *which legislates racism on both micro and macro levels;*

Media, *which legitimizes overrepresented and idealized representations of White Americans while marginalizing and minimizing people of color; and*

Passivism, *such that overlooking or denying the existence of racism encourages others to do the same. In short, they argue that the U.S. positions and empowers some over others, reinforces those differences through biased media, and then leaves those disparities and media in place.*"[216]

The methods of racism, discrimination and prejudice have changed over the years. Today racism and discrimination are more subtle than in the past, yet it still exists to a significant degree. The following illustration symbolically indicates the contemporary nature of racism in America.

Since the socialization process in many White families is ineffective in teaching their kids how to be void of *racist residue*, it is the responsibility of education institutions to give constructive direction to American society. It seems that many White families are teaching their kids to think and behave in the same ways of the parents. If America believes there is a future in racism, then the divisions in America will only continue and create the circumstances that make America weak and susceptible to outside influence and a threat to democracy. Outside influences will capitalize on the "divide and conquer" psychology. The same concept exists between democrats and republicans. Characters like Donald Trump make America weak because he creates divisions instead of cohesion. American leadership does not behave with concern about America. Too many American leaders are aligned with divisive ideologies. They only care about their own individual concerns, at the expense of America. "*Ask not what America can do for you, ask what you can do for America*" is a patriotic quote delivered by President John F. Kennedy in his 1960 Presidential Inauguration Speech. However, the practice of Americans is; "*Ask not what I can do for America, but what America can do for me.*" That attitude and psychology is destructive to the American people and to America.

There is obviously a continuity in the learning of prejudice behavior in America otherwise the systematic and institutional presence and establishment of racism would not exist today. For those who oppose Black Lives Matter (BLM), one way to get rid of BLM is to get rid of racism. Racist behaviors are a part of the socialization and development process, to a significant degree, in White culture. BLM is a logical and necessary response to racism. It can be argued that many Black organizations are only created in response to White racism (NAACP, The Black Panthers, The Black Muslims, The Nation of Islam, Black Lives Matter, Congress of Racial Equality - CORE, etc.). Racist traits are ingrained in White culture. Racism is learned behavior that begins when White people attend all white elementary schools; all White high schools, and have limited or no interaction with people of diverse backgrounds. Segregated environments reinforce racist's attitudes. How to break the cycle of prejudiced learned behavior is also a learning process.

America has evolved into a country that has veered off-course from the intentions of the founding fathers. Evidence of this is expressed in the following research data collected:

- A Majority of Americans have an unfavorable view of the Supreme Court. Voters Say decisions are based on political / personal views rather than on the Constitution, 63-30% [217]
- Trust in U.S. democracy has eroded across the political spectrum, a Times/Siena poll found, with 58% of voters saying the system needs reform. [218]
- Public Trust in Government: 1958-2022

Public trust in government remains low, as it has for much of the 21st century. Only two-in-ten Americans say they trust the government in Washington to do what is right "just about always" (2%) or "most of the time" (19%). Trust in the government has declined somewhat since last year, when 24% said they could trust the government at least most of the time. [219]

- Most in new poll say US government needs major reforms, complete overhaul. [220]

Malcolm X would say these pessimistic statements about the current state of America indicate the "chickens have come home to roost." The origin of this statement is from Hindu folklore. When a bird roosts somewhere, it is resting there. This rather old saying, 'chickens have come home to roost', is normally used to mean that the bad things that someone has done in the past have come back to bite or haunt the individual(s).[221] It is karma. One can argue the pessimistic perspective of America portrayed in various media is based on a conglomeration of American behaviors, racism being one primary detrimental behavior manifestation of White America. This perspective in the American media should concern every American who loves their country. These perspectives needs to change. These perspectives sound an alarm indicating America needs to reconcile its divisions. The psychology that prevails America has resulted in a number of related phenomena. For example, the way America handles and votes on the gun crisis phenomenon, the climate change / global warming crisis, the abortion issue, income inequality, racism, discrimination, and prejudice and in general, the divisions that keep Americans for respecting the rights of Americans are all part of the same psychology that overshadows America. Perspective on these issues are divided along political party lines. America is developing characteristics of a country influenced by demagogue psychology. Stereotypically, republicans are racists and democrats are liberals. Political party is not as important as the failure of republicans and democrats to collaborate and find common ground to their differences. The dysfunction in the interactive relationship between democrats and republicans is no surprise. It is characteristic of America's relationship with minorities. Conflict is the norm in political behavioral psychology. This is the same phenomenon between White and Black people. The issues central to America's problems and dysfunction are all related the American psychology that is manifested in America's behavior.

The Universities and colleges can make a significant contribution to the student body, the alumni, and the greater society and be an example for learning institutions around the world if they address the issue of racism and discrimination effectively. Effectively addressing the issues of racism and discrimination will only enhance the already esteemed reputation of renowned universities. Constructing positive racial perspectives is a necessary contribution to American society, an action that will save America from its self-destructive ignorance.

There is a concern that the general society and likewise universities of higher learning are not serious about addressing the issue of racism and discrimination, diversity, and inclusion. That the policy on discrimination, racism and diversity is only for show and not for remedy. I do not believe this and do not subscribe to this opinion. The problems of diversity are complex and challenging, often overwhelming. A case can also be made that White people do not know how to solve the problems of racism infecting our society. White society is reluctant to do the things that solve the problem. The same things that happen in White communities will solve the problems in Black communities (investment in the communities, investment in the infrastructure of Black communities, investment in jobs in the Black community, investment in education in the Black community, investment in health care in the Black community, investment in law enforcement that cares about the community and people therein). The answer is quite simple. However, White people who want to solve the race problem do not deal with the issues that solve the problem. While much of the solution lies in learning, there is also the aspect of motivating people to learn. There is the aspect of reinforcing what people learn, then for them to internalize the knowledge such that it is manifested in behavior. This applies to both Black and White individuals.

Racists are not going to change racist. Racist will only reinforce racism. People have known racism is a problem for centuries. Why does it still exist? Research found that White guilt, embarrassment, and disgust about how their group benefits from inequality, inspired Whites to act. However, participants only felt guilty if they believed that they could be efficacious in fighting institutional racism. Participants who felt low efficacy or helpless to make a difference rejected feelings of guilt and, consequently, exhibited less positive racial attitudes and less engagement in antidiscrimination action. A sense of efficacy needs to be incorporated into diversity training programs, to get people to act. No doubt combating racism is a challenging effort. The United States democracy is at stake. [222] People tend to ignore phenomena they rationalize as having a negative impact or no positive impact on their lives. A positive attitude about others reflects a positive attitude about oneself.

Racism, like most psychological issues, becomes clearer and better understood, when analyzed from multiple perspectives. There are multiple dimensions of White racism. One must wonder if White people understand why, they are racist. Analysis from a White intergroup relationship perspective gives insight into what Whites consider acceptable behavior. Some White theorists conclude that, to distance themselves from unpleasant thoughts and social affiliations is necessary. These people process racism ambiguously. Psychological theories of racial bias indicate that some White people are motivated to avoid appearing racist. Some Whites seek to avoid racial bias because of extrinsic pressures such as political correctness and fear of reprisal. Racism to some Whites conjure psychological impressions of thoughts of the anti-bellum south during slavery, resulting in a "fear of change syndrome." A subtle, ambiguous form of bias, and racist attributes involves political ideology. These people have a broader societal impact on racism. There is evidence that some Whites mitigate nonracial factors that could account for racial bias behavior but attempt to rationalize their racist bias based on what they consider overwhelming evidence. [223] The fallacy in the mitigation theory on race is that they attribute racism to White perceptions of Black and other minority individuals, even when Whites manifest those same identical behaviors.

Members of White culture often attribute pathological behavior toward non-White individuals is because of their illegal behavior. Increasing attacks against innocent Asian people have increased, mostly perpetrated by Whites, since Donald Trump coined the phrase "China virus." Statistics prove that Asians are the most law-abiding people in America, based on the incarceration statistics. Statistics based on one month's data but historically characteristic of Asia interaction with American society -- -- Last Updated: Saturday, 11 September 2021. [224] Why would a White person attack an innocent Asian person without cause? Why would any decent human being attack another human being without cause? The statistics below indicate who the real criminals are.

Race	# of Inmates	% of Inmates
Asian	2,331	1.5%
Black	59,313	38.2%
Native American	3,826	2.5%
White	89,965	57.9%

Racist White people are motivated by a pathological mentality causing them to behave in extreme and unacceptable ways. Their behavior is often a result of feelings they cannot control. It can be argued that the source of White hatred for minorities is based on a chronic, almost pathological jealousy, self-hatred, insecurity, or a genetic defect in White DNA.

According to FBI statistics on arrests by Race, 2010 and based on reports by 12,221 law enforcement agencies and a 2010 estimated population of 240,100,189 people in the United States of America.[227] White people commitment the most crimes. White people are the most arrested under 18 years of age and over 18 years of age. [228]

Total arrests					
Offense charged	Total	White	Black	American Indian or Alaskan Native	Asian or Pacific Islander
TOTAL	10,177,907	7,066,154	2,846,862	145,612	119,279

Percent distribution					
Offense charged	Total	White	Black	American Indian or Alaskan Native	Asian or Pacific Islander
TOTAL	100.0	69.4	28.0	1.4	1.2

These statistics indicate the truth and the *American Reality* of why White culture and the American media do not want the truth revealed. It shatters the stereotype myth and the lie that White people are law abiding and Black people are criminals. The truth is that all races have their share of criminal elements. It is just that the White race has many more than the other races.

White privilege, racism, and greed can obstruct the ethical and moral values of fairness and equality. An insight into another reason White people persist in their racism and prejudice to the extent of institutionalizing the suppression of Black and minority people can be found in an 1860 debate between two ministers. Reverend Fuller is a southern pro-slave minister and Reverend Wayland, an anti-slavery northern minister. Arguing the ethics and morals of slavery, Reverend Fuller expressed a fear of White people. White people fear that if Black people gained equality and political power, they would inflict the same suppression on Whites that Whites enacted on Blacks. This fear motivates White racism in some Whites. The fact that Whites fear reprisal is an indicator they are aware of their deplorable treatment of Black people. They know they are wrong yet persist in being so. That is the epitome of a low-life character. White fear is manifest in political voter suppression, economic repression, and education repression.[229]

For racist behavior to be reconciled, it must be understood. Some White people that have *racist residue* do not believe they are racist but are benign to the racism in White culture, as I believe, is the case with Sarah Nolan, Jackie Hennard and Joanne Nee. Ingrid Gould works for the University of Chicago and probably considers it her job to present the best possible image for the university. I do think they are unwilling or unable to evaluate racial situations with objectivity or they are too insecure to be honest. The question to ask is; does that really help the university to get better? Likewise, with the university General Counsel, who accepted the false results of Attorney Jackie Hennard without question. There is a racist attribute to compliance.

UC Berkeley professor John Powell stated that the country needs to combat white supremacy through collective action. He refers to *President Joe Biden's inaugural speech that clearly states, "his administration will make defeating white supremacy — as well as the rise of political extremism and domestic terrorism — a priority for his presidency."* However, Powell further advances that, "*Americans must focus on defeating white supremacist structures without condemning white people.*" [230] The American dogma that this is a country for "all of us" is what needs to be institutionally reinforced. White people organize around the synergy of their whiteness. One of the main factors that causes the marginalization of non-white people, people of a different color, different races, different religions, and those who are not White is because White people isolate themselves from other cultures, for the most part. White supremacy is based on the desire of White people to dominate and control. White supremacy is anti-democracy. It guarantees conflict. It is an important concern of democracy to make sure the needs of people are enfranchised, not disenfranchised; framing society interest in terms of Black and White causes an inevitable conflict. Framing society in terms of the needs of Americans presents a common interest that is the foundation of a democracy. Racists White supremacist have no interest in the common good nor are they concerned about the goals of United States of America as a democracy, to make room for all Americans. White supremacist are anti-democracy, anti-America, and criminals to America. White America needs to realize this for their own benefit and for the preservation of American democracy. "*Lifting up Black people, lifting up Native Indian people, lifting up Latinos and Asians, doesn't mean we're putting down white people. Truthfully, it will elevate White people to eliminate the racism in their culture. It does mean that there's a history of this country being organized around white supremacy.*" [231]

Antisemitic Incidents | U.S.
Hitting A New High in Reported Incidents

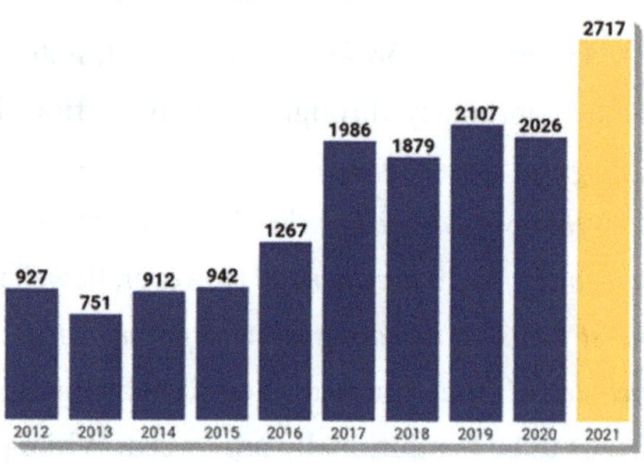

Re-constructing American institutions to serve the needs of all Americans equally does not mean White people will be disenfranchised. It means marginalized people will be enfranchised. It means White people are great Americans. In reality, White people believe they are ontologically threatened. They feel equality for minorities will diminish their rights. Whites believe they will become marginalized if equal opportunity and equal rights policies and civil rights laws are enacted in America. This is not true. This is a lie circulated among "Trump Type" politicians that spreads misinformation to cause divisions and conflict. Creating chaos is fertilizer for misleading people in the wrong directions. Ironically, Trump supporters, have strong White supremacist influence. Since Donald Trump became president, the antiemetic acts of violence have tripled over the past decade.[232] Trump supporters are low-income and out of work people. In addition, they are middle-class professionals. Ironically, many have the same profile and human condition as minorities. However, being honest, they need to get smarter and realize when political leaders are feeding them misinformation.

The purpose of White right-wing racists and extremist is to cause divisions that leads vulnerable, weak-minded White people to participate in insurrection against their country, as took place on January 6, 2021. How can America unite, as a country when they believe lies, as extreme as "that the election was fraudulent"? Belief in such a ridiculous lie indicates the lack of intelligence of factions of Americans and their ignorant weak-mindedness. When decent Americans are influenced to break the law and become criminals something is wrong. Actually, a lot is wrong, with the political leaders who promote lies and misinformation. Something is seriously wrong with the American citizens who believe the lies and act criminally based on falsehoods. While America needs to re-construct the institutions to be fair and inclusive, America also needs to recognize White supremacist are criminals with purpose to destroy American democracy. America needs to treat White supremacist as criminals and terrorist.

White culture created the myth, the lie, that they are superior (*"The Great White Lie"*). Most white people believe it because it boost their self-concept. The truth is that when an individual's self-concept is based on a lie, it is foundationally fragile. Logically a lie is easy to challenge. A lie does not align with common sense; therefore, significant and abundant dissonance is created resulting in insecurities. Belief in a lie under the pretense that is gives advantage or a strength to White culture does not even make sense, but that is the concept socialized into White culture. Realistically, living a lie is a severe weakness. To preserve and maintain their self-concept, White culture protects the lie built into their White cultural worldview; White culture becomes violent to other cultures. They become racist. White culture becomes prejudice and they discriminate. The truth is that the truth does not have to be protected. The truth is naturally conflictive with a lie. The entire relationship between Black and White people is based on protecting and manifesting the lie that White people are superior to Black people and to people of other races. White people will never have or realize the security of their lived experiences until they live in truth instead of living in myth, fantasy and a lie. That is a simple psychological law. A house built on lies will never have a stable foundation, until the house is reconstructed on the truth. If White culture continues to perpetuate the *"Great White Lie"*, they will protect it with violence against minorities, with racism, with discrimination and with prejudice and the conflict will be ongoing. The real damage to society is that most white people buy in to the lie to avoid the challenge of living the reality that all humans are created equal. It only emphasizes the weakness in the White cultural worldview and in White culture. This is what White culture socializes in White children.

It is important to state that the author recognizes and honestly believes, not all White people believe in, or are caught up in the *"Great White Lie"*. Many White people have escaped the racist *"Matrix"* that supports racism and dysfunction toward others. These individuals should take responsibility to educate and teach the dysfunctional factions of their race

White people who have escaped from the Matrix should accept the responsibility to rescue the rest of their culture who are still trapped in the racist "*Matrix*". White people need to evaluate their racism and behavior in terms of cost / benefit scale. They do not evaluate the anti-racist benefits to themselves.

Their fear of reprisal, the insecurity of their mindset cannot envision any other way of experiencing life. Think about it. Every indigenous culture White people have engaged has resulted in a conflictive disproportionate relationship. The relationship between African-American culture and White culture is conflictive. The relationship between Native American Indian culture and White culture is conflictive. The relationship between Native Hawaiian Indigenous culture and White culture is conflictive. Even the relationship between the Native Aborigine culture Indigenous to Australia and White culture is conflictive. The relationship between African Black culture Indigenous to South Africa and White culture is conflictive in South Africa. Everywhere European (White) culture has inhabited or migrated resulted in repression and oppression of the indigenous culture. The reason the conflict exist is that White culture does not respect other cultures. Frankly, White culture does not even respect its own culture. Think about it. The colloquial sayings, "Have gun will travel" synonymous with a 1960's television series of the same name and the saying, "every supply creates its own demand" is a formation of Say's law advanced by the economist John Maynard Keynes in 1936. [233] The potential for purchase (use) of a product is based on product supply (existence). Consider this concept in the context of nuclear weapons. What mindset of respect for life develops products that have the potential to destroy the human race, including the people who developed the nuclear weapons (products)? If White culture does not respect the existence, maintenance and perpetuation of their own culture, it is understandable why they do not respect other cultures. The countries with nuclear weapons are primarily White countries. Russia and the Western countries are conflictive. Russia has nuclear weapons and that is an exception of White culture conflicting with White culture, with itself. China has nuclear weapons as defense against the potential aggression of White culture. North Korea and Iran are vying to develop nuclear weapons for the same reason as China. The development of weapons of massive destruction, weapons with the potential to destroy humankind is because human beings do not get along with human beings and subconsciously do not respect himself or herself, or human life. If an individual had respect for something or someone, would they endanger it? The irony is that they rationalize the potential of their self-destruction, their destruction and dysfunction by saying it preserves world peace. That logic, whether used by individual gun owners or the military, is like putting sugar on shit and telling people to eat it (please excuse the use of this vulgar word, but it is in the dictionary). The negative dysfunction in the world is because White culture is a disrespectful culture with a foundation based on lies. Disrespect seeds disrespect even for oneself. Every supply creates its own demand and use. The existence of nuclear weapons is indication they will be used. Ironically, the only country that has ever used nuclear weapons on another country is the United States. During World War II, America bombed two cities in Japan (Hiroshima and Nagasaki). The intelligent humanitarian thing to do would have been to destroy the blueprint for nuclear weapons. To the contrary, the blueprints for nuclear weapons became the possession of countries around the world, giving numerous countries the ability to destroy humanity.

Considerable distress and deep anxiety can result from White culture addressing and telling the truth, so people perceive it is easier to live a lie than to be live in truth. [234] The problem with White culture is that they have lived a lie for so long, they themselves believe it and exorcising the lies from their culture is a transformation process. Acting in compliance with the "*Great White Lie*" is safe space, theoretically. It is more secure in the "*racist Matrix*" but that is only because White culture does not know the reality of the positive self-respect and security that comes from respecting other cultures. They have never exercised respect for others, in the entire history of their existence. White culture has never lived in truth. White history is rampant with and characterized by conflict, deception, larceny and violence.

Living a lie may also be a way to protect White culture from the painful realization of how bad things may actually be or actually how much of a negative influence White culture has had on the world, in contrast to beliefs they have concocted. One must not forget, however that White culture has also contributed "greatness to the world". Would the greatness of White contribution still have occurred if they did not inflict so much damage to other cultures? I think so and possible even more. More is produced from the elimination of conflict than from the maintenance of conflict. Positive thinking creates the freedom to thrive. Negative thinking and the perpetuation of dysfunction, inhibits real progress. Fear of consequences and shame is also a barrier to White culture dealing with their reality. Transformation can be managed as a positive process. However, as long as racists, White supremacist, or neo-Nazis, exists, cause violence and discriminate against others because of skin color, race, religion, gender identification, or culture, there will always be conflict.

The case study involving Discrimination against Dr. Barnes by the University of Chicago Alumni Association is an example of the *racist residue* that many White people harbor. By no means does the act of discrimination experienced by Dr. Barnes compare to acts caused by White supremacist ideology and White supremacy behavior. However, it is the presence and existence of White supremacist ideology in America that gives the "decent White people" freedom to express their "*racist residue*." **All White people are not bad people**. **Nor does Dr. Barnes consider most White people racist**. Dr. Barnes would suggest they might not be aware of the subconscious nature of their racist tendencies. This is a common attribute for many White people. Admittedly, White people are challenged and reluctant to reconcile their White privilege and engage behaviors that establish fairness and equal opportunity in our American society. One reason is that White racism is so deeply implanted in the White socialization process and has been for centuries. Even decent White people are reluctant to give up their White privilege. Diversity training on an ongoing basis, beginning in the elementary grades, will help White people understand and experience the benefits of eliminating racist behaviors and racist residue from their culture. The positive results will not only benefit Black people but White people, the American society, the students in elementary schools, high schools, colleges and universities, and the United States of America in general.

White people sometimes tend to respond to criticisms on White racism by using the "not all white people are racist" argument when racism is challenged. Often it distracts from the real issue that racism exist and is abundant in America to the extent that it impacts the lives of millions of Americans. The statement that "not all white people are racist" may have a tendency to give the impression that White racist behavior is rare. It is an excuse for White apathy on racism and serves as an adequate remorseful response to White racism. [235]

> *"There are many white people who mean right and in their hearts, wanna do right. If 10,000 snakes were coming down that aisle now, and I had a door that I could shut, and in that 10,000, 1,000 meant right, 1,000 rattlesnakes didn't want to bite me, I knew they were good... Should I let all these rattlesnakes come down, hoping that that thousand get together and form a shield? Or should I just close the door and stay safe?"*

Muhammed Ali gave a powerful response to the statement that 'Not All White People Are Racist' in 1971 on the BBC British Talk show, "Parkinson". [236] Explaining why the existence of some "good" white people isn't always enough, Muhammed Ali responded:

Support against racist and racism is the right position to take, the intelligent position to take, and is obviously important and necessary to ending racial injustice. Ali's words are still a pretty powerful reminder of the reality of being black in America. It is unfortunate and a pathetic testament to America that over 50 years later his words still resonate.

White people believe America belongs to them, even though they stole it from the Native American Indians. America was built on the backs of black slaves, and now America belongs to White culture. The irony in that perspective is that when someone steals something belonging to someone else, under the law and circumstances considered civilized, that is criminal behavior.

Another set of hypothesis one has to consider is that White culture knows it is racist. White America accepts that it is racist without intention or desire to change. White America is racist because it is the nature of the White cultural value system to denigrate others because they lack self-esteem. White culture has a frustration aggression complex and lack the ability to create and maintain a cultural depth that appreciates and values all human beings. How can an individual appreciate others when they have low self-appreciation or no appreciation for themselves? Outside of racism, it can be hypothesized that the psychological foundation in White culture influences other areas of society, such as school violence and killings. Our White legislators do not address substantial gun control measures because they care more about the bribes, the money; they receive from the gun lobbies and gun companies than they care about the lives of children. The second Amendment is smokescreen to cover the fact that Americas Republican legislators are taking bribes from the gun lobbies and gun companies to fight against any legislation that limits, restricts, or sets any controls on gun freedoms. The second amendment is satisfied if a family owned only one gun per household. Gun companies want to have unrestricted freedom to sell guns to anyone with money to buy them. Greed is the American way, even at the expense of killing kids or at the expense of kids killing kids. Regardless of the cost to America in Children's lives, gun companies, and Gun Company supported legislators do not care. They only care about the money and use the second Amendment to keep from telling the truth about their real motives. What is White culture's perspective on racism when lawmakers and American gun owners (many of whom are White racists) do not have real value for America's children? How is racism, White culture, gun ownership, and school violence connected? Most gun owners are White males, insecure, and "beset by racial fears".[237] A 2016 study from the University of Illinois at Chicago found that racial resentment among whites fueled opposition to gun control. This drives political affiliations.[238] A 2017 study in the *Social Studies Quarterly* found that gun owners had become 50 percent more likely to vote Republican since 1972—and that gun culture had become strongly associated with explicit racism".[239] Another study found that the people who felt most emotionally attached to their guns were 78% White and 65% male. White men who experienced financial problems and economic insecurity felt that owning a gun gave them a better self-image, security and made them a better person. This is a serious case of transference when an individual's self-concept is attached to gun ownership. Some White men who are economically insecure are also "irreligious". They view the gun as a symbol of power, independence and attached to their masculinity. A gun makes a White man feel like a man. They believe their manhood has been diminished because their economic status has become eroded. A significant number of these White men are less educated and have a lower level of intelligence. Minorities do not control the economy or influence the economic status of these insecure White men. White men are in control of the economy. The insecurity in White men is because the values in American society disregard the welfare of the general population in general. American society is dictated and constructed by and for the interest of corporations, the rich and the wealthy. The average American citizen is merely an afterthought; a secondary priority. White culture is the reason for the economic woes of White culture. White men control the American economic system. Poor, uneducated, ignorant, racist White people are pawns themselves to the corruption in America's political and economic systems. They are perfect targets used to create chaos that deflects attention from the real issues plaguing White America and minority America. They are perfect targets because they are White, uneducated, ignorant, racists and gullible. As long as they prevail in the gun war, used as pawns in the race conflicts, and embrace candidates like Donald Trump, they are absorbed in a cause that deflects their attention from restoring America to the ideology envisioned by the founding fathers. White poor uneducated people are deceived and motivated by the systematic apparatus that deceives and discriminates against minorities. An irony is that "these White men tend to see themselves as devoted patriots, but make a distinction between the federal government and the nation". To put things in perspective, Joe Biden summarized the dilemma between Trump followers and true Americans. President Biden stated: "you can't be pro-insurrection and pro-cop". "You can't be pro-insurrection and pro-American". [240] The difference between President Joe Biden and Donald Trump is like day and night. Their policies are polarized. Their communication skills and relational perspective about others are polar opposite. The experience in government is extensive for Biden, unqualified for Trump, according to many reputable sources. As a result, Trump nominates numerous unqualified people into government service that republicans approve. The characteristics of Trumps persona are comparable to the rise of Adolph Hitler. Individuals with similar profiles have a high propensity for terrorist and racists behaviors.

In summary, gun owners of this profile are more attached to their guns, and are more likely to believe guns are the solution to our social ills. They believe that more people with guns will reduce violence. This logic alone tells the story of how stupid these people are. White men of this profile get their self-image from extrinsic factors outside of their being, rather than from intrinsic factors inside of their being. [241] The problem with the entire scenario on White men and guns is that the people most likely to be killed by the guns of White men are not the "bad guys", criminals or terrorist. It is themselves, their families and other decent good people. The correlation between racism, insecure White men, racists, child killings and terrorist is a clear indication that America is not the country America thinks it is. America is a country with substandard legislators who make the laws, a country with legislators who value money more than they value children, and a country that allows racists the freedom to have voice and terrorize American citizens. Mostly, America is a country full of insecure inadequate scared White men. They say a great country is not destroyed from outside. A great country is destroyed from inside. If an individual is deplorable and dangerous without a gun, they will be more deplorable and dangerous with a gun. Too many deplorable racist people in America have guns. The thought that innocent babies will grow up to be deplorable racist should repulse every decent American. The phenomena of kids being killed by gun violence should be motivation to make sweeping changes to gun laws. Something is seriously wrong with America and the people in legislative positions when America's kids are being killed by gun violence and politicians pursue every remedy to the problem except the restriction of gun laws. What is the problem with American? The solution is to vote **only** for politicians who take **NO** gun money. That will give legislators responsibility to Americans and not the special interest of gun lobbyist and gun companies. A strong direct linkage exist between Whites who are ardent gun advocates and Whites who are racists. Racism in America should be criminalized, with severe penalties, similar to those suffered by 911 terrorist and sent to Guantanamo Bay. One hypothesis that would make for an interesting study is to study the degree that racism, White supremacy, prejudice and discrimination are characteristic in American society and the degree to which White racism influences America's problems, including crimes. Reconstructing American society to respect all Americans might seem to be a huge undertaking. However, it is not as difficult as people think; just eliminate the racist element in America. I do not mean literally. The racist element in America is a criminal element. They will commit crimes. When racists commit crimes that violate an individual's civil rights, they should be given the maximum penalty and prosecuted as terrorist, because they are. One way to accomplish this is to create a democracy and an American society that is inclusive instead of exclusive. An individual's thinking cannot be legislated but equal opportunity can. Racist will push back against equal opportunity for minorities and people who are non-White. Why allow people to influence the democratic process who are the same people who sabotage democracy and have purpose to overthrow democracy and act anti-democratic? Critical and most important, is to educate kids from the elementary through the college / university levels of learning to internalize diversity as a positive reality in our United States of America. That is the truth. America is multi-cultural. To have a misconception, and not giving a positive perspective on that reality is un-American, traitorous; it is democratic sabotage.

There are deplorable, low-life individuals in every race and culture. Good people have bad days. When the worse of their behavior is displayed, the good people regret their actions. That, too, is common to all races and cultures. We all have room to improve. Self-improvement is a life-long process that begins at the point people decide they want to become better human beings.

Race is a sensitive subject. Discussions of race and comments about race are often misunderstood and often have derogatory intent. Nevertheless, it is important for humans to overcome the tunnel of chaos that encases racial relationships, interactions and perspectives. Consider the speech given by Dr. Jill Biden, first lady of the United States of America. In her speech at the conference of Unidos US, the country's largest Latino advocacy group, Dr. Biden said the diversity of the Latino community — "as distinct as the bodegas of the Bronx, as beautiful as the blossoms of Miami and as unique as the breakfast tacos here in San Antonio — is your strength." Dr. Biden, in her mind, was being complimentary to the Hispanic community. However, her intent to deliver the speech as a compliment backfired. The Hispanic community pushed back against Dr. Biden with a negative reaction to her comments. The Hispanic crowd resented being compared stereotypically to tacos. Certainly, Dr. Biden had no racist intent, what so ever. Her intent was to be complimentary. This situation indicates the following: [242]

1. Whites do not understand racial sensitivities. A white person making an ethnic comment, regardless of how well-meaning, is subject to scrutiny. Dr. Biden is a fine woman, with a good heart. Most would say she has no ill intent toward others, yet it is common for White people to understand so little about minorities and ethnic differences that their "*racist residue*" blocks their diversity knowledge. *Racist residue* is common in White culture. Existing in a White environment for so long,

even good White people are challenged to eliminate their "*racist residue*."

2. There needs to be more discussion on race and a synergy developed between people of different ethnic backgrounds. White people need to become educated on diversity, ethnic history and learn the lies, fallacies and reasons behind the evolution of racism, prejudice and discrimination. Lack of knowledge is a stability in ignorance.
3. Hispanics, as well as African Americans have a heighten sensitivity regarding their racial perspectives and how others perceives them racially.
4. When someone makes a comment without ill intent but with well-meaning and the comment is taken offensively, that is an indication of miscommunication, no communication, misunderstanding and or lack of synergy between humans. It can also be a result of other problems that are not addressed such as economic inequalities, racism, discrimination and prejudice that heightens sensitivity to every issue and comment dealing with ethnic cultural analogies.
5. Dr. Biden's speechwriters, themselves, live in a vacuum unaware of racial sensitivities.

This situation gives voice to the realization that there is divisions between groups of people that need to be closed and reconciled. Dr. Biden is a wonderful person, a true American citizen, a patriot, a woman, who devotes her life to teaching kids. She is probably void of racist residue and believes all kids Black, White, Hispanic, Asian and other should have an equal opportunity to succeed in America. Nevertheless, racial sensitivities are so out of balance that even a patriot like Dr. Jill Biden is subject to criticism. The primary purpose of this book is to tell the truth, and to make our society

The primary purpose of this book is to tell the truth, and to make our society and world better.

The author wants to end this book with repeating his sincere belief that not all White human beings are deplorable people. White culture like all cultures are creations of God. Most people, of all races and cultures, are decent, law abiding, good people. All races and cultures have good people and bad people. It does not matter what the color of one's skin is. What matters is the content of an individual's character. Unfortunately, the American Reality is that White culture causes problems that keep America from becoming a great country. White Culture has too many racists.

Chapter XII
Final Thoughts

The final thoughts I want to leave with the reader are:

1. The vast majority of White people are wonderful decent people, great Americans and they love the United States of America.
2. The vast majority of White people are not prejudiced. They may have "*racist residue*" however, they recognize that human beings come in all sizes, shapes and colors. They have a basic respect for humanity and life, for everyone.
3. An estimated 40,000,000 to 50,000,000 people died during World War II (1939-1945). The death totals among the Allied countries were (estimates): [243]

Country	Military Deaths	Total Civilian and Military Deaths
Soviet Union	8,800,000-10,700,000	24,000,000
United Kingdom	383,600	450,700
United States	416,800	418,500
Yugoslavia	446,000	1,000,000
France	210,000	390,000
Poland	240,000	5,800,000

Death tolls in World War II are further put into perspective based on countries Allied Forces and Axis Forces. The Jewish people suffered the majority of deaths during WWII. The German Nazis killed over 6,000,000 Jews because of racism, hatred and prejudice. WWII was fought to prevent the racist Nazi Germans from spreading their evil and negative influence throughout in the World.

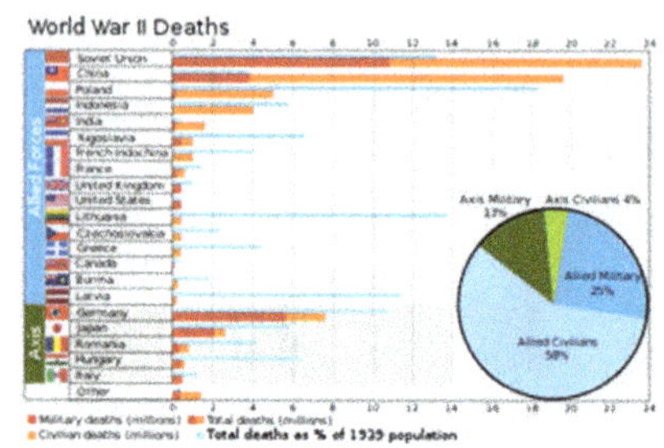

4. In the American Civil War an estimated 618,222 American citizens died, with 360,222 Union deaths and 258,000 Confederate deaths. The civil war fought on American soil, American against American, and brother against brother. The civil war was the deadliest and bloodiest of all American wars. Some consider a more accurate estimate of Civil War deaths is about 750,000, with a range from 650.000 to as many as 850,000 dead. [244]

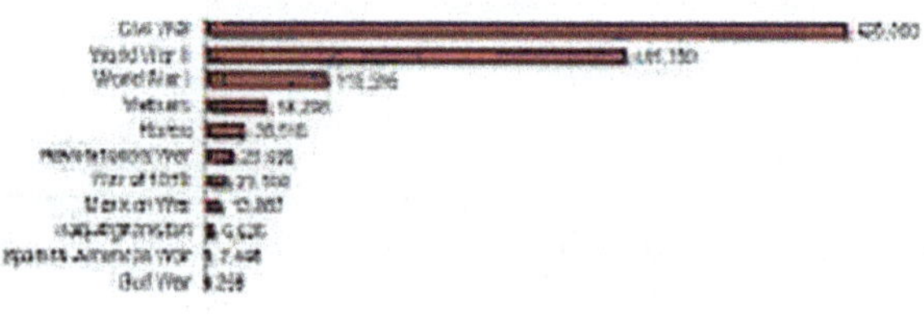

The adjacent chart represents the loss of life in the Wars America has fought. The American Civil was fought over a number of issues: 1) The Civil war was fought to keep the union together (Southern States wanted to succeed from the Union. 2) Another issue the Civil War was fought was over sectionalism, an superseding devotion to the interests of a region over those of a country as a whole. 3) The Civil War was fought over the issue of slavery and the inhuman treatment of people. Slavery was not what the dogma of America represented. It was an inhuman system of racism by White people using Black people as slaves and chattel, for economic gain.

Considering the economic and human cost of World War II and the cost of the Civil War, over 50 million lives lost between the two conflicts. American fought WWII to defeat Nazis. America fought the Civil War to free slaves and end racism. **Why in contemporary modern society, under God's skies does America allow Nazis, White Supremacist, White Nationalist and racists to exist, to have presence, and voice in our great country, the United States of America? The tragedy and sickness in American Reality is that millions of people worldwide and over a million Americans lost their lives fighting against racists and racism, yet the United States of America allows these destructive forces voice. What is the problem with White America?**

While the topics and subject matter of this book are about the deplorable and destructive influence of racism and racists on American society, one must also recognized the significant contributions of decent Americans. The constructive and positive efforts of decent Americans who fight for democracy and fight against the negative influence of racism and racist are prodigies for making America great. Without the efforts of decent Americans, America would be a cesspool. America has considerable more potential as a world example of positive leadership; however, because the decent influences in America tolerate the negative (racism and racists) influences, America is in a state of stifling conflict. Decent White people tolerate racists because they are not threatened by White racism. However, White people act with aggressive scrutiny toward innocent Muslims because they feel threatened by the imagery of Middle Eastern people. White people discriminate against innocent Muslims under the pretext of "*keeping Americas safe*". Safe for White people is the reality and basis of White discriminating behaviors against Muslims. Black people, Asians, Jews, Hispanics, and LBGTQ human beings. All are Americans. Until the focus of progress in America becomes the welfare of all American citizens; instead of focusing and giving priority to racists, the greed, the money, the things, and selfish interest based in extrinsic values, then America will always exist in conflict and imbalance. Otherwise, confronting the reality of the American mindset and behavior, Americans should just admit, we live in a sophisticated jungle. It is every person for themselves. God does not exist because; human actions do not acknowledge his existence. For those of you who think a harmonious society is senseless dreaming and fantasy, then the moon landing was faked. If America is predominantly a Christian country that tolerates religious freedom, then America should act like a religious country instead of being a country of hypocrisy.

Appendix I

Exhibit 1- Interview request from Ronald Barnes and refusals to participate from Sarah Nolan, Joanne Nee, Jackie Hennard and Ingrid Gould

Yahoo/Inbox

Ron Barnes

To: snolan@uchicago.edu

Mon, Jun 28 at 11:40 AM

Hello Sarah

If you recall in 2019 we had an encounter that banned me from the Alumni building. I am writing a book on that incident and I would like to interview you to understand your side of the equation. I harbor no ill feelings and my intention is not to lambast or defame anyone. I believe it is important to get your side of the story. I am an alumni of this great institution and it would be counterproductive and inaccurate for me to defame my alma-mater. I believe you are doing a great service for the University. Everyone has bad days. If you are willing, I would like for us to meet and openly discuss the matter. Please let me know what you think.

Sincerely

Ronald Barnes

Sarah Nolan <snolan@uchicago.edu>

To: Ron Barnes

Mon, Jul 12 at 9:11 AM

Mr. Barnes,

Thank you very much for reaching out and offering this opportunity. Unfortunately, I must respectfully decline.

I wish you the very best.
Warm regards,

Sarah

This message and its contents are confidential. If you received this message in error, do not use or rely upon it. Instead, please inform the sender and then delete it. Thank you.

Show original message

Ron Barnes

To: Sarah Nolan,Ingrid Gould,Joanne M. Nee, Kenton Rainey, stamatak@uchicago.edu and 1 more...

Cc: Angelo Chavers, Attorney Gray

Wed, Jul 14 at 12:29 PM

Hello Sarah

Thank you for responding. I understanding your decision to decline an interview. I want to inform you of my intentions to write a book on our incident and the phenomena that occurred. My intention is not to defame or advance any negative action upon anyone. I am a proud product of this great University of Chicago, both the high school and graduate school. I don't want to defame anyone associated with the school or the school. My intention is to present our encounter in a perspective that will contribute to the life long learning process we all experience.

Contrary to what some may think, I have no intention to sue the university. Frankly, I can make more money selling the book nationally and internationally.. I can also make a more significant contribution to the learning environment by presenting a perspective on human interactions in a diverse environment. The interactions between people in diverse environments is a dilemma in our society, even at the University of Chicago, otherwise there would not be a Diversity initiative, a Black Alumni Association, a Black student group, an Asian student group, an LGBTQ group and groups that meet the specific needs of diverse people. The challenge for the university of to create a positive synergy between the diverse entities on campus.

What I will do is give each of the individuals copied on this email a copy of the manuscript prior to publication. You will have 1 week to comment on the manuscript before I send it to the publisher. Providing feedback will be your decisions.

Sincerely

Ronald Barnes

Divinity School (2015)

Show original message

Ron Barnes

To:bcollier@uchicago.edu

Wed, Jul 14 at 2:09 PM

Sent from Yahoo Mail on Android

Show original message

Joanne M Nee <nee@uchicago.edu>

To:Ron Barnes

Thu, Jul 15 at 3:29 PM

Mr. Barnes,

I received your messages in a delayed fashion. I had been out of the office on personal business and apologize for the late response. I understand the nature of your project and wish you luck with it. However, I must decline your offer to participate. Thank you.

Confidentiality Notice: This document may contain confidential or legally privileged information intended only for the individual or entity named in this correspondence. If you are not the intended recipient, you are hereby notified that any disclosure, copying, distribution, or reliance upon the contents is strictly prohibited and may be unlawful. If you have received this in error please reply to the sender so that proper delivery may be arranged for and then please destroy the original and all copies.

Joanne M. Nee

Director of Professional Accountability

University of Chicago Department of Safety and Security

773.795.3882

nee@uchicago.edu

Thank you. No problem. I agree with you

RE: Ronald Barnes discrimination complaint2

Yahoo/UChicago Racism

Ingrid Gould <igould@uchicago.edu>

To:ron.barnes

Tue, Jun 1 at 4:54 PM

Hello, Ron,

I hope you had a good holiday weekend.

As my 8/14/2019 letter states, Jackie Hennard investigated and wrote to you about the race discrimination component of your complaint, and I separately reviewed your request to lift the no-trespass directive. My letter lifting the no-trespass directive said all I have to say.

It is not University policy or practice to provide its internal investigatory documents. If your attorney has questions, you may refer her to Ted Stamatakos, Senior Associate General Counsel, stamatak@uchicago.edu.

Kind regards,

Ingrid

Ingrid Gould <igould@uchicago.edu>

To: ron.barnes

Fri, Jun 4 at 6:20 PM

Hello, Ron,

Thank you for your kind words and invitation to participate in your research project. I do not wish to participate in an interview.

Kind regards,

Ingrid

Interview Request2

Yahoo/UChicago Racism

Jackie Hennard

Good afternoon Mr. Barnes, Thank you for reaching...

Tue, Oct 13, 2020 at 1:31 PM

Ron Barnes

To:jacquelineh1@uchicago.edu

Cc: Angelo Chavers

Tue, Oct 13, 2020 at 2:31 PM

Hello Jackie

Thank you for sending your investigation response. I am disappointed you have declined to participate in the case study. The times warrant as much understanding of racism in our society as possible. Racism is embedded, socialized and institutionalized into white culture. Even to the point that white people discriminate against non- whites and consider it justified normal behavior. White culture is often ignorant of their racist behavior and needs to be better educated in the ethics of diversity, especially in America, a heterogeneous society.

Your investigation spent more time investigating me than you did the person the complaint was levied against. While I believe your investigation was racist, in itself, I also believe that is the only way you know how to approach such matters. I believe that white culture needs to be better educated and learn about how to interface with people different from themselves. Racism is by an large, a white problem that has negative impact on our society and non- white people. Failure to participate in solution is complicit. You are in a position that needs to understand the overt and subtile aspects of racism. You cant get that insight without participation in learning how to transcend while racism.

I am conducting the case study, with or without participation from those involved. Non- participation does not surprise me. It was expected. However, it is fair and the right thing to get all viewpoints to arrive at mutual understanding.

Sincerely

Ronald Barnes

Interview Request2

Yahoo/UChicago Racism

Jackie Hennard <jacquelineh1@uchicago.edu>

To: Ron Barnes

Tue, Oct 13, 2020 at 1:31 PM

Good afternoon Mr. Barnes,

Thank you for reaching out this morning. I am going to decline to participate in an interview. During our conversation you mentioned that you had not received any communication regarding the findings of the previous investigation. For your convenience please find a copy of the outcome letter.

Please feel free to reach out if you have any concerns in the future.

Thanks,

Jacqueline Hennard

Associate Director/Lead Investigator, Office for Access and Equity
Office of the Provost

The University of Chicago
5525 S. Ellis Ave. |Chicago, IL 60637| 773-702-1032
equalopportunityprograms.uchicago.edu

Exhibit 2 – Article Dr. Barnes presented to the Alumni Association for publication in the UChicago Alumni magazine.

I have reached a plateau in my life that I never imagined prior to three years ago. I have never thought of myself as a scholar or academic. I do think of myself as a pragmatic person whose interest is to solve problems in society rather than talk or philosophize about them. However, even this self-concept is recent. In high school and undergraduate college, I was an athlete, All- conference in both high school and college in all years that I played basketball and small college All-American as a college senior. Academics and study did not interest me. Reflecting, my world was self-centered. As a star athlete, the praise, the accolade, and the cheers were addictive and can give a person misdirection in life. When the limelight dims, and the days of athletic prowess are over, the athlete often feels lost and is unprepared to have a substitute life direction that rivals the "glory days." It is like a period of withdrawal with a timeframe that varies from person to person, as does the severity of adjusting to life outside the limelight. The normalcy of day-to-day life and routine is a challenging adjustment. While sports taught me many useful life lessons such as the value of teamwork, the pride in winning, and the pain of how to be a good loser but learn from the experience and bounce back. The reality that even the best player on the team needs help from teammates to be successful is a primary phenomenon in sports. The one thing that is fleeting and difficult to replace is the passion in doing something that is totally consuming and absorbs every sense and emotion in the human nature. Replacing that is the most challenging dilemma for an athlete.

After working in corporate America for 15 years then going into business for 10 years and achieving a degree of monetary success, I decided to return to school. In high school and undergraduate college, I was an average student, boilerplate average. I never thought for a second, I was not smart, but I was aware that I did not apply myself and worse, it did not bother me. When I returned to school after over 25 years of reading nothing more enlightening than tales of mythology, business journals, and the sports pages, returning to school was transformational. At the University of Chicago, the academic demands were beyond my imagination and my lived experience. Professors assign 200-500 pages of reading per week per class. Taking three classes, that is 600 to 1500 pages of reading per week. What is wrong with these instructors? Don't they understand I have classes other than their class? They really do not care. The learning environment at the University of Chicago is intense, challenging, demanding and requires serious commitment. I was challenged, beyond my experience in sports. Study, reading, and writing essays was a new experience, new territory, serious work. Sports was play, fun. The seed of passion for sports is planted at an early age. Here I am now, middle aged, starting a new discipline, re-starting my brain or starting my brain, depending on perspective. While we suffered some losses in sports, we never failed and always competed at the top. Therefore, another thing that carried over from my sports days was that "failure was not an option." The adjustment in returning to school after years of absence, coupled with non-existent study habits, was like staring at the bottom of Mt. Everest then being told to climb. Re-orienting and conditioning the mind and the will power to focus on and value academic learning was a challenging adjustment, but I rose to the challenge. The experience was transformational for me. Having experienced a respectable academic success at the University of

Chicago graduate school was like a torch that ignited my passion for learning. I also realized the fulfillment, satisfaction and benefit in a life direction based on objectives that contribute to society, rather than those based on selfish goals. I attained a Master of Arts degree from the University of Chicago of which I am quite proud. I was inspired to the extent that I wrote a book entitled, *"Practice what you preach, Preach what you practice."* The book addresses areas of society in terms of religion, business, ethics, racism inequity, gender discrimination, greed, and idea on how to develop better society balance. Presenting Dr. Zimmer with a copy of my book was a highlight and made me proud because that experience exemplified what can be achieved when an individual puts their mind on positive accomplishment and indicated to me, the quality of my learning at this institution. I am finishing my second book, entitled, "The Pyrrhic State of America: Make America Great". I have two other books in publishing. With my knowledge and enthusiasm growing, I am writing a fourth and fifth books. One entitled, *"Everybody wants to go to heaven, but nobody wants to die"* and the other is entitled, *"The Three Fold Mimesis of Life". "Everybody wants to go to heaven, but nobody wants to die"* is about reconciling difficult and challenging situations in one's lived experience. More so, however, I developed a passion for learning, an experience that was new and exciting. In a sense, learning replaced the void left in me after the glory days of athletics was long gone. The University of Chicago experience motivated me to pursue a doctorate degree in psychology, which I will complete this year (2022). While I can't wait to earn the title of Dr. Ronald Barnes, PhD, the shining star in my achievement is that I was inducted into PSI CHI, (April 2019), the international honor society for psychology. That honor never came onto my radar. Two things I want to share from my journey and life experience:

1. The lack of clarity in life direction is an obstruction to achievement.
2. If I can do it, anybody can.

Ronald Barnes
University of Chicago Laboratory High School
University of Chicago Divinity School, Master of Arts in Religious Studies (2015)
Doctor of Philosophy in Psychology (2022)

Exhibit 3 - Email correspondence between Paul Casperson and Laura Demanski introducing Ronald Barnes

Email Exchanges between Dr. Barnes, Paul Casperson and Laura Demanski

Email # 1 – From Paul Casperson who connected Dr. Barnes with Laura Demanski

Making an Introduction6

Yahoo/Inbox

Paul Casperson

To: Laura Demanski

Cc: Ronald Barnes

Mar 29 at 1:54 PM

Laura,

I am emailing to introduce you to Ronald Barnes, a UChicago Alumnus. He was hoping to speak to you or someone else on the writing team about featuring a book he has written. I didn't get much in the way of details on the book or what exactly Ronald had in mind (I believe he mentioned some sort of feature, or at least an advertisement?) but I know he was hoping to alert alumni to the book. Ronald, hopefully you can elaborate here.

I'm happy to help you two connect further in any way I can.

Sincerley,

Paul

Email # 2 - To Laura Demanski and Paul Casperson

Ron Barnes <ron.barnes7@yahoo.com>

To: Laura Demanski,Paul Casperson

Cc: Ronald barnes

Mar 29 at 3:28 PM

Fantastic Paul ... and thank you very much

Exhibit 4 – Email correspondence between Laura Demanski and Ronald Barnes

Hi Laura

I want to communicate with my alumni mates and it's been a challenge navigating the proper avenues in UChicago ... and alumni ... to get things done. I was just approved as a member of PSI CHI, the psychologist national honor society .. that's one story I'm proud of but more so that I am positioning myself to make a positive contribution to society.

Please respond to me and let's set up a meeting so I can give you my spill.

Sincerely

Ronald Barnes

Divinity School Alumni (2015)

Email # 3 from Laura Demanski to me regarding meeting

Laura Demanski

To: Ron Barnes

Apr 9 at 6:42 PM

Dear Ronald,

Thanks for your note, and apologies for taking so long to respond. I would be happy to hear about your book and any other stories you have. I could speak to you on the phone this Wednesday or Friday, when I'm free most of the day, or else we could look at next week. Are there times tomorrow or Friday when you'll be free for me to give you a call?

Best wishes,

Laura

Laura Demanski, AM'94

Editor, University of Chicago Magazine

Email # 4 from Laura Demanski to me confirming indication a plan for information on my book to be in the magazine

Laura Demanski

To: Ron Barnes

Apr 22 at 9:38 AM

Dear Ron,

Thank you for sharing your story and news of your books and academic honors with the *University of Chicago Magazine*. We will include an abbreviated version in our Advanced Degree News section in the Summer 2019 issue of the *Magazine*, which will be published in mid-August. I know your fellow alumni will read it with interest.

Congratulations on all your achievements!

Best wishes,

Laura

Exhibit 5 – Email correspondence between Ronald Barnes and Sarah Nolan

Email # 5 from Sarah Nolan to Me

Re: Comments from alumni2

Yahoo/Drafts

Sarah Nolan <snolan@uchicago.edu>

To: ron.barnes

Apr 25 at 10:01 AM

Mr. Barnes,

Laura Demanski forwarded me your message from Monday, April 22. Thank you for reaching out to share comments/concerns from alumni. That falls under my purview more than Laura's and I would be happy to discuss with you. Here are some times when I am available for a call:

Today, Thursday, 1-1:30pm or 2-2:30pm

Friday, 9 – 11am

Please let me know if one of those times works for you and what number is the best to reach you.

Separately, I want to make sure we are in agreement about the appropriate ways to interact with this office. Access to Harper Court offices is restricted to staff and tenants of the building. According to the security rules of Harper Court, non-staff visitors must contact us ahead of time and make an appointment before visiting our offices. Alumni badges may not be used to access the building. I understand that you have come to our offices in Harper Court several times without an appointment, which is contrary to our security rules and is not possible for our staff to accommodate.

Maintaining these rules is essential for reasons of security. It is also important as a courtesy to our staff. Please do not visit us in person again unless you have a previously scheduled appointment.

Thank you again and I look forward to speaking with you by phone.

Sarah

Sarah Nolan
AVP for Alumni Communications
snolan@uchicago.edu

Exhibit 6 - Band Letter from Assistant Police Chief Joanne Nee

Police Department

6054 South Drexel Avenue
Chicago, Illinois 60637

May 2, 2019

By First Class and Electronic Mail

Mr. Ronald Barnes
P.O. Box 15322
Chicago, IL 60615-5143
ron.barnes7@yahoo.com

Re: No Trespass Notification

Dear Mr. Barnes:

As you know, you have repeatedly visited the University's Alumni Relations & Development Office (ARD) without an appointment, and on at least two occasions, bypassed access restrictions to enter their office. On April 25, 2019, Sarah Nolan sent you an email in which she reminded you of the building's access restrictions and notified you that you should not come to ARD's office without a previously scheduled appointment. Nevertheless, on April 30, you gained access to ARD's office by pretending to be a job fair participant. Your conduct has been disruptive to ARD's operations and cannot continue.

This letter is to notify you that you are forbidden – effective immediately – from entering the Harper Court office tower, 5235 South Harper Court, Chicago. **This prohibition is permanent and if you violate this ban, you will be arrested for criminal trespass under 720 ILCS 5/21-3.** If you wish to challenge this ban, you may do so by following the process set forth in the University's No-Trespass (Ban) Policy, which can be accessed here: https://provost.uchicago.edu/handbook/life/safety-and-security.

Sincerely,

Joanne M. Nee
University of Chicago Police Department

cc: Eric Heath, AVP for Safety and Security
Carlton Hughes, University of Chicago Police Department
Ingrid Gould, Associate Provost
Brett Leibsker, Director, Employee & Labor Relations (HR)
Sarah Nolan, AVP for Alumni Communications
Suzanne Baker, AVP, Alumni Relations & Development
Philip Gold, Executive Director of Commercial Real Estate
Gary Wenzel, McCaffery

Exhibit 7 -No Trespass Notification Email

Email from the Campus Police

No Trespass Notification

Yahoo/Inbox

Joanne M Nee <nee@uchicago.edu>

To:'ron.barnes

Cc: Eric Heath,Ingrid Gould,Carlton Hughes,Brett Leibsker,Sarah Nolanand 3 more...

May 2 at 1:20 PM

Mr. Barnes,

My name is Joanne Nee. I am the Deputy Chief of Police at the University of Chicago Police Department. Attached is a formal notification that you are forbidden to enter the Harper Court office tower, located at 5235 South Harper Court, Chicago. If you violate this ban, you will be arrested for criminal trespass under 720 ILCS 5/21-3.

A copy of this letter has also been sent to you via US mail. If you have any questions regarding this notification, contact me directly.

Joanne M. Nee

Deputy Chief

University of Chicago Police Department

773.795.3882 O

773.490.5369 C

Exhibit 8 - Response to No Trespass from Dr. Barnes to Sara Nolan and Joanne Nee

May 6, 2019

To: Sarah Nolan

Jennifer Nee

Re: Ronald Barnes Ban from Alumni

Hello Ms. Nolan and Ms. Nee

I took time and I wanted to be thoughtful in writing this letter. I do believe both of you acted irresponsibly. I believe that if I were a white person the response by Ms. Nolan would have been "what can I do to help you." Which is the customary response in this situation. Ms. Nee as a campus police officer should have investigated the situation before acting rashly and rushing to judgement. I further believe that to distribute the ban letter to so many people without knowing both sides of the story was counterproductive. Nevertheless, I would like to see this situation resolved amicably without having it escalate to the Provost office or the President's office. Frankly, I do not want my name and reputation cast in a negative light at that level. I have worked too hard and responsibly to build my name and reputation and I don't want it cast in a negative light, especially, under these unnecessary and irresponsible circumstances based on actions I consider racist, irresponsible and grossly over reactive. However, if we can resolve this issue amicable without escalating it to the executive levels of the university that would be my preference.

On the two occasions I entered the Alumni building without an appointment. I did stop at the security desk to ask them who I should contact. They searched the directory and did not know. The first time I entered the building was to inform the Alumni magazine about the book I wrote and to get space in the magazine. The second time was to inform the Alumni about my induction into Psi Chi, the psychology national honor society and have my story about how the university motivated my learning. On both of these occasions I stopped at the security desk to ask who I should contact. They did not know and the security **directed** me to go upstairs to inquire on both occasions. The third time I entered the building without an appointment was to wait for the shuttle. I noticed a job fair going on, made inquire and was signed up on the spot by the person at the desk. This person instructed to go to the 11th floor. At no time did I enter the building and go up without direction. Everything I have stated can be collaborated by the persons involved (100%). I do not lie or present a false impression. It is not my nature. I am proud of myself and what I have and am accomplishing. It insults me to have to deal with a matter such as this however, it would be worse for me to ignore it.

I want to suggest a meeting between myself, Ms. Nee and Ms. Nolan to resolve this matter in a mutually amicable manner to keep it from escalating to higher levels. Without us resolving the issue at our level, it will be appealled to the Provost office and the President's office. I do not think it should be necessary to take their time with a matter such as this that never should have been an issue in the first place.

Please respond and let me know by **Thursday May 9, 2019**, if you are agreeable to meeting and resolving this issue between ourselves. Otherwise, I will appeal to higher levels.

Please review the following attachments:

1. The Ban letter, you both have copies so it is not attached.
2. The email exchange is worth review because it documents my correspondence with people in the building (Exhibit 2 - Email Exchanges between myself, Paul Casperson and Laura Demanski).

3. The article I wanted to have published in the Alumni magazine and the reason for my second visit is attached (Exhibit 1).

4. Also attached are letters of recommendation from noteworthy people who know the person I am. The recommendations were recently written as an endorsement for my enrollment to receive my second doctorate in clinical psychology. My first doctorate is in psychology with a focus on integrating technology into the learning system. Frankly, I am the type of person the Alumni Association should embrace. The reason we have a Black Alumni Association is because the Alumni Association does not serve Alumni equally or fairly, otherwise there would be no need for two Alumni associations.

Cole Peterson (retired) - Vice President of Walmart HR, people division, in Charge of their 1 million people (employees).

Jeanette Altenau - Director of Community services for Tri-Health systems and board member of the Cincinnati Bengals professional football team.

Dr. Hoyland Ricks - Prominent physical in Atlanta Georgia

These people know my character and the person I am. I'm sure they would be totally shocked at the actions taking by Ms. Nee and Ms. Nolan. Nevertheless, these letters give you an insight into the person I am, at least they person they see me to be.

Personally, I believe it will be in all of our best interest to resolve this matter between us so I do not have to escalate the problem to higher levels but that is my opinion. What do you think? Ms. Nolan, I believe meeting was your initial suggestion per the email previous.

Ronald Barnes
University of Chicago Alumni (2015)

Exhibit 9 – Dr. Barnes Response to the Ban – Appeal Request

May 2, 2019

Re: Appeal of Ban from entering the University of Chicago Alumni Building at 5235 South Harper Court – No Trespass Notification (Exhibit A and Exhibit Al)

From: Ronald Barnes, Plantiff

To: **University of Chicago personnel:**

Eric Heath, AVP for Safety and Security

Carlton Hughes, University of Chicago Police Department

Ingrid Gould, Associate Provost

Brett Leibsker, Director Employee and Labor Relations

Sara Nolan, AVP for Alumni Communications

Suzanne Baker, AVP, Alumni Relations and Development

Philip Gold, Executive Director of Commercial Real Estate

Gary Wenzel McCaffery

Joanne M. Nee, University of Chicago Police Department

Laura Demanski,

ldemanski@uchicago.edu emheath@uchicago.edu chughes@uchicago.edu bleibsker@uchicago.edu i-gould@uchicago.edu snolan@uchicago.edu s-baker1@uchicago.edu philgold@uchicago.edu nee@uchicago.edu gwenzel@mccafferyinterests.com

Hello All,

I am writing this appeal with much embarrassment, complete astonishment, regret that I have to take the time to address this issue, some disgust that this is happening in the first place but also with a confrontation of the reality that individuals in our society resorts to negative acts of response to a situation before they look for positive reconciling solutions. I am referring to the fact that someone from the Alumni Association (Sarah Nolan) contacted the University Police and requested that I be banned from the Alumni building. That was a negative response to a completely benign and harmless situation. In my opinion, is was a gross over-reaction on the part of the Alumni Office personnel (Sarah Nolan) that issued the complaint. I do believe that if I were a white person instead of an African American this situation would never have occurred. Frankly, as a professional with a keen sense of instinct and insight, the situation strikes me as a racist reaction to a black person that never would have happened to a white person. Our society has seen many instances of victimization of African American people because of an over-reaction on the part of a white person. I do not want to have an incident such as this on my record. As a matter of record, I do not want my reputation tarnished by this incident and frankly, I regret having to take the time to address it, but it is important that I do. White hostility to Black people is raising its ugly head (Starbucks, Yale student in the dorm studying late at night and many more of which this is another) throughout America and, unfortunately, in Universities. I would have been courteously received and time would have been taken to talk with me and at least explain the policy requiring a prior appointment without any need to contact the Campus police and put a scar on my reputation, if I were white. To have such a high-profile incident of this type is embarrassing and signifies an incompetence and an inability to deal with situations in a conciliatory manner on the part of the Alumni personnel. Especially, since I am an alumnus of the University of Chicago. I also attended and graduated from the University of

Chicago Laboratory School. I am a part of this community since my teenage years. I am appalled at having to take the time to deal with this incident.

I graduated with a M.A. degree from the Divinity School in 2015. I am now writing my dissertation for my PhD in psychology. I have recently been inducted into Psi Chi, which is the International Honor Society for Psychology. My doctorate grade point average is 3.56 out of 4.0. I am not the kind of person that should have to deal with this kind of incident. In my opinion it is purely racial, racist.

The Ban states the following charges and I would like to respond to each one individually.

1. **I was charged with repeatedly visiting the Alumni Building without an appointment on at least two (2) occasions.**

The reason I visited the Alumni Building is because knowing who to contact is not easy. Navigating the Alumni personnel and departments is a challenge. I did visit the building on 2 occasions without an appointment. Both times was to find out the contact person for my purpose. I wanted to have my story told. Check the emails attached and it will explain the reasons for my visit. (Exhibit 2). The first visit was to have the fact I wrote a book published in the Alumni magazine. The book is entitled "Practice what you Preach, preach what you Practice." You can see a 1 minute overview on the book at:

https://www.youtube.com/watch?v=pBbttZXPh5w

The second time I went to the Alumni building was to have my story told about my doctoral journey and induction into Psi Chi. (See Exhibit 1).

I encountered Paul Casperson who helped me to find the right person. He put me in touch with Laura Demanski. You can check the email exchange between myself and Laura Demanski (Exhibit 2). There is nothing in our exchange that even gives the slightest hint of actions to warrant this extreme and hostile action to ban me from the building. I am an Alumni of the University and have every right to contact people in the building. They work for me. Also on each and every occasion I entered the building I stopped at the security guard desk, showed them my ID and they told me to go up, on each and every occasion. They tried to help me locate the person and department I needed to contact but even the security guards could not find the right people so they directed me to go up and find out for myself.

Please check the email exchanges between myself and Laura Demanski. There is nothing improper in those emails. They are professional and completely collaborative. (Exhibit 2).

I will comment that my interaction with Laura Demanski was cordial, professional and she was polite. It seemed that we had a good respectful conversation. I left appreciating our meeting.

2. **Sarah Nolan sent me an email in which she reminded me about the buildings access restrictions and notified me I should not visit ARD without a prior appointment.**

Sarah Nolan did send me an email (Exhibit 3) that I did not respond to because I was focused on research and writing my doctoral dissertation. I intended to respond after I got some daylight from my doctoral responsibilities. Her email is attached and initially there is nothing in the email that indicates she would act hostile toward me, as she obviously did.

She did indicate the policy on making an appointment prior to a visit but there is nothing that I thought indicated hostile action, as was taken.

I do think her hostile action was taken because of a comment I made to Laura Demanski about the lack of stories in the Alumni magazine on the accomplishments of Black people. I made the comment that the magazine writes and publishes stories on Black people who dance, who play music or who are artist. When it comes to the academic and intellectual accomplishments of Black people there are no articles. I also talked with two other alumni about this and mentioned it to Laura Demanski. It is my instinctive opinion that this incident was a cause of the hostile reaction. White people react defensive to comments regarding race and I believe this was such an incident. Instead of having discussion, the reaction was hostile and showed a lack of intelligence to handle controversy, controversy that is actively prevalent our contemporary society.

3 On April 30 I entered the ARD building by "pretending" to be a job fair participant.

The only way I can respond to this issue is that it is an **out and out blatant LIE.** I had an appointment at the Polsky center to present a product line I developed to get some guidance regarding how to get the product into the market. I brought 2 boxes on the shuttle to the Polsky center. After the appointment I went to catch a return shuttle and waited in the Alumni building (street level) until the shuttle arrived. When I went into the building I saw the desk for the Job Fair and made an inquiry. They told me that I had to register. I told them, distinctly, I was not registered. The lady at the Job fair desk told me to sign the sheet and go to the 11th floor. At no time did I "**pretend**" to be a participant. The fact that I went to the job fair was haphazard. Had I not waited for the shuttle I would not have known about the Job fair. Under no circumstances was I misleading. I specifically told the job fair representative I was not registered and she had me sign up on the spot. I went to the 11th floor and to no other location in the building. This charge / complaint is totally without substance and is a **misleading lie** regarding my presence in the building. Besides the job fair was open to the public anyway. Why this is an issue is an indication of the petty nature of this incident and the character of those who made this complaint.

4 My conduct has been disruptive to the ARD operations.

With all respect, I can understand how an unplanned visit can take a person out of their work routine, if it takes an undue amount of time. This is a total exaggeration of the situation and likewise misleading for the sake of the Alumni personnel making a discriminating argument. At no time was I given more than 1 minute of anyone's time that I saw, with the exception of Laura Demanski, with whom I met and Paul Carperson who helped me navigate the building to locate Laura Demanski. If the minute I spent with other people was disruptive, asking them questions regarding who handles the business I need then that person gets nothing done anyway. Again, if I were white this would never have been an issue. Besides, going into the Alumni building and witnessing the activity that goes on, one wonders, what do they do anyway. There is an abundance of idle activity. If they were professional, the response would have been: "What can I do to help you." Not banning me from the building that is supportive of my status as a University Alumni. The people who initiated this complaint need to revisit their purpose, their people skills and their racial ideology. I am not saying they are bad people. I am saying they are people who need training in interpersonal relationships and Alumni relations.

While I have every respect for the Campus police and highly appreciate the safe environment, they have created for the people in the University community, I do believe they could have acted more responsibly. Before issuing a statement banning me from the Alumni building, they should have heard my side of the story. They could have been a catalyst in resolving this problem without incident, instead of having it escalate to the level it has. I was proven guilty until proven guilty, which was all at once. It was not considered that learning my side of the story would have kept the incident from escalating. These are incidents that make even the most professional and intelligent African Americans see our society for what it is.

I am deeply touched by this matter and seriously insulted. Everyone who knows me on this University Campus can vouch for my character. I am confident the Police officers I've had the pleasure of knowing can vouch for the fact this incident does not align with my character. My professors, associates at the University, library personnel, students, everyone I know at this University, I am confident can vouch for the fact that this complaint is not aligned with the person I am. Investigate that.

Sincerely

Ronald Barnes
University of Chicago Divinity School (2015)

Exhibit 10 - Lift of the Ban Letter

The University of Chicago

OFFICE OF THE PROVOST
5801 SOUTH ELLIS AVENUE
CHICAGO • ILLINOIS 60637

Ingrid Gould
Associate Provost

TELEPHONE: (773) 702-8846
FAX: (773) 702-9595

14 August 2019

Mr. Ronald Barnes
PO Box 15322
Chicago, Il 60615-5143
ron.barnes7@yahoo.com

Dear Ron:

Thank you for meeting with me on 8 August. It was nice to meet your friend who preferred not to give his name. I write to recapitulate our discussion. Again, I apologize that you had to wait longer than the standard 30 days for the University to review your request to remove the no-trespass warning for the Harper Court office tower, 5235 S. Harper Court, Chicago. As I explained, we used a two-step process, first investigating your allegation that the warning was racially motivated and second considering if it should remain in place.

Jackie Hennard, Associate Director/Lead Investigator in the Office for Access and Equity, assessed the alleged discriminatory basis, finding no discrimination. Her rationale is, in part, that there is no evidence that those responsible for implementing the directive were aware of your race at the time. She also found evidence of a plausible non-discriminatory reason for the directive. I suggested that you speak with Melissa Gilliam about your Alumni Association & Development (ARD) concerns.

I reviewed the no-trespass warning itself, the reasons for its imposition, and the rationale for it to remain. I concluded that the no-trespass directive should be lifted. You are again welcome to enter the Harper Court office tower as long as you, like all other visitors, respect that building's rules, which are more restrictive than on other parts of campus.

Staff members of ARD gladly meet with people, especially alumni, by appointment. Theirs is not a drop-in operation, as some alumni affairs offices and centers are elsewhere. Thank you for agreeing to abide by ARD's practices should you wish to meet with someone in that office in the future; failing to do so may prompt reinstatement of your no-trespass warning.

Further, as I reviewed your petition, I learned that you sometimes drop in on others on campus. While some people enjoy an occasional impromptu visit as much as you do, many UChicago employees find it disrupts their work to receive surprise visitors. You would extend a courtesy by scheduling time to meet with Laboratory Schools, Divinity School, and other staff. You bridled at this suggestion and stated that Americia Huckabee, the Divinity School assistant to the dean of students and someone you described as a friend, welcomes your unscheduled visits. While you may be right, consider that her supervisor expects her to work during work hours. You would avoid problems by calling ahead.

If you have questions about this letter, please feel free to contact me for clarification.

Sincerely,

Ingrid Gould

cc: Suzanne Baker, ARD
Laura Demanski, ARD
Philip Gold, Commercial Real Estate
Jackie Hennard, Access and Equity
Eric Heath, UCPD
Carlton Hughes, UCPD
Brett Leibsker, HR
Joanne Nee, UCPD
Sarah Nolan, ARD
Gary Wenzel, McCaffery
Ellen Wetmore, OLC

The University of Chicago

OFFICE OF THE PROVOST
5801 SOUTH ELLIS AVENUE
CHICAGO • ILLINOIS 60637

Ingrid Gould
Associate Provost

TELEPHONE: (773) 702-8846
FAX: (773) 702-9595

14 August 2019

Mr. Ronald Barnes
PO Box 15322
Chicago, Il 60615-5143
ron.barnes7@yahoo.com

Dear Ron:

Thank you for meeting with me on 8 August. It was nice to meet your friend who preferred not to give his name. I write to recapitulate our discussion. Again, I apologize that you had to wait longer than the standard 30 days for the University to review your request to remove the no-trespass warning for the Harper Court office tower, 5235 S. Harper Court, Chicago. As I explained, we used a two-step process, first investigating your allegation that the warning was racially motivated and second considering if it should remain in place.

Jackie Hennard, Associate Director/Lead Investigator in the Office for Access and Equity, assessed the alleged discriminatory basis, finding no discrimination. Her rationale is, in part, that there is no evidence that those responsible for implementing the directive were aware of your race at the time. She also found evidence of a plausible non-discriminatory reason for the directive. I suggested that you speak with Melissa Gilliam about your Alumni Association & Development (ARD) concerns.

I reviewed the no-trespass warning itself, the reasons for its imposition, and the rationale for it to remain. I concluded that the no-trespass directive should be lifted. You are again welcome to enter the Harper Court office tower as long as you, like all other visitors, respect that building's rules, which are more restrictive than on other parts of campus.

Staff members of ARD gladly meet with people, especially alumni, by appointment. Theirs is not a drop-in operation, as some alumni affairs offices and centers are elsewhere. Thank you for agreeing to abide by ARD's practices should you wish to meet with someone in that office in the future; failing to do so may prompt reinstatement of your no-trespass warning.

Further, as I reviewed your petition, I learned that you sometimes drop in on others on campus. While some people enjoy an occasional impromptu visit as much as you do, many UChicago employees find it disrupts their work to receive surprise visitors. You would extend a courtesy by scheduling time to meet with Laboratory Schools, Divinity School, and other staff. You bridled at this suggestion and stated that Americia Huckabee, the Divinity School assistant to the dean of students and someone you described as a friend, welcomes your unscheduled visits. While you may be right, consider that her supervisor expects her to work during work hours. You would avoid problems by calling ahead.

If you have questions about this letter, please feel free to contact me for clarification.

Sincerely,

Ingrid Gould

cc: Suzanne Baker, ARD
Laura Demanski, ARD
Philip Gold, Commercial Real Estate
Jackie Hennard, Access and Equity
Eric Heath, UCPD
Carlton Hughes, UCPD
Brett Leibsker, HR
Joanne Nee, UCPD
Sarah Nolan, ARD
Gary Wenzel, McCaffery
Ellen Wetmore, OLC

Exhibit 11 – Recommendation for a Diverse Environment

September 22, 2019

Ms. Ingrid Gould, Associate Provost

The University of Chicago

5801 South Ellis Avenue

Chicago, Illinois 60637

Dear Ingrid

Thank you for taking the time to address and assist in the resolution of my appeal regarding being banned from the Alumni Building in Harper Court. I consider this situation a negative and unfortunate incident that is characteristic of phenomena that occurs in the lives of many minority individuals in America. What makes the difference in facing life challenges is not that they occur but how they are handled. It is my intention that this negative unfortunate incident results in a learning experience for myself, the University, Sarah Nolan (the Alumni Association, Jennifer Nee (the University Police Department, Jackie Hennard (in handling University discrimination complaints and for yourself (the Provost office and Executive Administration of the University).

I took considerable time composing this document and gave much thought before sending it. This document is sent to those who previous received information on the ban and individuals in the university who need to be award of the situation and are in position to make improvements. This document is also sent to those who have no relevance to the investigation but were contacted, irresponsibly, by investigators to get background information on Ronald Barnes.

Please understand the directness and unfiltered content of this correspondence is because the point of the communication would be diluted if wrong, racist and discriminatory actions were "sugar coated." I want to state from the outset that I am not angry nor vindictive. My intention in writing this communication is to inform the University of Chicago how it can improve the environment. I'm sure I am not saying anything that is not known. I'm sure that if I state the investigation was prejudiced and only covers up hostile actions on the part of the University Alumni Association, these are facts already known by the persons involved. Therefore, accept that I am stating the obvious for the purpose of moving forward toward solution (See Exhibit I to understand the sequence of events)

I considered myself a member (longstanding) of the university community. I went to the University of Chicago Laboratory School. My sister went to the University of Chicago Laboratory School. I graduated from the University of Chicago Divinity School with a M.A. in Religious Studies. Because I considered myself a longstanding member of this community is a reason the action taken by Sarah Nolan (Alumni Department) against me, did not anger me so much as it hurt me and challenged my security of being an accepted member of the university community. As a Black person, the situation was even more profound because it was an example of a White person, irresponsibly and prejudicially, taking unwarranted negative aggressive action against a Black person, which is a common phenomenon in our American society, past and present. Based on the actions that led to me being banned from the Alumni building, if I were a White man her response would have been, "may I help you Mr. Barnes." Being a Black man her response was to ban me from the Alumni Building. This hypocrisy in the way White people and Black people are dealt with is an issue this University has not resolved and does not deal with effectively. Certainly, the University did not deal with my situation in a just manner nor in a manner that will resolve the problem. Not only am I a graduate of the university but also a member of the Alumni Association, which makes the ban all the more ridiculous and racist. I am a Black man who has a Master degree from this university. I am completing my PhD in psychology. I have a doctoral GPA of 3.6. I have been inducted into Psi Chi, the international honor society for psychology and I have written my first book with 3 more in the cue to be out by second quarter of 2020 (See Exhibit II). The only difference between myself and any other accomplished person who never would have encountered this incident is that I am a Black male. A White person never would have encountered this incident based on the circumstances. This incident is categorically indicative and analogous to two other high profile incidents that have occurred in our contemporary times:

1. When Muhammed Ali was given the Medal of Freedom, the highest honor an American Citizen can be awarded by the government, by President George W. Bush, he was congratulated by his Muslim Brother, Minister Louis Farrakhan. Muhammed Ali's response was; "Still a nigger."

2. Labron James, one of the best basketball players of today, built a school for kids. In an interview with a TV host, he expressed concern that our country leadership was not adequate. Laura Ingram, a Fox news anchor, made the statement; "Shut up and just dribble the basketball."

These statements are expressions of viewpoints that give insight into White and Black perspectives on racism, discrimination and prejudice in our country. The statement by Muhammed Ali, indicates what Black people perceive about race relations. The second statement indicates what White people perceive about race relations. Both statements have alignment with the fact that racism, White privilege and prejudice are openly prevalent issues and beliefs in our American Society. The question then becomes, should it be accepted, condoned and allowed to exist without scrutiny or should it be changed otherwise.

The ban letter issued by Joanne Knee of the UCPD stated that I "have repeatedly visited the University Alumni Relations & Development Office without an appointment and on at least two occasions bypassed access restrictions to enter the office." This statement reflects the lack of knowledge on the part of

Joanne Knee and reflects on her professional ability or lack thereof. The statement is not true. On each and every occasion I entered the building and went beyond the lobby I was instructed to do so. Had Joanne Knee exercised professional investigative skills, she would have known this. Instead, she merely took the word and false accusation of Sarah Nolan without getting my side of the story. I would think this is police training 101, to get both sides of the story before taking action in minor incidents of misunderstanding. As far as an appointment goes, the security could not tell me the proper person to see or contact. I was advised to go up, on each and every occasion. The Alumni office is so disorganized that the security does not have personnel information. The reason for my entering the Alumni Building was to inform them of my book, with hope to gain recognition in the Alumni Magazine (first time entering the building). The second time I entered the building was to present an article to the Alumni I wanted published, giving credit and expressing my sincere gratitude to the University of Chicago for playing a significant role in the development and emergence of my latent intellectual ability, as a result of my experience at this institution (See exhibit III). The third time I entered the building was to attend a job recruitment event open to the public. It was thereafter, Sarah Nolan of the Alumni Department notified Jennifer Knee of the UCPD to have me barred from the building. This was a ridiculous, ignorant and unwarranted reaction on the part of Sarah Nolan and Jennifer Knee. It is my opinion that Sarah Nolan's "hot button" was pushed because I stated to her staff member Laura Demanski, that the Magazine does not publish articles on the professional and academic accomplishments of Black people and it does not. The Alumni Association does not serve the needs of the minority University Alumni community. They are only interested in serving the needs of the White University Alumni. A prime example and result of this is the establishment of the Black Alumni Association (UCABA). If the Alumni Association served the needs of the entire Alumni there would be no need for auxiliary Alumni associations.

The actions against me by Sarah Nolan also indicate and reinforce the attitude of the Alumni Association toward Black Alumni. Even good White people have subtle tendencies of racism because they allow racism and racist ideology to exist. This is evident in my particular case, herein, White people who conduct the investigation, cover up racist acts and make ridiculous nonsensical excuses for racist behavior on the part of their White counterparts who demonstrate racist behavior. How do you expect the problem to be solve by dealing with it in a protective manner? It will only perpetuate and become more ingrained in White society, culture and specifically in the University of Chicago. White society and culture is a racist culture, essentially. Please understand I am not saying this in anger but in truth. History substantiates this statement. A problem is only resolved when it is acknowledged and addressed in a resolve manner. The university failed in this case to do that. I am grateful and appreciative the ban was lifted. Thank you, Ingrid. However, that the ban was lifted is a strong indication it never should have been placed in the first place and the action taken by Sarah Nolan was racist and at the very least unwarranted, irrational and unnecessary. Bad judgement is an indication that people are not responsible in their job position. Additionally, Joanne Knee (UCPD) was used by Sarah Nolan to execute the unjust ban. Joanne Knee as the Deputy Director of the UCPD was irresponsible in that she merely took the word of Sarah Nolan without investigating the facts. This is a subtle characteristic of racism. White people use the police to reinforce racist behavior who unquestionable accept the word of other White people when the object is a Black person. This is a problem in society and obviously on this University Campus.

One of the most ridiculous aspects of the investigation of the ban against me was that the University investigation, investigated me. As stated in your lifting of the ban letter, the university investigated my interactions with the Lab school and found that I sometimes "drop in" without notice. This really makes me laugh with a realization of how people search for straws. The first time I "dropped in" on the Lab School Alumni director was to get information on my lab school counselor, Carolyn Smith to thank her for the input she gave me and my parents about which college I should attend. That turned out to be a decision in the crossroad of my life that made a critical difference in where I am today. I wanted to thank her for paying attention to me at that stage in my life. The second time I "dropped in" to the Lab school Alumni office was because I had an appointment with them to acknowledge my book and give me recognition in the Lab school Alumni magazine. The third time I "dropped in" to the Lab school Alumni office was to ask the "new" alumni director if he could help me locate Ms. Carolyn Smith because the prior Alumni director was not helpful. If these incidents are used to determine my pattern of behavior, then you need to question your value system and your ability to assess behavior. If I were white this would have been irrelevant and a non-issue. More so the Lab school never complained. Frankly, both times the Lab School director demonstrated a positive attitude that I was an Alumni who visited.

It was also stated that I demonstrate likewise, "drop in" behavior at the Divinity School. I have "dropped in" on the Divinity school. My reasons have been to give a copy of my book to the Dean of student's secretary, Americus Huckabee. Occasionally, I will "drop in" to say hello but only when my initial reason was to get a sandwich at the Ground of Being café. These incidents were a maximum of 5 minutes. You mentioned in our meeting that these "drop in" incidents cause disruptions to their work. I do expect a more intelligent evaluation of my "drop in" behavior from a University of Chicago executive. If it causes a work stoppage by me dropping in for 3-5 minutes to say hello to Divinity School personnel, of which I am an Alumni and because they are past associates and friends, then it shameful to find fault with my behavior to justify the ban. Besides, they never complained and were happy to see me. The important point in this investigation procedure is that the investigation involved investigating me. Did the investigation probe into the background and activity of Sarah Nolan as deeply as it did mine? This is a prime case of the accuser being treated as the accused. A case of White people covering up for White people by developing a case against the Black man to justify the racism of the White person. This behavior on the part of the investigation was shallow, ridiculous and far beneath any professional standard for resolving important issues. Frankly, I question the practical intelligence of how the entire investigation was handled. What did the investigation do in investigation Sarah Nolan? Did the investigation probe into Sarah Nolan's background as deeply as they did mine? If not, the investigation was racist. The investigation was conducted in a racist manner. With all respect, my purpose is to point out some shortcomings that are ingrained in White people and White culture and socialized into their culture when addressing Black and White issues. This is an example of good White people having racist tendencies. White people are so blinded by White privileges that they lack a clear lens by which to fairly investigate racist incidents. White people perceive some incidents of racism against Black people as justifiable behavior and find reasons to justify White racist behavior. It is easier to justify White racism when it is subtle. This case does have some subtle and overt racist incidental behaviors. This case would have been stronger if the Alumni publishes an article stating that they will not publish articles about Black accomplishment or if they had a "Black Face" day in the office or if a noose was found hanging from the Alumni Building elevator. Then my case would have been easier to prove. The truth is that White people are not qualified to evaluate or investigate racist behavior because they have no significant experience with the phenomena of racism.

Again, my purpose is to provide insight and understanding that hopefully will make this university environment better. Numerous complaints on racism have been placed against this institution by African American, Islamic students, LGBT students and even Asian students do comfortably integrate into this university environment. The University of Chicago environment does not make a comfortable integration space for all of its student body and obviously, neglects a significant population of its Alumni, the African American alumnus. The American Psychological Association (APA) just published a guide to provide a 'safe' space environment for transgender, gay, lesbian and bisexual student,

(https://www.breitbart.com/politics/2019/10/17/american-psychological-association-publishes-guide-to-provide-safe-environment-for-transgender-students/).

African Americans are not the only group discriminated against in our society and our learning institutions. Discrimination on college campuses is recognized by authority organizations who are concerned with problems in our society, organizations such as the APA.

If the University wants to change and improve this, I have recommendations. My purpose is to contribute positive to this university. I am a product of this environment since high school. I believe I have a responsibility to contribute positive to my Alma Mater. Having the university become recognized not only for academic excellence but for social excellence enhances my pride in the school and my status as being an Alumni of a school that strives for excellence in all areas of responsibility.

My recommendations:

1. Provide extensive and periodic ongoing diversity training for University personnel on a regular basis. Especially personnel in a position that deal with minority and diversity encounters, (The Alumni department personnel, The University police for starters). Diversity training, Black history and White privilege should be a mandatory prerequisite entry level course for all incoming freshmen. Diversity education on LGBT issues, Asian issues, African American issues, Islamic issues and Caucasian issues. Asian students, for the most part, are a close-knit group and find comfort in their own group settings. However, Asians have

much to offer this university and all students herein. Many Asians are in the STEM programs; few African Americans are in STEM programs. Asians can contribute to all students in providing insight into what gives them the academic focus they possess. This insight will be helpful to all learners in this institution. As long as there is isolation and discrimination in this university environment, without a committed and qualified program and effort to bring people together for the purpose of enhancing learning and improving the conditions on campus and in society, the University of Chicago has only achieved mediocre success in contributing to society. There is more to teaching and training the complete human being than book knowledge. The lack of social skills and acceptance of all human beings regardless of race, color, creed or gender orientation still makes book smart people stupid and ignorant.

2. Dedicate at least 5 pages in the Alumni Magazine that addresses the accomplishments of Black individuals who are university Alumni or fund a Magazine to be published by the Black Alumni Association so they can acknowledge the accomplishments of Black Alumni and address issues relevant to Black Alumni. If White Alumni and people in the university Alumni department were aware of the many accomplishments of Black alumni, then possibly their perspective and behavior will change for the better. Individuals who graduate from this great institution have tools and skills to accomplish great things and the vast majority of University of Chicago alumni do just that, including the Black Alumni.
3. Another alternative is for the Alumni Association to have the other University Alumni associations, UCABA for example, housed in the Alumni Building, along with dedicated staff, and under the same umbrella to address the needs of the entire alumni student body. This will give the image of unity instead of presenting a fraction among the

White University Alumni and the minority University Alumni. The Alumni associations will be able to work more closely and as one, instead of as many.

4. With all respect, White people are not qualified to investigate White racism. The person who should investigate racism complaints should be a black person or someone of minority status who has background and understand of the overt and subtle acts of racism. In my opinion, the people investigating racist complaints are not qualified to understand the realm of racist behaviors. Being white their perspective is influenced with a "White empathy" that is skewed with a skeptical perspective of Black behavior that would be totally acceptable were White people behaving in the same manner. White people are more prone to cover up racist acts of White people rather than condemn White racism or provide education that gives more understanding to the problem.

5. If Black people felt the University was more responsible to their needs and more opened to Black participation, then Black contributions to the University would increase. I've talked to a number of Black Alumni who have no interest in giving money to this University. They feel the score is even. I got the great education I wanted and the University got paid. Even score. In my opinion, this attitude on the part of both parties needs to change. It is in everyone's best interest to see this university flourish and as great as this university is, it can get better. The more resources the university has the better it can get. However, improvement also involves improving the cultural values and the mindset. This can only be done when racist incidents are addressed in a strong resolved manner. My case was handled to protect the culprit and rationalize (in a very weak manner) justification for the ban. However, if the ban was justified it would not have been lifted. This incident that happened to

me is an example of why Black Alumni do not have any monetary empathy for this institution after they graduate. I would like to see this changed.

6. The behavior demonstrated by Sarah Nolan was comparable to behavior by the Nazis against the Jews (metaphorically speaking and as an analogy). The police reinforce the racist ideology. That the UCPD takes action on complaints such as the one described herein against me is indicative of neophyte police work. There was no investigation to learn both sides of the story and find a positive resolution more amenable than negative. I even sent an email to Joanne Knee and Sarah Nolan requesting that we resolve this matter without having it escalate to the level of the Provost office. It's embarrassing being cast in this way. "First impressions people have of me, who were made aware of the incident, that do not know me, is their first impression. My reputation is at stake. My professional image is at stake. All of which could have been prevented. Both, Joanne Knee and Sarah Nolan refused to resolve the matter before it escalated to the current level. This demonstrates a lack of ability to resolve conflict with mindful intelligence. If they had approached this incident in a more intelligent manner it would have reflected positive on the University. Problem and conflict resolution is an area that the UCPD and obviously, persons of leadership positions in the university need to learn. The university should have ongoing training in the area of problem and conflict resolution for its management and it will be a good idea to have students take seminars on this topic. This is a diverse environment, with different cultures, ideologies, religions and views. Learning tolerance and understanding individual differences only creates and enhanced the learning environment. It is also an area the University of Chicago can take leadership thus enhancing it's already established reputation for academic excellence.

It is really quite shameful and pathetic that this incident occurred. It is an example of very good intentions on my part being sabotaged by discriminating and racist ideology. My intention was to give praise to the university and express my appreciation to this university for motivating my academic mind. Instead, my good intentions were turned into a ban from the alumni building and an appeal to the Provost office to have the ban lifted. Absolutely incredible. If they were boiling water, it would have burned.

There are some insights and issues the University needs to consider for future investigations on racism and discrimination claims as a result of this investigation on racism and discrimination

1. The first issue raises the concern that the University of Chicago is not serious about addressing the issue of racism and discrimination on the campus. That the policy on discrimination, racism and diversity is only for show and not for remedy. How many complaints have been received by Jackie Hennard's office? How many were resolved where discrimination was found? How many were resolved where discrimination was not found?

2. Had this incident been handled properly it never would have escalated to this point. Both Joanne Knee and Sarah Nolan had the opportunity for us to discuss this matter and resolve it between us. They declined to do so. I sent them both an email requesting not to let this matter escalate. They ignored my request. This is an example of how White individuals exercise wrong and racist behavior and feel justified to stand behind their irresponsible decisions. Pathetic.

3. A damaging aspect of this incident, banning Ron Barnes from the Alumni building is that Jennifer Knee sent a copy of the ban letter to multiple people. What was the purpose of this? Before even knowing the facts and issues for which Sarah Nolan, Jennifer Knee took the lib-

erty to distribute the ban against Ronald Barnes to multiple sources in the university community. This was a lack of good judgement, incompetence and "bad police." The reputation and name of Ronald Barnes was slandered without just cause. The ban letter was a first impression of Ronald Barnes for people who received the ban letter. The problem is that the ban has been revoked but how do you revoke first impressions. I am not saying that Jennifer Knee is incompetent in all of her professional responsibilities. I am saying that in this particular incident, she was incompetent. Procedures need to be installed that provide guidelines for UCPD to handle complaints of this nature.

4. The manner in which the investigation was conducted and the findings are questionable. The investigators investigated the person making the complaint. What investigation was conducted against the person on whom the complaint was made? Did the investigators delve into the background of the person against whom the complaint was filed? Did they investigate the background of the person against whom the complaint was filed as deeply as they investigated the background of the complainant? This gives the impression the entire investigation was conducted in a racist and discriminating manner.

5. The details and reasoning for the findings were never disclosed to the complainant. The complainant was merely told there was no finding of discrimination or racism without being given any details. The complainant received more details on his own background than he did on the investigation procedures and details on how the findings were determined. This raises the issue that the entire investigation was racist and prejudicial.

6. The issue of the competence and ability of the investigators to handle racism and discrimination complaints is in question. The manner in

which the investigation was conducted and the findings demonstrates the investigators have no substantial understanding of racism or discrimination behaviors. White culture is socialized to consider it normal behavior to be skeptical about the behavior of Black people even when Black behavior is the same as White behavior. 1) Either the investigators are compliant with racist and discrimination behavior. 2) Either the investigators do not understand the subtle behavior of racism. 3) Either the investigators do not have the ability or skillset to address the issue of racism and discrimination. Or 4) The investigators are just plain stupid and do not know how to deal with racism and discrimination. To present such a weak case that focuses on the behavior of the complainant rather than the behavior of the person the complaint was made against is ridiculous. To present a rational for action taken against the complainant such as: "he has a habit of dropping in" is ridiculous. In other words, to stop by and say hello to people that are former associates and valuable to the complainants learning process, is objectionable behavior. Being that was the only rational the investigators could come up with for the ban placed against the complainant is so ridiculous that I have to pity the people who defend White racist behavior rather that solve the problem in a professional manner.

The objective is not to use this situation as a punishment but as a learning experience so the University can teach its personnel, employees, staff and even students how to deal with each other with respect. Unless racism and discrimination is addressed with resolve to eliminate the behavior on this campus, it will exist, perpetuate, and increase.

7. The University does not need partisan investigators addressing these claims. The university needs people who have knowledge of overt and subtle forms of racism and discrimination to address the claims. The

> purpose of finding racism and discriminating behavior is not be punish the person demonstrating racism but to educate the racist and help them to identify the subtle racist and discriminatory characteristics in their behavior. I have no doubt that all people involved in this situation are decent and good people, under normal circumstances. However, racist behaviors are a part of the socialization and development process in White culture. It is learned behavior that begins when White people attend all white elementary schools and is reinforced by segregation environments. How to break the cycle of wrong learned behavior is also a learning process. This university can make a significant contribution to the student body, the alumni and be an example for learning institutions around the world if they address the issue of racism and discrimination effectively. Effectively addressing the issues of racism and discrimination will only enhance the already esteemed reputation of this university. There is a serious question that the university does not take the issue of racism and discrimination seriously. The university professes and declares their position against racist and discriminating behavior but their actions do not align with what they say. By not taking it seriously, the university supports the behavior.

I hope this correspondence gives the university a better understanding of how to deal with discrimination on campus, improve the learning environment, and improve student and alumni participation, present and post university attendance. Again, I want to reintegrate my purpose is to see the university get better. I am a member of this great institution and the better it gets the more students and alumni benefit from being associated with the University of Chicago.

I realize the initial reaction on the part of some who receive this letter may be anger and create a defensive reaction to their cultural worldview. To these people, I want to suggest that you take an objective view and consider the facts, the reason the ban was placed, the fact the ban was lifted and the reality and the fact we live in a society that has racism socialized into White culture and institutionalized into American society. If you don't like it, then change it.

Sincerely
Ronald Barnes (Alumni 2015)

Exhibit 12 - Correspondence between Dr. Barnes' Attorney and the University of Chicago General Counsel

Attorney Gray

To:ron.barnes

Mon, Jul 5 at 8:09 PM

---------- Forwarded message ---------

From: **Theodore C. Stamatakos** <stamatak@uchicago.edu>

Date: Wed, Jun 9, 2021 at 10:52 AM

Subject: Re: Ronald Barnes, 2019

To: Atrorney Gray

Dear Ms. Gray,

Thank you for your message.

By way of background, I understand that Mr. Barnes believes that the University of Chicago discriminated against him by banning him in May 2019 from the Harper Center. He was banned after he made repeated unscheduled visits to a University business office (Alumni Relations and Development (ARD)) that does not have drop-in hours, and did so on at least two instances after bypassing access control restrictions to gain access to the office. Even after being reminded in writing of the building's access restrictions and the need to make an appointment, he again accessed the office, this time under the guise of being a job fair participant.

The University's ban/no-trespass policy contains an appeals process, which is designed to give the banned person an opportunity to provide a complete explanation for the conduct that precipitated the no-trespass directive and share the basis for a desire to be on University property in the future. The process also enables the University to assess whether the conduct that precipitated the directive has abated and whether there is a different way to address any risk posed by the presence of the person who has been banned. Associate Provost Ingrid Gould reviewed Mr. Barnes's request, interviewed him in-person, and, using reasoned judgment, agreed to lift the no-trespass directive. In her August 2019 outcome letter to Mr. Barnes, she felt compelled to underscore for him the need to make an appointment if he wishes to visit ARD's offices and to call ahead before visiting other offices, as impromptu visits can be disruptive. Mr. Barnes also alleged that the decision to ban him was motivated by racial animus. The Office for Access and Equity (OAE) investigated his claim and found no evidence to support the claim, a conclusion that Ms. Gould shared with Mr. Barnes in her letter to him.

Mr. Barnes recently requested a copy of OAE's investigative materials. Ms. Gould declined the request. Your message clarifies that, in the alternative, Mr. Barnes would like "an explication of various testimony said against him as stated in the report."

I write to confirm that, as a private entity, the University only provides third parties with internal, confidential documents or summaries of those documents when required to do so by law (e.g., by statute or in response to a validly issued and served subpoena), and thus the Office of Legal Counsel, too, declines the request. If you believe Mr. Barnes is legally entitled to the records, I'm happy to consider any case law, statute or regulation that supports that contention. I know that this is not the outcome that Mr. Barnes is seeking but I wanted to be clear about the University's decision about this matter. If you wish to communicate with the University in the future about this matter, please do so only through me.

Regards,

Ted

Theodore C. Stamatakos
Senior Associate General Counsel
University of Chicago

Edward H. Levi Hall
5801 South Ellis Avenue
Chicago, Illinois 60637

This message may be privileged and/or confidential. If you received it in error, please promptly notify me by return email and then delete the message. Thank you.

From: Atrorney Gray

Date: Monday, June 7, 2021 at 7:29 PM

To: "Theodore C. Stamatakos" <stamatak@uchicago.edu>

Subject: Ronald Barnes, 2019

Hello Mr. Stamatakos,

I hope this email finds you well. I am an attorney writing on behalf of Ronald Barnes, who holds a Master's degree from University of Chicago, and is now completing his PhD off campus.

In 2019 Mr. Barnes, an African American male, was wrongfully banned from a University of Chicago campus building under a no-trespassing directive. Provost Ingrid Gould very justly lifted the ban against my client. As you can imagine, the incident unfortunately, greatly disappointed my client as he was and still is proud to be a University of Chicago alumni. However, Mr. Barnes hopes there will be room for awareness in such discriminatory matters so that incidents like what he experienced, do not happen again within University of Chicago administrative culture.

I am writing to respectfully request a copy of the investigative report against Mr. Barnes. However, it is my understanding that it is against University policy to disclose such a report. My question now is, is there a way Mr. Barnes can receive not the entire report, but perhaps an explication of various testimony said against him as stated in the report?

Your guidance will be greatly appreciated.

Very sincerely,

Attorney Gray

Atorney. Gray, Esq.
Attorney Gray, J.D.

Appendix 2

American Association of University Publishers (AAUP) – Exclusion of Minority Authors.

Dear Ronald Barnes,

I want to thank you for sending your recent letter and related materials inquiring about our interest in publishing your manuscript, *An American Reality: White People ... LOL.* I have now reviewed your project and discussed it with our editorial colleagues, and I regret to report that we have decided not to pursue the work for publication at Illinois Press.

Our response in no way reflects on the potential merit of your manuscript. Far from it. In choosing books to fill the limited number of places in our publishing program we must necessarily be very selective to maintain balanced booklists that reflect our established publishing interests and plans for our list.

Again, thank you for allowing us the opportunity to consider your work. Wishing you all the best in placing *An American Reality* with a suitable publisher.

Warmly,

Dominique

***Please note that publication decisions are final.

When submitting materials, please be sure to copy Ellie Hinton on your correspondences: ehinton2@illinois.edu

Dominique J. Moore | Acquisitions Editor
she/her/hers
The University of Illinois Press

1325 S Oak St., Champaign, IL 61820
217.265.8109 moore53@uillinois.edu
Check Out Our Fall 2021 Catalog!
Then Follow Me On Twitter: @DomTheEditor

Dear Dr. Barnes,

Thank you for your interest in Princeton University Press and for your patience. This is a fascinating and important topic, but regretfully this is not quite a fit for the list here at Princeton. I'm sorry not to have a more optimistic response, but I have no doubt you'll be able to find a good home for this, perhaps at Oxford or Cambridge, with their much larger programs. Please keep us in mind for future projects.

Many thanks,

Alena

Dear Ronald,

Thank you for your inquiry. I have read the materials you enclosed and determined that your proposed book project would not be a good fit for Cornell's list. I wish you every success in finding a more suitable publisher.

Sincerely,

Mahinder S. Kingra, Editorial Director
Cornell University Press
msk55@cornell.edu | cornellpress.cornell.edu

Knowledge knows no boundaries. Read free ebooks at Cornell Open.

Dear Ronald,

Thank you for reaching out to Baylor University Press. We appreciate the opportunity to consider your proposal; however, while the issue of racial justice is deeply important to us, our emphases are primarily theological rather than sociological.

We wish you all success with the book, and thank you for your contribution to this crucial conversation.

Regards,

Cade

Dear Dr. Barnes,

Thank you for your inquiry. This seems like a very interesting and important project, but I fear it's simply out of scope for our publishing program. Being a small press, Kent State has to focus on a few specific subject areas, and we do not have a list in higher education.

We certainly wish you all the best in placing your work with an appropriate publisher.

Sincerely,

Susan Wadsworth-Booth

Susan Wadsworth-Booth
Director, Kent State University Press
1118 University Library
Phone: 330-672-8099
Email: swadswo2@kent.edu

Dear Dr Barnes,

Thank you for your enquiry and for your interest in publishing with Cambridge University Press. I'm afraid this project is not quite right for the Psychology list, so I must respectfully decline.

I am sorry not to be able to respond more positively but wish you well with your project.

Best wishes,

Janka

Ms Janka Romero
Commissioning Editor, Psychology
Cambridge University Press
+44 (0)7956 046992
jjromero@cambridge.org
www.cambridge.org/psychology
Twitter: @jankaromero

Dear Ron,

Thank you for sending your materials to our attention. While I agree with you that racism is a topic that is very important to address on college campuses and in American life more widely, I'm afraid that your book doesn't quite fit into our publishing program. I suggest perhaps sending it to SUNY Press which has an extensive education list as well as books on race, or perhaps Routledge. I do wish you all the best with it.

Sincerely,

Kim Guinta

Kimberly Guinta (she/her)
Editorial Director
Rutgers University Press
106 Somerset St.New Brunswick, NJ 08901
848-445-7786
kimberly.guinta@rutgers.edu

Dear Dr. Barnes,

Thank you very much for sending your manuscript, *A Theory on Universal Continuity and Sustainability*. We are grateful for the opportunity to consider your work.

I've consulted with Elizabeth Branch Dyson and Karen Darling, and I'm afraid we are not going to pursue your project for publication. Our publishing commitments are extensive, and we must consciously limit the number of projects we take on. Other publishers will have different considerations, and we hope you will be able to find the right match very soon.

Thank you again for reaching out, and we wish you all the best.

Sincerely,

Susannah Engstrom
Assistant Editor
University of Chicago Press
1427 East 60th Street
Chicago, IL 60637
sengstrom@uchicago.edu
773-702-5051

APPENDIX 3
ABORTION STATISTICS

One of the conspiracies White supremacist, White nationalist, White extremist and racist use is the "Great Replacement Theory". This theory states that minorities and others are replacing Whites and subjugating the rights of the White race. That Whites will become a minority. Whites blame their foreseen future as minorities on current minorities. The reason Whites are projected to become a minority is because the birth rate among Whites is decreasing. **The majority of Women who get abortions are White.** The reason Whites are projected to become minorities is not the fault of anyone but Whites, themselves. The statistics below prove this out and tell the truth, debunking one of the many lies and deceptive conspiracies theories that are circulated by White fear mongers.

Year	LIVE BIRTHS				
	TOTAL	WHITE, NON-HISPANIC	BLACK, NON-HISPANIC	HISPANIC	OTHER
1971	3,555,970	2,661,000	565,000	259,000	71,000
1974	3,159,958	2,296,000	507,000	280,000	77,000
1977	3,326,632	2,389,000	544,000	302,000	91,000
1980	3,612,258	2,612,000	568,000	324,000	104,000
1983	3,638,933	2,550,000	563,000	396,000	129,000
1986	3,756,547	2,551,000	593,000	468,000	139,000
1989	4,040,968	2,670,000	660,000	541,000	170,000
1990	4,158,212	2,705,000	673,000	602,000	178,000
1991	4,110,907	2,631,000	673,000	628,000	180,000

1992	4,065,014	2,518,000	663,000	649,000	236,000
1993	4,000,240	2,506,000	648,000	662,000	185,000
1994	3,952,767	2,467,000	625,000	672,000	189,000
1995	3,899,589	2,419,000	597,000	690,000	193,000
1996	3,891,494	2,394,000	587,000	711,000	200,000
1997	3,880,894	2,368,000	590,000	719,000	204,000
1998	3,941,553	2,392,000	600,000	743,000	207,000
1999	3,959,417	2,377,000	596,000	772,000	215,000
2000	4,058,814	2,389,000	611,000	823,000	236,000
2001	4,025,933	2,341,000	593,000	857,000	235,000
2002	4,021,726	2,313,000	581,000	882,000	246,000
2003	4,089,950	2,338,000	579,000	919,000	254,000
2004	4,112,052	2,315,000	582,000	954,000	260,000
2005	4,138,349	2,296,000	587,000	993,000	262,000
2006	4,265,555	2,325,000	621,000	1,047,000	273,000
2007	4,316,233	2,327,000	631,000	1,071,000	287,000
2008	4,247,694	2,284,000	627,000	1,051,000	286,000
2009	4,130,665	2,227,000	614,000	1,008,000	282,000
2010	3,999,386	2,176,000	593,000	953,000	277,000
2011	3,953,590	2,160,000	586,000	926,000	282,000
2012	3,952,841	2,149,000	587,000	917,000	300,000
2013	3,932,181	2,143,000	587,000	909,000	293,000
2014	3,988,076	2,164,000	593,000	923,000	309,000
2015	3,978,497	2,146,000	593,000	934,000	306,000
2016	3,945,875	2,117,000	572,000	949,000	308,000
2017	3,855,500	2,051,000	575,000	928,000	301,000

Live Births in the United States by race
by Wm. Robert Johnston
last updated 14 April 2019
Retrieved from: https://www.johnstonsarchive.net/policy/abortion/usa_abortion_by_race.html

Year	ABORTIONS (ESTIMATED)				
	TOTAL	WHITE, NON-HISPANIC	BLACK, NON-HISPANIC	HISPANIC	OTHER
1971	486,000	356,000	102,000	20,000	9,000
1974	904,000	567,000	244,000	62,000	25,000
1977	1,317,000	793,000	384,000	96,000	44,000
1980	1,554,000	971,000	410,000	123,000	50,000
1983	1,573,000	929,000	426,000	156,000	65,000
1986	1,568,000	864,000	458,000	181,000	71,000
1989	1,613,000	828,000	495,000	206,000	84,000
1990	1,629,000	828,000	501,000	219,000	78,000
1991	1,590,000	783,000	500,000	228,000	76,000
1992	1,565,000	735,000	500,000	240,000	85,000
1993	1,512,000	697,000	498,000	235,000	79,000
1994	1,435,000	647,000	476,000	225,000	85,000
1995	1,361,000	583,000	463,000	229,000	86,000
1996	1,364,000	585,000	460,000	231,000	88,000
1997	1,326,000	571,000	442,000	230,000	84,000
1998	1,302,000	565,000	426,000	228,000	83,000
1999	1,277,000	538,000	413,000	238,000	85,000
2000	1,313,000	530,000	431,000	262,000	91,000
2001	1,289,000	506,000	419,000	267,000	98,000
2002	1,271,000	488,000	411,000	274,000	99,000
2003	1,252,000	469,000	422,000	259,000	102,000
2004	1,221,000	447,000	416,000	257,000	102,000
2005	1,209,000	433,000	415,000	259,000	103,000
2006	1,235,000	434,000	423,000	277,000	102,000
2007	1,210,000	438,000	406,000	275,000	91,000

2008	1,213,000	427,000	416,000	277,000	93,000
2009	1,154,000	405,000	398,000	263,000	88,000
2010	1,104,000	384,000	379,000	254,000	87,000
2011	1,060,000	366,000	360,000	247,000	86,000
2012	1,010,000	349,000	344,000	232,000	85,000
2013	959,000	322,000	333,000	220,000	84,000
2014	927,000	323,000	317,000	204,000	83,000
2015	896,000	308,000	309,000	197,000	82,000
2016	875,000	294,000	303,000	200,000	79,000
2017	851,000	280,000	295,000	195,000	77,000

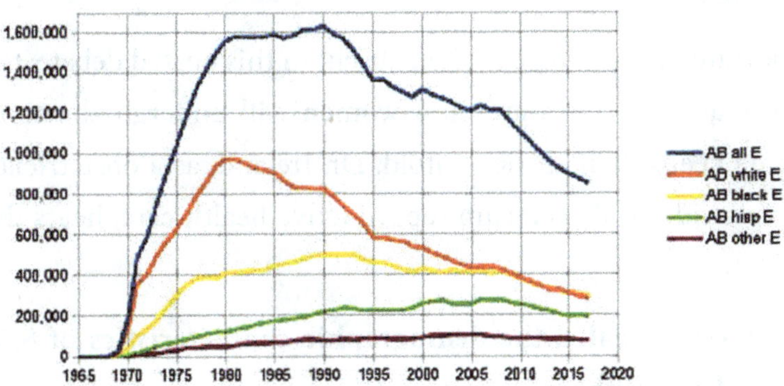

Abortions in the United States by race
by Wm. Robert Johnston
last updated 14 April 2019
Retrieved from: https://www.johnstonsarchive.net/policy/abortion/usa_abortion_by_race.html

Year	LIVE BIRTHS		ABORTIONS		ABORTION PERCENTAGE
	NUMBER	% OF TOTAL	NUMBER	% OF TOTAL	
white	**2,051,000**	**53.2**	**280,000**	**32.9**	**12.0**
black	575,000	14.9	295,000	34.7	33.9
Hispanic	928,000	24.1	195,000	23.0	17.4

Asian	260,000	6.7	68,000	8.0	20.8
American Indian/ Alaskan Native	31,300	0.8	7,000	0.8	18.4
Pacific Islander	10,400	0.3	2,400	0.3	18.6
TOTAL	3,855,500	100.0	851,000	100.0	18.1

by Wm. Robert Johnston
last updated 14 April 2019
Retrieved from: https://www.johnstonsarchive.net/policy/abortion/usa_abortion_by_race.html

Women obtaining abortions

One important group's voice is often absent in this heated debate: the women who choose abortion. While 1 in 4 women will undergo abortion in her lifetime, stigma keeps their stories untold. Dr. Ireland, as a obstetrician/gynecologist who provides full spectrum reproductive health care, hears these stories daily.

A 2014 survey revealed the demographic characteristics of 8,380 U.S. women who had abortions.

Age group	
Under 20	11.9%
20 to 24	33.6%
25 to 29	26.5%
30 to 34	15.9%
35 to 39	9.1%
40 or older	3.1%
Race/ethnicity	
White	38.7%
Black	27.6%

Hispanic	24.8%
Asian/Pacific Islander	5.5%
Other	3.4%
Educational attainment	
No high school diploma	8.9%
High school graduate/GED	27.0%
Some college/associate degree	40.9%
College graduate	23.1%
Number of prior births	
0	40.7%
1	26.2%
2 or more	33.1%
Religious affiliation	
Mainline Protestant	17.2%
Evangelical Protestant	12.8%
Roman Catholic	23.7%
Other	8.2%
None	38.0%
Family income level	
<100% of federal poverty level	49.3%
100-199% of federal poverty level	25.7%
200% or more of federal poverty level	25.0%

Chart: The Conversation, CC-BY-ND

Source: Guttmacher . The Guttmacher Institute, a research and policy institute in New York City, has been tracking these data for the last 50 years.

This 2014 survey indicates that the majority of abortions are White women and women between the ages of 20-34, women in the prime of child bearing age.

Ironically approximately ¼ of the abortions are women who are Roman Catholic, a traditionally anti-abortion religion.

Why women have abortions

In a 2004 survey of 957 women having an abortion, one in four said their most important reason for having the procedure was that they weren't ready for a child or the timing was wrong.

Not ready for a(nother) child/Timing is wrong	**25%**
Can't afford a baby now	**23%**
Have completed my childbearing/Have other people depending on me/Children are grown	**19%**
Don't want to be a single mother or am having relationship problems	**8%**
Don't feel mature enough to raise another child/Feel too young	**7%**
Would interfere with education or career plans	**4%**
Physical problem with my health	**4%**
Possible problems affecting the health of the fetus	**3%**
Other	**6%**

The following categories were chosen by fewer than 0.5 percent of respondents and are not shown:
"Was a victim of rape",
"Husband or partner wants me to have an abortion",
"Parents want me to have an abortion",
"Don't want people to know I had sex or got pregnant"

Chart: The Conversation, CC-BY-ND Source: Guttmacher

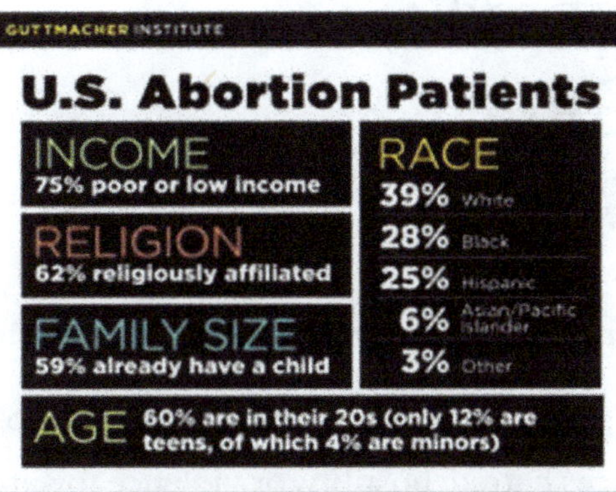

GUTTMACHER INSTITUTE
U.S. Abortion Patients
INCOME
75% poor or low income
RELIGION
62% religiously affiliated
FAMILY SIZE
59% already have a child
RACE
39% White
28% Black
25% Hispanic
6% Asian/Pacific Islander
3% Other
AGE
60% are in their 20s (only 12% are teens, of which 4% are minors)
guttmacher.org
©2016

Jones, Rachael K. (2022). United States Abortion DEMOGRAPHICS. Guttmacher Institute. Retrieved from: https://www.guttmacher.org/united-states/abortion/demographics

Appendix 4
Hate Groups

Compiled by the Southern Poverty Law Center. Retrieved from: https://www.splcenter.org/fighting-hate/extremist-files/groups

The following is comprised of hate groups of all ideologies. A **hate** group is a social group that advocates and practices hatred, hostility, or violence towards members of a race, ethnicity, nation, religion, gender, ...

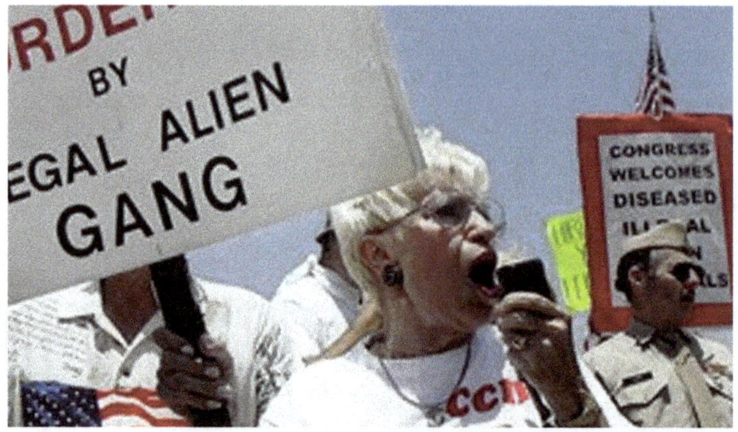

National Coalition for Issue Reform

The California Coalition for Immigration Reform (CCIR) was founded in 1994 by Barbara Coe . Its original purpose was to serve as a co-sponsor for California's Proposition 187, which would have denied social and medical benefits to undocumented immigrants and their children. The initiative passed,...

Knights of the Ku Klux Klan

The group's leaders, from Duke to current chief Thomas Robb, have been plagued by their own racist views, which inevitably shine through the smoke-screen, and by the attacks of other Klan members who view their interest in mainstream media and politics as hypocritical and counterproductive. In Its...

National Vanguard
Toward a New Consciousness; a New Order; a New People.

National Vanguard

Formed in 2005 by longtime activist Kevin Strom, National Vanguard was a breakaway group from the neo-Nazi National Alliance, the most dominant neo-Nazi group from the 1970s until 2002, when its founder died. National Vanguard was increasing its membership and its prestige in white supremacist...

EURO

Beyond hosting a website, whitecivilrights.com, and staging an occasional conference, EURO is a paper tiger, serving primarily as a vehicle to publicize Duke's writing and sell his books. In Its Own Words "The Jewish media and Jews in general will attack us for wanting to restore White America. The...

Blood & Honour

One faction, known as Blood & Honour America Division, was "reestablished" in North America by the skinhead group Volksfront in 2005 and includes skinhead, neo-Nazi and Christian Identity adherents in its ranks. The other group , which became known as Blood & Honour Council USA, was...

Aryan Nations

In its heyday in the 1980s and early 1990s, neo-Nazis, racist skinheads, Klansmen and other white nationalists convened regularly at the group's Idaho compound for its annual world congresses. In 2000, AN began to fall apart after losing a civil lawsuit brought by the Southern Poverty Law Center...

Jewish Defense League

The JDL's position with regard to Israel is denial of any Palestinian claims to land and the calling for the removal of all Arabs from the "Jewish-inherited soil." The group has orchestrated countless terrorist attacks in the U.S. and abroad, and has engaged in intense harassment of foreign...

Brotherhood of Klans

Where most present-day Klan groups splash pictures and news of their activities on their websites and online forums, the Brotherhood of Klans is exceptionally secretive, in the tradition of Klan groups of yesteryear, offering scant details of its actions online and conducting serious background...

Keystone United

While its members attempt to project a mediagenic image of being part of a new breed of more sophisticated and less spasmodically violent skins, the truth is that the group's members have been convicted of a string of remarkably violent attacks dating back to at least 1998, ranging from bar brawls...

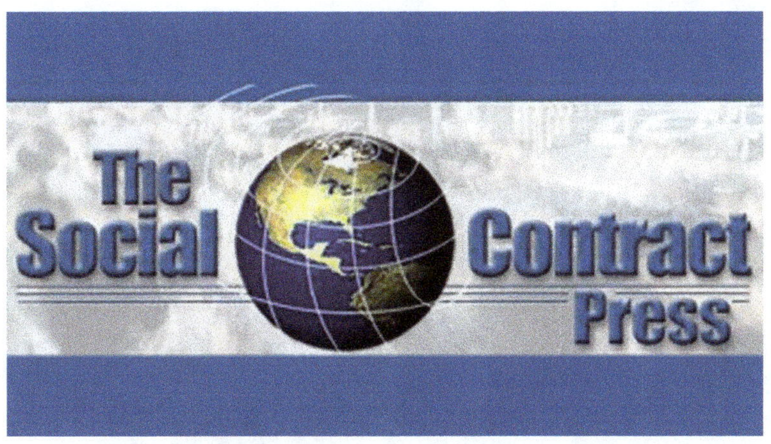

The Social Contract Press

Recent articles in its main product, The Social Contract , have propagated the myth that Latino activists want to occupy and 'reclaim' the American Southwest, argued that no Muslim immigrants should be allowed into the U.S., and claimed that multiculturalists are trying to replace "successful Euro-...

Nuwaubian Nation of Moors

Nuwaubians refer to their belief system – which mixes black supremacist ideas with worship of the Egyptians and their pyramids, a belief in UFOs and various conspiracies related to the Illuminati and the Bilderbergers, as "Nuwaubianism" – not as theology, but as "factology, "Right Knowledge," or a...

National Alliance

Explicitly genocidal in its ideology, NA materials call for the eradication of the Jews and other races — what a principal foundational document describes as "a temporary unpleasantness" — and the creation of an all-white homeland. Founded by William Pierce in 1970, the group produced assassins,...

Imperial Klans of America

IKA's headquarters and compound in Dawson Springs, Ky., have long served as the venue for the hate-rock gathering Nordic Fest. In Its Own Words "WE BELIEVE that the Man Adam (a Hebrew word meaning: ruddy, to show Blood, flush, turn rosy) is father of the White Race only. As a son of God (Luke 3:38...

White Revolution

In some ways, the group has turned out to be little more than a club for founder Billy Roper and a handful of friends. In Its Own Words "Always remember that it is up to us to save our race, no one else is going to do it for us! Evolution is not a spectator sport." — White Revolution website "We...

New Black Panther Party

Founded in Dallas, the group portrays itself as a militant, modern-day expression of the black power movement. Although it frequently engages in armed protests of alleged police brutality, non-racist, left wing members of the original Black Panther Party of the 1960s and 1970s have rejected the new...

Church of the National Knights of the Ku Klux Klan

As disorganized as the Indiana-based group may be, it is still dangerous, as evidenced by a 2001 murder and plot linked to National Knights members in North Carolina. In Its Own Words "What We Believe. The WHITE RACE: The irreplaceable hub of our nation, our Christian Faith, and the high levels of...

Vinlanders Social Club

The Vinlanders relished a reputation for drinking, brawling and following a racist version of Odinism, a form of ancient paganism once practiced by Vikings. In Its Own Words "Our beliefs stem from being deprived of our individual freedoms and from our witnessing of the decline of western...

American Family Association

Initially founded as the National Federation for Decency, the American Family Association (AFA) originally focused on what it considered indecent television programming and pornography. The AFA says it promotes "traditional moral values" in media. A large part of that work involves "combating the...

Fundamentalist Church of Jesus Christ of Latter-Day Saints

After concealing itself from the public eye for decades by virtually taking over and occupying small towns on the Utah-Arizona border, the intensely secretive FLDS finally started coming under scrutiny in the mid-2000s due to widespread allegations of organized welfare fraud and sexual abuse of...

American Freedom Party

The group is now led by a coterie of prominent white nationalists, including corporate lawyer William D. Johnson, virulent anti-Semite Kevin MacDonald and white nationalist radio host James Edwards. David Duke's former right-hand man, Jamie Kelso , helps with organizing. The party has big plans to...

America's Promise Ministries

Located in a section of the Pacific Northwest that was a notorious hotbed of white supremacist activity in the 1990s, America's Promise Ministry is both a Christian Identity church and a major publisher and distributor of right-wing extremist tracts. Its current leader, Dave Barley, peddles a "soft...

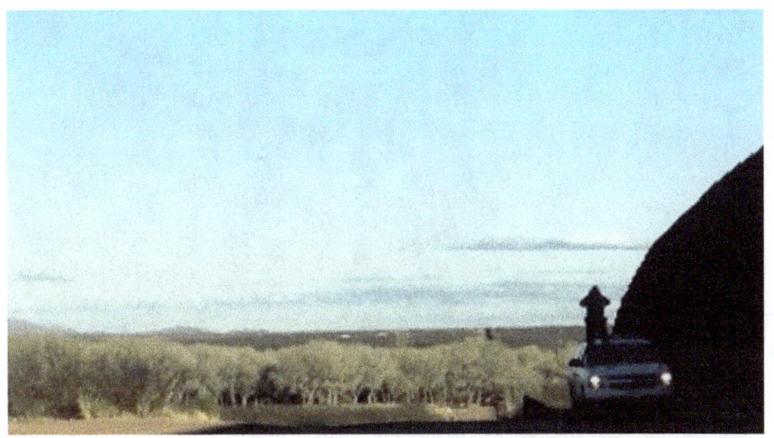

American Border Patrol/American Patrol

On the American Patrol website and in self-produced videos, the group rails against Mexican immigrants, accusing them of bringing to the U.S. crime, drugs and squalor and of practicing "immigration via the birth canal." Mexicans, in the words of group founder Glenn Spencer , are a "cultural cancer...

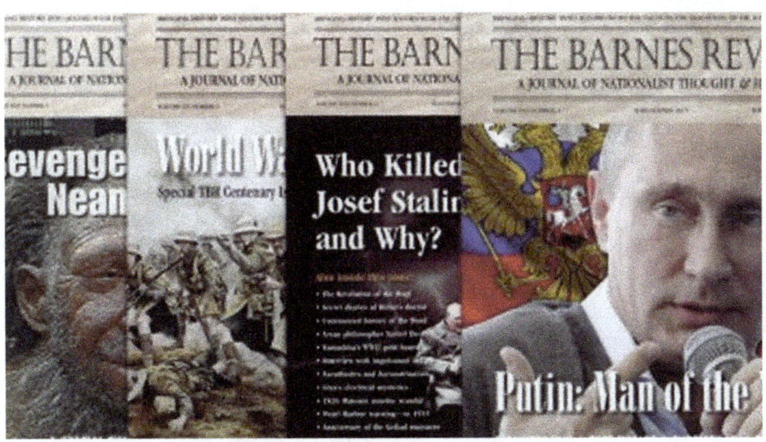

Barnes Review/Foundation for Economic Liberty, Inc.

The organization is also a moneymaking enterprise. Besides journal subscriptions, its TBR Book Club and online bookstore promote and sell a wide range of extremist books and publications. The Barnes Review also hosts nearly annual conferences that attract an international crowd of antigovernment...

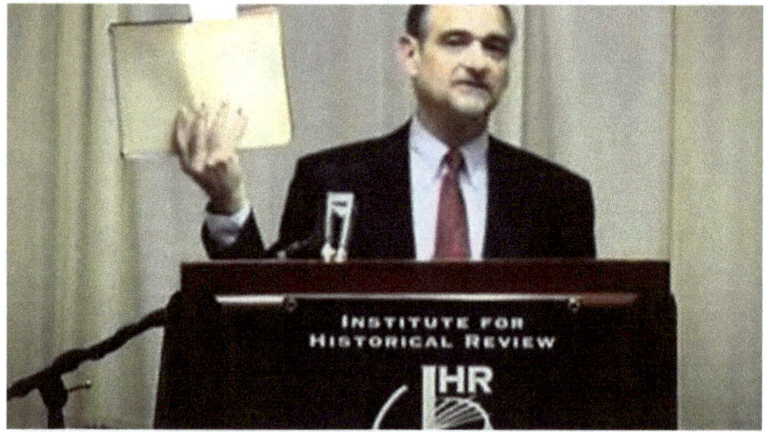

Institute for Historical Review

Once a prominent voice in extremist circles, the IHR has been on the decline, unable to publish its anti-Semitic Journal of Historical Review or sponsor major international Holocaust denial conferences since 2004. The organization still runs its website, where it peddles extremist books and other...

Kingdom Identity Ministries

It functions primarily as a publishing house, churning out Identity Bible study courses, tracts and books, including foundational texts by early Identity leaders like Wesley Swift. The ministry teaches that Judgment Day will arrive in the form of a sanctified race war, a theory widely popular with...

Occidental Quarterly

Its editors and advisory board members have constituted a "Who's Who" of the radical right, and its regular publication of extremists' articles has made it a favorite among academic racists in America. In Its Own Words "Nations and races provide the seedbed in which families can flourish over many...

Pioneer Fund

Today, it still funds studies of race and intelligence, as well as eugenics, the "science" of breeding superior human beings that was discredited by various Nazi atrocities. The Pioneer Fund has supported many of the leading Anglo-American race scientists of the last several decades as well as anti...

Family Research Council

The FRC often makes false claims about the LGBTQ community based on discredited research and junk science. The intention is to denigrate LGBTQ people as the organization battles against same-sex marriage, hate crime laws, anti-bullying programs and the repeal of the military's "Don't Ask, Don't...

American Renaissance

Founded by Jared Taylor in 1990, the New Century Foundation is a self-styled think tank that promotes pseudo-scientific studies and research that purport to show the inferiority of blacks to whites — although in hifalutin language that avoids open racial slurs and attempts to portray itself as...

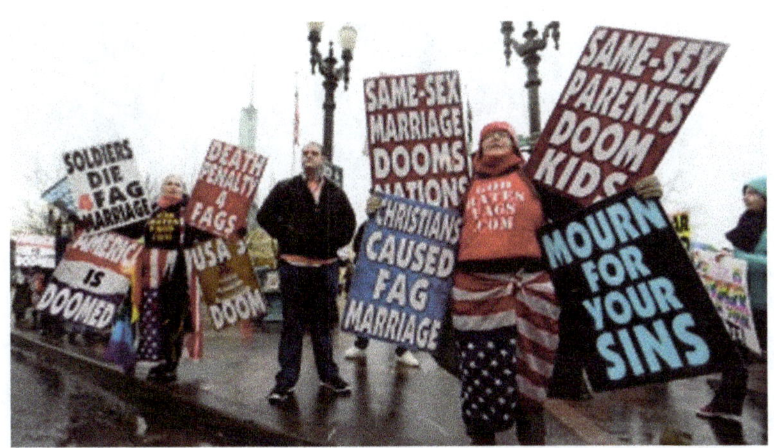

Westboro Baptist Church

The group is basically a family-based cult of personality built around its patriarch, Fred Phelps. Typified by its slogan, "God Hates F---," WBC is known for its harsh anti-gay beliefs and the crude signs its members carry at their frequent protests. In Its Own Words "Filthy sodomites crave...

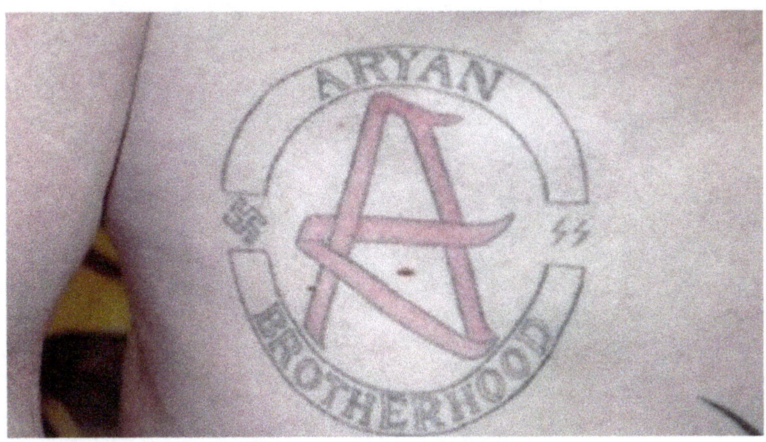

Aryan Brotherhood

Its motto is simple – "blood in, blood out." AB chapters can be found in most major federal and state prisons in the country. As a crime syndicate, the AB participates in drug trafficking, male prostitution rings, gambling, and extortion inside prison walls. On the streets, the AB is involved in...

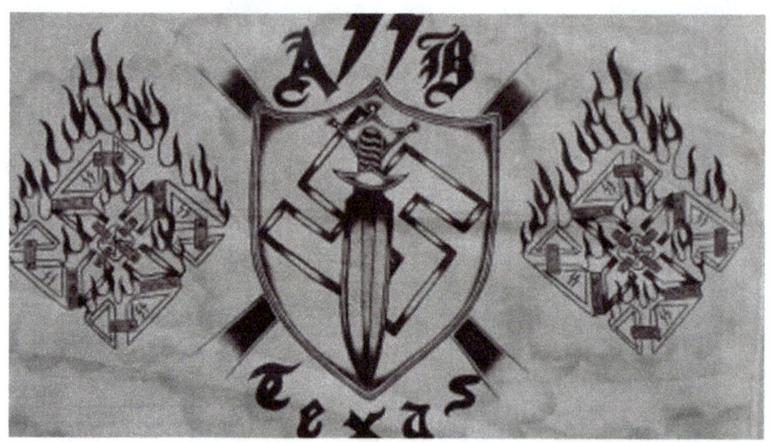

Aryan Brotherhood of Texas

The gang follows the late terrorist David Lane's "14 Words," a white supremacist motto: "We must secure the existence of our people and a future for White children." Unlike many other more flamboyant racist prison gangs, members of the ABT pride themselves on anonymity and their ability to blend in...

Creativity Movement

After the 1993 suicide of Ben Klassen, who initially formed the group in 1973 as the Church of the Creator and wrote a number of foundational texts, new leader Matt Hale renamed it the World Church of the Creator (WCOTC) in 1996. The group, largely composed of racist skinheads, developed a...

Stormfront

But a series of reverses — the 2008 assertion by Black's wife that she was not a racist, a similar declaration by his son in 2010, and the Southern Poverty Law Center's exposure of the identity of many Stormfront funders and the fact its registered users have been behind almost 100 murders — have...

Council of Conservative Citizens

Among other things, its Statement of Principles says that it "oppose[s] all efforts to mix the races of mankind." Created in 1985 from the mailing lists of its predecessor organization, the CCC, which initially tried to project a "mainstream" image, has evolved into a crudely white supremacist...

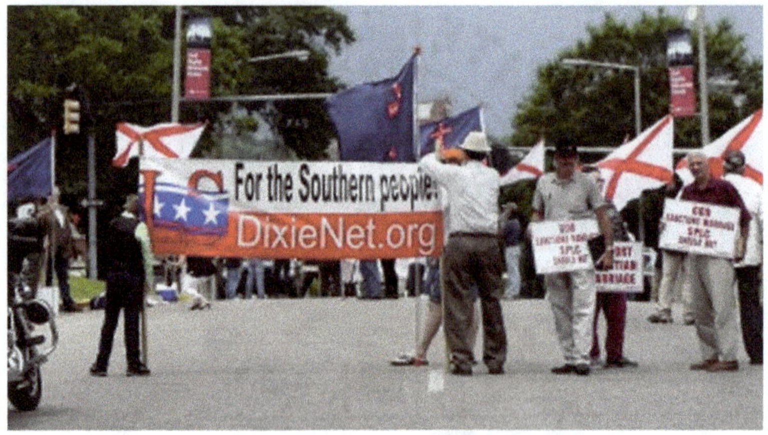

League of the South

Originally founded by a group that included many Southern university professors, over the years the group lost its academic luster as it became more explicitly racist. The League denounces the federal government and Northern and Coastal states as part of a materialist and anti-religious society...

Liberty Counsel

The Liberty Counsel was founded by conservative activists Mathew ("Mat") Staver – an attorney and former dean at Liberty University School of Law – and his wife Anita. The Counsel bills itself as a non-profit litigation, education and policy organization that provides legal counsel and pro bono...

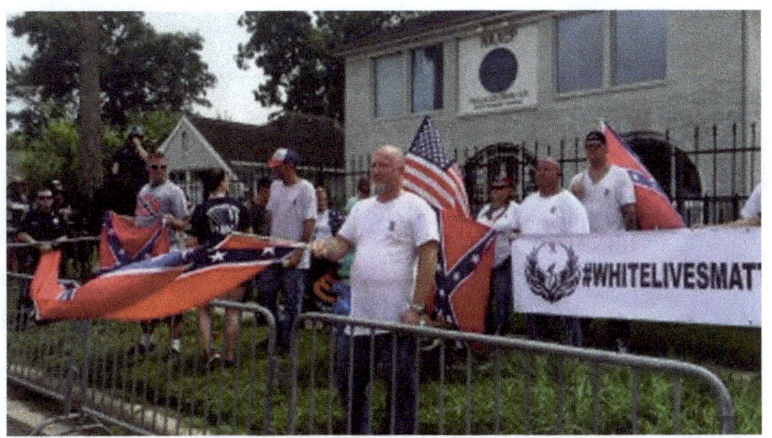

White Lives Matter

In Its Own Words "What happens to blacks in this country at the hand of law enforcement is none of our concern ... other than to prepare to restore order and rebuild our neighborhoods taking back our lands one community at a time. When the enemy destroys ... we guard our town borders and make our...

Alliance Defending Freedom

Founded by some 30 leaders of the Christian Right, the Alliance Defending Freedom is a legal advocacy and training group that has: Supported the recriminalization of sexual acts between consenting LGBTQ adults in the U.S. and criminalization abroad Defended state-sanctioned sterilization of trans...

Proud Boys

The Proud Boys' actions belie their disavowals of bigotry: Rank-and-file Proud Boys and leaders regularly spout white nationalist memes and maintain affiliations with known extremists. They are known for anti-Muslim and misogynistic rhetoric. Proud Boys have appeared alongside other hate groups at...

Family Watch International

Founded in 1999 as Global Helping to Advance Women (Global HAWC), Family Watch International (FWI) is based in Gilbert, Arizona, and claims to be a nonprofit international educational organization. FWI is under the leadership of founder and longtime anti-LGBT and anti-choice activist Sharon Slater...

Ruth Institute

The group is largely a vehicle for spreading the Catholic right-wing Gospel of its founder, Jennifer Roback Morse, a former hardline libertarian and professor of economics at George Mason University, where she was mentored by fellow economist and Nobel Prize-winner James Buchanan , one of the...

Identity Evropa/American Identity Movement

Identity Evropa members insist they're not racist, but "identitarians" who are interested in preserving Western culture. The group owes its style and ideology to the European identitarian movement . Founded in 2016 by Iraq war veteran Nathan Damigo , Identity Evropa has always operated with an eye...

Fraternal Order of Alt-Knights (FOAK)

Formed as the "tactical defense arm" of the Proud Boys, the Fraternal Order of Alt-Knights (FOAK) has become an accelerant for violence at right-wing rallies. The group's founder, repeat-felon Kyle Chapman, organized FOAK after a melee with counter-protestors in Berkeley, California, to "protect...

Pacific Justice Institute

Founded in 1997 by attorney Brad Dacus, who is currently its president, the Pacific Justice Institute (PJI) calls itself a "legal organization specializing in the defense of religious freedom, parental rights, and other civil liberties." Throughout its existence PJI has proved to be a hate group ,...

American College of Pediatricians

ACPeds opposes adoption by LGBTQ couples, links homosexuality to pedophilia, endorses so-called reparative or sexual orientation conversion therapy for homosexual youth, believes transgender people have a mental illness and has called transgender health care for youth child abuse. In its own words...

World Congress of Families

The World Congress of Families (WCF) was formed in 1997 in a meeting in Russia between American academic and Reagan appointee to the National Commission on Children, Allan Carlson, and the Russian intellectuals Anatoly Antonov and Viktor Medkov. Though its origins are in the American Christian...

Family Security Matters

For example, a 2016 article on the FSM website stated bluntly , "Fighting and attacking others with knives and other sharp objects appears to be in the Muslim DNA." FSM's longtime president Carol Taber was also a vocal proponent of the racist "Birther" conspiracy theory. In its own words "It is...

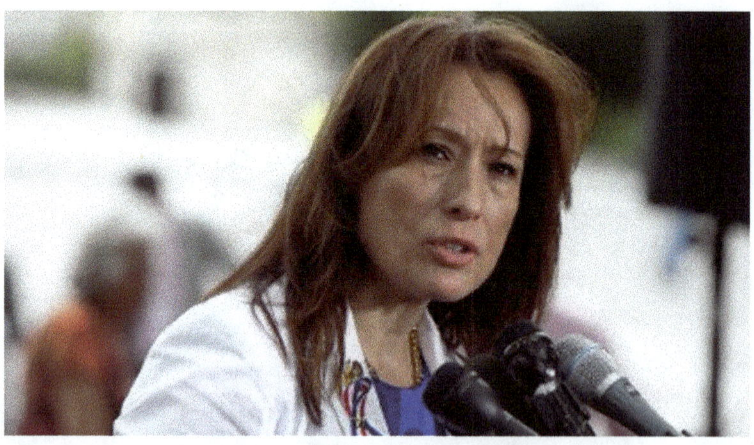

The Remembrance Project

The Remembrance Project was founded by Texas couple Maria Espinoza and Tim Lyng in 2009. Espinoza was active on the conservative circuit in her native Houston, serving as president of the Houston chapter of the Eagle Forum , a right-wing group founded by Phyllis Schlafly , widely considered to be...

Patriot Front

Patriot Front is an image-obsessed organization that rehabilitated the explicitly fascist agenda of Vanguard America with garish patriotism. Patriot Front focuses on theatrical rhetoric and activism that can be easily distributed as propaganda for its chapters across the country. In its own words "...

Rise Above Movement

In Its Own Words "We had them completely surrounded. I hit like 5 people." — RAM member Benjamin Drake Daley, 25, of Redondo Beach, California, referring to the "Unite the Right" rally in Charlottesville, Virginia, in August 2017 in a social media chat on Aug. 11, 2017 "Death to antifa!" — RAM...

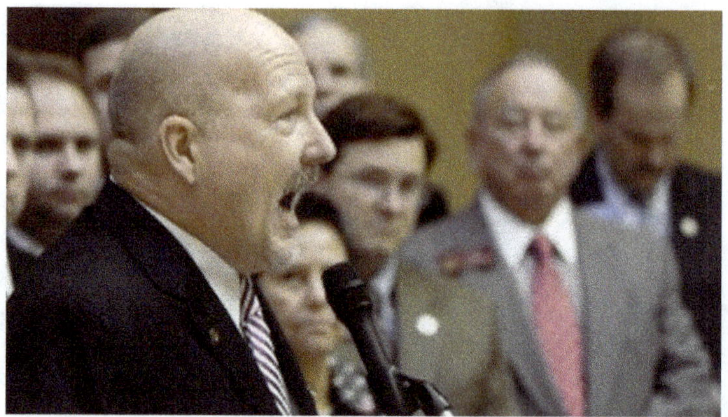

Dustin Inman Society

The Dustin Inman Society is a Georgia-based anti-immigrant hate group founded and led by activist D.A. King. The Southern Poverty Law Center lists it as an anti-immigrant hate group because it denigrates immigrants and supports efforts to make the lives of immigrants so hard that they leave on...

New Black Panther Party for Self Defense

In its own words "My Blood Brother Joseph, was killed on 9/11/01 and the white-man proves over and over to be the master of deception, even more so when he is teamed-up with the extremely deceptive white woman. Ahmeen." – Imam Akbar, former minister of justice, Sept. 12, 2018 "NO GOOD COPS JUST THE...

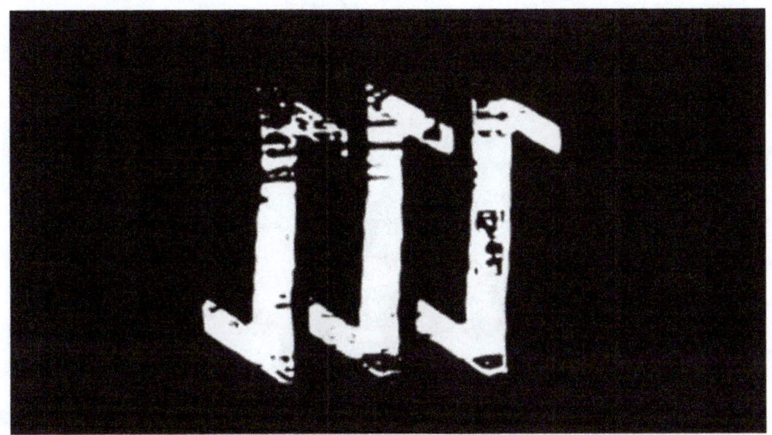

The Base

Made up of small, terroristic cells, The Base believes society should be pushed to collapse so a white ethnostate can arise out of the ruins. It is not an organization that seeks to build popular appeal. Instead, groups like The Base seek to inspire a small number of actors to commit themselves...

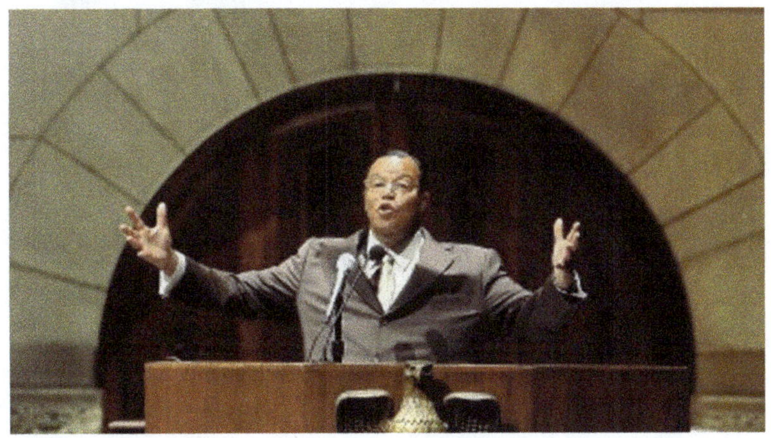

Nation of Islam

Since its founding in 1930, the Nation of Islam (NOI) has grown into one of the wealthiest and best-known organizations in black America, offering numerous programs and events designed to uplift African Americans. Nonetheless, its bizarre theology of innate black superiority over whites – a belief...

WorldNetDaily

Among its enduring storylines is the "birther" theory advanced by columnist Jerome Corsi, who asserts that President Obama is ineligible to serve because he was not born in America, a baseless claim long since abandoned by most of the political right. In Its Own Words "It's important to understand...

ACT for America

Brigitte Gabriel, born Hanan Qahwaji, claims ACT for America was launched as a response to the 9/11 attacks and "educates citizens and elected officials to impact policy involving national security and defeating terrorism." ACT has stayed true to its mission by working to advance anti-Muslim...

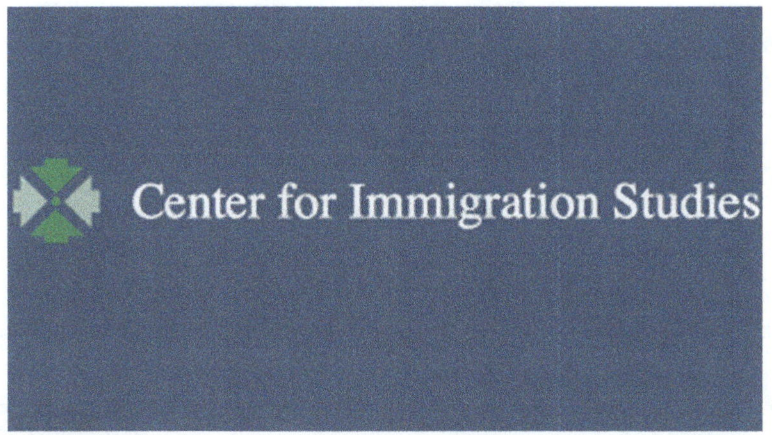

Center for Immigration Studies

While CIS and its position within the Tanton network have been on the Southern Poverty Law Center's (SPLC) radar for years, what precipitated listing CIS as an anti-immigrant hate group for 2016 was its repeated circulation of white nationalist and antisemitic writers in its weekly newsletter and...

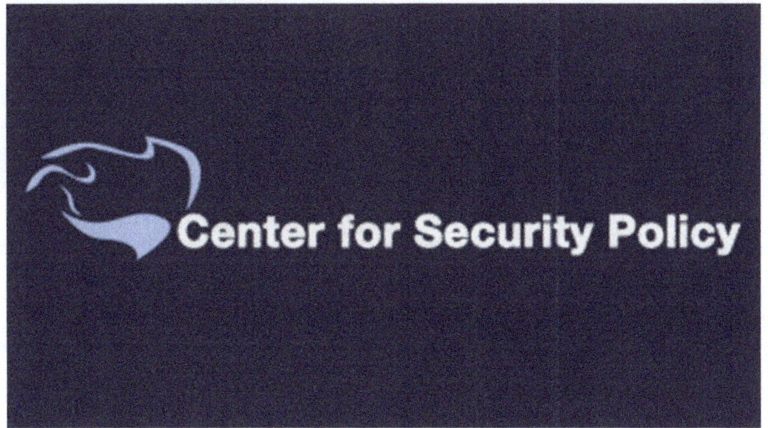

Center for Security Policy

Known for its accusations that a shadowy "Muslim Brotherhood" has infiltrated all levels of government and warnings that "creeping Sharia," or Islamic religious law, is a threat to American democracy, Center for Security Policy (CSP) founder Frank Gaffney has called for Congressional hearings along...

Atomwaffen Division

AWD is organized as a series of terror cells that work toward civilizational collapse. Its members, who can be fairly described as accelerationists, believe that violence, depravity and degeneracy are the only sure way to establish order in their dystopian and apocalyptic vision of the world. AWD's...

Radical Hebrew Israelites

Disclaimer: SPLC uses the term Radical Hebrew Israelite to differentiate from the greater Hebrew Israelite faith. Hebrew Israelites should not be confused with Black Jews or Jewish individuals of color. SPLC no longer refers to these groups as solely Black Hebrew Israelites, as there are Latin and...

Federation for American Immigration Reform

FAIR leaders have ties to white supremacist groups and eugenicists and have made many racist statements. Its advertisements have been rejected because of racist content. FAIR's founder, the late John Tanton , has expressed his wish that America remain a majority-white population: a goal to be...

Traditionalist Worker Party

The Traditionalist Worker Party (TWP) was a neo-Nazi group that advocated for racially pure nations and communities and blamed Jews for many of the world's problems. The group was intimately allied with other prominent neo-Nazi and other hard-line racist organizations espousing unvarnished white...

National Socialist Movement

The group is notable for its violent antisemitic rhetoric, its racist views and its policy allowing members of other racist groups to join NSM while remaining members of other groups. NSM became the largest membership-based neo-Nazi group in this country through the 2000s and into the following...

VDARE

In recent years, VDARE's audience has grown to include not just more mainstream anti-immigrant groups, but also other prominent figures on the right, ranging from Fox News hosts to the Trump administration. Drawing on Brimelow's previous stature in the conservative movement, along with the...

Asatru Folk Assembly

Founded by Stephen McNallen in Northern California, the AFA reached 24 U.S.-based chapters , or kindreds, in 2021 with numerous other chapters around the world. Members of the AFA subscribe to a belief that pre-Christian Norse and Germanic religions can only be practiced by individuals with...

Three Percenters

Three Percenters often draw parallels between the U.S. government today and the British government in the 1700s, arguing that the current U.S. government is tyrannical and actively working to infringe on Americans' Constitutional rights and liberties. They believe a small force of armed individuals...

National Liberty Alliance

Although their website claims not to be affiliated with the sovereign citizen movement, the NLA, and in its former incarnation as the New York Liberty Alliance (NYLA), has propagated antigovernment conspiracy theories and other radical beliefs commonly found among sovereign citizens, such as Agenda...

Moorish Sovereign Citizens

Members of the Moorish sovereigns, called Moors, have come into conflict with federal and state authorities over their refusal to obey laws and government regulations. Recently, Moorish sovereign citizens have engaged in violent confrontations with law enforcement. They have also been known to...

United Constitutional Patriots

In its own words "If these people make it to here, it's going to be a war in our own country and it's coming. We're going to have a war on the border." – Larry Hopkins (Johnny Horton Jr.), "United Constitutional Patriots Radio Live Stream," YouTube, April 1, 2019 "These people (migrants) obviously...

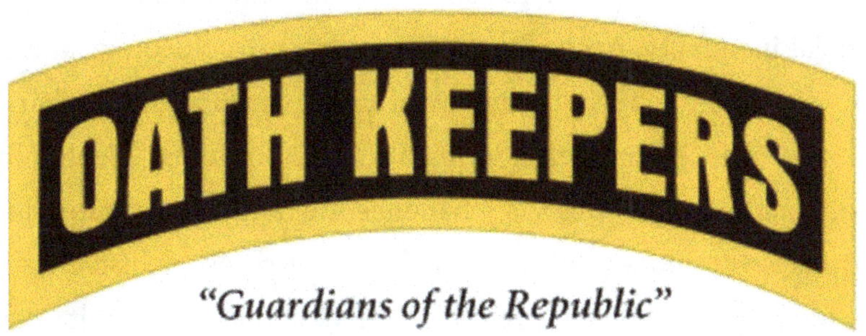

Oath Keepers

The Oath Keepers organization claims to be defending the U.S. Constitution and fighting tyranny, but as former Oath Keepers spokesman Jason Van Tatenhove describes, the group is actually "selling the revolution." The threats to American liberties that Oath Keepers say the federal government is...

Appendix 5

Professional Research Studies and Articles that give perspective to White Racism And A Relational Perspective to Black / White Intelligence

1. Abstract - Are Smart People Less Racist? Verbal Ability, Anti-Black Prejudice, and the Principle-Policy Paradox

It is commonly hypothesized that higher cognitive abilities promote racial tolerance and a greater commitment to racial equality, but an alternative theoretical framework contends that higher cognitive abilities merely enable members of a dominant racial group to articulate a more refined legitimizing ideology for racial inequality. According to this perspective, ideological refinement occurs in response to shifting patterns of racial conflict and is characterized by rejection of overt prejudice, superficial support for racial equality in principle, and opposition to policies that challenge the dominant group's status. This study estimates the impact of verbal ability on a comprehensive set of racial attitudes, including anti-black prejudice, views about black-white equality in principle, and racial policy support. It also investigates cohort differences in the effects of verbal ability on these attitudes. Results suggest that high-ability whites are less likely than low-ability whites to report prejudicial attitudes and more likely to support racial equality in principle. Despite these liberalizing effects, high-ability whites are no more likely to support a variety of remedial policies for racial inequality. Results also suggest that the ostensibly liberalizing effects of verbal ability on anti-black prejudice and views about racial equality in principle emerged slowly over time, consistent with ideological refinement theory.

Keywords: racial attitudes, prejudice, affirmative action, group conflict, verbal ability

Geoffrey T. Wodtke (2016). Are Smart People Less Racist? Verbal Ability, Anti-Black Prejudice, and the Principle-Policy Paradox. *Soc Probl.* Author manuscript; available in PMC 2017 Jan 8.

Published in final edited form as: Soc Probl. 2016 Jan 8; 63(1): 21–45. doi: 10.1093/socpro/spv028. Retrived from: https://www.ncbi.nlm.nih.gov/pmc/articles/PMC4845100/

2. Abstract - The psychology of American racism

American racism is alive and well. In this essay, we amass a large body of classic and contemporary research across multiple areas of psychology (e.g., cognitive, developmental, social), as well as the broader social sciences (e.g., sociology, communication studies, public policy), and humanities (e.g., critical race studies, history, philosophy), to outline seven factors that contribute to American racism: (a) Categories, which organize people into distinct groups by promoting essentialist and normative reasoning; (b) Factions, which trigger in-group loyalty and intergroup competition and threat; (c) Segregation, which hardens racist perceptions, preferences, and beliefs through the denial of intergroup contact; (d) Hierarchy, which emboldens people to think, feel, and behave in racist ways; (e) Power, which legislates racism on both micro and macro levels; (f) Media, which legitimize overrepresented and idealized representations of White Americans while marginalizing and minimizing people of color; and (g) Passivism, such that overlooking or denying the existence of racism obscures this reality, encouraging others to do the same and allowing racism to fester and persist. We argue that these and other factors support American racism, and we conclude with suggestions for future research, particularly in the domain of identifying ways to promote antiracism.

Roberts, S., & Rizzo, M. (2020, June 1). The Psychology of American Racism. https://doi.org/10.31219/osf.io/w2h73

MLA. Retrieved from: https://osf.io/w2h73/ ; https://pubmed.ncbi.nlm.nih.gov/32584061/

3. **Abstract - The Racism of Intelligence: How Mental Testing Practices Have Constituted an Institutionalized Form of Group Domination**

This article focuses on intelligence testing and discusses its role in the process of group domination between whites and blacks and more generally between the haves and the have-nots. The article first argues that standardized testing, from its inception, has constituted an institutionalized arrangement aimed at expropriating resources from dominated groups to maintain dominant groups' privileges. For this purpose, the article reviews what is considered to be the main steps in the history of intelligence testing. It then argues that the concepts of merit and intelligence have played a major role as control ideologies in sustaining the long-term expropriative relationship between blacks and whites. This form of ideological control can be called the racism of intelligence, the main characteristics of which are delineated.

Keywords: intelligence testing, racism, group domination, standardized testing, expropriative relationship, ideological control

Jean Claude Croizet (2012). The Racism of Intelligence: How Mental Testing Practices Have Constituted an Institutionalized Form of Group Domination. *Edited by Lawrence D. Bobo, Lisa Crooms-Robinson, Linda Darling-Hammond, Michael C. Dawson, Henry Louis Gates Jr., Gerald Jaynes, and Claude Steele*. Print Publication Date: May 2012. Subject: Political Science, U.S. Politics, Political Behavior, Online Publication Date: Sep 2012 DOI: 10.1093/oxfordhb/9780195188059.013.0034. Retrieved from: https://www.oxfordhandbooks.com/view/10.1093/oxfordhb/9780195188059.001.0001/oxfordhb-9780195188059-e-34

4. The Black-White Test Score Gap: Why It Persists and What Can Be Done.

Psychologists, sociologists, and educational researchers have devoted far less attention to the black-white test score gap over the past quarter-century than they should have. Cowed by the hostile reaction to Daniel Patrick Moynihan's 1965 report on the status of the black family and to Arthur Jensen's 1969 article arguing that racial differences in test performance were likely to be partly innate, most social scientists have chosen safer topics and hoped the problem would go away. We can do better.

Christopher Jencks and Meredith Phillips (1998). The Black-White Test Score Gap: Why It Persists and What Can Be Done. *Brookings Institute*. Retrieved from: https://www.brookings.edu/articles/the-black-white-test-score-gap-why-it-persists-and-what-can-be-done/

5. Abstract - Scientific Racism: The Politics of Tests, Race and Genetics

RECENTLY PUBLISHED BOOK, The Bell Curve (Herrnstein & Murray 1994), revives a centuries old controversy regarding alleged genetic differences in the respective intellectual capacities of Americans of Euro- pean and African descent. The credibility of this argument rests on several interdependent assumptions related to the validity of: group intelligence (and other standardized) tests; comparisons between the average test scores of different racial groups; and interpreting the results of these comparisons in genetic terms. Before proceeding with a discussion of these assumptions, some background is needed to establish both the social science and the historical context of the controversy itself. Since the administration of earliest "intelligence" tests (Binet & Simon

1916), particularly the Army Intelligence tests during World War I, African Americans, Hispanic Americans and Native Americans have scored consistently and significantly lower (one standard deviation lower, in statistical terms) than whites (Bond 1924a; Brigham 1923; Gould 1981). This does not suggest that persons of color do not score in the highest score ranges or that whites do not score in the lowest, only that the average scores differ by race. Some researchers, including Herrnstein and Murray, have interpreted these differences to mean that - just as skin and eye color, hair texture, and some anatomical features (e.g., shape of head, nose, lips) are genetically transmitted "racial" characteristics - different levels of ability to perform certain mental tasks must somehow be genetically transmitted as well (Brigham 1923; Burt 1972a, 1972b; Jensen 1967, 1969; Terman 1916). However, the vast preponderance of social science and genetic research over several generations indicates that this conclusion, when examined closely, is inherently illogical and baseless - and that differences in test score patterns reflect differences in how racial groups are educated and/ or treated (Bond 1924a, 1924b, 1934; Crummell 1898; Du Bois 1914; Gould 1981; Grubb 1992; Hilliard 1992; Kamin 1973; Long 1923; Price 1934; Thomas 1934; Thompson 1982).

Hudson, J. B. (1995). Scientific Racism: The Politics of Tests, Race and Genetics. *The Black Scholar*, *25*(1), 3–10. http://www.jstor.org/stable/41068539. Retrieved from: https://www.jstor.org/stable/41068539?seq=1

6. Abstract - "Scientific" racism and the evidence on race and intelligence.

Examines the controversy over genetic determinants of racial intelligence, and criticizes points raised by Eysenck in Race, Intelligence and Education. Several lines of evidence are presented that refute biological studies of IQ differences: (a) anatomical studies of brain structure reveal no differences in blacks and whites, while structural differences have been produced in animals by nutritional manipulation, suggesting that environmental factors outweigh genetic factors; (b) 75% of American blacks have some white ancestry with no correlation between degree of white ancestry and IQ; and (c) compensatory education of disadvantaged black children significantly increases IQ. 5 biasing factors in comparisons of American Indian and Negro performance on culture-fair intelligence tests are discussed: (a) Indian studies are based on urban samples; (b) Indians typically attend white schools, unlike blacks; (c) social-distance studies reveal more discrimination against blacks than Indians; (d) blacks have been denied identification with their cultural heritage; and (e) blacks may "pass" for Indians. (32 ref) (PsycINFO Database Record (c) 2016 APA, all rights reserved)

Colman, A. M. (1972). "Scientific" racism and the evidence on race and intelligence. *Race, 14*(2), 137–153. https://doi.org/10.1177/030639687201400202. Retrieved from: https://psycnet.apa.org/record/1974-29373-001. Retrieved from: https://journals.sagepub.com/doi/pdf/10.1177/030639687201400202

7. The IQ Myth

Hilary Rose and Steven Rose (1978). The IQ Myth
Retrieved from:
https://journals.sagepub.com/doi/pdf/10.1177/030639687802000104

8. Abstract - Racial differences in intelligence: The importance of the executive system

The race-IQ controversy arose at a time when psychometric views of intelligence dominated. Little attention was paid to more process-oriented models in spite of the fact they provide alternative perspectives on the causes of individual differences in problem-solving. We hypothesized that much of the IQ spread commonly observed between black and white children can be attributed to differences in components of their executive systems, including the knowledge base, control processes, and metacognitive states. To test this possibility, black and white children who differed significantly on fluid and crystallized intelligence were tested on multiple tasks reflecting components of the executive systems as well as on perceptual efficiency tasks. Striking group differences were observed in metamemory, strategy use, and general knowledge, but few reliable differences were found in perceptual efficiency. Regression analyses showed that different factors predicted fluid and crystallized intelligence, with meta-memory predicting the latter but not the former. An implication of these findings has potential educational significance: training directed at executive skills, introduce at an early age, might elevate learning and problem-solving skills in black children, thereby reducing racial differences in crystallized intelligence.

John G. Borkowski, Audrey Krause (1983). Racial differences in intelligence: The importance of the executive system, *Intelligence, Volume 7, Issue 4, 1983, Pages 379-395,*

ISSN 0160-2896, https://doi.org/10.1016/0160-2896(83)90012-0..

Retrieved from:

https://www.sciencedirect.com/science/article/pii/0160289683900120

9. Abstract - Research on group differences in intelligence: A defense of free inquiry

In a very short time, it is likely that we will identify many of the genetic variants underlying individual differences in intelligence. We should be prepared for the possibility that these variants are not distributed identically among all geographic populations, and that this explains some of the phenotypic differences in measured intelligence among groups. However, some philosophers and scientists believe that we should refrain from conducting research that might demonstrate the (partly) genetic origin of group differences in IQ. Many scholars view academic interest in this topic as inherently morally suspect or even racist. The majority of philosophers and social scientists take it for granted that all population differences in intelligence are due to environmental factors.

The present paper argues that the widespread practice of ignoring or rejecting research on intelligence differences can have unintended negative consequences. Social policies predicated on environmentalist theories of group differences may fail to achieve their aims. Large swaths of academic work in both the humanities and social sciences assume the truth of environmentalism and are vulnerable to being undermined. We have failed to work through the moral implications of group differences to prepare for the possibility that they will be shown to exist.

Nathan Cofnas (2020) Research on group differences in intelligence: A defense of free inquiry, Philosophical Psychology, 33:1, 125-147, DOI: 10.1080/09515089.2019.1697803. Retrieved from: https://www.tandfonline.com/doi/full/10.1080/09515089.2019.1697803

10. Is Racism Just a Form of Stupidity?

Empirical evidence has consistently linked low intelligence with prejudice.

Scientists have measured intelligence in a variety of ways, and the main conclusion always holds up. In one study of white children, for example, some were less able to see that a short wide glass holds the same amount of water as a taller skinnier glass. This ability is known as "conservation" in the jargon of the field, and it's widely considered an important mental ability. In this study, the kids who lacked this ability also held more negative views of black children. Other researchers conducted an ambitious meta-analysis—a statistical aggregation of findings from many studies—and this also documented a link between cognitive style and ability, on the one hand, and authoritarian attitudes on the other.

Wray Herbert. Is Racism Just a Form of Stupidity? Association for Psychological Science (aps). Retrieved from: https://www.psychologicalscience.org/news/were-only-human/is-racism-just-a-form-of-stupidity.html

11. Abstract - Does Lower Cognitive Ability Predict Greater Prejudice?

Historically, leading scholars proposed a theoretical negative association between cognitive abilities and prejudice. Until recently, however, the field has been relatively silent on this topic, citing concerns with potential confounds (e.g., education levels). Instead, researchers focused on other individual-difference predictors of prejudice, including cognitive style, personality, negativity bias, and threat. Yet there exists a solid empirical paper trail demonstrating that lower cognitive abilities (e.g., abstract-reasoning skills and verbal, nonverbal, and general intelligence) predict greater prejudice. We discuss how the effects of lower cognitive ability on prejudice are explained (i.e., mediated) by greater endorsement of right-wing socially conservative attitudes. We conclude that the field will benefit from a recognition of, and open discussion about, differences in cognitive abilities between those lower versus higher in prejudice. To advance the scientific discussion, we propose the Cognitive Ability and Style to Evaluation model, which outlines the cognitive psychological underpinnings of ideological belief systems and prejudice.

Dhont, K., & Hodson, G. (2014). Does Lower Cognitive Ability Predict Greater Prejudice? *Current Directions in Psychological Science, 23*(6), 454–459. https://doi.org/10.1177/0963721414549750. Retrieved from: https://journals.sagepub.com/doi/10.1177/0963721414549750

12. Stanford psychologist identifies seven factors that contribute to American racism

"One of the most important steps for future research will be to shift our attention away from how people become racist, and toward the contextual influences, psychological processes and developmental mechanisms that help people become anti-racist," Roberts and Rizzo wrote. "In a state of increasing racial inequality, we hope to find future students and scholars, both in the U.S. and beyond, well-versed and embedded within a psychology of anti-racism."

Sandra Feder (2020). Stanford psychologist identifies seven factors that contribute to American racism

Stanford News. Retrieved from: https://news.stanford.edu/2020/06/09/seven-factors-contributing-american-racism/

Appendix 6

PAULO FREIRE
PEDAGOGY OF THE OPPRESSED

Translated by Myra Bergman Ramos

With an Introduction by Donaldo Macedo

https://envs.ucsc.edu/internships/internship-readings/freire-pedagogy-of-the-oppressed.pdf

Overview of the Chapters

Chapter 1

The justification for a pedagogy of the oppressed; the contradiction between the oppressors and the oppressed, and how it is overcome; oppression and the oppressors; oppression and the oppressed; liberation: not a gift, not a self-achievement, but a mutual process.

Chapter 2

The "banking" concept of education as an instrument of oppression— its presuppositions—a critique; the problem-posing concept of education as an instrument for liberation—-its presuppositions; the "banking" concept and the teacher-student contradiction; the problem-posing concept and the supersedence of the teacherstudent contradiction; education: a mutual process, world-mediated; people as uncompleted beings, conscious of their incompletion, and their attempt to be more fully human.

Chapter 3

Dialogics—the essence of education as the practice of freedom; dialogics and dialogue; dialogue and the search for program content; the human-world relationship, "generative themes," and the program content of education as the practice of freedom; the investigation of "generative themes" and its methodology; the awakening of critical consciousness through the investigation of "generative themes"; the various stages of the investigation.

Chapter 4

Antidialogics and dialogics as matrices of opposing theories of cultural action: the former as an instrument of oppression and the latter as an instrument of liberation; the theory of antidialogical action and its characteristics: conquest, divide and rule, manipulation, and cultural invasion; the theory of dialogical action and its characteristics: cooperation, unity, organization, and cultural synthesis.

Endnotes

1

Rea, Shilo (2015). Researchers Find Everyone Has a Bias Blind Spot. *Carnegie Mellon University.* Retrieved from: https://www.cmu.edu/news/stories/archives/2015/june/bias-blind-spot.html

2

Eileen Sullivan and Katie Benner (2021). Top law enforcement officials say the biggest domestic terror threat comes from white supremacists. Retrieved from: https://www.nytimes.com/2021/05/12/us/politics/domestic-terror-white-supremacists.html

3

Roza, David (2021). Air Force finally boots prominent white supremacist after months of review. Retrieved from: https://taskandpurpose.com/news/air-force-white-supremacist-shawn-mccaffrey/

4

KHALEDA RAHMAN **(2019).** Full List of 229 Black People Killed by Police Since George Floyd's Murder. Retrieved from: https://www.newsweek.com/full-list-229-black-people-killed-police-since-george-floyds-murder-1594477

Julie Tate, Jennifer Jenkins and Steven Rich (2022). David Fallis and Danielle Rindler (Ed) 956 people have been shot and killed by police in the past year. Retrieved from: https://www.washingtonpost.com/graphics/investigations/police-shootings-database/

5

Rene Ater (2020). IN MEMORIAM: I CAN'T BREATHE. RETRIEVED FROM: HTTPS://WWW.RENEEATER.COM/ON-MONUMENTS-BLOG/TAG/LIST+OF+UNARMED+BLACK+PEOPLE+KILLED+BY+POLICE

6

Lett, E., Ngozi Asabor, E., Corbin, T., and Boatright, D. (2021). Racial inequity in fatal US police shootings, 2015–2020. *J Epidemiol Community Health* 2021;**75:**394-397. Retrieved from: https://www.bmj.com/company/newsroom/fatal-police-shootings-of-unarmed-black-people-in-us-more-than-3-times-as-high-as-in-whites/

7

Arlin Cuncic and Cara Lustik (2022). The Psychology Behind Police Brutality. *Verywell.* Retrieved from: https://www.verywellmind.com/the-psychology-behind-police-brutality-5077410

8

DeVylder J, Lalane M, Fedina L. (2019). The association between abusive policing and PTSD symptoms among U.S. police officers. *J Soc Soc Work Res*. 2019;10(2):261-273. doi:10.1086/703356

Arlin Cuncic (2022). The Psychology Behind Police Brutality. *VeryWell Mind.* Retrieved from: https://www.verywellmind.com/the-psychology-behind-police-brutality-5077410#citation-1 ;

https://www.verywellmind.com/the-psychology-behind-police-brutality-5077410

9

DeVylder J, Lalane M, Fedina L. (2019). The association between abusive policing and PTSD symptoms among U.S. police officers. *J Soc Soc Work Res*. 2019;10(2):261-273. doi:10.1086/703356

10

DeVylder J, Lalane M, Fedina L. (2019). The association between abusive policing and PTSD symptoms among U.S. police officers. *J Soc Soc Work Res*. 2019;10(2):261-273. doi:10.1086/703356

Falkenbach D, Balash J, Tsoukalas M, Stern S, Lilienfeld SO. (2018). From theoretical to empirical: Considering reflections of psychopathy across the thin blue line. *Personal Disord Theor Res Treat.* 2018;9(5):420-428. doi:10.1037/per0000270

Arlin Cuncic (2022). The Psychology Behind Police Brutality. *VeryWell Mind.* Retrieved from: https://www.verywellmind.com/the-psychology-behind-police-brutality-5077410#citation-1 ;

https://www.verywellmind.com/the-psychology-behind-police-brutality-5077410

11

Edwards F, Lee H, Esposito M. Risk of being killed by police use of force in the United States by age, race-ethnicity, and sex. *PNAS.* 2019;116(34):16793-16798. doi:10.1073/pnas.1821204116

Arlin Cuncic (2022). The Psychology Behind Police Brutality. *VeryWell Mind.* Retrieved from: https://www.verywellmind.com/the-psychology-behind-police-brutality-5077410#citation-1 ;

https://www.verywellmind.com/the-psychology-behind-police-brutality-5077410

12

Elle Lett , Emmanuella Ngozi Asabor , Theodore Corbin , Dowin Boatright (2020). Racial inequity in fatal US police shootings, 2015–2020. *Journal of Epidemiology & Community Health.* Retrieved from: https://jech.bmj.com/content/jech/75/4/394.full.pdf

https://www.bmj.com/company/newsroom/fatal-police-shootings-of-unarmed-black-people-in-us-more-than-3-times-as-high-as-in-whites/

13

(2022). Movement for Black Lives Responds to Biden's Plan to Allow Cities to Use Federal Stimulus Money to Increase Funding for Police Departments. Retrieved from: https://m4bl.org/statements/bidens-plan-stimulus-money-funding-police/

14

Wodtke, Geoffrey (2016). Are Smart People Less Racist? Verbal Ability, Anti-Black Prejudice, and the Principle-Policy Paradox. Soc Probl. 2016, Jan 8; 63(1): 21–45. doi: 10.1093/socpro/spv028. Retrieved from: https://www.ncbi.nlm.nih.gov/pmc/articles/PMC4845100/

15

Wodtke, Geoffrey (2016). Are Smart People Less Racist? Verbal Ability, Anti-Black Prejudice, and the Principle-Policy Paradox. Soc Probl. 2016, Jan 8; 63(1): 21–45. doi: 10.1093/socpro/spv028. Retrieved from: https://www.ncbi.nlm.nih.gov/pmc/articles/PMC4845100/

16

Clair, M. and Denis, Jeffrey, S. (2015). *Sociology of Racism.* Retrieved from: https://scholar.harvard.edu/files/matthewclair/files/sociology_of_racism_clairandenis_2015.pdf

17

Clair, M. and Denis, Jeffrey, S. (2015). *Sociology of Racism.* Retrieved from: https://scholar.harvard.edu/files/matthewclair/files/sociology_of_racism_clairandenis_2015.pdf

18

Carmichael, S., & Hamilton, C. V. (1967). Black power: The politics of liberation in America. New York: Vintage Books.

19

Clair, M. and Denis, Jeffrey, S. (2015). *Sociology of Racism.* Retrieved from: https://scholar.harvard.edu/files/matthewclair/files/sociology_of_racism_clairandenis_2015.pdf

20

McLeod, Saul (2008). **Prejudice and Discrimination. Simply Psychology. Retrieved from:** https://www.simplypsychology.org/prejudice.html

21

Chamberlain, Jamie (2004). What's behind prejudice? American Psychological Association, October 2004, Vol 35, No. 9, p. 34. Retrieved from: https://www.apa.org/monitor/oct04/prejudice

22

Fernald LD (2008). *Psychology: Six perspectives* (pp.12–15). Thousand Oaks, CA: Sage Publications.

Hockenbury & Hockenbury (2010). *Psychology*. Worth Publishers.

23

Clair, M. and Denis, Jeffrey, S. (2015). *Sociology of Racism.* Retrieved from: https://scholar.harvard.edu/files/matthewclair/files/sociology_of_racism_clairandenis_2015.pdf

24

Cornell, S., Hartmann, D. (2006). *Ethnicity and Race: Making Identities in a Changing World,* second ed. Pine Forge Press, Thousand Oaks, CA.

25

Pager, Devah and Shepherd, Hana (2008). The Sociology of Discrimination: Racial Discrimination in Employment, Housing, Credit, and Consumer Markets. Annu Rev Sociol. 2008 Jan 1; 34: 181–209. Retrieved from: https://www.ncbi.nlm.nih.gov/pmc/articles/PMC2915460/

26

Pager, D and Shepherd, H. (2008). The Sociology of Discrimination: Racial Discrimination in Employment, Housing, Credit, and Consumer Markets. Annu Rev Sociol. 2008 Jan 1; 34: 181–209. Retrieved from: https://www.ncbi.nlm.nih.gov/pmc/articles/PMC2915460/

27

ADL. Racism. Race and Racial Justice. Retrieved from: https://www.adl.org/racism

28

APA. What is Racism? Racism, bias, and discrimination resources. American Psychological Association. Retrieved from: https://www.apa.org/topics/racism-bias-discrimination

29

APA (2020). The psychology of American racism and how to work against it. American Psychological Association. Retrieved from: https://www.apa.org/pubs/highlights/spotlight/issue-189

Roberts, S. O., & Rizzo, M. T. (2020). The psychology of American racism. *American Psychologist*. Advance online publication. https://doi.org/10.1037/amp0000642

Roberts, S. O., & Rizzo, M. T. (2021). The psychology of American racism. *American Psychologist, 76*(3), 475-487. http://dx.doi.org/10.1037/amp0000642. Retrieved from: https://psycnet.apa.org/fulltext/2020-45459-001.html

30

Wilson, W.J. (1999). *The Bridge over the Racial Divide: Rising Inequality and Coalition Politics.* University of California Press, Berkeley. P. 14.

31

Clair, M. and Denis, Jeffrey, S. (2015). *Sociology of Racism.* Retrieved from: https://scholar.harvard.edu/files/matthewclair/files/sociology_of_racism_clairandenis_2015.pdf

32

Kochman, T. (1976). Perceptions along the Power Axis: A Cognitive Residue of Inter-Racial Encounters. *Anthropological Linguistics, 18*(6), 261–273. http://www.jstor.org/stable/30027582. Retrieved from: https://www.jstor.org/stable/30027582?seq=1

33

Irene Scopelliti, Carey K. Morewedge, Erin McCormick, H. Lauren Min, Sophie Lebrecht, Karim S. Kassam (2015). Bias Blind Spot: Structure, Measurement, and Consequences. *Management Science Volume 61, Issue 10, October 2015, Pages iv-vii, 2281-2547, Published Online: 24 Apr 2015,* https://doi.org/10.1287/mnsc.2014.2096. Retrieved from: https://pubsonline.informs.org/doi/abs/10.1287/mnsc.2014.2096

34

Rea, Shilo (2015). Researchers Find Everyone Has a Bias Blind Spot. *Carnegie Mellon University.* Retrieved from: https://www.cmu.edu/news/stories/archives/2015/june/bias-blind-spot.html

35

Wijeysinghe, C. L., Griffin, P, and Love, B. (1997). Racism Curriculum Design. In M. Adams, L. A. Bell, & P. Griffin (Eds.), Teaching for diversity and social justice: A sourcebook (pp. 82-109). New York: Routledge. Retrieved from: https://www.vanderbilt.edu/oacs/wp-content/uploads/sites/140/Key-Terms-Racism.pdf

36

SPLC. WHITE NATIONALIST. SOUTHERN POVERTY LAW CENTER. RETRIEVED FROM: HTTPS://WWW.SPLCENTER.ORG/FIGHTING-HATE/EXTREMIST-FILES/IDEOLOGY/WHITE-NATIONALIST

37

Healthline. What is a Superiority Complex? *Healthline Media*. Retrieved from: https://www.healthline.com/health/mental-health/superiority-complex

38

Roberts, Anyssa (2021). Why Black People Are Top Consumers But Lack Wealth. Campaign Monitor. Retrieved from: https://www.campaignmonitor.com/blog/email-marketing/why-black-people-are-top-consumers/

39

McKinsey Global Institute (2021). The Economic State of Black American: What is and what could be. *McKinsey & Company*. Retrieved from: https://www.mckinsey.com/featured-insights/diversity-and-inclusion/the-economic-state-of-black-america-what-is-and-what-could-be

40

Melancon, Merritt (2021). Consumer buying power is more diverse than ever. *UGA Today (University of Georgia)*. Retrieved from: https://news.uga.edu/selig-multicultural-economy-report-2021/

41

(Masci, 2018; Pew Research Center, 2015; *Sahgal & Smith, 2009;* Taylor, Chatters and Brown, 2015).

Masci, D. (2018). 5 facts about the religious lives of African Americans. *Pew Research Center*. Retrieved from: http://www.pewresearch.org/fact-tank/2018/02/07/5-facts-about-the-religious-lives-of-african-americans/

Pew Research Center (2015). Importance of religion and religious beliefs, chapter 1, U.S. public becoming less religious. *Pew Research Center*.

Retrieved from: http://www.pewforum.org/2015/11/03/chapter-1-importance-of-religion-and-religious-beliefs/

Pew Research Center (2015). America's changing religious landscape. Retrieved from: http://www.pewforum.org/2015/05/12/americaschanging-religious- landscape/

Sahgal N., Smith, G. (2009). A religious portrait of African Americans, *Pew Research Center: Religion and Public life*. Retrieved from: http://www.pewforum.org/2009/01/30/areligious-portrait-of-African- Americans/

Taylor, R. J., Chatters, L. M., and Brown, R. K. (2014). African American religious participation. *Rev Relig Res. 2014 Dec; 56(4): pp. 513–538*. Published online 2013 Dec 10. doi: 10.1007/s13644-013-0144-z.

Retrieved from: https://www.ncbi.nlm.nih.gov/pmc/articles/PMC4285628/

42

White, Walter F. (August 23, 2001). "Tulsa, 1921". The Nation. Archived from the original on June 12, 2018. Retrieved September 16, 2018.

Branigin, Anne (2019). "Nearly 100 Years Later, Tulsa Begins Search for Mass Graves From 1921 Black Wall Street Massacre". *The Root. Archived from the original on October 9, 2019. Retrieved October 9, 2019. Retrieved from:* https://www.theroot.com/nearly-100-years-later-tulsa-begins-search-for-mass-gr-1838883790

Ellsworth, Scott *(2009)*. "Tulsa Race Riot". The Encyclopedia of Oklahoma History and Culture. Archived *from the original on June 13, 2020*. Retrieved December 31, *2016.*

Parshina-Kottas, Yuliya; Singhvi, Anjali; Burch, Audra D. S.; Griggs, Troy; Gröndahl, Mika; Huang, Lingdong; Wallace, Tim; White, Jeremy; Williams, Josh (May 24, 2021). «What the Tulsa Race Massacre Destroyed». The New York Times. ISSN 0362-4331. Retrieved March 16, 2022.

Huddleston Jr, Tom (July 4, 2020). "'Black Wall Street': The history of the wealthy black community and the massacre perpetrated there". CNBC. Retrieved August 30, 2020.

43

Wallace Greene. (1984). The Holocaust Hoax: A Rejoinder. *Jewish Social Studies*, *46*(3/4), 263–276. http://www.jstor.org/stable/4467263. Retrieved from: https://www.jstor.org/stable/4467263#metadata_info_tab_contents

Holocaust Denial. Southern Poverty Law Center. Retrieved from: https://www.splcenter.org/fighting-hate/extremist-files/ideology/holocaust-denial

44

Notes later obtained from the defense give a different story, with Bryant earlier claiming she was "insulted" but not mentioning him touching her. (*Mitchell, Jerry (September 4, 2017). "Emmett Till eyewitness dies; saw 1955 abduction of his cousin". Chicago Sun-Times. USA Today. Retrieved July 13, 2018.*)

45

Many years later, there were allegations that Till had been castrated. (Mitchell, 2007) John Cothran, the deputy sheriff who was at the scene where Till was removed from the river testified, however, that apart from the decomposition typical of a body being submerged in water, his genitals had been intact. (FBI [2006]: Appendix Court transcript, p. 176.) Mamie Till-Mobley also confirmed this in her memoirs. (Till-Bradley and Benson, p. 135.)

46

When *Jet* publisher John H. Johnson died in 2005, people who remembered his career considered his decision to publish Till›s open-casket photograph his greatest moment. Michigan congressman Charles Diggs recalled that for the emotion the image stimulated, it was «probably one of the greatest media products in the last 40 or 50 years». (Dewan, 2005)

47

Weller, Sheila (January 26, 2017). "How Author Timothy Tyson Found the Woman at the Center of the Emmett Till Case". Vanity Fair.

Pérez-Peñajan, Richard (January 27, 2017). "Woman Linked to 1955 Emmett Till Murder Tells Historian Her Claims Were False". The New York Times. Retrieved October 23, 2017.

48

Seed, Patricia. American Pentimento [electronic Resource] : The Invention of Indians and the Pursuit of Riches / Patricia Seed.Minneapolis: University of Minnesota Press, 2001. Print.

Bonch-Bruevich, Xenia. "Ideologies of the Spanish Reconquest and Isidore's Political Thought." Mediterranean Studies, vol. 17, 2008, pp. 27–45. JSTOR, www.jstor.org/stable/41167390. Accessed 12 Nov. 2020.

Forsythe, David P. (2009). Encyclopedia of Human Rights, Volume 4. Oxford University Press. p. 297. ISBN 978-0-19-533402-9.

David E. Stannard (1993-11-18). American Holocaust: The Conquest of the New World. Oxford University Press, USA. p. 146. ISBN 978-0-19-508557-0.

Seed, Patricia. Ceremonies of possession in Europe's conquest of the New World, 1492-1640. United Kingdom, Cambridge University Press, 1995.

49

Pager, Devah and Shepherd, Hana (2008). The Sociology of Discrimination: Racial Discrimination in Employment, Housing, Credit, and Consumer Markets. Annu Rev Sociol. 2008 Jan 1; 34: 181–209. Retrieved from: https://www.ncbi.nlm.nih.gov/pmc/articles/PMC2915460/

50

Pager, Devah and Shepherd, Hana (2008). The Sociology of Discrimination: Racial Discrimination in Employment, Housing, Credit, and Consumer Markets. Annu Rev Sociol. 2008 Jan 1; 34: 181–209. Retrieved from: https://www.ncbi.nlm.nih.gov/pmc/articles/PMC2915460/

51

Sternberg RJ, Grigorenko EL, Kidd KK. (2005). Intelligence, race, and genetics. Am Psychol. 2005 Jan;60(1):46-59. doi: 10.1037/0003-066X.60.1.46. PMID: 15641921. Retrieved from: https://pubmed.ncbi.nlm.nih.gov/15641921/

52

Rosenberg, Eli (2019). I believe in white supremacy': John Wayne's notorious 1971 Playboy interview goes viral on Twitter. Retrieved from: https://www.washingtonpost.com/arts-entertainment/2019/02/20/i-believe-white-supremacy-john-waynes-notorious-playboy-interview-goes-viral-twitter/

Sandler, Rachel (2020). USC To Remove John Wayne Exhibit After Renewed Protests Over Actor's Racist Remarks. *Forbes.* Retrieved from: https://www.forbes.com/sites/rachelsandler/2020/07/10/usc-to-remove-john-wayne-exhibit-after-renewed-protests-over-actors-racist-remarks/?sh=5e4859293181

Andone Dakin (2020). USC will remove a John Wayne exhibit after actor's racist comments resurfaced. *CNN.* Retrieved from: https://www.cnn.com/2020/07/12/us/john-wayne-exhibit-usc-trnd/index.html

Shafer, Ellise (2020). John Wayne Exhibit to be removed at USC following protest over actor's racist remarks.

Variety.com. Retrieved from: https://variety.com/2020/film/news/john-wayne-exhibit-removed-usc-racist-1234704108/

53

Davis, Ronald, L. (May 1, 2001). *Duke: The Life and Image of John Wayne*. University of Oklahoma Press. ISBN 978-0-8061-3329-4.

54

Wodtke, Geoffrey T. (2016). Are Smart People Less Racist? Verbal Ability, Anti-Black Prejudice, and the Principle-Policy Paradox. *Social Problems*, Volume 63, Issue 1, February 2016, Pages 21–45, https://doi.org/10.1093/socpro/spv028. Retrieved from: https://academic.oup.com/socpro/article/63/1/21/1846173

55

Wodtke, Geoffrey T. (2016). Are Smart People Less Racist? Verbal Ability, Anti-Black Prejudice, and the Principle-Policy Paradox. *Social Problems*, Volume 63, Issue 1, February 2016, Pages 21–45, https://doi.org/10.1093/socpro/spv028. Retrieved from: https://academic.oup.com/socpro/article/63/1/21/1846173

56

Wodtke, Geoffrey T. (2016). Are Smart People Less Racist? Verbal Ability, Anti-Black Prejudice, and the Principle-Policy Paradox. *Social Problems*, Volume 63, Issue 1, February 2016, Pages 21–45, https://doi.org/10.1093/socpro/spv028. Retrieved from: https://academic.oup.com/socpro/article/63/1/21/1846173

57

Piaget(1965). The child's conception of number. New York: W. Norton Company & Inc.

Siegler, R., DeLoache, J., & Eisenberg., N. (2003). How children develop. New York: Worth Publishers.

58

Wubbena, Zane (2013). "Mathematical fluency as a function of conservation ability in young children". *Learning and Individual Differences*. **26**: 153–155. doi:10.1016/j.lindif.2013.01.013.

Ojose, B. Applying Piaget's Theory of cognitive development to mathematics instruction. *The Mathematics Educator*, 18 (1), 26-30.

59

Wray Herbert. Is Racism Just a Form of Stupidity? Association for Psychological Science (aps). Retrieved from: https://www.psychologicalscience.org/news/were-only-human/is-racism-just-a-form-of-stupidity.html

Dhont, Kristof and Hodson (2014). Gordon. Does Lower Cognitive Ability Predict Greater Prejudice? Sage Journals, Current Directions in Psychological Science, First Published December 16, 2014 Research Article

https://doi.org/10.1177/0963721414549750. Retrieved from: https://journals.sagepub.com/doi/10.1177/0963721414549750

60

Dhont, Kristof and Hodson (2014). Gordon. Does Lower Cognitive Ability Predict Greater Prejudice? Sage Journals, Current Directions in Psychological Science, First Published December 16, 2014 Research Article

https://doi.org/10.1177/0963721414549750. Retrieved from: https://journals.sagepub.com/doi/10.1177/0963721414549750

61

Wray Herbert. Is Racism Just a Form of Stupidity? Association for Psychological Science (aps). Retrieved from: https://www.psychologicalscience.org/news/were-only-human/is-racism-just-a-form-of-stupidity.html

Dhont, Kristof and Hodson (2014). Gordon. Does Lower Cognitive Ability Predict Greater Prejudice? Sage Journals, Current Directions in Psychological Science, First Published December 16, 2014 Research Article

https://doi.org/10.1177/0963721414549750. Retrieved from: https://journals.sagepub.com/doi/10.1177/0963721414549750

62

Wray Herbert. Is Racism Just a Form of Stupidity? Association for Psychological Science (aps). Retrieved from: https://www.psychologicalscience.org/news/were-only-human/is-racism-just-a-form-of-stupidity.html

Dhont, Kristof and Hodson (2014). Gordon. Does Lower Cognitive Ability Predict Greater Prejudice? Sage Journals, Current Directions in Psychological Science, First Published December 16, 2014 Research Article

https://doi.org/10.1177/0963721414549750. Retrieved from: https://journals.sagepub.com/doi/10.1177/0963721414549750

63

Wodtke, Geoffrey (2016). Are Smart People Less Racist? Verbal Ability, Anti-Black Prejudice, and the Principle-Policy Paradox. Soc Probl. 2016, Jan 8; 63(1): 21–45. doi: 10.1093/socpro/spv028. Retrieved from: https://www.ncbi.nlm.nih.gov/pmc/articles/PMC4845100/

64

Clair, Matthew and Denis, Jeffery, S. (2015). Sociology of Racism. Harvard University. Retrieved from: https://scholar.harvard.edu/files/matthewclair/files/sociology_of_racism_clairandenis_2015.pdf

65

Schrader, Jessica (2017). The Psychology of Hate: Why do we hate? Psychology Today. Retrieved from: https://www.psychologytoday.com/us/blog/nurturing-self-compassion/201703/the-psychology-hate

King, Ben (2020). You hate in others what you dislike in yourself. Retrieved from: https://medium.com/@BensEthos/you-hate-in-others-what-you-dislike-in-yourself-483829770571

66

Taylor, Steve, PhD (2018). The Psychology of Racism. Psychology Today. Retrieved from: https://www.psychologytoday.com/us/blog/out-the-darkness/201801/the-psychology-racism

67

Peace Learning Center (2020). What is implicit bias? Retrieved from: https://peacelearningcenter.org/implicit-bias-workshops/?gclid=EAIaIQobChMIudbQkavb8QIVDh6tBh05lgGbEAMYAyAAEgKVTPD_BwE

68

Powell, Aisha, (2021). Powell, Aisha, (2021). Black principal calls out racism after he was told to remove photo kissing white wife. Retrieved from: https://www.yahoo.com/news/black-principal-calls-racism-told-160504944.html ; https://www.yahoo.com/news/colleyville-heritage-principal-posts-racial-020525445.html

69

Cory Shaffer, Cory (2021). White woman who stole $250K gets probation, while Black woman who stole $40K goes to jail. Disparate sentences spark calls for reform. *Courts and Justice*. Retrieved from: https://www.cleveland.com/court-justice/2021/08/cuyahoga-county-judges-disparate-sentences-for-white-black-women-who-stole-public-money-sharpens-calls-for-statewide-sentencing-database.html

70

Cornell Law School. What does equal protection mean in the 14th Amendment? *Legal Information Institute, Equal Protection | Wex | US Law | LII / Legal Information Institute*

Retrieved from: https://www.law.cornell.edu/wex/equal_protection

71

Beals, Monique (2021). Black couple sues appraiser for valuing home at $500,000 more when 'whitewashed'. The Hill. Retrieved from: https://thehill.com/homenews/state-watch/584993-black-couple-sues-appraiser-for-valuing-home-at-500000-more-when-white/

Johns, Joe and Robinson, Laura (2021). A Black couple had a White friend show their home and its appraisal rose by nearly half a million dollars. CNN. Retrieved from: https://www.cnn.com/2021/12/09/business/black-homeowners-appraisal-discrimination-lawsuit/index.html

72

Hall, Ellie (2021). A Woman Who Ran Her Car Into Two Children Because Of Their Race Has Been Sentenced To 25 Years In Prison. Retrieved from: https://www.buzzfeednews.com/article/ellievhall/iowa-woman-hit-children-car-sentence-hate-crime

Department of Justice (2021). Iowa Woman Sentenced to 304 Months in Prison for Hate Crimes Involving Attempting to Kill Two Children Because of their Race and National Origin. Department of Justice, Civil Rights Division, Hate Crimes. Retrieved from: https://www.justice.gov/opa/pr/iowa-woman-sentenced-304-months-prison-hate-crimes-involving-attempting-kill-two-children

73

Rob Frehse and Laura Studley (2022). Video showing how police treat Black and White teens in mall fight sparks outrage. *CNN*. Retrieved from: https://www.cnn.com/2022/02/16/us/video-new-jersey-police-black-and-white-teen-fight-outrage/index.html

https://www.nbcnews.com/news/us-news/police-response-nj-mall-fight-sparks-outrage-black-teen-cuffed-white-t-rcna16459

Kenneth Garger (2022). NJ police under fire after cuffing black teen in mall fight as white teen watches. *NY Post*. Retrieved from: https://nypost.com/2022/02/16/nj-police-cuff-black-teen-in-mall-fight-as-white-teen-watches/

Joe Hernandez (2022). N.J. police are under scrutiny for racial bias after breaking up a fight between teens. *NPR*. Retrieved from: https://www.npr.org/2022/02/16/1081155557/nj-police-fight-mall-teenagers-black-white

74

Vera, Amir and Frehse, Rob (2022). 2 Black girls were charged with hate crimes after allegedly hitting a woman on a bus and making 'anti-White' statements, police say. *CNN*. Retrieved from: https://www.cnn.com/2022/07/26/us/nypd-black-girls-anti-white-hate-crime-reaj/index.html

75

Edwards, G. S. and Rushin, Stephen (2018). The Effect of President Trump's Election on Hate Crimes. Retrieved from: https://papers.ssrn.com/sol3/papers.cfm?abstract_id=3102652

Edwards, Griffin Sims and Rushin, Stephen, The Effect of President Trump's Election on Hate Crimes (January 14, 2018). Available at SSRN: https://ssrn.com/abstract=3102652 or http://dx.doi.org/10.2139/ssrn.3102652

Williamson, Vanessa and Gelfrand, Isabella (2022). Trump and racism: What do the data say? Brookings Institute. Retrieved from: https://www.brookings.edu/blog/fixgov/2019/08/14/trump-and-racism-what-do-the-data-say/

76

Yam, Kimmy (2021). Anti-Asian hate crimes increased by nearly 150% in 2020, mostly in N.Y. and L.A., new report says. Retrieved from: https://www.nbcnews.com/news/asian-america/anti-asian-hate-crimes-increased-nearly-150-2020-mostly-n-n1260264

77

Koski, Susan V. and Bantley, Kathleen (2020). DOG WHISTLE POLITICS: THE TRUMP ADMINISTRATION'S INFLUENCE ON HATE CRIMES. Retrieved from: https://scholarship.shu.edu/cgi/viewcontent.cgi?article=1157&context=shlj

78

(2018-2020). THE TRUMP ADMINISTRATION'S RECORD OF RACISM, part 1. Retrieved from: https://democracyincolor.com/recordofracism

79

Dorman, John, L. (2022). New York Post editorial board throws cold water on a 2024 Trump campaign, calling him 'unworthy' to serve in the White House for another term. Business Insider. Retrieved from: https://www.businessinsider.com/trump-new-york-post-editorial-board-unworthy-2024-white-house-2022-7

80

Cillizza, Chris (2022). 11 Trump associates have now been charged with crimes. 11! *CNN Politics*. Retrieved from: https://amp.cnn.com/cnn/2021/07/21/politics/tom-barrack-trump-arrested/index.html

81

Miller, Cassie (2018). The Biggest Lie in the White Supremacist Propaganda Playbook: Unraveling the Truth About 'Black-on-White Crime'. *The Southern Poverty Law Center.* Retrieved from: https://www.splcenter.org/20180614/biggest-lie-white-supremacist-propaganda-playbook-unraveling-truth-about-%E2%80%98black-white-crime#modern

82

Itkowitz, Colby (2020). Trump again uses racially insensitive term to describe coronavirus. The Washington Post. *Retrieved from*: https://www.washingtonpost.com/politics/trump-again-uses-kung-flu-to-describe-coronavirus/2020/06/23/0ab5a8d8-b5a9-11ea-aca5-ebb63d27e1ff_story.html

83

Phillips, Amber (2017). 'They're rapists.' President Trump's campaign launch speech two years later, annotated. *The Washington Post.* Retrieved from: https://www.washingtonpost.com/news/the-fix/wp/2017/06/16/theyre-rapists-presidents-trump-campaign-launch-speech-two-years-later-annotated/

84

Phillips, Amber (2017). 'They're rapists.' President Trump's campaign launch speech two years later, annotated. *The Washington Post.* Retrieved from: https://www.washingtonpost.com/news/the-fix/wp/2017/06/16/theyre-rapists-presidents-trump-campaign-launch-speech-two-years-later-annotated/

85

Dale, Daniel and Kaczynski, Andrew (2019). Fact check: Trump falsely claims, again, to have opposed the invasion of Iraq. *CNN Politics.* Retrieved from: https://www.cnn.com/2019/10/29/politics/fact-check-trump-false-claim-opposed-iraq-invasion

86

FBI (2020). 2020 Hate Crime Statistics. The United States of America Department of Justice. Retrieved from: https://www.justice.gov/hatecrimes/hate-crime-statistics

87

Hightower E. (1997). Psychosocial characteristics of subtle and blatant racists as compared to tolerant individuals. J Clin Psychol. 1997 Jun;53(4):369-74. doi: 10.1002/(sici)1097-4679(199706)53:4<369::aid-jclp10>3.0.co;2-e. PMID: 9169392. Retrieved from: https://pubmed.ncbi.nlm.nih.gov/9169392/

88

Torrey, John (2020). This Harvard Test Reveals Sub-Conscious Racial Biases. Retrieved from: https://medium.com/be-unique/this-harvard-test-reveals-sub-conscious-racial-biases-f50a8032baea

89

Pew Research Center (2016). On Views of Race and Inequality, Blacks and Whites Are Worlds Apart. Retrieved from: https://www.pewresearch.org/social-trends/2016/06/27/on-views-of-race-and-inequality-blacks-and-whites-are-worlds-apart/

90

2021 Best Global Universities Rankings. U.S. News and World Report. Retrieved from: https://www.usnews.com/education/best-global-universities/rankings

The 100 Best Universities in the World Today. The Best Schools. Retrieved from: https://thebestschools.org/rankings/best-universities-world-today/

91

UChicago (2021). Diversity and Inclusion. University of Chicago. Retrieved from: https://diversityandinclusion.uchicago.edu/

92

Cone, James (2009). *Black Theology*.

93

BYRNE, JOHN, A. (2020). Chicago Booth MBA Loses Her Job After Racist Behavior Goes Viral. Retrieved from: https://poetsandquants.com/2020/05/26/chicago-booth-mba-loses-her-job-after-being-accused-of-racist-behavior/?pq-category=business-school-news

Reluctant Activist (2020). I got the same racist education as Central Park Karen. You probably did too. Retrieved from: https://medium.com/@reluctantlyurs/i-got-the-same-racist-education-as-central-park-karen-you-probably-did-too-f132ab41307a

Vera, Amir and Ly, Laura (2020). White woman who called police on a black man bird-watching in Central Park has been fired. *CNN*. Retrieved from: https://www.cnn.com/2020/05/26/us/central-park-video-dog-video-african-american-trnd/index.html

94

Reluctant Activist (2020). I got the same racist education as Central Park Karen. You probably did too. Retrieved from: https://medium.com/@reluctantlyurs/i-got-the-same-racist-education-as-central-park-karen-you-probably-did-too-f132ab41307a

95

Reluctant Activist (2020). I got the same racist education as Central Park Karen. You probably did too. Retrieved from: https://medium.com/@reluctantlyurs/i-got-the-same-racist-education-as-central-park-karen-you-probably-did-too-f132ab41307a

96

McCluskey, Neal (2022). Report on Indian Boarding Schools: A Sad and Important Reminder. CATO Institute. Retrieved from: https://www.cato.org/blog?utm_campaign=Cato%20at%20Liberty%20Newsletter&utm_medium=email&_hsmi=213071923&_hsenc=p2ANqtz--Dx_-OZkbxruf1b-20nzZETfKaNBKkFWYM_ggdfbL-JHKMV3Du8YfAH5Rhw3QlV1uvKbcTzbhgCSccZJyO-zFZt-KALOrw&utm_content=213071923&utm_source=hs_email

97

98

McCluskey, Neal (2022). Report on Indian Boarding Schools: A Sad and Important Reminder. *CATO Institute*. Retrieved from: https://www.cato.org/blog?utm_campaign=Cato%20at%20Liberty%20Newsletter&utm_medium=email&_hsmi=213071923&_hsenc=p2ANqtz--Dx_-OZkbxruf1b-

20nzZETfKaNBKkFWYM_ggdfbL-JHKMV3Du8YfAH5Rhw3QlV1uvKbcTzbhgCSccZJyO-zFZ-tKALOrw&utm_content=213071923&utm_source=hs_email

Newland, Brian (2022). Federal Indian Boarding School Initiative Investigative Report. *United States Department of the Interior.* Retrieved from: https://www.bia.gov/sites/default/files/dup/inline-files/bsi_investigative_report_may_2022_508.pdf?utm_campaign=Cato%20at%20Liberty%20Newsletter&utm_medium=email&_hsmi=213071923&_hsenc=p2ANqtz-8ZNXBCzP4SvtBk35d-8QlUcZW6i8itLXc_DwCdtYEhL540RPOq0CSZH3duja4Z0bC1iI1UJ-yXQPFZbHHlPEi8TF_9ik-w&utm_content=213071923&utm_source=hs_email

Chalabi, Mona (2020). Tim Scott says 'America is not a racist country' – the data says otherwise. *Atlanta Daily World.* Retrieved from: https://atlantadailyworld.com/2021/06/11/sen-tim-scott-says-america-is-not-a-racist-country/

99

Ray, Rashawn (2021). Is the United States a racist country? *Brookings Institute*. Retrieved from: https://www.brookings.edu/blog/how-we-rise/2021/05/04/is-the-united-states-a-racist-country/

100

Simon, Clea (2021). An unflinching look at racism as America's caste system. *The Harvard Gazette.* Retrieved from: https://news.harvard.edu/gazette/story/2021/02/viewing-racism-as-americas-caste-system/

101

Ray, Rashawn (2021). Is the United States a racist country? *Brookings Institute*. Retrieved from: https://www.brookings.edu/blog/how-we-rise/2021/05/04/is-the-united-states-a-racist-country/

102

103

WMMT Staff (2022). Police: 12-year-old boy commits armed robbery in broad daylight. Retrieved from: https://www.kold.com/2022/06/06/police-12-year-old-boy-commits-armed-robbery-broad-daylight/

"Attorney General Lynch Statement Following the Federal Grand Jury Indictment Against Dylann Storm Roof" (Press release). United States Department of Justice. July 22, 2015.

Dustin Waters & Mark Berman (December 15, 2016). "Dylann Roof found guilty on all counts in Charleston church massacre trial". Washington Post.

Alan Blinder & Kevin Sack (December 15, 2016). "Dylann Roof Found Guilty in Charleston Church Massacre". New York Times.

Sack, Kevin; Blinder, Alan (January 5, 2017). "No Regrets From Dylann Roof in Jailhouse Manifesto". The New York Times. Retrieved September 19, 2020.

Groll, Elias (June 18, 2015). "Was the Charleston Massacre an Act of Terrorism?". Foreign Policy. Retrieved January 27, 2021.

Hartmann, Margaret (June 19, 2015). "Why the Charleston Shooter Should Be Called a Terrorist". New York Magazine.

Dahl, Julia (June 19, 2015). "Was the South Carolina shooting a hate crime or a terrorist attack?". CBS News.

Friedersdorf, Conor (June 22, 2015). "Why It Matters That the Charleston Attack Was Terrorism". The Atlantic.

Norris, Jesse J. (March 30, 2017). "Why Dylann Roof Is a Terrorist under Federal Law, and Why It Matters". Harvard Journal on Legislation. ***54*** *(1): 501–541.*

Ghansah, Rachel Kaadzi (August 11, 2017). "A Most American Terrorist: The Making Of Dylann Roof". GQ. Retrieved January 27, 2021.

McCord, Mary B. (August 21, 2017). "Criminal Law Should Treat Domestic Terrorism as the Moral Equivalent of International Terrorism". Lawfare.

104

Bleiberg, J., Spagat, E., and Vertuno, J. (2022). Uvalde shooter's final 90 minutes fuel questions about police delays *PBS*. Retrieved from: https://www.pbs.org/newshour/education/uvalde-shooters-final-90-minutes-fuel-questions-about-police-delays

105

Prokupecz, Shimon; Moshtaghian, Artemis; Maxouris, Christina; and Beech Samantha (2022). What we know about Buffalo supermarket shooting suspect Payton Gendron. *CNN*. Retrieved from: https://www.cnn.com/2022/05/15/us/payton-gendron-buffalo-shooting-suspect-what-we-know/index.html

Eric Levenson, Sarah Jorgensen, Polo Sandoval and Samantha Beech (2022). Mass shooting at Buffalo supermarket was a racist hate crime, police say. CNN. Retrieved from:

https://www.cnn.com/2022/05/15/us/buffalo-supermarket-shooting-sunday/index.html

Lou Michel , Ben Tsujimoto , Maki Becker (2022). Buffalo's worst mass shooting takes 10 lives, leaves 3 wounded; attack called 'a racially motivated hate crime'. The Buffalo News. Retrieved from: https://buffalonews.com/news/local/crime-and-courts/buffalos-worst-mass-shooting-takes-10-lives-leaves-3-wounded-attack-called-a-racially-motivated/article_6e8132fa-d3b7-11ec-a714-2b3f-beaf848c.html

106

Taguieff, Pierre-André *(2015). La revanche du nationalisme: Néopopulistes et xénophobes à l'assaut de l'Europe (in French). Presses Universitaires de France. ISBN 978-2-13-072950-1.*

Verstraet, Antoine (2017). "C'est ça que tu veux ? !". Savoirs et Clinique (in French). **23** *(2): 55. doi:10.3917/sc.023.0055. ISSN 1634-3298. [transl. from French] This theory states that the indigenous French ("Français de souche") could soon be demographically replaced by non-European peoples, especially from the Maghreb and sub-Saharan Africa.*

Önnerfors, Andreas; Krouwel, André (2021). *Europe: Continent of Conspiracies: Conspiracy Theories in and about Europe. Routledge. ISBN 978-1-000-37339-4.*

Fourquet, Jérôme *(2016). Accueil ou submersion ?: Regards européens sur la crise des migrants (in French). Éditions de l'Aube.* ISBN 978-2-8159-2026-1.

107

Frey, William H. (2018). The US will become "minority White in 2045, Census projections. Brookings Institute. Retrieved from: https://www.brookings.edu/blog/the-avenue/2018/03/14/the-us-will-become-minority-white-in-2045-census-projects/

108

Kesich, Greg (23 June 2019). "The View From Here: Conspiracy theory takes hold in Maine GOP". Portland Press Herald. Archived from the original on 7 October 2019. Retrieved 7 October 2019.

109

Biesecker, Michael; Dunklin, Reese; Kunzelman, Michael (4 August 2019). "El Paso suspect appears to have posted anti-immigrant screed". *Associated Press.*

110

Bump, Philip (14 April 2021). "Tucker Carlson's toxic 'replacement' rhetoric gets picked up in the House". *The Washington Post.*

Haltiwanger, John (23 September 2021). "Tucker Carlson peddled a white supremacist conspiracy theory while attacking Biden over the Haitian migrant crisis". *Business Insider*. Retrieved 23 September 2021.

111

Hullinger, Logan (2021). ICYMI: Rep. Perry pushes 'replacement theory' during committee hearing. York Dispatch. Retrieved from: https://www.yorkdispatch.com/story/news/politics/2021/04/15/rep-perry-pushes-replacement-theory-during-committee-hearing/7229074002/

112

Bump, Philip (2022). Nearly half of Republicans agree with 'great replacement theory'. Washington Post. Retrieved from: https://www.washingtonpost.com/politics/2022/05/09/nearly-half-republicans-agree-with-great-replacement-theory/

113

Bump, Philip (2022). Nearly half of Republicans agree with 'great replacement theory'. Washington Post. Retrieved from: https://www.washingtonpost.com/politics/2022/05/09/nearly-half-republicans-agree-with-great-replacement-theory/

114

Jackson, J. P., & Winston, A. S. (2021). The Mythical Taboo on Race and Intelligence. *Review of General Psychology*, *25*(1), 3–26. https://doi.org/10.1177/1089268020953622. Retrieved from: https://journals.sagepub.com/doi/full/10.1177/1089268020953622

115

ERLC Staff (2022). The demographics of abortion in America. Retrieved from: https://erlc.com/resource-library/articles/the-demographics-of-abortion-in-america/

116

Dollard, J., Miller, N. E., Doob, L. W., Mowrer, O. H., & Sears, R. R. (1939). Frustration and aggression.

Nickerson, Charlotte (2021). Frustration- Aggressopm Hupothesis. Simply Psychology. Retrieved from: https://www.simplypsychology.org/frustration-aggression-hypothesis.html

117

Leonhardt, David (2022). The Right's Violence Problem. The New York Times. Retrieved from: https://www.nytimes.com/2022/05/17/briefing/right-wing-mass-shootings.html

Anti-Defamation League

118

Trac Reports (2017). Retrieved from: https://trac.syr.edu/tracreports/crim/481/

Jones, Seth, G. (2022). The Evolution of Domestic Terrorism. *Center for Strategic & International Studies.*

Retrieved from: https://www.csis.org/analysis/evolution-domestic-terrorism

FBI. What we investigate: Terrorism. Retrieved from: https://www.fbi.gov/investigate/terrorism

119

Peiser, Jaclyn, Students punished for labeling water fountains 'Whites only,' 'Blacks only'. Washington Post. Retrieved from: https://www.washingtonpost.com/nation/2022/05/19/racist-signs-water-fountain-ohio/

120

FBI. What we investigate: Terrorism. Retrieved from: https://www.fbi.gov/investigate/terrorism

121

NIJ (2022). Domestic Extremists and Social Media: Study Finds Similarities, Differences in Web Habits of Those Engaged in Hate Crimes Vs. Violent Extremism. Department of Justice, National Institute of Justice. Retrieved from: https://nij.ojp.gov/topics/articles/domestic-extremists-and-social-media-study-finds-similarities-differences-web

Thomas J. Holt, Joshua D. Freilich, Steven M. Chermak & Gary LaFree (2018) Examining the utility of social control and social learning in the radicalization of violent and non-violent extremists, Dynamics of Asymmetric Conflict, 11:3, 125-148, DOI: 10.1080/17467586.2018.1470661

122

Irwin Katz, Irwin (1991). *Gordon Allport's "The Nature of Prejudice".* Political Psychology , Mar., 1991, Vol. 12, No. 1 (Mar., 1991), pp. 125-157. Published by: International Society of Political Psychology, https://www.jstor.org/stable/3791349. https://doi.org/10.2307/3791349

Retrieved from: https://www.jstor.org/stable/pdf/3791349.pdf?refreqid=excelsior%3A1e99a1cc26d1eeb8065a6b008307e6db

Allport, Gordon (1949). *The Nature of Prejudice.* Addison Wesley Publishing Company. Retrieved from: https://faculty.washington.edu/caporaso/courses/203/readings/allport_Nature_of_prejudice.pdf

123

Irwin Katz, Irwin (1991). *Gordon Allport's "The Nature of Prejudice".* Political Psychology , Mar., 1991, Vol. 12, No. 1 (Mar., 1991), pp. 125-157. Published by: International Society of Political Psychology, https://www.jstor.org/stable/3791349. https://doi.org/10.2307/3791349

Retrieved from: https://www.jstor.org/stable/pdf/3791349.pdf?refreqid=excelsior%3A1e99a1cc26d1eeb8065a6b008307e6db

Allport, Gordon (1949). *The Nature of Prejudice.* Addison Wesley Publishing Company. Retrieved from: https://faculty.washington.edu/caporaso/courses/203/readings/allport_Nature_of_prejudice.pdf

124

Rene Ater (2020). IN MEMORIAM: I CAN'T BREATHE. RETRIEVED FROM: HTTPS://WWW.RENEEATER.COM/ON-MONUMENTS-BLOG/TAG/LIST+OF+UNARMED+BLACK+PEOPLE+KILLED+BY+POLICE

125

Ross, Matt (2017). Study finds that white families live in less diverse areas. Retrieved from: https://dailytrojan.com/2017/03/22/study-finds-white-families-live-less-diverse-areas/

Gersema, Emily (2017). White families with kids are drawn to less diverse neighborhoods and schools. *USC Dornsife, College of Letters Arts and Sciences.* Retrieved from: https://dornsife.usc.edu/news/stories/2550/white-families-with-kids-are-drawn-to-less-diverse-neighborhoods/

Owens, Ann (2017). Racial Residential Segregation of School-Age Children and Adults: The Role of Schooling as a Segregating Force. The Russell Sage Foundation, Journal of Social Sciences, February 2017, 3 (2) 63-80; DOI: https://doi.org/10.7758/RSF.2017.3.2.03. Retrieved from: https://www.rsfjournal.org/content/3/2/63

126

John D. Bransford, Ann L. Brown, and Rodney R. Cocking, editors. Committee on Developments in the Science of Learning with additional material from the

Committee on Learning Research and Educational Practice, M. Suzanne Donovan, John D. Bransford, and James W. Pellegrino, editors (2004). How People Learn Brain, Mind, Experience, and School. *Commission on Behavioral and Social Sciences and Education*

National Research Council. Retrieved from: https://www.depauw.edu/files/resources/howpeoplelearn.pdf

127

John D. Bransford, Ann L. Brown, and Rodney R. Cocking, editors. Committee on Developments in the Science of Learning with additional material from the

Committee on Learning Research and Educational Practice, M. Suzanne Donovan, John D. Bransford, and James W. Pellegrino, editors (2004). How People Learn Brain, Mind, Experience, and School. *Commission on Behavioral and Social Sciences and Education*

National Research Council. Retrieved from: https://www.depauw.edu/files/resources/howpeoplelearn.pdf

128

Cavanagh, Ben (2015). What works to reduce prejudice and discrimination? - A review of the evidence. A review of international evidence on prejudice reduction interventions. Retrieved from: https://www.gov.scot/publications/works-reduce-prejudice-discrimination-review-evidence/pages/4/

129

John D. Bransford, Ann L. Brown, and Rodney R. Cocking, editors. Committee on Developments in the Science of Learning with additional material from the

Committee on Learning Research and Educational Practice, M. Suzanne Donovan, John D. Bransford, and James W. Pellegrino, editors (2004). How People Learn Brain, Mind, Experience, and School. *Commission on Behavioral and Social Sciences and Education*

National Research Council. Retrieved from: https://www.depauw.edu/files/resources/howpeoplelearn.pdf

130

Reskin B.F. (2005) Including Mechanisms in our Models of Ascriptive Inequality. In: Nielsen L.B., Nelson R.L. (eds) Handbook of Employment Discrimination Research. Springer, Dordrecht. https://doi.org/10.1007/1-4020-3455-5_4. Retrieved from: https://link.springer.com/chapter/10.1007/1-4020-3455-5_4

131

Reskin B.F. (2005) Including Mechanisms in our Models of Ascriptive Inequality. In: Nielsen L.B., Nelson R.L. (eds) Handbook of Employment Discrimination Research. Springer, Dordrecht. https://doi.org/10.1007/1-4020-3455-5_4. Retrieved from: https://link.springer.com/chapter/10.1007/1-4020-3455-5_4

132

FBI. Federal Bureau of Investigation. Retrieved from: https://www.fbi.gov/investigate/civil-rights/hate-crimes

133

Fischer, A., Halperin, E., Canetti, D., & Jasini, A. (2018). Why We Hate. *Emotion Review*, *10*(4), 309 320. https://doi.org/10.1177/1754073917751229. Retrieved from: https://journals.sagepub.com/doi/full/10.1177/1754073917751229

https://journals.sagepub.com/doi/pdf/10.1177/1754073917751229

134

Fischer, A., Halperin, E., Canetti, D., & Jasini, A. (2018). Why We Hate. *Emotion Review*, *10*(4), 309 320. https://doi.org/10.1177/1754073917751229. Retrieved from: https://journals.sagepub.com/doi/full/10.1177/1754073917751229

https://journals.sagepub.com/doi/pdf/10.1177/1754073917751229

135

Fischer, A., Halperin, E., Canetti, D., & Jasini, A. (2018). Why We Hate. *Emotion Review*, *10*(4), 309 320. https://doi.org/10.1177/1754073917751229. Retrieved from: https://journals.sagepub.com/doi/full/10.1177/1754073917751229

https://journals.sagepub.com/doi/pdf/10.1177/1754073917751229

136

Andrea Mathews LPC, NCC (2022). Why Do We Hate. Psychology Today. Retrieved from:https://www.psychologytoday.com/us/blog/traversing-the-inner-terrain/201608/why-do-we-hate

137

Rohini Radhakrishnan and Shaziya Allarakha, MD (2021). Why Do People Hate? *Medicine Net*. Retrieved from: https://www.medicinenet.com/why_do_people_hate/article.htm

138

Rohini Radhakrishnan and Shaziya Allarakha, MD (2021). Why Do People Hate? *Medicine Net*. Retrieved from: https://www.medicinenet.com/why_do_people_hate/article.htm

139

Allison Abrams, LCSW-R (2017). The Psychology of Hate: Why do we hate? Psychology Today. Retrieved from: https://www.psychologytoday.com/us/blog/nurturing-self-compassion/201703/the-psychology-hate

140

Allison Abrams, LCSW-R (2017). The Psychology of Hate: Why do we hate? Psychology Today. Retrieved from: https://www.psychologytoday.com/us/blog/nurturing-self-compassion/201703/the-psychology-hate

141

Allison Abrams, LCSW-R (2017). The Psychology of Hate: Why do we hate? Psychology Today. Retrieved from: https://www.psychologytoday.com/us/blog/nurturing-self-compassion/201703/the-psychology-hate

142

Rohini Radhakrishnan and Shaziya Allarakha, MD (2021). Why Do People Hate? *Medicine Net.* Retrieved from: https://www.medicinenet.com/why_do_people_hate/article.htm

143

Kelsey-Sugg, Anna (3 April 2021). "Misogynistic 'radicalisation' of boys online has these experts calling for change". *ABC News.* Life Matters. Australian Broadcasting Corporation. Retrieved 5 April 2021.

144

Halevy, N.; Bornstein, G.; Sagiv, L. (2008). ""In-group love" and "out-group hate" as motives for individual participation in intergroup conflict". *Psychological Science.* **19** (4): 405–11. doi:10.1111/j.1467-9280.2008.02100.x. PMID 18399895. S2CID 6869770.

145

Parker, M.T.; Janoff-Bulman, R. (2013). "Lessons from morality-based social identity: the power of outgroup "hate," not just ingroup "love"". *Social Justice Research.* **26**: 81–96. doi:10.1007/s11211-012-0175-6. S2CID 144523660.

146

Stephan, W.G.; Stephan, C.W. (2000). "An integrated theory of prejudice". *Reducing Prejudice and Discrimination: The Claremont Symposium on Applied Social Psychology*: 23–45.

147

Riek, B.M.; Mania, E.W.; Gaertner, S.L. (2006). "Intergroup threat and outgroup attitudes: a meta-analytic review". *Personality and Social Psychology Review.* **10** (4): 336–53. doi:10.1207/s15327957pspr1004_4. PMID 17201592. S2CID 144762865.

148

Sherif, M., & Sherif, C.W. (1969). *Social psychology*. New York: Harper & Row. pp. 221–66.

149

McConahay, J.B. "Self-interest versus racial attitudes as correlates of anti-busing attitudes in Louisville: Is it the buses or the blacks?". *Journal of Politics.* **441**: 692–720.

150

Kinder, D.R.; Sears, D.O. (1981). "Prejudice and politics: Symbolic racism versus racial threats to the good life". *Journal of Personality and Social Psychology*. **40** (3): 414–31. doi:10.1037/0022-3514.40.3.414.

151

Stephan, W.G.; Stephan, C.W. (2000). "An integrated theory of prejudice". *Reducing Prejudice and Discrimination: The Claremont Symposium on Applied Social Psychology*: 23–45.

152

Riek, B.M.; Mania, E.W.; Gaertner, S.L. (2006). "Intergroup threat and outgroup attitudes: a meta-analytic review". *Personality and Social Psychology Review*. **10** (4): 336–53. doi:10.1207/s15327957pspr1004_4. PMID 17201592. S2CID 144762865.

153

Ho, C.; Jackson, J.W. (2001). "Attitudes toward Asian Americans: Theory and measurement". *Journal of Applied Social Psychology*. **31** (8): 1553–81. doi:10.1111/j.1559-1816.2001.tb02742.x.

154

Eagley, A.H.; Mladinic, A. (1989). "Gender stereotypes and attitudes toward women and men". Personality and Social Psychology Bulletin. ***15*** *(4): 543–58. doi:10.1177/0146167289154008. S2CID 145550350.*

155

"2003 FBI Law Enforcement bulletin". 2003. Archived from the original *on 2013-08-18.*

Schafer, J.R. (2006). "The seven-stage hate model: the psychopathology of hate groups". Cultic Studies Review. ***5****: 73–86.*

156

Schafer, J.R. (2006). "The seven-stage hate model: the psychopathology of hate groups". *Cultic Studies Review*. **5**: 73–86.

Schafer, John R, Navarro, Joe (2003). Seven-Stage Hate Model: The Psychopathology of Hate Groups.

NCJ Number 199742, Journal *FBI Law Enforcement Bulletin* Volume: 72 Issue: 3 Dated: March 2003 Pages: 1-8. Retrieved from: https://www.ojp.gov/ncjrs/virtual-library/abstracts/seven-stage-hate-model-psychopathology-hate-groups

157

Sternberg, R.J. (2005). *The Psychology of Hate*. Washington, D.C.: American Psychological Association. pp. 61–63.

158

Allison Abrams, LCSW-R (2017). The Psychology of Hate: Why do we hate? Psychology Today. Retrieved from: https://www.psychologytoday.com/us/blog/nurturing-self-compassion/201703/the-psychology-hate

Roberts, S. O., & Rizzo, M. T. (2020). The psychology of American racism. *American Psychologist*. Advance online publication. https://doi.org/10.1037/amp0000642

159

Roberts, S. O., & Rizzo, M. T. (2020). The psychology of American racism. *American Psychologist*. Advance online publication. https://doi.org/10.1037/amp0000642

Allison Abrams, LCSW-R (2017). The Psychology of Hate: Why do we hate? Psychology Today. Retrieved from: https://www.psychologytoday.com/us/blog/nurturing-self-compassion/201703/the-psychology-hate

160

Roberts, S. O., & Rizzo, M. T. (2020). The psychology of American racism. *American Psychologist*. Advance online publication. https://doi.org/10.1037/amp0000642

161

Roberts, S. O., & Rizzo, M. T. (2020). The psychology of American racism. *American Psychologist*. Advance online publication. https://doi.org/10.1037/amp0000642

Allison Abrams, LCSW-R (2017). The Psychology of Hate: Why do we hate? Psychology Today. Retrieved from: https://www.psychologytoday.com/us/blog/nurturing-self-compassion/201703/the-psychology-hate

162

Dorman, John (2022). New York Post editorial board throws cold water on a 2024 Trump campaign, calling him 'unworthy' to serve in the White House for another term. *Insider.* Retrieved from: https://www.businessinsider.com/trump-new-york-post-editorial-board-unworthy-2024-white-house-2022-7

163

Roberts, S. O., & Rizzo, M. T. (2020). The psychology of American racism. *American Psychologist*. Advance online publication. https://doi.org/10.1037/amp0000642

APA (2020). The Psychology of American Racism and how to work against it. American Psychological Association. Retrieved from: https://www.apa.org/pubs/highlights/spotlight/issue-189

164

Alsharif, Mirna and The Associated Press (2022). A woman flashed a 'white privilege' card after being pulled over. Now, officers are in trouble for letting her go. Retrieved from: https://www.nbcnews.com/news/us-news/woman-flashed-white-privilege-card-pulled-now-officers-are-trouble-let-rcna41700

165

Kerry Coddett, Kerry (2015). White on White Crime: An Unspoken Tragedy. *Huffington Post.* Retrieved from: https://www.huffpost.com/entry/white-on-white-crime-an-u_b_6771878

166

Peter Salovey and John D. Mayer (2021). Emotional Intelligence. *Psychology* Today. Retrieved from: https://www.psychologytoday.com/us/basics/emotional-intelligence

167

Study Mode (2021). My Social Location. Referenced from: https://www.studymode.com/essays/My-Social-Location-47318433.html

168

Federal Bureau of Prisons (2021). Statistics. Retrieved from: https://www.bop.gov/about/statistics/statistics_inmate_race.jsp

NBC News (2020). White Woman in NYC Confrontation With Black Birdwatcher Made False Assault Charge: DA. *NBC News.* Retrieved from: https://www.nbcnewyork.com/news/local/white-woman-in-central-park-confrontation-with-black-birdwatcher-made-false-assault-charge-da-says/2667375/

169

170

Ansell, Amy (2008). "Critical Race Theory". In Schaefer, Richard T. (ed.). *Encyclopedia of Race, Ethnicity, and Society, Volume 1*. SAGE Publications. pp. 344–346.

171

Lee Hale, Sami Yenigun, Brent Baughman, Leah Donnella. and Cara Tallo (2021). How Critical Race Theory Went From Harvard Law To Fox News. *NPR*. Retrieved from: https://www.npr.org/2021/07/02/1012696188/how-critical-race-theory-went-from-harvard-law-to-fox-news

172

The Constitutional Rights Foundation (2021). The Southern "Black Codes" of 1865-66. Retrieved from: https://www.crf-usa.org/brown-v-board-50th-anniversary/southern-black-codes.html

173

Quinn, Karl (2020). Are all white people racist? Why Critical Race Theory has us rattled. The Sydney Morning Herald. Retrieved from: https://www.smh.com.au/culture/books/are-all-white-people-racist-why-critical-race-theory-has-us-rattled-20201105-p56bwv.html

174

Ray, Rashawn (2021). Is the United States a racist country? *Brookings Institute*. Retrieved from: https://www.brookings.edu/blog/how-we-rise/2021/05/04/is-the-united-states-a-racist-country/

175

David Miguel Gray (2021). **Critical race theory: What it is and what it isn't. Retrieved from:** https://theconversation.com/critical-race-theory-what-it-is-and-what-it-isnt-162752

176

David Miguel Gray (2021). **Critical race theory: What it is and what it isn't. Retrieved from:** https://theconversation.com/critical-race-theory-what-it-is-and-what-it-isnt-162752

177

David Miguel Gray (2021). **Critical race theory: What it is and what it isn't. Retrieved from:** https://theconversation.com/critical-race-theory-what-it-is-and-what-it-isnt-162752

178

Ray, Rashawn (2021). Is the United States a racist country? *Brookings Institute*. Retrieved from: https://www.brookings.edu/blog/how-we-rise/2021/05/04/is-the-united-states-a-racist-country/

179

NBC News (2020). White Woman in NYC Confrontation With Black Birdwatcher Made False Assault Charge: DA. *NBC News.* Retrieved from: https://www.nbcnewyork.com/news/local/white-woman-in-central-park-confrontation-with-black-birdwatcher-made-false-assault-charge-da-says/2667375/

UChicago (2021). The University of Chicago Diversity and Inclusion. Retrieved from: https://diversityandinclusion.uchicago.edu/ ; https://diversityandinclusion.uchicago.edu/commitment/

180

UChicago (2021). The University of Chicago Diversity and Inclusion. Retrieved from: https://diversityandinclusion.uchicago.edu/ ; https://diversityandinclusion.uchicago.edu/commitment/

181

UChicago (2021). Our Approach. University of Chicago Diversity and Inclusion. Retrieved from: https://diversityandinclusion.uchicago.edu/commitment/approach/

182

Duke University. Duke Center for Truth, Racial Healing & Transformation. *Duke University.* Retrieved from: https://trht.duke.edu/

183

Rutgers University. Truth, Racial Healing & Transformation Center. *Rutgers University.* Retrieved from: https://www.newark.rutgers.edu/truth-racial-healing-and-transformation-center

184

Ayana, Archie (2022). Harvard releases report detailing its ties to slavery, plans to issue reparations. *NPR.* Retrieved from: https://www.npr.org/2022/04/27/1094971897/harvard-university-report-slavery-slave-trade-reparations-students

Moscufo, Michela (2022). Harvard sets up $100 million endowment fund for slavery reparations. *Reuters.* Retrieved from: https://www.reuters.com/world/us/harvard-sets-up-100-million-endowment-fund-slavery-reparations-2022-04-26/

185

Richard Fuller and Francis Wayland. DOMESTIC SLAVERY CONSIDERED AS A SCRIPTURAL INSTITUTION. *Mercer University Press.* Retrieved from: https://lib.tcu.edu/staff/bellinger/60013/Wayland.pdf

186

Llopis, Glenn (2021). The Cultural Demographic Shift Is In Full Force.

Forbes. Retrieved from: https://www.forbes.com/sites/glennllopis/2020/08/29/the-cultural-demographic-shift-is-in-full-force/?sh=64baf6716ad8

187

Jonathan Vespa, Lauren Medina, and David M. Armstrong (2020). Demographic Turning Points for the United States: Population Projections for 2020 to 2060. Retrieved from: https://www.census.gov/content/dam/Census/library/publications/2020/demo/p25-1144.pdf

188

189

Dovidio, John F., Kawakami, Kerry and Gaertner, Samuel L. (2001). Implicit and Explicit Prejudice and Interracial Interaction. INTERPERSONAL RELATIONS AND GROUP PROCESSES. Retrieved from: https://equity.ucla.edu/wp-content/uploads/2016/11/Dovidio-Kawakami-Gaertner-2002.pdf

Salovey P, Mayer JD. Emotional intelligence. *Imagin Cogn Pers*. 1990;9(3):185-211. doi:10.2190/DUGG-P24E-52WK-6CDG

190

Srovastava, Kalpana (2013). Emotional intelligence and organizational effectiveness. Ind Psychiatry J. 2013 Jul-Dec; 22(2): 97–99. doi: 10.4103/0972-6748.132912. Retrieved from: https://www.ncbi.nlm.nih.gov/pmc/articles/PMC4085815/

191

Srovastava, Kalpana (2013). Emotional intelligence and organizational effectiveness. Ind Psychiatry J. 2013 Jul-Dec; 22(2): 97–99. doi: 10.4103/0972-6748.132912. Retrieved from: https://www.ncbi.nlm.nih.gov/pmc/articles/PMC4085815/

192

Srovastava, Kalpana (2013). Emotional intelligence and organizational effectiveness. Ind Psychiatry J. 2013 Jul-Dec; 22(2): 97–99. doi: 10.4103/0972-6748.132912. Retrieved from: https://www.ncbi.nlm.nih.gov/pmc/articles/PMC4085815/

193

Srovastava, Kalpana (2013). Emotional intelligence and organizational effectiveness. Ind Psychiatry J. 2013 Jul-Dec; 22(2): 97–99. doi: 10.4103/0972-6748.132912. Retrieved from: https://www.ncbi.nlm.nih.gov/pmc/articles/PMC4085815/

194

Schmalor, A., & Heine, S. J. (2021). Subjective Economic Inequality Decreases Emotional Intelligence, Especially for People of High Social Class. *Social Psychological and Personality Science*. https://doi.org/10.1177/19485506211024024. Retrieved from: https://journals.sagepub.com/doi/pdf/10.1177/19485506211024024

https://journals.sagepub.com/doi/full/10.1177/19485506211024024

Ellwood, Beth (2021) People with higher socioeconomic status have lower emotional intelligence, especially at high levels of inequality. *PsyPost*. Retrieved from: https://www.psypost.org/2021/10/people-with-higher-socioeconomic-status-have-lower-emotional-intelligence-especially-at-high-levels-of-inequality-61942

195

Schmalor, A., & Heine, S. J. (2021). Subjective Economic Inequality Decreases Emotional Intelligence, Especially for People of High Social Class. *Social Psychological and Personality Science*. https://doi.org/10.1177/19485506211024024. Retrieved from: https://journals.sagepub.com/doi/pdf/10.1177/19485506211024024

https://journals.sagepub.com/doi/full/10.1177/19485506211024024

Ellwood, Beth (2021) People with higher socioeconomic status have lower emotional intelligence, especially at high levels of inequality. *PsyPost.* Retrieved from: https://www.psypost.org/2021/10/people-with-higher-socioeconomic-status-have-lower-emotional-intelligence-especially-at-high-levels-of-inequality-61942

196

Schmalor, A., & Heine, S. J. (2021). Subjective Economic Inequality Decreases Emotional Intelligence, Especially for People of High Social Class. *Social Psychological and Personality Science.* https://doi.org/10.1177/19485506211024024. Retrieved from: https://journals.sagepub.com/doi/pdf/10.1177/19485506211024024

https://journals.sagepub.com/doi/full/10.1177/19485506211024024

Ellwood, Beth (2021) People with higher socioeconomic status have lower emotional intelligence, especially at high levels of inequality. *PsyPost.* Retrieved from: https://www.psypost.org/2021/10/people-with-higher-socioeconomic-status-have-lower-emotional-intelligence-especially-at-high-levels-of-inequality-61942

197

Srovastava, Kalpana (2013). Emotional intelligence and organizational effectiveness. Ind Psychiatry J. 2013 Jul-Dec; 22(2): 97–99. doi: 10.4103/0972-6748.132912. Retrieved from: https://www.ncbi.nlm.nih.gov/pmc/articles/PMC4085815/

198

MURPHY, BILL(2021). Why Emotionally Intelligent Leaders Use the 9 Secret Rules of Winning Arguments. Retrieved from: https://www.inc.com/bill-murphy-jr/why-emotionally-intelligent-leaders-use-9-secret-rules-of-winning-arguments.html

Cherry, Kendra (2020), 9 Signs of Low Emotional Intelligence. Reviewed by Amy Morin, LCSW. *Verywellmind.* Retrieved. from: https://www.verywellmind.com/signs-of-low-emotional-intelligence-2795958

Srovastava, Kalpana (2013). Emotional intelligence and organizational effectiveness. Ind Psychiatry J. 2013 Jul-Dec; 22(2): 97–99. doi: 10.4103/0972-6748.132912. Retrieved from: https://www.ncbi.nlm.nih.gov/pmc/articles/PMC4085815/

Ellwood, Beth (2021) People with higher socioeconomic status have lower emotional intelligence, especially at high levels of inequality. *PsyPost.* Retrieved from: https://www.psypost.org/2021/10/people-with-higher-socioeconomic-status-have-lower-emotional-intelligence-especially-at-high-levels-of-inequality-61942

Schmalor, A., & Heine, S. J. (2021). Subjective Economic Inequality Decreases Emotional Intelligence, Especially for People of High Social Class. *Social Psychological and Personality Science.* https://doi.org/10.1177/19485506211024024. Retrieved from: https://journals.sagepub.com/doi/full/10.1177/19485506211024024 ; https://journals.sagepub.com/doi/pdf/10.1177/19485506211024024.

199

MURPHY, BILL(2021). Why Emotionally Intelligent Leaders Use the 9 Secret Rules of Winning Arguments. Retrieved from: https://www.inc.com/bill-murphy-jr/why-emotionally-intelligent-leaders-use-9-secret-rules-of-winning-arguments.html

Cherry, Kendra (2020), 9 Signs of Low Emotional Intelligence. Reviewed by Amy Morin, LCSW. *Verywellmind.* Retrieved. from: https://www.verywellmind.com/signs-of-low-emotional-intelligence-2795958

Srovastava, Kalpana (2013). Emotional intelligence and organizational effectiveness. Ind Psychiatry J. 2013 Jul-Dec; 22(2): 97–99. doi: 10.4103/0972-6748.132912. Retrieved from: https://www.ncbi.nlm.nih.gov/pmc/articles/PMC4085815/

Ellwood, Beth (2021) People with higher socioeconomic status have lower emotional intelligence, especially at high levels of inequality. *PsyPost.* Retrieved from: https://www.psypost.org/2021/10/people-with-higher-socioeconomic-status-have-lower-emotional-intelligence-especially-at-high-levels-of-inequality-61942

Schmalor, A., & Heine, S. J. (2021). Subjective Economic Inequality Decreases Emotional Intelligence, Especially for People of High Social Class. *Social Psychological and Personality Science.* https://doi.org/10.1177/19485506211024024. Retrieved from: https://journals.sagepub.com/doi/full/10.1177/19485506211024024 ; https://journals.sagepub.com/doi/pdf/10.1177/19485506211024024.

200

Shapiro, Ari (2020). 'There Is No Neutral': 'Nice White People' Can Still Be Complicit In A Racist Society. NPR. Retrieved from: https://www.npr.org/2020/06/09/873375416/there-is-no-neutral-nice-white-people-can-still-be-complicit-in-a-racist-society

201

Mallory Yu and Sarah Handel produced and edited the interview broadcast into text information. Beth Novey adapted it for the web. 'There Is No Neutral': 'Nice White People' Can Still Be Complicit In A Racist Society. NPR. Retrieved from: https://www.npr.org/2020/06/09/873375416/there-is-no-neutral-nice-white-people-can-still-be-complicit-in-a-racist-society

Shapiro, Ari (2020). 'There Is No Neutral': 'Nice White People' Can Still Be Complicit In A Racist Society. NPR. Retrieved from: https://www.npr.org/2020/06/09/873375416/there-is-no-neutral-nice-white-people-can-still-be-complicit-in-a-racist-society

202

Mallory Yu and Sarah Handel produced and edited the interview broadcast into text information. Beth Novey adapted it for the web. 'There Is No Neutral': 'Nice White People' Can Still Be Complicit In A Racist Society. NPR. Retrieved from: https://www.npr.org/2020/06/09/873375416/there-is-no-neutral-nice-white-people-can-still-be-complicit-in-a-racist-society

Shapiro, Ari (2020). 'There Is No Neutral': 'Nice White People' Can Still Be Complicit In A Racist Society. NPR. Retrieved from: https://www.npr.org/2020/06/09/873375416/there-is-no-neutral-nice-white-people-can-still-be-complicit-in-a-racist-society

203

DiAngelo, Robin (2018). *White Fragility.* Beacon Press

204

Colton, Emma (2021). Professor singles out 'average White guy' in lecture, says skin color benefits him over Black students. Retrieved from: https://www.foxnews.com/us/professor-average-white-black-students

205

Cancian, Mark (2022). What Does $40 Billion in Aid to Ukraine Buy? Center for Strategic and International Studies. Retrieved from: https://www.csis.org/analysis/what-does-40-billion-aid-ukraine-buy

206

Janofsky, Michael. "Thurmond Kin Acknowledge Black Daughter", The New York Times, December 16, 2004.

Washington-Williams, Essie Mae (2005). Dear Senator: A Memoir by the Daughter of Strom Thurmond. Harper

Crenshaw, Kimberlé Williams (February 26, 2004). "Was Strom a Rapist?". The Nation. ISSN 0027-8378. Retrieved November 1, 2020.

207

Brandt, Chris (2017). Harvard Researcher Says Africans Are 100% Pure Human Than The Rest. Retrieved from: https://www.universityherald.com/articles/70130/20170321/harvard-researcher-says-africans-are-100-pure-human-than-the-rest.htm

208

Owens, James (2007). Modern Humans Came Out of Africa, "Definitive" Study Says. Retrieved from: https://www.nationalgeographic.com/history/article/modern-humans-came-out-of-africa-definitive-study-says

209

Pavid, Katie (2018). Rethinking our human origins in Africa. *Natural History Museum*. Retrieved from: https://www.nhm.ac.uk/discover/news/2018/july/the-way-we-think-about-the-first-modern-humans-in-africa.html

Wong, Jenny and Hendry, Lisa. Human Evolution: The origin of our species. Natural History Museum. Retrieved from: https://www.nhm.ac.uk/discover/the-origin-of-our-species.html

210

Coyne, Jerry A. (2009). *Why Evolution is True*. Viking. pp. 8–11. ISBN 978-0-670-02053-9.

211

Thanm, Ker, Taylor, Ashley, P., and Garner, Tom (2021). What is Darwin's Theory of Evolution? Live Science. Retrieved from: https://www.livescience.com/474-controversy-evolution-works.html

212

Stinson, S., ECOLOGICAL DIVERSITY AND MODERN HUMAN ADAPTATIONS. HUMAN RESOURCES AND THEIR DEVELOPMENT – Vol. II – Ecological Diversity and Modern Human Adaptations - S. Stinson. Retrieved from: https://www.eolss.net/sample-chapters/c11/E1-10-03-02.pdf

213

Thanm, Ker, Taylor, Ashley, P., and Garner, Tom (2021). What is Darwin's Theory of Evolution? Live Science. Retrieved from: https://www.livescience.com/474-controversy-evolution-works.html

214

Feder, Sandra (2020). Stanford psychologist identifies seven factors that contribute to American racism. Stanford News. Retrieved from: https://news.stanford.edu/2020/06/09/seven-factors-contributing-american-racism/

215

Feder, Sandra (2020). Stanford psychologist identifies seven factors that contribute to American racism. Stanford News. Retrieved from: https://news.stanford.edu/2020/06/09/seven-factors-contributing-american-racism/

216

Feder, Sandra (2020). Stanford psychologist identifies seven factors that contribute to American racism. Stanford News. Retrieved from: https://news.stanford.edu/2020/06/09/seven-factors-contributing-american-racism/

217

(2022). Majority Have Unfavorable View of Supreme Court; Voters Say Decisions Based on Political Views Rather than Constitution, 63-30%. *Siena College Research institute.* Retrieved from: https://scri.siena.edu/2022/07/13/majority-have-unfavorable-view-of-supreme-court-voters-say-decisions-based-on-political-views-rather-than-constitution-63-30/.

218

Epstein, Reid, J. (2022). As Faith Flags in U.S. Government, Many Voters Want to Upend the System. *Siena College Research institute.* Retrieved from: https://www.nytimes.com/2022/07/13/us/politics/government-trust-voting-poll.html.

219

Pew Research Center (2022). Public Trust in Government: 1958-2022

Retrieved from: https://www.pewresearch.org/politics/2022/06/06/public-trust-in-government-1958-2022/.

LEE RAINIE, SCOTT KEETER AND ANDREW PERRIN (2019). Trust and Distrust in America. Pew Research Center. Retrieved from: https://www.pewresearch.org/politics/2019/07/22/trust-and-distrust-in-america/.

220

Mueller, Julia (2022). Most in new poll say US government needs major reforms, complete overhaul. *The Hill.* Retrieved from: https://www.yahoo.com/news/most-poll-us-government-needs-192911414.html.

221

222

Upendran, S. (2011). What is the meaning of 'chickens have come home to roost'? *The Hindu*. Retrieved from: https://www.thehindu.com/books/know-your-english/what-is-the-meaning-of-chickens-have-come-home-to-roost/article2669218.ece

Tracie Stewart (2010). Motivation to End Racism Relies on 'Yes We Can' Approach. *Association for Psychological Science*. Retrieved from: https://www.psychologicalscience.org/news/releases/motivation-to-end-racism-relies-on-yes-we-can-approach.html

223

Samuel R. Sommers and Michael I. Norton (2006). Lay Theories About White Racists: What Constitutes Racism (and What Doesn't). *Group Processes & Intergroup Relations 2006 Vol 9(1) 117–138. Retrieved from: https://www.Lay Theories About White Racists: What Constitutes Racism (and What Doesn't)*

224

225

Eberhardt, J. L., & Randall, J. L. (1997). The essential notion of race. *Psychological Science, 8*, 198–203.

226

Kennedy, R. F. (1966). Suppose God is Black. *Look, 30*, 45.

227

FBI (2010). Crime in the United States. United States *Department of Justice: FBI*. Retrieved from: https://ucr.fbi.gov/crime-in-the-u.s/2010/crime-in-the-u.s.-2010/tables/table-43

FBI (2010). Crime in the United States. United States *Department of Justice: FBI*. Retrieved from: https://ucr.fbi.gov/crime-in-the-u.s/2010/crime-in-the-u.s.-2010/tables/table-43

228

229

FBI (2010). Crime in the United States. United States *Department of Justice: FBI*. Retrieved from: https://ucr.fbi.gov/crime-in-the-u.s/2010/crime-in-the-u.s.-2010/tables/table-43

Fuller Rev. Richard and Wayland Rev. Francis, Domestic Slavery considered as a Scriptural Institution, Sheldon & Company, New York, 1860. Retrieved from: https://archive.org/stream/domesticslavery05waylgoog#page/n36/mode/2up, p. 136

230

Natividad, Ivan (2021). To end white supremacy, attack racist policy, not people. Berkeley news, UC Berkley. Retrieved from: https://news.berkeley.edu/2021/01/25/to-end-white-supremacy-attack-racist-policy-not-people/

231

Natividad, Ivan (2021). To end white supremacy, attack racist policy, not people. Berkeley news, UC Berkley. Retrieved from: https://news.berkeley.edu/2021/01/25/to-end-white-supremacy-attack-racist-policy-not-people/

232

2021 Audit of Antiemetic Incidents (2021). Anti-Defamation League. Retrieved from: https://www.adl.org/audit2021w

233

Investopedia (2022). Say's Law of Markets. Retrieved from: https://www.investopedia.com/terms/s/says-law.asp

234

Shaffer, Alyssa (2019). The truth about lies. American Psychological Association. May 2019, Vol 50, No. 5. Print version: page 38. Retrieved from: https://www.apa.org/monitor/2019/05/truth-lies

235

Picknell, Kyle (2018). WATCH: Muhammad Ali's perfect reply to being told 'not all white people are racist'. Retrieved from: https://www.joe.co.uk/life/muhammad-ali-had-the-perfect-reply-to-the-not-all-white-people-are-racist-argument-169358

236

Picknell, Kyle (2018). WATCH: Muhammad Ali's perfect reply to being told 'not all white people are racist'. Retrieved from: https://www.joe.co.uk/life/muhammad-ali-had-the-perfect-reply-to-the-not-all-white-people-are-racist-argument-169358

237

Smith Jeremy Adam (2018). Why Are White Men Stockpiling Guns? Scientific American. Retrieved from: https://blogs.scientificamerican.com/observations/why-are-white-men-stockpiling-guns/

238

Josslyn, Mark R., Haider-Market, Donald P., Baggs, Michael, and Bilbo, Andrew (2017). Emerging Political Identities? Gun Ownership and Voting in Presidential Elections. *Social Science Quarterly*

Volume 98, Issue 2 p. 382-396. First published: 15 June 2017

https://doi.org/10.1111/ssqu.12421. Retrieved from: https://onlinelibrary.wiley.com/doi/full/10.1111/ssqu.12421

Filindra, Alexandra and Kaplan, Noah, L. (2016). Racial Resentment and Whites' Gun Policy Preferences in Contemporary America. *Polit Behav (2016) 38:255–275* DOI 10.1007/s11109-015-9326-4. Retrieved from: https://link.springer.com/content/pdf/10.1007/s11109-015-9326-4.pdf ; https://link.springer.com/article/10.1007/s11109-015-9326-4

239

Filindra, Alexandra and Kaplan, Noah, L. (2016). Racial Resentment and Whites' Gun Policy Preferences in Contemporary America. *Polit Behav (2016) 38:255–275* DOI 10.1007/s11109-015-9326-4. Retrieved from: https://link.springer.com/content/pdf/10.1007/s11109-015-9326-4.pdf ; https://link.springer.com/article/10.1007/s11109-015-9326-4

Josslyn, Mark R., Haider-Market, Donald P., Baggs, Michael, and Bilbo, Andrew (2017). Emerging Political Identities? Gun Ownership and Voting in Presidential Elections. *Social Science Quarterly*

Volume 98, Issue 2 p. 382-396. First published: 15 June 2017 https://doi.org/10.1111/ssqu.12421. Retrieved from: https://onlinelibrary.wiley.com/doi/full/10.1111/ssqu.12421

240

Chen, Shawna (2022). Biden slams Trump: "You can't be pro-insurrection and pro-American". *Axios.* Retrieved from: https://www.axios.com/2022/07/25/joe-biden-donald-trump-jan-6-inaction

241

Mencken, F., Carson and Froese, Paul (2017). Gun Culture in Action. *Social Problems, Volume 66, Issue 1, February 2019, Pages 3–27,* https://doi.org/10.1093/socpro/spx040

Published: 20 November 2017. Retrieved from: https://academic.oup.com/socpro/article/66/1/3/4643202.

242

Bennett, Kate and Blaine, Kyle (2022). Jill Biden apologizes after citing 'bodegas' and 'breakfast tacos' to praise Hispanic diversity. *CNN.* Retrieved from: https://www.cnn.com/2022/07/12/politics/jill-biden-breakfast-tacos/index.html.

Gamboa, Suzanne (2022). Jill Biden's Texas speech fires up debate over breakfast tacos: A Latino stereotype or a point of local pride. *ABC News.* Retrieved from: https://www.nbcnews.com/news/latino/jill-bidens-texas-speech-fires-debate-breakfast-tacos-latino-stereotyp-rcna37866.

Rascon, Jacob (2022). We are not tacos': First Lady Dr. Jill Biden criticized for comparing Latinos to tacos in speech. ABC Eyewitness News. Retrieved from: https://abc11.com/dr-jill-biden-2022-unidosus-annual-conference-speech-san-antonio-breakfast-tacos-first-lady-criticized-for-on-hispanic-equity/12045894/.

243

World War II Casualties. Retrieved from: https://en.wikipedia.org/wiki/World_War_II_casualties

244

Zeller, Bob (2022). How Many Died in the American Civil War? History: A&E Television Networks. Retrieved from: https://www.history.com/news/american-civil-war-deaths

Hacker, J. David,Dr. (2011). "A Census-Based Count of Civil War Dead," in the scholarly quarterly, *Civil War History.*

Faust, Drew, Gilpin. Death and Dying. National Park Service, U.S. Department of Interior (Npr.gov). Retrieved from: https://www.nps.gov/nr/travel/national_cemeteries/death.html

245

World War II Casualties. Retrieved from: https://en.wikipedia.org/wiki/World_War_II_casualties

www.ingramcontent.com/pod-product-compliance
Lightning Source LLC
Chambersburg PA
CBHW062112020426
42335CB00013B/936

* 9 7 8 1 9 5 7 1 1 4 5 0 7 *